This book will make you angry. Very angry.

When I read *Grand Illusions,* I was so outraged that I immediately called Wolgemuth & Hyatt, Publishers and committed to distribute at least ten thousand copies, even if I had to give them away. This book is that important.

I thought I knew Planned Parenthood. I was aware that they promoted, financed, and participated in baby-killing. But this corrupt organization is dedicated to not only killing America's babies, but also destroying America's cornerstone—the family. And they have been frighteningly successful.

But Planned Parenthood's days are numbered—Christians are *awakening* to the threat.

Planned Parenthood, however, will not be defeated easily. Recently, a Planned Parenthood spokesman has said that they "will crush Operation Rescue within one year." ("He who sits in the heavens laughs," said the Psalmist.) We will have to fight to topple this empire of bloodshed and guile. And to win any war, you must know your enemy. *Grand Illusions* will arm you with the truth about Planned Parenthood and the practical means by which you can rid your community of this menace.

When I read this book, I envisioned Planned Parenthood as a large, luxurious ocean liner cruising the open seas. I saw the leadership of Planned Parenthood on the deck, smug and defiant, smiling and waving to passing boats, confident that their ship could never be sunk. They felt an impact, heard an explosion, but continued smiling and waving, arrogantly self-assured that it was a minor problem. Meanwhile, below the surface, the lower decks were filling with water, the engine room was on fire, and the ship was irreparably damaged—doomed to sink. It had been hit by one brilliantly designed and perfectly aimed torpedo—*Grand Illusions.* Read it, praise the Lord, and pass the ammunition.

Randall A. Terry
Founder / Operation Rescue

GRAND ILLUSIONS

Other books by George Grant

Bringing in the Sheaves:
Transforming Poverty into Productivity, 1985

In the Shadow of Plenty:
Biblical Principles of Welfare and Poverty, 1986

The Dispossessed:
Homelessness in America, 1986

The Changing of the Guard:
Biblical Principles of Political Action, 1987

A Christian Response to Dungeons and Dragons:
The Catechism of the New Age, 1987
(with Peter Leithart)

GRAND ILLUSIONS

The Legacy of Planned Parenthood

George Grant

Wolgemuth & Hyatt, Publishers, Inc.
Brentwood, Tennessee

Unless otherwise noted, all Scripture quotations are either the
author's own, or are from the New King James Version of the
Bible, copyrighted 1984 by Thomas Nelson, Inc., Nashville,
Tennessee.

Wolgemuth & Hyatt, Publishers, Inc.
P.O. Box 1941, Brentwood, Tennessee 37027.

Printed in the United States of America.

First printing, July, 1988
Second printing, November, 1988
Third printing, August, 1989

Library of Congress Cataloging-in-Publication Data

Grant, George, 1954-
     Grand illusions.

Includes index.
     1. Birth control — United States — Societies, etc.
     2. Birth control — Religious aspects — Christianity.
     3. Pro-choice movement — United States.
     4. Pro-life movement — United States.   I. Title.

HQ776.5.U5G69 1988   363.9'6'0973   88-14333
ISBN 0-943497-08-6

To Uz and Jair
Beyond our Grasp
But not Beyond God's
and to Karen, Kathe, and Suzanne
Beyond the Beyond.

CONTENTS

AUTHOR'S NOTE

All the stories and vignettes in this book are true. In some, names have been changed, in others editorial liberties have been taken to combine certain events for purposes of clarity or illustration. But in all instances, the events and conversations accurately reflect factual situations.

Many thanks are due to the hundreds of women I have talked with and interviewed over the years. I owe a special debt of gratitude to the women of the Crisis Pregnancy Center of Houston, of the HELP Services Women's Center in Humble, and of the WEBA (Women Exploited By Abortion) chapters in Houston and around the country. These stories are their stories.

ACKNOWLEDGMENTS

ars n'est celare pas artem

I suspect that those who have read some of my other books will be a little surprised by this one. I am a little surprised by it myself.

The great literary critic Northrup Frye once remarked that "the written word is far more powerful than simply a reminder: it recreates the past in the present, and gives us, not the familiar remembered thing, but the glittering intensity of a summoned up passion." This book, as it has been transformed from research and remembrance into text, has been like that for me. It has surprised me with its fervid fervor.

Certainly, there are advantages afforded by that kind of passion. Urgency, duty, and sacrifice all make for better writing. And for quicker writing. But they can also devolve that writing into the tangential ravings of the fantastic.

Fortunately, there were several people who girded me round about all through the process of writing. They kept the fires of passion stoked. But they also lent me the balance, stability, and security necessary to check my ever-increasing alacrity.

Robert Ruff was an indispensable counselor, researcher, and friend throughout this project. Without him, not only would it never have gotten finished, it would never have begun.

Terri and Kevin Larkin, Lynn and Steve Hawley, Karen and Greg Mead, Robin and Randy Rogers, Karen and Michael Chakerian, Elaine and Jim Hime, Karen and Kelly Hartman, Emily and Nina Neisig, and Maggie and Ben Huggins likewise served sacrificially in providing research materials and in insuring the manuscript's accuracy, fidelity, and practicality.

My spiritual yokefellows Frank Marshall, Kemper Crabb, Dave Marshall, and Brian Martin along with the entire congregation of ChristChurch in Houston guarded me with their prayers and love. No thanks can ever compensate.

Pastor Gordon Walker, and all the presbyters of the Church of the Holy Trinity in Nashville, afforded me a haven of rest and refuge and courageously cast their lot with me when all convention demanded otherwise.

Similarly, Jamie O'Rourke, Tom Singleton, Dave Jones, Bev Lewis, Bill Baumgartner, David Shepherd, and the rest of the "vagabond recons" in Nashville threw their support behind me and this project early on. They have been a gracious provision of Almighty God.

My publishers Robert Wolgemuth, Dan Wolgemuth, and Michael Hyatt not only believed in this project from the start, but they put their reputations and their livelihoods on the line for it. I know they will receive their reward in Heaven, but I hope they get a taste of it here, too.

Several wise and judicious colleagues read the manuscript along the way: Josh McDowell and Joe Scheidler to ensure ministry applicability, Lars Berthoud and Jim Jordan to ensure theological orthodoxy, Dr. Reed Bell and Dr. Jack Willke to ensure medical accuracy, Marvin Olasky and Connie Marshner to ensure journalistic fairness, Sandy McKasson and Gary North to ensure ideological astuteness, and Curtis Brown and Dick Schmude to ensure legal viability.

Michael Card, Leo Kottke, Bourgeois Tagg, Charlie Peacock, Spin 180, Dennis Welch, Michael W. Smith, Til Tuesday, and Bob Bennett helped the project immensely by providing the soundtrack, while Garrison Keillor, Tim Powers, K. W. Jeter, Steve Lawhead, George Alec Effinger, P. J. O'Rourke, John Skipp, and Craig Spector supplied the midnight musings. Thanks, you are artists, all.

Finally, my dear friends Kathe Salazar, Suzanne Martin, David Dunham, and Bruce Tippery, as well as my wonderful family, have stood by me from day one. To them I must offer my sincerest and deepest thanks.

Whatever subjectivity born of passion that somehow was able to sneak past this heavenly host must be ledgered to my ac-

count. Whatever glittering intensity remains must be ledgered
to theirs.

Feast of the Holy Innocents
Nashville, Tennessee

To be or not to be, that is the question.

William Shakespeare

AD VITUM

apologia pro vita

Why Planned Parenthood?

Why a whole book dedicated to examining — and quite apparently exposing — one of the largest and most respected social service providers in our nation's history?

Sour grapes?

Spite?

Uninformed animosity?

Guilt?

Religious vendetta?

No, the fact is that despite a full three quarters of a century of controversy and conflict surrounding Planned Parenthood, there has never been a comprehensive examination of the organization's history, policies, procedures, and programs available to the public.[1]

This book then is an attempt to fill that vast void.

The question of why the void has existed for so long is one that has plagued me for many years. It was only as I undertook the massive task of researching Planned Parenthood that any kind of answer to that question began to surface.

For one thing, Planned Parenthood is actually not an organization. Instead, it is a loose affiliation of several hundred separately incorporated, separately administered, and separately financed organizations. These separate organizations share a common history, a common philosophy, a common agenda, and a common public image. They all pay annual affiliation fees and dues to national and international bureaucratic entities. And they all cooperate in various educational, political, judicial, and financial concerns. But, they all maintain distinctives that make detailed analysis and blanket assessments very difficult indeed.

Beyond the structural and institutional dilemma, the fact is
that though the name *Planned Parenthood* is a registered service-
mark,[2] it always has been — and probably always will be — the
generic name of a movement as well. For several decades following World War II, central figures in the organization were
encouraging the use of the name *Planned Parenthood* to identify
the entire birth control-abortion-population control social phenomenon.[3] Although there are vast areas of agreement between
the many individuals and institutions in this generic movement,
widespread diversity again makes detailed analysis and blanket
assessment terribly tenuous.[4]

Finally, the frenetic litigal character of Planned Parenthood —
both as an institutional association and as an instrumental movement — has no doubt discouraged previous serious investigations.
Most authors and most publishers tend to shy away from legal
entanglements.[5] Despite these serious difficulties, I became
convinced that I needed to write a comprehensive exposé of
Planned Parenthood.

That conviction was confirmed when several pro-life activists
from around the country came knocking on my door with several hundred thousand never before disclosed Planned Parenthood documents: internal memorandums, clinic visit records,
medical charts, financial statements, publicity files, confidential
correspondence, and meeting minutes. Frankly, I was flabbergasted by what I saw as I thumbed through those documents. I
had been deeply immersed in the pro-life movement for more
than a decade, and I was still shocked.

So I set myself to the task. You have before you the result.

But be apprised, this book is by no means the last word on
Planned Parenthood. Believe it or not, I eliminated five chapters
from the manuscript text to conserve space.[6] And even at that, I
have only just skimmed the surface.[7] A full treatment of Planned
Parenthood's international activities, its political connections, its
judicial agenda, its research manipulations, its propaganda techniques, and its theological orientation will have to be taken up at
a later date.[8]

Presuppositions

Several kind reviewers have asked me why I chose to make
my manuscript openly and overtly Christian. Their concern was

simply that the book might be quickly dismissed and its message ignored in the marketplace of ideas. They felt that it might be perceived as impractical, apolitical, and unpragmatic when in point of fact it is none of those things. In a milieu where traditional values have been exiled to a desolate cultural outback and where the proponents of those values have voluntarily sequestered themselves in a squalid spiritual and intellectual ghetto, those concerns are not at all unwarranted.

Even so, I feel that the *only* appropriate response to Planned Parenthood is a distinctively Christian response. And I am entirely at ease in announcing that from the start.

G. K. Chesterton once quipped that any new book of modern social inquiry is bound to be dullardly predictable in both form and function: "It begins as a rule with an analysis, with statistics, tables of population, decrease of crime among Congregationalists, growth of hysteria among policemen, and similar ascertained facts; it ends with a chapter that is generally called *The Remedy*. It is almost wholly due to this careful, solid, and scientific method that *The Remedy* is never found. For this scheme of medical question and answer is a blunder; the first great blunder of sociology. It is always called stating the disease before we find the cure. But it is the whole definition and dignity of man that in social matters we must actually find the cure before we find the disease."[9]

This book is obviously an exploration, explanation, and exposition of the disease of Planned Parenthood. But as Chesterton has said, we need not approach our subject medically. In this case, it is entirely appropriate for us to announce the cure before we engage in examination and diagnosis. The cure is, very simply, the Word of God. The Scriptures. The Bible.

The Bible is God's own revelation of wisdom, knowledge, understanding, and truth. It is not simply a marvelous collection of quaint sayings and inspiring stories. It is God's message to man. It is God's instruction. It is God's direction. It is God's guideline, His plumb line, and His bottom line.

All those who in faith have gone on before us — forefathers, fathers, patriarchs, prophets, apostles, preachers, evangelists, martyrs, confessors, ascetics, and every righteous spirit made pure in Christ — have always looked to the Bible as the blueprint for living. They have always taken it seriously, studying it, applying it, and obeying it. That is because they have comprehended the reality that from Genesis to Revelation the Bible is indeed God's Word. And that God's Word is hope for the hopeless, help for the helpless, salve for the sick, balm for the broken, and strength for the stricken. It is the cure.

The doctors, lawyers, politicians, social scientists, judges, psychologists, bureaucrats, and various and sundry other experts who have harnessed their disciplines for the Planned Parenthood movement, certainly cannot be faulted for their concern over the plight of women and children—if indeed their concern is genuine. Where they have gone astray is in taking matters into their own hands, seeking out their own new and novel cure. Instead of adhering to the wise and inerrant counsel of the Bible—walking along the well-trod path of the Saints—they have done "what was right in their own eyes" (Judges 21:25). They have completely ignored—and as a consequence violated—God's Wisdom. Their policies, proposals, and programs have been blatantly *man centered*. In other words, they have been *humanistic*.

Humanism is, according to the Russian iconodule Aleksandr Solzhenitsyn, "the proclaimed and practiced autonomy of man from any higher force above him."[10] Or, as theologian Francis Schaeffer has said, it is "the placing of man at the center of all things and making him the measure of all things."[11] According to humanistic dogma, there is no notion of absolute right or wrong. There are no clear-cut standards. Morality is relative. And problem solving is entirely subjective.[12]

The problem is that humanism is entirely out of sync with reality:

> To the Law and to the Testimony! If they do not speak according to this Word, it is because they have no dawn (Isaiah 8:20).

To attempt to solve the perilous problems of modern society without hearing and heeding the clear instructions of the Bible is utter foolishness (Romans 1:18-23). It is an invitation to inadequacy, incompetency, irrelevancy, and impotency (Deuteronomy 28:15). All such attempts are doomed to frustration and failure.

Humanism cannot work because humanism ignores the fabric of reality (Ephesians 5:6). It is fraught with fantasy (Colossians 2:8). Only the Bible can tell us of things as they *really* are (Psalm 19:7-11). Only the Bible faces reality squarely, practically, completely, and honestly (Deuteronomy 30:11-14). Thus, only the Bible can provide genuine solutions to the problems that plague mankind (Psalm 119:105).

Jesus was forever reminding His disciples of these facts. He made it clear to them that the Bible was to be their ultimate standard—for life and godliness, for faith and practice, and for profession and confession:

> It is written, "Man shall not live by bread alone, but on every Word that proceeds out of the mouth of God" (Matthew 4:4).

> But it is easier for heaven and earth to pass away than for one stroke of a letter of the Law to fail (Luke 16:17).

> Whoever then annuls one of the least of these Commandments, and so teaches others, shall be called least in the Kingdom of Heaven; but whoever keeps and teaches them, he shall be called great in the Kingdom of Heaven (Matthew 5:19).

Again and again He affirmed the truth that "all Scripture is God breathed" (2 Timothy 3:16), that it is useful for "teaching, rebuking, correcting, and training in righteousness" (2 Timothy 3:17), and that it "cannot be broken" (John 10:35):

> All His Precepts are sure. They are upheld forever and ever; they are performed in truth and uprightness (Psalm 111:7-8).

All men know this. Even the diligent and studied humanists in Planned Parenthood know this. The work of God's Law is written on the hearts of all men (Romans 2:14-15). They must actively restrain or suppress this Truth in order to carry on with their novelties (Romans 1:18). Though they know what is right, they deliberately debase themselves with futile thinking, foolish passions, and filthy behavior (Romans 1:19-24, 26-27). They purposefully betray reality, exchanging God's Word for lies (Romans 1:25). Though they know the Ordinances of Life, they consciously choose the precepts of death (Romans 1:28-31). And then they attempt to impose their conjured insanity on the rest of us, proposing it as the solution to all our earthly ills (Romans 1:32).

So, despite their desperate ravings to the contrary, the only way that we will be able to develop compassionate solutions to the tough dilemmas of crisis pregnancies, poor maternal health, overextended family resources, teen promiscuity, and venereal diseases is if we submit ourselves to the eternal, established, and effectual Word of Truth (Psalm 119:152). The only way we will be able to develop genuine and dynamic alternatives to the humanistic programs of Planned Parenthood is if we yield ourselves to the solitary, supreme, and sufficient Word of Life (Proverbs 6:23).

> "For My Thoughts are not your thoughts, neither are your ways My Ways," declares the Lord. "For as the heavens are higher than the earth, so are My Ways higher than your ways, and My Thoughts than your thoughts. For as the rain and the snow come down from heaven, and do not return there without watering the earth, and making it bear and sprout, and furnishing seed to the sower and bread to the eater; so shall My Word be which goes forth from My mouth; it shall not return to Me empty, without accomplishing what I desire, and without succeeding in the matter for which I sent it" (Isaiah 55:8-11).

Throughout this book, as we survey the landscape Planned Parenthood has laid waste, this will ever be before us.

The Cure Applied

In the first two chapters we will look at Planned Parenthood — both the generic movement and the institutional association — in very general terms. We will basically be getting a lay of the land. Concepts and controversies introduced in these chapters will be dealt with in much greater detail later in the book.

In Chapter 3 we will begin to examine the history of Planned Parenthood. I say "begin" simply because the historical context of the organization's policies, programs, principles, priorities, plans, and procedures is an important theme that we will return to again and again throughout the book.

In Chapter 4 we will look into the medical practices of Planned Parenthood. Abortion, birth control, and sterilization are at the heart of the organization's work. Just how safe are these practices?

In Chapter 5 we will examine the very controversial subject of prejudice and discrimination. Is Planned Parenthood a racist movement?

In Chapter 6 we will look at Planned Parenthood's crusade to bring comprehensive sex education to every man, woman, and child in America. Just what does sex education actually accomplish? How effective is it in combating teen pregnancy, runaway promiscuity, venereal diseases, and interpersonal irresponsibility?

In Chapter 7 we will closely examine the finances of Planned Parenthood. Where do the funds to run this massive coast-to-coast, international, cross-cultural phenomenon come from? And how are they spent?

In Chapter 8 we will take a look at the many different organizations and institutions that actively support and cooperate with Planned Parenthood's program for social transformation.

In Chapter 9 the media will be our concern. How does the established media deal with Planned Parenthood? And why?

In Chapter 10 we will turn our attention to the Church. Is there a connection between the Church's actions — or inactions — and Planned Parenthood's tremendous influence?

With Chapter 11 we will begin to look at specific strategies to deal with the problems raised by Planned Parenthood. First, we will determine what we must *be* in order to confront evil.

Then in Chapter 12, we will determine what we must *do* in order to confront evil.

Finally, in the last two chapters, we will look at some positive, constructive alternatives to the Planned Parenthood juggernaut.

The book closes with several practical resources to enable faithful Christians to make a real difference in their families, in their communities, and in their world.

In ancient Alexandria, a school of literary interpretation was developed that analyzed texts on three different levels simultaneously: the physical or literal level, the intellectual or philosophical level, and the spiritual or allegorical level. This book was written to conform to that Alexandrian model. Thus it operates on all three of those levels. So, for instance, the various affiliate statistics, personal stories, and historical overviews are to be taken quite literally. The sociological analysis, the Biblical theology, and the institutional suppositions are to be understood philosophically. And the literary allusions, Spielbergian feints, and Latin puzzles are allegorical indicators. Each level is *true*, but each level has its own perspective of and approach to that truth — a truth ultimately summed up and encapsulated in Christ Jesus alone: the Truth (John 14:6).

Ad Maiorem Dei Gloriam.

PART ONE

THE ILLUSION

Ah! The temper of the true liar! With his frank, fearless statements, his superb irresponsibility, his healthy,
natural disdain of proof of any kind! After all, what is a
fine lie? Simply that which is its own evidence.

Oscar Wilde

April is the cruelest month, breeding
Lilacs out of the dead land, mixing
Memory and desire, stirring
Dull roots with spring rain.

T. S. Eliot

IN THE HEAT
OF THE FIGHT

casus belli

I heard him coming.

Who wouldn't?

Stumbling over the piles of rubbish, refuse, and overgrowth that littered the alley, his stealth was extremely questionable.

But his determination certainly wasn't. Nor was his destination. He was headed right for me.

I looked up, peering between the cracks of broken boards. The dilapidated fence gave me momentary vantage and advantage. And I saw him. He was a perfect picture of spit and polish. His crisp blue uniform played a stark contrast against the alley's cudulent clutter. The gleam of chrome and polished leather threw flitting reflections of sunlight on the ground, shattered triangles of morning brightness skipping across the discarded baubles and forgotten fascinations that composed the heaps of garbage between him and me.

"Hey. Hey you!"

The moment of decision. And I was frozen in indecision.

"Hey. Get out of there."

I did. Clambering over the edge of the wretched and rusted bin, I hoisted a bulky sack to my shoulder and skirted around the fence.

"Stop. Right where you are."

I didn't. As best I could, I began to run, my indecision washed away in a tidal wave of adrenalin.

"Stop, dammit. I said *stop*."

I was running as fast as I could now, burden upon my back, fire in my lungs, and passion in my heart.

"I'm warning you. Stop."

I ran as if my life depended on it.

"I'll shoot you down."

I was straining, my heart bursting at my chest, my fear stabbing at my soul.

"I mean it. I'll shoot, dammit."

He swore vilely. He swore again. And again. And then he opened fire. Just as I reached the end of the alley and rounded the corner, he shattered the Saturday morning stillness with a furious report.

I was panic stricken.

I ran harder and faster. But he was gaining on me anyway.

In desperation I threw myself toward the street, still clutching my precious sackload. Another shot erupted overhead. And another.

I ran. I prayed. I made for the parking lot ahead.

Ducking past a retainer wall and stumbling over a guardrail, I burst into a small crowd of men, women, and children pacing back and forth along a thirty foot stretch of sidewalk between the lot and the street. My friends. Safety.

"Get me out of here," I screeched.

Gawking, uncomprehending, they just stood there.

Breathless and terrified, I lunged toward a car. "The keys. I need the keys. Now!"

Just then, the security guard came charging toward us from behind the retainer wall.

"The keys. I need the keys."

I stuffed my sack through the window and jumped behind the wheel. Honking wildly and screaming madly, I finally snapped their spell of astonishment, and several men sprang into action.

One tossed me the keys. Two others piled into the back seat. I skidded away from the curb just as another blast echoed round about us.

"Which way do I go?" I was gasping for air. My senses were numb. "Which way?"

"Uh, I dunno. Uh, head for the freeway I guess."

"Which way is that?" Impatient, I swerved around the corner, leaving a trail of dust clouds and flaying skree.

As they steered me in the right direction, I glanced back. The security guard was not about to let us get away. Of that, I was sure. He roared after us in an ominous and carnivorous pickup. It was the kind of truck that young boys drool over: jacked high off the ground, and gaudily adorned with fog lamps, mud gear, and massive chrome mags. It lurched into view just a block and a half behind us.

The chase was on.[1]

Facing the Anomaly

Day had just begun and I was already off the mark. The vast unending midwestern sky was crystalline blue and cloudless. Songbirds filled the air with sweetness and delight. The fresh aroma of turned soil and amber waves of grain beckoned from the outskirts of town. And here I was, careening down the freeway like a scalded cat.

Not quite my idea of a pleasant Saturday morning out.

It had all started out innocently enough, though. I was in town for a couple of speaking engagements. Several pro-life advocates, including the two men currently playing "Elliot Ness" in the back seat of my "getaway car," had invited me to participate in their regular Saturday morning picket of a local abortion clinic.[2] Such invitations for me are like the bite of a silk piranha. I accepted.

The night before, my hosts had taken me out and about town to show me the sights. We visited some of the great architectural icons of America's heartland: an imposing Sullivan warehouse, an eclectic Graves showroom, a landmark Wright home, a daunting Jahn office tower, and a sterling Johnson theater. We reveled in the gloriously sculpted bridges and the marvelously restored depots. We stopped by the farmers' market where a furious cacophony of sights, sound, and smells drenched us with the delirium of business-as-usual. Neon, granite, and steel combined with flesh and blood to proclaim with unmistakable clarity the vibrancy and vitality of this community.

The city was alive. It pulsed with an assured urgency. It bore in its breast that brash existential exuberance that demarcates American society.

As a last stop on our whirlwind tour, my hosts drove me past the site of the picket scheduled for the next morning: the abortuary.

Suddenly, I was confronted with the central anomaly of these modern times: a liberal lust for life, a lavish love of life, a luxuriant litany of life, and yet, simultaneously, a leaden loathing of life. I was struck by the complex absurdity of our cultural dance: a compulsive rehearsal of the rite of life confused and confounded by a chronic denial of the right to life.[3]

Back in my hotel room, alone with my thoughts, a haunting refrain rang in my ears:

We must cry out for the young
How long must this crime go on?
Until we see
The Church in unity?

We must cry out for the young
Sound the warning, make it strong
And move as one
The time has come.
The time has come.[4]

I caught myself pining. Maudlin moments.[5]

I shook the mood before it took hold, though. I decided to put on my "Matt Scudder Cap"[6] and do a bit of research.[7] The time had come.

It didn't take me long to get the ball rolling, even at that late hour. I perused the phone directory. I made several calls to hospitals, pathology labs, disposal services, and emergency clinics — adding to my hotel bill an obscene fifty cents apiece. And I asked a few key questions of a few key people.[8]

Within half an hour I knew with a fair amount of certainty what I would find in the morning. It would not be pleasant.

A shiver went up and down my spine.

In the Belly of the Beast

Dawn broke tawny as a lion and somnolent as a hearthside tom. A belvedere weekend, teal true and rumor red, beckoned through the hotel window sheers.

I hastily went through my regular morning ritual: shower, shave, devotions, and a frantic search for my wallet. I always try to put my money in a "safe place" when I'm away from home.

Invariably, I forget where that "safe place" is and am forced to spend precious moments racking my still anesthetized brain in order to discover how "clever" I was the night before. On this particular morning, I hunted through drawers, in closets, and under mattresses for almost twenty minutes before I remembered that I had hidden the wallet in the ice bucket. I've since been told that's one of the first places a thief checks when he's casing a room.

I didn't have time for breakfast now, so I went down to the lobby to await my ride to the picket.

The drive was pleasant and uneventful. Talk ranged from baseball scores to department stores, from amusement parks to broken hearts, from movie releases to dry-cleaned creases. No one said a word about the dark portent of danger that we all felt. I, for one, was trying to ignore it, hoping that it would just go away.

But it wouldn't.

And I knew why.

I knew what would be waiting for us at the clinic. And no amount of hoping could erase that knowledge.

We parked just across from the old building. It was a real oddity in the once distinguished neighborhood. Situated on the main street in town, it was down four or five blocks from where the commercial section began, in an area that had long ago sported wide lawns and overarching elms. Now, all those trees were gone, victims of Dutch Elm disease, and the grand promenade had an exposed, befuddled air. Gallant English gardens and proud Tudor homes had given way to a barren wasteland of asphalt and gaudy metal warehouses.[9] The clinic occupied a remnant of the past. It was once a stately mansion — brownstone and ivy, leaded glass and cedar shakes. It was an island of antiquity amidst a sea of modernity.

When it was built around the turn of the century, it was serious and simple to excess. Contemporary men rarely appreciate that style. They prefer the esoteric eccentricity of modernism. No doubt they are right, since they are restless space-time nomads.[10] But men and women who have lived long and are tired of wandering — who want rest, who have done with temporal aspirations and ambitions, whose life in the urban Negev has been a broken arch—feel its repose and self-restraint as they feel nothing else.[11] The quiet strength of its curved lines, the solid support of its tall columns, the moderate proportions of its gables and transepts, even its absence of display, of effort, and of self-consciousness, satisfy them as no other art does. They come back to it to rest, after a long circle of pilgrimage—the cradle of rest from which their forefathers started.[12]

Here though, they find that rest none too deep.

The apex of the brownstone rose like a sugarloaf forty feet above the foundations, majestic and unfettered. But the foundations below had been despoiled by the creeping convenience of contemporaneity.[13]

The bottom floor of the building was apparently remodeled sometime during the irreverent days of the sixties in order to accommodate the clinic. A false facade and broad spans of plate glass invited clients into a sterile beige foyer. The renovations of the sixties, like the buildings of the sixties, show bland economy, and sometimes worse. The world grew cheap, as the world's world must.[14]

Contemporary men may like it all the better for being less serious, less heroic, and more what the French call "bourgeois"—just as they may like the style of Louie Louie better than that of Louis XIV, Madonna better than Montesquieu, and videos better than Videossis—for taste is as free as will. Athanasius called such freedom "captivity." Luther called it "bondage." Calvin called it "depravity." Basil called it "vanity." Chrysostom called it "debauchery." And Solzhenitsyn called it "irresponsibility." Sin's shackles severely limit the latitude of both taste and will.[15]

A scraggly line of picketers were already doing their paces back and forth in front of the building. They made for a motley crew. A sweetly attired grandmother was walking with a fully festooned college student. A young mother pushing a double stroller and carrying a gargantuan sign was accompanied by a teenager who preened a tragically hip haircut and a phosphorescently decorated t-shirt. A middle aged couple, perfectly type-cast fundamentalists, were engrossed in a conversation with three nuns. Several young families, who looked as if they had suddenly been sidetracked from a trip to the zoo or a picnic in the park supervised childrens' activities. Two men, in whose veins flowed zealot's blood, were taking turns reading passages of Scripture over a megaphone. One was dressed in a banker's gray flannel suit. The other wore ragged jeans and a chambray work shirt. Hardly heterogeneous, yet they testified as one that the old building bore the sorry stains not only of bad taste, but of bad will as well.[16]

I joined them.[17]

Every thirty minutes for the next two and a half hours, we watched as a fresh clutch of doe-eyed girls were whisked into the clinic by "pro-choice escorts." They met the girls at their cars and quickly aimed them up the sidewalk. They snarled at our offers of help and batted away our literature. If a girl displayed the least hint of hesitation, the "escorts" would take her by the arm and rush her toward the door. So much for "choice."[18]

When despite their best efforts, a frightened and confused teen slipped their grasp and turned aside to talk to one of the protesters, to read a Gospel tract, the "escorts" flew into a frenzied rage. They lunged at the picket line. Taunting, jeering, cursing, and reviling, they tried to recapture their prey. One turned her contorted, wild-eyed gaze toward me.

"You pig," she sputtered. "You damned, chauvinist pig. Let the girl go."[19]

I looked over my shoulder where the girl was kneeling in the grass, quietly praying with several picketers, utterly incognizant of the efforts of this thrashing, yammering champion for "choice."[20]

"Why don't you go home? Mind your own business?" She was right in my face, yelling in my ear, shoving, red-faced, and livid. "You're traumatizing the girl, you pig."

She went on and on, clichés repeated like a worn out record. But all to no avail. The girl was walking away, arm in arm with her new found friends. She said she was keeping her baby.[21]

Frustrated, the "escorts" retreated to the building. A quick conference ensued with the clinic director, two nurses, and a security guard. They were clearly disturbed and kept gesturing in our direction with stabbing fingers and malevolent stares. After a few moments of haggling between themselves, they dispatched the guard, presumably to "restore order" to this now thoroughly unpleasant Saturday morning.

As he sauntered toward us, calling us to attention, he struck me as an anguished, angry man. But his anger was hidden and subversive. It was tucked neatly into the dark folds of his uniform like a murderer's knife hidden inside an old coat on a closet shelf. On his breath was what the philosophic observer was free to regard as either his last drink on Friday or his first on Saturday. Certainly, *he* was not particular.

"Look here, people. Don't you think you've caused enough of a ruckus here today? Why don't you just go on home?"

Most of the picketers ignored him. They resumed their march back and forth on the sunset side of the building, while the banker with the megaphone and the sweetly attired grandmother explained Scriptural profundities to him.[22]

"I don't wanna hear your spiel. I just want you to leave. Now."

Unperturbed, the banker continued reading from his well-worn Bible.

"Hey, come on. Give me a break, will ya? I don't need this grief."

Now, it was the grandmother's turn. She quoted Scripture by memory. King's English. Perfect inflection.

"You people are impossible."

At that, both protesters turned tender and tried to reason with the guard.[23] But, there was no reasoning with him. Stern faced, anger no longer hidden, he harumphed a few moments longer. And then thoroughly flustered, he turned to go.

Suddenly, all was quiet on the western front.

I decided it was now or never.

Hell's Ballad

I left the sidewalk and rounded the corner of the building. A long retainer wall dropped off to the parking lot. The concrete there was overlaid with graffiti, years of abbreviated manifestos, twisting into a single metascrawl of rage and indignation.[24] I crossed the lot and ducked behind an old fence into a service alley.

Before me was a large garbage dumpster. The object of my reconnaissance. I stood before its reeking hulk and paused. Uncertain. Hesitant. And skittish.

I felt faint and foolish. "What on earth am I getting myself into?" I wondered.[25]

It was the same sensation that I'd felt standing on the free throw line in the Pershing Elementary School gym a quarter century earlier. We were one point behind, and I knew that with seven seconds to go I held the district championship in my hands. But all I wanted to do was to crawl up under the old pine bleachers and throw up. I didn't want to bravely face my destiny. I didn't want to take my free throws.

I knew what was in that dumpster just as surely as I knew that I would miss those shots.

Memory is a madman that hoards my colored rags and throws away my precious gems. Prescience is a school-marm that belabors what I ought to be and ignores what I thought to be. I took a deep breath and climbed into the bin.[26]

The stench was overwhelming. Rotten fruit, stale tobacco, fetid beer, and hospital astringent assaulted my senses. Bile rose up like a knot in my throat.

But, the sight was worse even than the smell. It was horrid. A scene like a ballad come to life. A ballad composed about the tragic events in some border hell.

Several garbage bags had spilled their contents out into the open bin. Mixed with the empty Coke cans, fast food wrappers, cigarette butts, and office litter were bundles of surgical gauze and laminaria matted with blood. And wrapped in those bundles were the broken bodies of several dozen children. Dismembered arms and legs. Crushed skulls. Mutilated corpses. Unseeing eyes. The leering look of death was all around me.

They tell me that comparisons with the Nazi Holocaust are inappropriate. Hyperbole, they say. Apparently, such people have never been inside this dumpster. Their comprehension of the abortion issue is theoretical. It is political. Or, sociological. But, this dumpster is as inescapable as Auschwitz. Its evidence is as irrefutable. As damnable.[27]

I reached across the carnage and opened one of the plastic bags. Even with all that I'd seen thus far I was entirely unprepared for this. There were no bloody limbs. There were no brutal decapitations. There were no broken spines, disemboweled bodies, or shredded extremities. Instead, what I saw in this bag was a *perfect* baby. Whole. Unblemished. Brown haired and olive skinned. The sort of child you'd make silly faces at through the maternity ward window. The sort of child you'd expect to see in a bassinet, snuggled into a fluffy pink blanket.

I caught my breath. Stunned.

The Greek gods tossed men like dice. Invoking spirits from the vast deep or calling up enormities from earthen elements, they made a rude fetish of cruelty. Their diabolism knew no bounds. But, even they would have strained to conjure a decadence as ugly as this.[28]

I lightly brushed the child's cheek with the back of my hand and marveled at the delicacy of life. Like hymning angels chime, I whispered a prayer. And tears fell from my eyes like rain.[29]

Just then, I heard the security guard coming. I bundled the child up in her crude plastic sarcophagus and made my mad dash to safety.[30]

Insomnia's Clarity

"Why was that guy shooting?"

"Can he really get away with that?"

"Shouldn't we report him to the police?"

"Or was he the police?"

"Do you think we could prosecute?"

"Would the DA even believe our story?"

"How many actual witnesses do we have?"

"How did you know what you'd find in the garbage?"

"It's not legal to throw babies out like that, is it?"

"What do we do now?"

"Are you sure he's not still following us?"

We were weaving through light traffic on the freeway. The security guard had apparently broken off the chase and we were headed back to my hotel. The immediate crisis was past and my "getaway" accomplices were full of questions.

I didn't have a whole lot of answers.

I knew that I would find a mass grave in the dumpster, I told them, because of the little bit of telephone work the night before.[31] It appeared that neither the state nor the city had fetal disposal ordinances. There were no pathology labs in town that had business dealings with the clinic. There were no bio-medical incinerator services. Like so many other abortuaries around the country, this clinic had little choice but to hurl its victims into the garbage. Offered up on the Altar of Convenience, they are indignantly heaped upon Gehenna.[32] That, I'd expected. The guard, the gun, the chase—well, that was another story altogether. I had heard of incidents, from time to time, of overwrought clinic operators or staff doctors wildly wielding handguns in the face of pro-life opposition. I had seen gruff and overbearing security guards stretch the letter of the law, pushing, shoving, and baiting picketers. I had seen District Attorneys refuse to take up, or even consider, legitimate charges against clinic personnel in extremely abusive situations. I had even witnessed the exercise of raw judicial power in an attempt to quash pro-life activities. But, in all my days, I had never seen a more reckless or foolhardy display.[33]

Back at the hotel, we all got busy tying up loose ends. We called a lawyer for legal counsel. We called a local pastor so that the baby could be properly buried. We called our families, our friends, our contacts, and the media. Over the next several hours, we were subjected to interviews, accusations, charges, and countercharges. But as the day wore on, it became all too apparent that the "powers that be" considered the baby in the dumpster and the shots in the alley nothing more than a tempest in a teapot. A soon-to-be-forgotten unfortunate incident.

By the next evening I was on a plane headed home. The flight was long and tiresome. I tried to catch a quick nap, but the perfect recall and vivid clarity of insomnia wreaked havoc on my repose. My mind was haunted by insane images of twisted lifeless bodies, faces recoiling in terror, and sprays of gunfire scoring the ground around me with deep fury.[34]

When at last I arrived at home, all the lights were out and everyone was fast asleep in their beds. I went from room to room looking at each of my children as they slept. I sat on the edge of the bed where my youngest was snuggled up with his special blanket clutched tight to his breast.

I gazed at him lying there for a long moment. Awestruck. I lightly brushed his cheek with the back of my hand and marveled at the delicacy of life. Like hymning angels chime, I whispered a prayer. And tears fell from my eyes like rain.

Only then did I feel some measure of relief.

And resolve.

From where Winston stood, it was just possible to read, picked out on its face in elegant lettering, the three slogans of the party:

WAR IS PEACE
FREEDOM IS SLAVERY
IGNORANCE IS STRENGTH

The Ministry of Truth contained, it was said, three thousand rooms above ground level, and corresponding ramifications below.

George Orwell

TWO

ALL THAT GLITTERS

ecce signum

Abortion is nasty business. And it is big business.

Since its decriminalization less than twenty years ago, abortion has grown into a five hundred million dollar a year industry in the United States,[1] and an estimated ten billion dollars a year worldwide.[2] More than one hundred and twenty thousand women each day, almost fifty million per year, resort to abortion and then to its various birth control subsidiaries.[3] It has thus become the most frequently performed surgical operation.[4] Though propaganda still hangs like a ground mist over the already complicated issue, these statistics make one thing quite certain: The mind-numbing vastness of the market, the opportunities for a wildly profitable stock-in-trade, and the cataclysmic effects on the social fabric have catapulted abortion to the forefront of our social, economic, political, and ethical concerns.

And standing out like the Nephilim in the midst of those concerns is Planned Parenthood.[5]

Planned Parenthood is the world's oldest, largest, and best-organized provider of abortion and birth control services.[6] From its humble beginnings around the turn of the century, when the entire shoestring operation consisted of a two-room makeshift clinic in a rundown Brooklyn neighborhood[7] staffed by three untrained volunteers,[8] it has expanded dramatically into a multi-billion dollar international conglomerate with programs and activities in one hundred twenty nations on every continent.[9] In the United States alone, it employs more than twenty thousand staff personnel and volunteers[10] in over eight hundred clinics,[11] nearly two hundred affiliates,[12] and more than fifty chapters[13] in every major metropolitan area, coast to coast.[14]

23

Utilizing this considerable wealth, manpower, and influence, Planned Parenthood has muscled its way into virtually every facet of modern life. It now plays a strategic role in the health and social services community.[15] It is actively involved in both advertising and programming in the mass media.[16] It exerts a major influence on public and private education.[17] It carries considerable political clout through lobbying, legislation, advocacy, campaigning, and litigation.[18] It is involved in publishing,[19] research,[20] medical technology,[21] judicial activism,[22] public relations,[23] foreign affairs,[24] psychological counseling,[25] sociological planning,[26] demographic investigation,[27] curriculum development,[28] pharmacological distribution,[29] theological reorientation,[30] and public legal service provision.[31]

But despite this nearly omnipresent intrusion into family, Church, state, and culture, Planned Parenthood has somehow managed to manufacture for itself a sterling reputation. It has brokered its abortion trade into a public image that is very nearly unassailable.

It has a reputation for providing effective and professional social services for the needy.

It has a reputation for developing honest and insightful educational programs for the young.

It has a reputation for maintaining the rights and liberties of the weak, the desperate, the frightened, and the downtrodden.

It has a reputation for advocating low-cost, readily available counseling and health care services for women.

It has a no-nonsense, tough-as-nails, down-to-earth, where-the-rubber-meets-the-road kind of reputation that has made it a glittering star in the grand constellation of the American social service field.

All that glitters, however, is not gold.

Just as Planned Parenthood's wealth and prestige has been built on death, defilement, and destruction, its reputation has been built on deception, disinformation, and distortion. It is a reputation built on illusions.

Planned Parenthood is not all that it is cracked up to be. In fact, it is not *anything* that it is cracked up to be. It is not even close.

The Pro-Choice Illusion

Planned Parenthood claims to advocate the freedom of women to choose if and when they will have children, without government interference. [32] But that is an illusion. [33]

Planned Parenthood is anything *but* a "pro-choice" organization. And it is anything *but* a populist, non-interventionist champion of liberty against governmental coercion.

The truth is that from its very inception, Planned Parenthood has sought mandatory population control measures — measures carefully designed to *deny* the freedom to choose. [34] Over the years it has proposed that our government implement such things as "compulsory abortion for out-of-wedlock pregnancies," [35] federal entitlement "payments to encourage abortion," [36] "compulsory sterilization for those who have already had two children," [37] and "tax penalties" for existing large families. [38]

Although Planned Parenthood's sterilization crusade has seen ready acceptance in the United States from time to time, especially among the ill, the infirm, the poor, and the incarcerated, [39] most of its other coercive programs have been embraced enthusiastically in a number of other countries.

China, for example, has taken Planned Parenthood's suggestions to heart, launching a brutal, no-holds-barred, one-child-per-couple policy. [40] Nearly one hundred million forced abortions, mandatory sterilizations, and coercive infanticides later, [41] Planned Parenthood continues to maintain that the communist government's genocidal approach to population control is a "model of efficiency." [42] It has fought to maintain United States funding of the Chinese operation, [43] and has continued to increase its own funding and program support involvement [44] despite widespread reports of human rights atrocities. [45]

Similar draconian measures have been implemented at Planned Parenthood's behest in dozens of countries throughout the Third World. [46] Providing many of these countries with detailed restraints and quotas, suggested compulsory incentives and disincentives, and assistance in circumventing public opinion and moral opposition, Planned Parenthood has taken the lead in the international campaign to crush the rights of women to choose if and when they will have children. [47]

The slow advance of Planned Parenthood's coercive programs has eroded freedom of choice in the United States as well.

Parents often *cannot choose* to obtain full medical disclosure for their minor children.[48] Fathers often *cannot choose* to save the lives of their unborn babies.[49] Pro-life advocates often *cannot choose* to exercise their first amendment rights in front of aborturaries and clinics.[50] Alternative centers for women with crisis pregnancies often *cannot choose* to counsel, lobby, solicit, or advertise on an equal basis with abortuaries.[51] Medical personnel often *cannot choose* to abstain from abortion, infanticide, fetal harvesting and euthanasia procedures.[52] Cities and states often *cannot choose* to unilaterally regulate commercial abortion activities within their jurisdictions.[53] Even the President of the United States *cannot choose* to develop a pro-life administration policy program.[54] All this, thanks to the diligence of Planned Parenthood and its insistence on government interference into the personal lives of men, women, and children everywhere.[55]

In a recent survey of women who had received abortions at Planned Parenthood, sixty percent stated that their counselor had "very strongly encouraged them to choose abortion as the *best* solution to their problem."[56] This is especially significant in light of the fact that over ninety percent of those encouraged to abort by their Planned Parenthood counselor said that "there was a strong chance" they would have chosen *against* the abortion if they "had not been so strongly encouraged to abort."[57] Over sixty percent were "still hoping to find an alternative" when they went in for counseling.[58] Only twenty-five percent were already "firm in their decision" to obtain an abortion.[59] So what did the "champions of choice" at Planned Parenthood do to help these women through the agonizing decision-making process? Did they lay out all the options? Did they discuss all the available alternatives? Did they go over all the possible risks, hazards, and complications? Did they offer women a *real* choice? Hardly. Ninety-five percent of the women said that their Planned Parenthood counselors gave "little or no biological information about the fetus which the abortion would destroy."[60] Eighty percent said that their counselors gave "little or no information about the potential health risks which might follow the surgery."[61] Sixty-eight percent felt that "the procedure was not described with any degree of depth or clarity."[62] And eighty-nine percent said that their counselor was "strongly biased in favor of the abortion."[63]

Far from advocating choice then, Planned Parenthood has become, over the years at home and abroad, the most valiant crusader against choice since Madame Mao and the "Gang of Four" conducted the Cultural Revolution.

Planned Parenthood is *not*, by any stretch of the imagination, a "pro-choice" organization. It is instead one of the most vicious opponents of choice in the world today. It knows no *glasnost*. We simply cannot contend or pretend otherwise.

The Charity Illusion

Planned Parenthood claims to serve the needs of poor women and low-income families.[64] But that is an illusion.[65]

Planned Parenthood's pose as a champion of the underprivileged is a cruel hoax foisted on the uninformed and unsuspecting.

The truth is, Planned Parenthood appears to want to *eliminate* the poor, not *serve* them.[66] Animosity toward the weak and lowly has been its hallmark from its earliest days.[67] In fact, its entire program of family limitation was designed to foster an elitist pogrom against the underclasses.[68]

In 1922, Margaret Sanger, founder of Planned Parenthood, chided social workers, philanthropists, and churchmen for perpetuating "the cruelty of charity."[69] She argued that organized attempts to help the poor were the "surest sign that our civilization has bred, is breeding, and is perpetuating constantly increasing numbers of defectives, delinquents, and dependents."[70] She went on to write that the most "insidiously injurious philanthropy" was the maternity care given to poor women.[71] She concluded her diatribe by describing all those who refused to see the necessity of severely regulating the fertility of the working class as "benign imbeciles, who encourage the defective and diseased elements of humanity in their reckless and irresponsible swarming and spawning."[72]

Her alternative to charity was "to *eliminate* the stocks" that she felt were most detrimental "to the future of the race and the world."[73] To that end, Planned Parenthood has always targeted minorities, the unwanted, and the disadvantaged for family limitation, contraception, abortion, and sterilization.[74] "More children from the fit, less from the unfit," Sanger pined, "that is the chief issue of birth control."[75]

To this day the thrust of Planned Parenthood's literature focuses on the terrible *burden* that the poor place on the rich.[76] It continually reminds us of the costs that welfare mothers incur for the elite.[77] It constantly devises new plans to penetrate Black, Hispanic, and ethnic communities with its crippling message of Eugenic racism.[78] It seems that its only use for the deprived and rejected is as bait for huge federal subsidies and foundation grants. "If we must have welfare," Sanger argued, "give it to the rich, not to the poor."[79] Her organization has for years attempted to translate that philosophy into public policy.

Among measures Planned Parenthood has recently spotlighted in its literature are such things as the elimination of child care, medical attention, scholarships, housing, loans, and subsidies to poor families.[80] In addition it has given voice to such notions as maternity benefits being drastically reduced or even eliminated, substantial, across-the-board marriage and child taxes being imposed, and large families *not* being given preferential charitable relief.[81]

Planned Parenthood is *not*, by any stretch of the imagination, an advocate of the poor. It is instead a great oppressor and exploiter of the poor. Its image-conscious rhetoric of compassion is a paragon of Orwellian doublespeak. We simply cannot contend or pretend otherwise.

The Private Funding Illusion

Planned Parenthood claims to be a privately funded, non-profit family planning organization.[82] But that is an illusion.[83]

First of all, Planned Parenthood is *not* an "organization"—it is instead an association of more than three hundred separately incorporated organizations worldwide.[84] Second, it is *not* involved primarily in "family planning"—it is instead involved in "family banning."[85] Finally, and perhaps most importantly, it is by no means "privately" funded, either.[86]

The truth is, a vast proportion of Planned Parenthood's funding at every level—from the local level to the international level—comes right out of the American taxpayer's pocket. It has become for all intents and purposes an unofficial—and thus unrestrained and unrestricted—branch of the federal government.

It is widely known that Planned Parenthood receives tens of millions of tax dollars through the Title X appropriations of the

Public Health Service Act.[87] In fiscal 1987, Title X funds amounted to a whopping $142.5 million.[88] In 1988, that sum was upped to $146 million.[89] Dispensed as a virtual block grant, to be spent in whatever way Planned Parenthood and the other beneficiaries see fit, this Title X money is obviously a major source of income for the aborturies and birth control clinics of our land.[90]

What is not widely known, however, is that those Title X appropriations represent only a small proportion of Planned Parenthood's taxpayer largess. There are some eighteen additional federal statutes[91] as well as hundreds of state and local measures that authorize public expenditures and support for "family planning" programs, policies, and procedures.[92] So for instance, during the "pro-life" Reagan administration, Planned Parenthood clinics, affiliates, and chapters received annual federal funding under the seventeen million dollar Title V provision of the Social Security Maternal and Child Health Program.[93] Each year they received federal funding under the nine million dollar Medicaid appropriations bill. In addition, those clinics, affiliates, and chapters benefited each year from the government's eight million dollar contraceptive development splurge,[94] its three million dollar expenditure for a contraceptive evaluation project,[95] its sixty-six million dollar spending spree for "reproductive sciences,"[96] its fourteen million dollars spent on demographic and behavioral research,[97] and its twenty-seven million dollars budgeted for community services block grants.[98] Internationally, various Planned Parenthood agencies have been able to skim the cream off of virtually every United States foreign aid package. This includes a lion's share of the more than two hundred million dollars in International Population Assistance funds,[99] and the more than one hundred million dollars in contraceptive and abortifacient research appropriations.[100] Additionally, Planned Parenthood gets a larger part of the untold billions in grants, contracts, and cooperative agreements of the United Nations Fund for Population Activities, the World Bank, and the Agency for International Development.[101]

That is a lot of money. That is a lot of *your* money. And a lot of *my* money.

Planned Parenthood is *not*, by any stretch of the imagination, a privately funded, non-profit family planning organization. It is instead one of the largest—if not the largest—*publicly funded* multi-national collectives the world has ever seen. We simply cannot contend or pretend otherwise.

The Birth Control Illusion

Planned Parenthood claims that its system of birth control is safe and effective. [102] But that is an illusion. [103]

Planned Parenthood's blind faith in its chemical and mechanical methodology is completely and entirely unfounded. [104] The truth is, Planned Parenthood's program of birth control has failed to inhibit unwanted pregnancies, and it has dramatically increased the risk of severe medical problems for the women who follow it. [105] Ninety percent of the fifty-five million women of reproductive age in the United States use some form of contraception, [106] including as many as seventy-nine percent of all sexually active teens. [107] Even so, more than three million unwanted pregnancies are reported every year. [108] More than fourteen million cases of venereal disease are reported every year. [109]

The number of reported complications and side effects increases with every passing day. [110] All this is *directly* attributable to Planned Parenthood's cult of contraception. [111]

According to Planned Parenthood's own figures, the annual in-use failure rate for the Pill is as high as eleven percent. [112] For the diaphragm, the normal failure rate is nearly thirty-two percent. [113] For the inter-uterine device (IUD), it is almost eleven percent. [114] For "safe sex" condoms, it is over eighteen percent. [115] And for the various foam, cream, and jelly spermicides, it can range as high as thirty-four percent. [116] That means that a sexually active fourteen-year-old girl who faithfully uses the Pill has a forty-four percent chance of getting pregnant at least once before she finishes high school. [117] She has a sixty-nine percent chance of getting pregnant at least once before she finishes college. [118] And she has a thirty percent chance of getting pregnant two or more times. [119] If she relies on "safe sex" condoms, the likelihood of an unwanted pregnancy while she is in school rises to nearly eighty-seven percent. [120] In other words, the Planned Parenthood system virtually *guarantees* that women will get pregnant—and that they will then be "forced" to fall back on the birth control lynch pin: abortion.

Safe and effective? Not by a long shot. Planned Parenthood's program of birth control is nothing but foreplay for abortion. Besides the fact that it is fraught with awful side effects, complications, and medical risks, it is incapable of preventing unwanted pregnancies as well. Planned Parenthood's entire myth is an empty charade. We simply cannot contend or pretend otherwise.

The STD Illusion

Planned Parenthood claims that it is in the forefront of the battle against sexually transmitted diseases.[121] But that is an illusion.[122]

Planned Parenthood is not only not in the *forefront* of the battle, it is not even *in* the battle. The truth is, Planned Parenthood's efforts have been tragically counterproductive. It has become a veritable Typhoid Mary, actually encouraging the *spread* of syphilis, gonorrhea, chlamydia, herpes, hepatitis, granuloma, chancroid, and even AIDS at an alarming rate. Besides the fact that it constantly exhorts youngsters to flaunt a ribald and irresponsible promiscuity,[123] it continually promotes an alarmingly "unsafe" exercise of that promiscuity. Instead of affording its fornicating disciples with the slim security of barrier devices, it primarily peddles the entirely unguarded prescription birth control methods. Eighty percent of Planned Parenthood's clients receive non-barrier contraceptives,[124] and eighty-eight percent of those who previously practiced "safe sex" are *dissuaded* from continuing.[125]

Admittedly, barrier devices such as condoms offer only limited protection against venereal infection.[126] Due to in-use mechanical failure—leaks, breaks, tears, slippage, and spillage—their effectiveness has been estimated to be *at best* eighty-two percent.[127] But the Pill offers *no* protection whatsoever. Neither does the IUD or the diaphragm or spermicides or contraceptive sponges or any of the other non-barrier birth control devices that Planned Parenthood favors. Worse, recent studies indicate that not only do these methods fail to guard *against* venereal infection, they may actually *enhance* the risks.[128] "Apparently," says demographic analyst Robert Ruff, "Planned Parenthood believes that safe sex is a lot less important than free sex."[129]

Planned Parenthood is *not*, by any stretch of the imagination in the forefront of the battle against venereal disease. It is instead part of the problem, serving as a conduit for "unsafe" sexual practices. We simply cannot contend or pretend otherwise.

The Sex Education Illusion

Planned Parenthood claims that sex education is a necessary and effective means of preventing teen pregnancies.[130] But that is an illusion.[131]

Planned Parenthood's multi-million dollar, tax-funded educational efforts have proven to be anything but necessary and effective.

The truth is, Planned Parenthood's sex education programs have backfired, actually *increasing* teen pregnancies. According to its own survey, conducted in 1986 by the Louis Harris pollsters, teens who have taken "comprehensive" sex education courses have a fifty percent *higher* rate of sexual activity than their "unenlightened" peers.[132] And yet the courses had no significant effect on their contraceptive usage.[133] The conclusion, one that even Planned Parenthood researchers have been unable to escape, is that sex education courses only exacerbate the teen pregnancy problem.[134]

In an effort to denounce the threat that such a conclusion poses to its precious empire, Planned Parenthood has erected a scaffold of spurious statistics, studies, and surveys.[135] A long fusillade of figures come clamoring out of it. Fresh salvos of arithmetic are marshalled to the cause. But all to no avail. The cold hard facts like granite tetons straddling its path have forced Planned Parenthood to go on a quixotic offensive.[136]

In 1970 fewer than half of the nation's school districts offered sex education curricula and none had school-based birth control clinics.[137] Today more than seventy-five percent of the districts teach sex education and there are more than one hundred clinics in operation.[138] Yet the percentage of illegitimate births has only increased during that time, from a mere fifteen percent to an astonishing fifty-one percent.[139]

In California, the public schools have required sex education for more than thirty years, and yet the state has maintained one of the highest rates of teen pregnancy in the nation.[140]

According to the Harris poll, the only things that effectively impact the teen pregnancy problem are frequent Church attendance and parental oversight,[141] the very things that Planned

Parenthood has been railing against for three quarters of a century—the very things that sex education courses are designed to circumvent.[142]

Planned Parenthood's program of sex education is *not*, by any stretch of the imagination, a necessary or effective means of preventing teen pregnancies. Instead, it does just the opposite. We simply cannot contend or pretend otherwise.

The Abortion Illusion

Planned Parenthood claims that its efforts to provide abortion services have at last removed the specter of dangerous back alley abortions from our land.[143] But that is an illusion.[144]

The specter remains, darker and more ominous than ever before.

The truth is, many of the butchers who ran the old back alley operations have simply moved uptown to ply their grisley trade for Planned Parenthood.[145]

The same unsafe techniques, the same lecherous motivations, and the same twisted and perverse ethics that marred their criminal careers continue to haunt them.[146] The 1973 *Roe v. Wade* decision did nothing to change that. Planned Parenthood's "efforts" do nothing to change it, either.

Abortions are dangerous. Planned Parenthood's own liability release forms say so—in very fine print, of course.[147] There is no such thing as a "safe and legal" abortion. *Legal*, yes.[148] *Safe*, no way.[149]

Recently the Centers for Disease Control conducted a study of maternal deaths and discovered that abortion is now the sixth most common cause. The results of the study, released in the May 1985, issue of *Obstetrics and Gynecology*, admitted that those abortion-related deaths may be under-reported by as much as fifty percent.[150]

According to a Johns Hopkins University study, nearly twenty percent of all mid-trimester abortions result in serious genital tract infections.[151] And a study conducted by two UCLA Obstetrical and Gynecological professors concluded that "abortion can be a killer," due to "pelvic abscess, perforation of the uterus, and sometimes also of the bowel."[152] But even if such infections and abscesses do not prove to be fatal, they can cause serious and permanent medical complications. According to one physician, writing in the *British Journal of Venereal Disease*, "infection in the womb and tubes often does permanent damage. The Fallopian tube is a fragile organ, a very tiny bore tube. If infection injures it, it often seals shut. The typical infection involving these organs is pelvic inflammatory disease, or PID."[153] This condition affects nearly fifteen percent of all those who submit to induced abortion.[154]

Other medical complications of abortion include sterility (as many as twenty-five percent of all women receiving mid-trimester abortions);[155] hemorrhaging (nearly ten percent of all cases require transfusions);[156] viral hepatitis (occurring in ten percent of all those transfused);[157] embolism (in as many as four percent of all cases);[158] cervical laceration, cardio-respiratory arrest, acute kidney failure, and amniotic fluid embolus (occurring in as many as forty-two percent of all Prostaglandin abortions).[159]

As a result of these complications, women in America have seen a massive increase in the cost of medical care.[160] While the average cost of normal health maintenance for men has increased nearly twelve percent over the last eight years due to inflation, the average cost for women has skyrocketed a full twenty-seven percent.[161]

Planned Parenthood has not removed the specter of dangerous back alley abortions. Not by any stretch of the imagination. As the world's number one abortion provider and promoter, it has instead extended that dark and dismal shadow all across the land.[162] We simply cannot contend or pretend otherwise.

The Population Illusion

Planned Parenthood claims that its birth control, sex education, and abortion juggernaut is essential to control rapid population growth.[163] But that is an illusion.[164]

Its justifications ring hollow. Planned Parenthood is simply grasping at straws.

The truth is that there *is no* rapid population growth for Planned Parenthood to control. There *is no* population crisis. There *is no* population explosion. There aren't *too many* people.[165] If anything, there aren't *enough* people. Instead of worrying about Planned Parenthood's "population bomb,"[166] many researchers are concerned about a "birth dearth."[167]

Fertility in the United States has been steadily declining for two centuries.[168] And it has been below replacement level since 1972.[169] In Western Europe, the figures are even more frightening: The Netherlands saw its fertility rate plunge fifty-three percent in just twenty years.[170] The French rate has dropped thirty-two percent in just eleven years.[171] Only Finland has been able to avoid the suicidal bent of the rest of the continent,[172] prompting France's Prime Minister Jacques Chirac to exclaim, "Europe is vanishing . . . soon our countries will be empty."[173] In the Third World regions of Asia, Africa, and Latin America, fertility rates are now declining almost as rapidly.[174] As a result, the world wide birthrate is now falling faster than the mortality rate for the first time in recorded history.[175] And the trend appears to be accelerating.[176] Despite this, Planned Parenthood persists in issuing frantic invectives against overcrowding and overpopulation.[177] False figures tumble out of it like the dry rush of a grain chute.[178] It is lost in a don't-confuse-me-with-the-facts kind of oblivion.[179] Like Don Quixote it is madly crashing across foggy moors, jousting with phantoms, wind churns, and vain imaginations. But of course, the joke is on *us*, because Planned Parenthood pursues its folly at our expense. Spending our money, stealing our future, and wasting our hope, it careens down the path of death and destruction.

Planned Parenthood's attempt to justify its birth control, sex education, and abortion schemes by appealing to the threat of a population explosion has been a brilliant but desperate public relations assault on reality. Flying in the face of the facts, its campaign has been as false as the shimmering sands of the Sahara. We simply cannot contend or pretend otherwise.

The Big Lie

Lies. Lies. Lies. All lies.[180]

One after another, Planned Parenthood's lies,[181] hallowed in near sanctity, blaze forth in a positive conflagration of revered shibboleths. Taken together, those lies comprise *the lie*. The Big Lie. The Grand Illusion. The Myth of Planned Parenthood.

Myths, according to theologian J. I. Packer, are "stories made up to sanctify social patterns."[182] They are lies, carefully designed to reinforce a particular philosophy or morality within a culture. They are instruments of manipulation and control.

When Jeroboam splintered the nation of Israel after the death of Solomon, he thought that in order to consolidate his rule over the northern faction he would have to wean the people from their spiritual and emotional dependence on the Jerusalem temple. So he manufactured myths. He lied.

> And Jeroboam said in his heart, "Now the kingdom will return to the house of David. If this people go up to offer sacrifices in the house of the Lord at Jerusalem, then the heart of this people will return to their lord, even to Rehoboam king of Judah; and they will kill me and return to Rehoboam king of Judah." So the king consulted, and made two golden calves, and he said to them, "It is too much for you to go up to Jerusalem; behold your gods, O Israel, that brought you up from the land of Egypt." And he set one in Bethel, and the other he put in Dan. Now this thing became a sin, for the people went to worship before the one as far as Dan. And he made houses on high places, and made priests from among all the people who were not of the sons of Levi. And Jeroboam instituted a feast in the eighth month on the fifteenth day of the month, like the feast which is in Judah, and he went up to the altar; thus he did in Bethel, sacrificing to the calves which he had made. And he stationed in Bethel the priests of the high places which he had made. Then he went up to the altar which he had made in Bethel on the fifteenth day in the eighth month, even in the month which he had devised in his own heart; and he instituted a feast for the sons of Israel, and went up to the altar to burn incense (1 Kings 12:26-33).

Jeroboam instituted a false feast at a false shrine, attended by false priests, before false gods, and all on a false pretense. But his lies succeeded in swaying the people. Jeroboam's mythology sanctified a whole new set of social patterns. What would have been *unthinkable* before — idolatry, apostasy, and travesty — became almost overnight not only thinkable or acceptable, but conventional and habitual. As a result, the new king was able to manipulate and control his subjects.

The powerful, the would-be-powerful, and the wish-they-were-powerful have always relied on such tactics. Plato and Thucidides observed the phenomenon during Greece's classical era.[183] Plutarch and Augustine identified it during the Roman epoch.[184] Sergios Kasilov and Basil Argyros noted it during the Byzantine millennium.[185] Niccolo Machiavelli and Thomas More recognized its importance during the European renaissance.[186] And Aleksandr Solzhenitsyn and Colin Thubron have pointed it out in our own time.[187] Most of the myth-makers never actually *believed* in the gods upon Olympus, across the River Styx, or within the Kremlin Palace. After all, they knew all too well from whence those lies came. But as high priests of deceit, they *used* the lies to dominate the hearts and minds and lives of the masses.

The Bible says that such men are full of deceitful words (Psalm 36:3). Their counsel is deceitful (Proverbs 12:5). Their favor is deceitful (Proverbs 27:6). And their hearts are deceitful (Mark 7:22). They defraud the unsuspecting (Romans 16:18), displaying the spirit of anti-Christ (2 John 7), all for the sake of wealth, prestige, and prerogative (Proverbs 21:6).

Such puissance is in the long run all too fleeting, however (Revelation 21:8), because myth-makers do not go unpunished (Proverbs 19:5). Ultimately, their sin finds them out (Jeremiah 17:11).

Still, because their lies wreak havoc among the innocent (Micah 6:12), it is essential that we not be taken in. Not only are we to be alert to deception (Ephesians 4:14), testing the words and deeds of the myth-makers against the Truth (1 John 4:1-6), but we are to *expose* their deceptions as well (Ephesians 5:11).

Planned Parenthood, not at all unlike Jeroboam and the other infamous myth-makers throughout history, has thus far been able to parlay its deception into a substantial empire. But now, the truth must be told. The illusion must be exposed. The Big Lie must be demythologized.

Woe to the bloody city, completely full of lies and pillage; Her prey never departs (Nahum 3:1).

PART TWO

THE LEGACY

There were much glare and glitter and piquancy and phantasm. . . . There were delirious fancies as the madman fashions. There were much of the beautiful, much of the wanton, much of the bizarre, something of the terrible, and not a little of that which might have excited disgust.

Edgar Allan Poe

Vice is a monster
Of so frightful mien,
As, to be hated,
Needs but to be seen;
Yet seen too oft,
Familiar with her face,
We first endure,
Then pity, then embrace.

                              Alexander Pope

THREE

BAD SEED: THE HISTORICAL LEGACY

dux femina facti

On January 1, 1900, most Americans greeted the twentieth century with the proud and certain belief that the next hundred years would be the greatest, the most glorious, and the most glamorous in human history. They were infected with a sanguine spirit. Optimism was rampant. A brazen confidence colored their every activity.

Certainly there was nothing in their experience to make them think otherwise. Never had a century changed the lives of men and women more dramatically than the one just past. The twentieth century has moved fast and furiously, so that those of us who have moved in it feel sometimes giddy, watching it spin; but the nineteenth moved faster and more furiously still. Railroads, telephones, the telegraph, electricity, mass production, forged steel, automobiles, and countless other modern discoveries had all come upon them at a dizzying pace, expanding their visions and expectations far beyond their grandfathers' wildest dreams. It was more than unfounded imagination, then, that lay behind the *New York World's* New Year's prediction that the twentieth century would "meet and overcome all perils and prove to be the best that this steadily improving planet has ever seen."[1]

Most Americans were cheerfully assured that control of man and nature would soon lie entirely within their grasp and would bestow upon them the unfathomable millennial power to alter the destinies of societies, nations, and epochs. They were a people of purpose. They were a people of manifest destiny.

What they did not know was that dark and malignant seeds were already germinating just beneath the surface of the new century's soil. Josef Stalin was a twenty-one-year-old seminary student in Tiflis, a pious and serene community at the crossroads of Georgia and the Ukraine. Benito Mussolini was a seventeen-year-old student teacher in the quiet suburbs of Milan. Adolf Hitler was an eleven-year-old aspiring art student in the quaint upper Austrian village of Brannan. And Margaret Sanger was a twenty-year-old shy and out-of-sorts nurse-probationer in White Plains, New York. Who could have ever guessed on that ebulently auspicious New Year's Day that those four youngsters would, over the span of the next century, spill more innocent blood than all the murderers, warlords, and tyrants of past history *combined*? Who could have ever guessed that those four youngsters would together ensure that the hopes and dreams and aspirations of the twentieth century would be smothered under the weight of holocaust, genocide, and triage?

As the champion of the proletariat, Stalin saw to the slaughter of at least fifteen million Ukrainian kulaks. As the popularly acclaimed Il Duce, Mussolini massacred as many as four million Ethiopians, two million Eritreans, and a million Serbs, Croats, and Albanians. As the wildly lionized Führer, Hitler exterminated more than six million Jews, two million Slavs, and a million Poles. As the founder of Planned Parenthood and the impassioned heroine of feminist *causes celebre*, Sanger was responsible for the brutal elimination of more than twenty million children in the United States and as many as one and a half billion worldwide.[2]

No one in his right mind would want to rehabilitate the reputations of Stalin, Mussolini, or Hitler. Their barbarism, treachery, and debauchery will make their names live on in infamy forever. Amazingly though, Sanger has escaped their wretched fate. In spite of the fact that her crimes against humanity were no less heinous than theirs, her place in history has somehow been sanitized and sanctified. In spite of the fact that she openly identified herself in one way or another with their aims, intentions, and movements—with Stalin's Sobornostic Collectivism,[3] with Hitler's Eugenic Racism,[4] and with Mussolini's Agathistic Distributism[5]—she somehow managed to establish an independent reputation for the perpetuation of her memory.

In life and death, she has been lauded as a "radiant"[6] and "courageous"[7] reformer.[8] She was heralded by friend and foe alike as a "heroine,"[9] a "champion,"[10] a "saint,"[11] and a "martyr."[12] Honored by men as different and divergent as H. G. Wells[13] and Martin Luther King,[14] George Bernard Shaw[15] and Harry Truman,[16] Bertrand Russell[17] and John D. Rockefeller,[18] Albert Einstein[19] and Dwight Eisenhower,[20] the "woman rebel"[21] somehow was able to secret away her perverse atrocities, emerging in the annals of history vindicated and victorious.

That this could happen is a scandal of grotesque proportions.

Growing Up Wrong

Margaret Sanger was born on September 14, 1879, in the small industrial community of Corning in upstate New York, the sixth of eleven children.[22] Her father, Michael Higgins, was an Irish Catholic immigrant who fancied himself a freethinker and a skeptic. As a youngster he had enlisted in General William Sherman's Twelfth New York Cavalry, and proudly participated in the infamous campaign that ravaged and ravished the South, across Tennessee, through Atlanta, and to the sea.[23] He worked sporadically as a stone mason and a tombstone carver but was never willing or able to provide adequately for his large family.[24] Margaret's mother, Anne Purcell, was a second generation American from a strict Catholic family. She was frail and tuberculous but utterly devoted to her improvident husband and her ever growing brood of children.

The family suffered cold, privation, and hunger. They also suffered scorn, shame, and isolation because of Michael's radical Socialist ideas and activities. Margaret would later describe her family's life together as "joyless and filled with drudgery and fear."[25]

Clearly, theirs was an impoverished life. But, not only did the Higgins suffer socially and materially, they were spiritually deprived as well. One day when Margaret was on her knees saying the Lord's Prayer, she came to the phrase "Give us this day our daily bread," and her father cut in. "Who were you talking to?" he asked. "To God," she replied. "Well tell me, is God a baker?" With no little consternation, she said, "No, of course not. But He makes the rain, the sunshine, and all the things that make the wheat, which makes the bread." After a thoughtful pause her father rejoined, "Well, well, so that's the idea. Then why didn't you just say so? Always say what you mean, my daughter, it is much better."[26]

In spite of Michael's concerted efforts to undermine Margaret's young and fragile faith, her mother had her baptized in St. Mary's Catholic Church on March 23, 1893. A year later, on July 8, 1894, she was confirmed. Both ceremonies were held in secret—her father would have been furious had he known. For some time afterward she displayed a zealous devotion to spiritual things, but gradually the smothering effects of Michael's cynicism took their toll. By the time she was seventeen her passion for Christ had collapsed into a hatred of the Church—a hatred that would be her spiritual hallmark for the rest of her life.[27]

Margaret moved away from her unhappy home as soon as she could. First, she went away to a boarding school, Claverack College of the Hudson River Institute, where she got her first taste of freedom. And what a wild and intoxicating freedom it was: She plunged into radical politics, suffragette feminism, and unfettered sex.[28] When she could no longer afford the tuition, she moved home only long enough to gather her belongings and set her affairs in order. She had drunk from the cup of concupiscence and would never again be satisfied with the quiet virtues of domestic tranquillity.

She decided to move in with her older sister in White Plains, taking a job as a kindergarten teacher. Assigned to a class made up primarily of the children of new immigrants, she found that her pupils couldn't understand a word that she said. She quickly grew tired of the laborious routine of teaching day in and day out, and quit after two terms. Next, she tried nursing. But hospital work proved to be even more vexing and taxing than teaching. She never finished her training.[29] She escaped from the harsh "bondage" of labor and industry in the only way a poor girl could in those "unenlightened" days when the Puritan Work Ethic was still ethical: She married into money.

The Winter of Her Discontent

William Sanger wasn't exactly rich, but he was close enough for Margaret. He was a young man of great promise. An architect with the famed McKim, Mead, and White firm in New York

City, he had already made a name for himself while working on the plans for Grand Central Station and the Woolworth building. He met Margaret at a party in White Plains and immediately fell head over heels in love. He courted her with a single-minded zeal, promising her devotion, leisure, and a beautiful home — the fulfillment of her most cherished dreams.

Within a few months, they were married.

The Sangers settled into a pleasant apartment in Manhattan's upper east side and set up housekeeping. But housekeeping appealed to Margaret even less than teaching or nursing. She quickly grew restless. Her doting husband began casting about, trying to find a way to satisfy her passions. He sent her off for long vacations in the Adirondacks. He hired maids and attendants. He bought her expensive presents. He even built her an extravagant home in the suburbs. Nothing seemed to suit his temperamental bride.

In short order they had three children, two boys and a girl — Margaret thinking that *they* would be the keys to her fulfillment. But alas, they too proved to be but temporary diversions. After nearly a decade of undefined domestic dissatisfaction, Margaret convinced William to sell all they had, including their suburban estate, and move back into the Manhattan hubbub.

She quickly threw herself into the fast-paced social life of the city: shopping, dining, reveling, and theater going. She attempted to drown her rootless discontent in the wastrel champagne of improvidence.

Meanwhile, William began to renew old ties in radical politics by attending Socialist, Anarchist, and Communist meetings down in Greenwich Village. From time to time, when she bored of her patrician activities, Margaret would tag along. Before long, she could think of little else. She suddenly shed her bourgeois habits and took to Bohemian ways. Instead of whiling the hours away in the elegant shops along Fifth Avenue, she plunged headlong into the maelstrom of rebellion and revolution.

The Woman Rebel

At first, William was thrilled by Margaret's conversion. It seemed that his bride had at last found fulfillment. Her commitment was rabid. She was forever attending rallies, meetings, and caucuses, getting acquainted with the foremost radicals of the day: John Reed, Eugene Debs, Clarence Darrow, Will Durant, Upton Sinclair, Julius Hammer, and Bill Haywood.[30] She joined the Socialist Party and attended all of its functions. She even volunteered as a women's organizer for Local Number Five, speaking at labor organization meetings and writing for the Party newspaper, *The Call*.

By this time, virtually all the revolutionary elements of American political life had been unified in the Socialist Party: the Radical Republicans, the Reformist Unitarians, the Knights of Labor, the Mugwumps, the Anarchists, the Populists, the Progressivists, the Suffragettes, the Single Taxers, the Grangers, and the Communists.[31] From ten thousand members in 1901, it had swollen to fifty-eight thousand by 1908, and more than twice that number were recorded four years later.[32] And its voting strength was many times greater even than that, accounting for more than six percent of all the votes cast in the national elections of 1912. When Margaret and William Sanger entered the fray that year, the Party had elected twelve hundred public officials in thirty-three states and one hundred and sixty cities, and it regularly published over three hundred periodicals.[33] Especially enticing to Margaret was the fact that no other political movement in American history had fought so consistently for women's suffrage, sexual liberation, feminism, and birth control.

While William was happy that Margaret had finally found a cause that satisfied her restless spirit, he gradually became concerned that she was taking on too much too soon. Their apartment was in a perpetual state of disarray. Their children were constantly being farmed out to friends and neighbors. And their time alone together was non-existent.

But then when Margaret fell under the spell of the militant utopian Emma Goldman, William's husbandly concern turned to extreme disapproval. Margaret had gone from an arch-typical "material girl" to a revolutionary firebrand almost overnight. And now she was taking her cues from one of the most controversial insurrectionists alive. It was just too much.

Goldman was a fiery renegade who had close connections with revolutionaries the world over: Bolsheviks in Russia, Fabians in England, Anarchists in Germany, and Malthusians in France.

She lectured around the country, drawing large crowds, discoursing on everything from the necessity of free love to the nobility of incendiary violence, from the evils of capitalism to the virtues of assassination, from the perils of democracy to the need for birth control. She made her living selling her Anarchist magazine *Mother Earth* and by distributing leaflets on contraception and liberated sex.[34]

Margaret was completely overwhelmed. She hung on Goldman's every word and began to read everything in Goldman's library including the massive seven volume *Studies in the Psychology of Sex* by Havelock Ellis, which stirred in her a new lust for adventure. She told William that she needed emancipation from every taint of Christianized capitalism, including the strict bonds of the marriage bed.

He was shocked.

William too was committed to the revolution, but only to a point. In a desperate attempt to save their marriage, he rented a cottage on Cape Cod and took Margaret and the children for a long vacation.

By the time they returned, Goldman had departed the Bohemian scene in Greenwich Village for a speaking tour, and Margaret's attentions were deflected from promiscuity, at least for the moment. She continued reading the radical and sensual literature of Ellis and others, but her activism took a different turn.

A strike of textile workers in Lawrence, Massachusetts drew the attentions of Socialist sympathizers all over the country. Sponsored by a militantly Marxist union, the Industrial Workers of the World (IWW), the strike was seen as a tremendous chance to bring the revolution to the streets of America. Bill Haywood, the labor leader who had opportunistically formed the union after a series of "sweat shop" disasters, came to the Village looking for professional organizers to help him manage the strike.

Margaret jumped at the chance.

Her great tenacity and innocent winsomeness proved to be a tremendous asset for Haywood. She was able to stir up a great deal of sympathetic publicity, and as a result the strike was a tremendous success. In fact, it was really *too* successful. It had attracted the support of Governors, Congressmen, and even President Taft. The battle was won, but the war was lost — the revolution never made it to the streets because the anger of the rebellion was diffused by the acceptance of the establishment. The IWW was unable to recover from its victory and was never again able to stage a successful strike. Margaret returned to William and the children, despondent and discouraged.

In the weeks that followed, she occupied herself by dabbling in midwifery by day and by holding court in Mabel Dodge's salon by night.

Dodge was a wealthy young divorcée, recently returned from France, where she had spent most of her married years. She had a stunning Fifth Avenue apartment where she started a salon modeled after those in the Palais Royale and Paris's Left Bank. Her series of evenings were opportunities for intellectuals, radicals, artists, actors, writers, and activists to gather, mingle, debate, aspire, and conspire. Each night had its own theme: sometimes it would be politics, sometimes drama, or perhaps poetry or economics or art or science. Ideas and liquor flowed freely until midnight, when Dodge would usher in a sumptuous meal of the finest meats, poultry, cheeses, and French pastries.

Margaret's topic of discussion was always sex. Her detour into labor activism had done little to dampen her interest in the subject. When it was her turn to lead an evening, she held Dodge's guests spellbound, ravaging them with intoxicating notions of "romantic dignity, unfettered self-expression, and the sacredness of sexual desire."[35] Free love had been practiced quietly for years by the avant-garde intellectuals in the Village. Eugene O'Neill took on one mistress after another, immortalizing them in his plays. Edna St. Vincent Millay "hopped gaily from bed to bed and wrote about it in her poems."[36] Max Eastman, Emma Goldman, Floyd Dell, Rockwell Kent, Edgar Lee Masters, and many others had for some time enjoyed unrestrained sexploits.[37] But no one had championed sexual freedom as openly and ardently as Margaret.[38] When she spoke, the others became transfixed. Dodge was especially struck by her sensuous didactae. Later she would write in her memoirs:

> Margaret Sanger was a Madonna type of women, with soft brown hair parted over a quiet brow, and crystal-clear brown eyes. . . . It was she who introduced us all to the idea of birth control, and it, along with other related ideas about sex, became her passion. It was as if she had been more or less arbitrarily chosen by the powers that be to voice a new gospel of not only sex-knowledge in regard to conception, but sex-knowledge about copulation and its intrinsic importance.
>
> She was the first person I ever knew who was openly an ardent propagandist for the joys of the flesh. This, in those days, was radical indeed when the sense of sin was still so indubitably mixed with the sense of pleasure. . . . Margaret personally set out to rehabilitate sex. . . . She was one of its first conscious promulgators.[39]

Everyone seemed to be delighted by Margaret's explicit and brazen talks. Everyone except her husband, that is. William began to see the Socialist revolution as nothing more than "an excuse for a Saturnalia of sex."[40] He decided he had best get Margaret away once again.

This time, he took Margaret and the children to Paris. He could pursue his interests in modern art. Margaret could study her now keen fascination with the advanced contraceptive methods widely available in France. And together they could refresh their commitment to each other in the world's most romantic city. Again though, he would be disappointed. After two weeks, Margaret became anxious for her Village friends and lovers. She begged William to return. He refused, so she simply abandoned him there, and returned to New York with the children.

Without her husband to support her every whim and fancy, Margaret was forced to find some means of providing an income for herself and the children. She had continued to write for *The Call* and found some degree of satisfaction in that, so she decided to try her hand at writing and publishing a paper herself.

She called it *The Woman Rebel*. It was an eight sheet pulp with the slogan "No Gods! No Masters!" emblazoned across the masthead. She advertised it as "a paper of militant thought," and militant it was indeed. The first issue denounced marriage as a "degenerate institution," capitalism as "indecent exploitation," and sexual modesty as "obscene prudery."[41] In the next issue, an article entitled "A Woman's Duty" proclaimed that "rebel women" were to "look the whole world in the face with a go-to-hell look in the eyes."[42] Another article asserted that "rebel women claim the following rights: the right to be lazy, the right to be an unmarried mother, the right to destroy . . . and the right to love."[43] In later issues, she published several articles on contraception, several more on sexual liberation, three on the necessity for social revolution, and two defending political assassinations.[44]

The Woman Rebel was militant, alright. In fact, it was so militant that Margaret was promptly served with a subpoena indicting her on three counts for the publication of lewd and indecent articles in violation of the federal Comstock Laws.

The Comstock Laws had been passed by Congress in 1873. Their purpose was to close the mails to "obscene and lascivious" material, particularly the erotic postcards and pornographic magazines from Europe which, during the confused post-Civil War period, were flooding the country. Anthony Comstock, its sponsor, was appointed a special agent of the Post Office, with the power to see that it was strictly enforced. For nearly half a century he fought a single-handed campaign to "keep the mails clean" and to "ensure just condemnation for the purveyors of filth, eroticism, and degeneracy."[45]

If convicted — and conviction was almost certain — Margaret could be sentenced to as much as five years. Frightened, she obtained several extensions of her court date. But then, deciding that her case was hopeless, she determined to flee the country under an assumed name. She had her Socialist friends forge a passport, provide her with connections in Canada and England, and take charge of her children. As a final gesture, just before she slipped over the border, she had them print and distribute one hundred thousand copies of a contraband leaflet she had written on contraception called *Family Limitation*. It was lurid and lascivious, designed to enrage the postal authorities and titillate the masses. But worse, it was dangerously inaccurate, recommending such things as Lysol douches, bichloride of mercury elixirs, heavy doses of laxatives, and herbal abortifacients.[46]

Margaret Sanger's illustrious career as the "champion of birth control" was now well underway.

Sex Education

Margaret spent more than a year in England as a fugitive from justice. But she made certain that the time was not wasted. She had found her cause: Revolutionary Socialism. She had found her niche in the cause: Sexual Liberation. And now she would further that cause with a single-minded zeal.

As soon as she came ashore, Margaret began to make contact with the various radical groups of Britain. She began attending Socialist lectures on Nietzsche's moral relativism, Anarchist lectures on Kropotkin's subversive pragmatism, and Communist lectures on Bakunin's collectivistic rationalism. But she was especially interested in developing ties with the Malthusians.

Thomas Malthus was a nineteenth-century professor of political economy whose theories of population growth and economic stability quickly became the basis for national and international social policy throughout the West. According to his scheme, population grows exponentially over time, while production only grows arithmetically. Poverty, deprivation, and hunger are thus evidence of a population crisis. It follows that the only responsible social policy is one that addresses the unnatural problem of population growth. In fact, Malthus argued, to deal with sickness, crime, privation, and need in any other way simply aggravates the problems further.

In his magnum opus, *An Essay on the Principle of Population*, published in six editions from 1798 to 1826, Malthus wrote:

> All children born, beyond what would be required to keep up the population to a desired level, must necessarily perish, unless room be made for them by the deaths of grown persons. . . . Therefore . . . we should facilitate, instead of foolishly and vainly endeavoring to impede, the operations of nature in producing this mortality; and if we dread the too frequent visitation of the horrid form of famine, we should sedulously encourage the other forms of destruction, which we compel nature to use. Instead of recommending cleanliness to the poor, we should encourage contrary habits. In our towns we should make the streets narrower, crowd more people into the houses, and court the return of the plague. In the country, we should build our villages near stagnant pools, and particularly encourage settlements in all marshy and unwholesome situations. But above

all, we should reprobate specific remedies for ravaging diseases; and restrain those benevolent, but much mistaken men, who have thought they were doing a service to mankind by projecting schemes for the total extirpation of particular disorders.[47]

Malthus's disciples — the Malthusians and the Neo-Malthusians — believed that if Western civilization were to survive, the physically unfit, the materially poor, the spiritually diseased, the racially inferior, and the mentally incompetent had to be eliminated. And while Malthus was forthright in recommending plague, pestilence, and putrification, his disciples felt that the subtler approaches of education, contraception, sterilization, and abortion were more practical ways to ease the pressures of over-population.

As historian Paul Johnson has shown, the Malthusians "were not men of action."[48] Instead, "they tried to solve the problems of the world in the quiet of their studies, inside their own heads. . . . They produced a new vocabulary of mumbo-jumbo. It was all hard-headed, scientific, and relentless."[49] Even so, their doctrines were immensely appealing to the intellectual elite. According to Johnson, "All the ablest elements" in Western society, "the trendsetters in opinion, were wholly taken in by this monstrous doctrine of unreason. Those who objected were successfully denounced as obscurantists, and the enemies of social progress. They could no longer be burned as heretical subverters of the new orthodoxy, but they were successfully and progressively excluded from the control of events."[50] This, despite the fact that the Malthusian mathematical scheme had been proven by historical verities to be utterly obsolete, if not entirely false.[51]

Margaret immediately got on the Malthusian bandwagon. She was not philosophically inclined, nor was she particularly adept at political, social, or economic theory, but she did recognize in the Malthusians a kindred spirit and a tremendous opportunity. She was also shrewd enough to realize that her notions of Radical Socialism and Sexual Liberation would not ever have the popular support necessary to usher in the revolution without some appeal to altruism and intellectualism. She needed somehow to capture the moral and academic "high ground." Malthusianism, she thought, just might be the key to that ethical and intellectual posture. If she could argue for birth control using the scientifically verified threat of poverty, sickness, racial tension, and over-population as its backdrop, then she would have a much better chance of making her case. So she began to absorb as much of the Malthusian dogma as she could.

Margaret also immersed herself in the teachings of each of the Malthusian off-shoots. If a little bit of something is a good thing, then a lot is even better. There were the Phrenologists, the Eugenicists, and the Social Darwinists. There were Oneidians, Polygenists, Craniometricists, Recapitulationists, Lambrosians, Binetists, Hereditarians, Freudians, and Neotenists.[52] From each group she picked up a few popular slogans and concepts that would permanently shape her crusade.

But even more important than these institutional and intellectual connections, Margaret's English exile gave her the opportunity to make some critical interpersonal connections as well. Her bed became a veritable meeting place for the Fabian upper crust: H. G. Wells, George Bernard Shaw, Arnold Bennett, Arbuthnot Lane, and Norman Haire. And of course, it was then that she began her unusual and tempestuous affair with Havelock Ellis.

Ellis was the iconoclastic grandfather of the Bohemian sexual revolution. The author of nearly fifty books on every aspect of concupiscence from sexual inversion to auto-eroticism, from the revolution of obscenity to the mechanism of detumescence, from sexual periodicity to pornographic eonism,[53] he had provided the free love movement with much of its intellectual apologia. Much to his chagrin however, he himself was sexually impotent, so he spent his life in pursuit of new and ever more exotic sensual pleasures. He staged elaborate orgies for his Malthusian and Eugenicist friends; he enticed his wife into innumerable lesbian affairs while he quietly observed; he experimented with mescaline and various other psychotropic and psychedelic drugs; and he established a network for both homosexual and heterosexual encounters.

To Margaret, Ellis was a modern day saint. She adored him at once, both for his radical ideas and for his unusual bedroom behavior. The two of them began to plot a strategy for Margaret's cause. Ellis emphasized the necessity of political expediency. Margaret would have to tone down her pro-abortion stance. She would, he said, have to distance herself from revolutionary rhetoric. The scientific and philanthropic-sounding themes of Malthus and Eugenics would have to replace the politically charged themes of old-line labor Anarchism and Socialism.

By the time her year in England was over, Margaret's ideas were firmly in place, her strategy was thoroughly mapped out, and her agenda was carefully outlined.

She set out for America with a demonic determination to alter the course of Western civilization.

Ultimately, she succeeded.

Planned Parenthood Is Conceived

Margaret's first task after crossing the Atlantic was to face the legal charges against her. Using the skills she developed in the IWW, she immediately began a brilliant public relations campaign that so rallied public support for her cause that the authorities were forced to drop all charges.

She had won her first victory.

Then, in order to capitalize on all the publicity that her victory had generated, she embarked on a three and a half month, coast-to-coast speaking tour. She was a stunning success, drawing large, enthusiastic crowds.

Another victory.

Next, she decided to open a birth control clinic. Papers, pamphlets, and speeches could only do so much to usher in the revolution. Following her Malthusian and Eugenic instincts, she opened her clinic in the Brownsville section of New York, an area populated by newly immigrated Slavs, Latins, Italians, and Jews.

But there would be no victory for Margaret Sanger in this venture. Within two weeks, the clinic had been shut down by the authorities. Margaret and her sister Ethel were arrested and sentenced to thirty days each in the workhouse for the distribution of obscene materials and the prescription of dangerous medical procedures.

Margaret was undeterred, of course. As soon as she was released, she founded a new organization, the Birth Control League, and began to publish a new magazine, *The Birth Control Review.* She was still intent on opening a clinic, but her time in

jail had convinced her that she needed to cultivate a broader following before she made another attempt at that. The new organization and magazine would help her do just that.

And she was right.

Though she was now drawing severe public criticism from
such men as the fiery popular evangelist Rev. Billy Sunday, the
famed Catholic social reformer Msgr. John Ryan, and the gallant
former president Theodore Roosevelt, Margaret was gaining
stature among the urbane and urban intelligentsia. Money began
to pour into her office as subscriptions and donations soared.
And the fact that articles from influential authors like H. G. Wells,
Pearl Buck, Julian Huxley, Karl Menninger, Havelock Ellis, and
Harry Emmerson Fosdick appeared on the pages of the *Review*
only boosted Margaret's respectability that much more.

By 1922 her fame and fortune were unshakably secure. She
had won several key legal battles, had coordinated an international conference on birth control, and had gone on a very successful round-the-world lecture tour. Her name had become a
household word and one of her numerous books had become an
instant bestseller in spite of—or perhaps because of—the tremendous controversy it had caused.

Entitled *The Pivot of Civilization*, it was one of the first popularly written books to openly expound and extol Malthusian and
Eugenic aims. Throughout its 284 pages, Margaret unashamedly
called for the elimination of "human weeds," for the cessation of
charity, for the segregation of "morons, misfits, and the malad-
justed" and for the sterilization of "genetically inferior races."[54]
Published today, such a book would be labeled immediately as
abominably racist and totalitarian. But writing when she did,
Margaret only gained more acclaim.

Her cause seemed unstoppable now. The revolution had
truly begun.

Even so, Margaret was miserable. Her private life was in utter shambles. Her marriage had ended. Her daughter caught
cold and ultimately died of pneumonia. Her boys were neglected
and forgotten. And her once ravishing beauty was fading with
age and abuse.

Desperate to find meaning and happiness, she lost herself in
a profusion of sexual liaisons.[55] She went from one lover to

another, sometimes several in a single day. She experimented with innumerable erotic fantasies and fetishes, but satisfaction always eluded her grasp. She began to dabble in the occult, participating in seances and practicing Eastern meditation. She even went so far as to apply for initiation into the mysteries of Rosicrucianism and Theosophy.

When all else failed, she turned to the one thing that she knew would bring her solace: once again, she married into money.

J. Noah Slee was the president of the Three-in-One Oil Company and a legitimate millionaire. A conservative Church-going Episcopalian, he opposed everything that Margaret stood for, but found her irresistible anyway.

At first, Margaret resisted his pleas for marriage. She still believed that it was a "degenerate institution." But nine million dollars was a mighty temptation. It was a temptation she simply could not resist.

But just to make certain that the new relationship would not interfere with her affairs and her cause, she drew up a prenuptial agreement that Slee was forced to sign just before the wedding ceremony. It stipulated that Margaret would be free to come and go as she pleased with no questions asked. She was to have her own apartment and servants within her husband's home, where she could entertain "friends" of her own choosing, behind closed doors. Furthermore, Slee would have to telephone her from the other end of the house even to ask for a dinner date.

Margaret told her lovers that with that document, the marriage would make little or no difference in her life—apart from the convenience of the money, of course.[56] And she went out of her way to prove it; she flaunted her promiscuity and infidelity every chance she could get.

She was still terribly unhappy, but at least now she was terribly rich, too.

Immediately, Sanger set herself to the task of using her new wealth to further the cause. She opened another clinic—this time calling it a "Research Bureau" in order to avoid legal tangles.[57] Then she began to smuggle diaphragms into the country from Holland.[58] She waged several successful "turf" battles to maintain control over her "empire."[59] She campaigned diligently to win over the medical community.[60] She secured massive foundation grants from the Rockefellers, the Fords, and the Mellons.[61] She took her struggle to Washington, testifying before several congressional committees, advocating the liberalization of contraceptive prescription laws.[62] And she fought for the incorporation of reproductive control into state programs as a form of social planning.[63] With her almost unlimited financial resources, she was able to open doors and pull strings that had heretofore been entirely inaccessible to her.

Margaret was also able to use her new-found wealth to fight an important public relations campaign to redeem her reputation.

Because of her Malthusian and Eugenic connections, she had become closely associated with the scientists and theorists who put together Nazi Germany's "race purification" program. She had openly endorsed the euthanasia, sterilization, abortion, and infanticide programs of the early Reich. She published a number of articles in the *Birth Control Review* that mirrored Hitler's Aryan-White Supremacist rhetoric. She even commissioned Dr. Ernst Rudin, the director of the Nazi Medical Experimentation program, to write for *The Review* himself.

Naturally, when World War II broke out and the grisly details of the Nazi programs began to come to light, Margaret was forced to backpedal her position and cover up her complicity. The Great Depression had been a boon for racist and Eugenic arguments, but those days were now past. Charges of anti-Semitism had been harmlessly hurled at her since her trial in 1917, but now that Auschwitz and Dachau had become very much a part of the public conscience, she realized she would have to do something, and quickly.

Her first step toward redeeming her public image was to change the name of her organization.[64] "Planned Parenthood" was a name that had been proposed from within the birth control movement since at least 1938. One of the arguments for the new name was that it connoted a positive program and conveyed a clean, wholesome, family-oriented image. It diverted attention from the international and revolutionary intentions of the movement, focusing instead on the personal and individual dimensions of birth control. By 1942, it was decided. The organization would be called the Planned Parenthood Federation of America.

Next, she embarked on an aggressive affiliation program that brought hundreds of local and regional birth control leagues under the umbrella of a national organization, and then dozens of national organizations were brought under the umbrella of an international organization. This enabled Margaret to draw on the integrity and respectability of grassroots organizations, solidifying and securing her place at the top.

Finally, she initiated a massive propaganda blitz aimed at the war-weary, ready-for-prosperity middle class. Always careful to hide her illicit affairs and her radical political leanings, her campaign emphasized patriotism and family values.

Before long, Margaret's brilliant strategy had won for her, and Planned Parenthood, the admiration and respect of virtually the entire nation, and certainly of the entire social services community.

Of course, these tremendous successes did little to ease the ache of her perpetual unhappiness. She continued her sordid and promiscuous affairs even after old age and poor health had overtaken her.[65] Her pathetic attraction to occultism deepened.[66] And perhaps worst of all, by 1949 she had become addicted to both drugs and alcohol.[67]

By the time she died on September 6, 1966, a week shy of her eighty-seventh birthday, Margaret Sanger had nearly fulfilled her promise to spend every last penny of Slee's fortune.[68] In the process, though, she had lost everything else: love, happiness, satisfaction, fulfillment, family, and friends. In the end, her struggle was for naught, "for what does it profit a man to gain the whole world, but to lose his own soul? Or what shall a man give in exchange for his soul?" (Mark 8:36-37).

The Continuing Legacy

Just as a nation's "head" defines the character and vision of that nation, so an organization's "head" defines the character and vision of that organization.

This is a very basic Biblical principle. It is the principle of "legacy." It is the principle of "inheritance."

The Canaanite people were perverse and corrupt. They practiced every manner of wickedness and reprobation. Why were they so dissolute? The answer, according to the Bible, is that their founders and leaders passed evil onto them as their *legacy*, as their *inheritance* (Genesis 9:25; Leviticus 18:24-25; Amos 1:3-12).

Similarly, the Moabites and the Ammonites were a rebellious and improvident people. They railed against God's Law and God's People. Why were they so defiant? Again, the Bible tells us that their founders and leaders passed insurrection onto them as their *legacy*, as their *inheritance* (Genesis 19:30-38; Numbers 21:21-23; Amos 1:13-15; Amos 2:1-3). A seed will always yield its own kind (Genesis 1:11). Bad seed brings forth bitter harvest (Ezra 9:2; Isaiah 1:4; Isaiah 14:20). You reap what you sow (Galatians 6:7). A nation or an organization that is sown, nurtured, and grown by deceit, promiscuity, and lawlessness, cannot help but be evil to the core (Hosea 8:7).

Planned Parenthood is a paradigmatical illustration of this principle. Margaret Sanger's character and vision are perfectly mirrored in the organization that she wrought. She intended it that way. And the leaders that have come after her have in no wise attempted to have it another way.

Dr. Alan Guttmacher, the man who immediately succeeded her as president of Planned Parenthood Federation of America once said, "We are merely walking down the path that Mrs. Sanger carved out for us."[69] Faye Wattleton, the current president, has claimed that she is "proud" to be "walking in the footsteps" of Margaret Sanger.[70]

Thus, virtually everything that she believed, everything that she aspired to, everything that she practiced, and everything that she aimed for is somehow reflected in the organization and program of Planned Parenthood, even today. The frightening thing about Planned Parenthood's historical legacy is that the legacy is not just historical. It is as current as tomorrow morning's newspaper.

Abortion. In her book *Women and the New Race*, Margaret Sanger asserted that "the most merciful thing a large family can do to one of its infant members is to kill it."[71] Today, Planned Parenthood's commitment to that philosophy is self-evident. The organization is the world's number one abortion provider.[72] It has aggressively fought the issue through the courts.[73] It has made killing infant members of large families its highest priority.[74] Bad seed brings forth bitter harvest. The legacy continues.

Promiscuity. Like her mentors Emma Goldman and Havelock Ellis, Margaret Sanger was not content to keep her lascivious and concupiscent behavior to herself. She was a zealous evangelist for free love. Even in her old age, she persisted in proselytizing her sixteen-year-old granddaughter, telling her that kissing, petting, and even intercourse were fine as long as she was "sincere," and that having sex about "three times a day" was "just about right."[75] Today, Planned Parenthood's commitment to undermining the moral values of teens is evident in virtually all its literature. It teachs kids to masturbate.[76] It endorses premarital fornication.[77] It approves of homosexuality.[78] It encourages sexual experimentation.[79] It vilifies Christian values, prohibitions, and consciences.[80] Bad seed brings forth bitter harvest. The legacy continues.

Socialism. Margaret Sanger was committed to the revolution. She wanted to overthrow the old order of Western Christendom and usher in a "New Age." Though in her latter years she toned down her radical rhetoric, she never wavered from that stance. Today, Planned Parenthood continues to carry the banner for big government, big spending, freewheeling liberal causes and agendas.[81] Even the normally sedate *Wall Street Journal* had to admit that "Planned Parenthood's love affair with Socialism has become more than a harmless upper middle-class hobby and now borders on the ludicrous."[82] Bad seed brings forth bitter harvest. The legacy continues.

Greed. When Leon Trotsky came to the United States briefly in 1917, he met Margaret Sanger and her friends and came away with a feeling of great revulsion.[83] In his memoirs, he recorded nothing but distaste for the rich, smug Socialists he encountered in the Village.[84] He said they were little better than "hypocritical Babbits," referring to the Sinclair Lewis character who used his parlor-room Socialism as a screen for personal ambition and self-aggrandisement.[85] Sanger and the other Village elitists were revolutionaries only to the extent that Socialism did not conflict with wealth, luxury, and political influence.[86] Today, Planned Parenthood's commitment to the revolution continues to hinge on that unswerving pursuit of "filthy lucre."[87] From its dogged preoccupation with government contracts, grants, and bequests, to its commercial ventures, investments, and vocations, its mercenary avariciousness is everywhere apparent.[88] Bad seed brings forth bitter harvest. The legacy continues.

Religion. In her first newspaper, *The Woman Rebel*, Margaret Sanger admitted that "Birth control appeals to the advanced radical because it is calculated to undermine the authority of the Christian Churches. I look forward to seeing humanity free someday of the tyranny of Christianity no less than Capitalism."[89] Today, Planned Parenthood is continuing her crusade against the Church. In its advertisements,[90] in its literature,[91] in its programs,[92] and in its policies,[93] the organization makes every attempt to mock, belittle, and undermine Biblical Christianity. Bad seed brings forth bitter harvest. The legacy continues.

Deceit. Throughout her life, Margaret Sanger developed a rakish and reckless pattern of dishonesty.[94] She twisted the truth about her qualifications as a nurse,[95] about the details of her work,[96] and about the various sordid addictions that controlled her life.[97] Her autobiographies were filled with exaggerations, distortions, and out-and-out lies.[98] She even went so far as to alter the records in her mother's family Bible in order to protect her vanity.[99] Today, Planned Parenthood faithfully carries on her tradition of disinformation. The organization continually misrepresents the facts about its lucrative birth control,[100] sex education,[101] and abortion enterprises.[102] Bad seed brings forth bitter harvest. The legacy continues.

A recent Planned Parenthood report bore the slogan "Proud of Our Past — Planning the Future."[103] If that is true — if the organization really is *proud* of its venal and profligate past, and if it really is planning the future — then we all have much to be concerned about.

> Those who plow iniquity and those who sow trouble harvest it. By the breath of God they perish, and by the blast of His anger they come to an end. (Job 4:8-9)

To affect, yea to effect their owne deaths, all living are importun'd. Not by nature only which perfects them, but by Art and Education which perfects her.

John Donne

FOUR

BACK ALLEY BUTCHERS: THE MEDICAL LEGACY

aegrescit medeno

The overcast sky hung in gray strips over the city—pale where the sun nearly broke through the clouds, darker where stubborn patches of rain rode the currents of a lolling stormy breeze. The glaze of the heavens permitted no shadows, only a darkening of color here and there, and a dulling of perception.

Caroline Ness told me that her life was like that now. "Dreary," she said. "Sad and dreary."

Her thick blonde hair fell in long, loose waves to her shoulders. Her eyes were as blue as poker chips. Backlit by bright neon, her slim and elegant frame bore an aristocratic beauty. But her expression was as dim and distant as a star in half light.

"I feel like a caged animal—trapped by a terrible and tragic past." She turned, her cold gaze piercing me. "And there's no way out."

We had just climbed the stairs from the Columbus Circle station into the mid-Manhattan bustle near Lincoln Center. The long clackety IRT ride from Wall Street through Soho, Greenwich Village, Chelsea, the Garment District, Times Square, and the Theater District had afforded us a unique opportunity to observe the city's teeming crush of variety. And it had afforded us a unique opportunity to talk. Anonymity and privacy are never so available than when surrounded by thousands of strangers on a New York subway.

Caroline was twenty-two when she had her first abortion. Eight months later, she had another. "The first one seemed to go just fine," she told me. "There was a little bleeding and some pain for the next few weeks. Nothing serious, though."

But it *was* serious. That became readily apparent when she went in for the second abortion. "There was quite a bit of scar tissue in my cervix. The physician seemed hesitant at first, but decided to go ahead with the procedure."

That was not the last mistake that the doctor would make that day. His sharp, blindly wielded curette inadvertently perforated Caroline's already scarred cervix. When he inserted the suction apparatus, it passed through to the body cavity. The shearing force of the suction then seriously lacerated the bladder and tore loose the right ureter—the tube that carries urine from the kidneys to the bladder. The delicate parametrium and peritoneum membranes were ruptured and a pooling hematoma surrounded the entire right renal system.

Completely unaware of the damage he had caused, the doctor finished the procedure, sent Caroline to the recovery room, and turned his attentions to other matters. After a forty-five minute rest, he released her.

"I collapsed on the subway on my way home. I think I was in shock," she said. She was suffering from a lot more than shock. An emergency room examination revealed heavy hemorrhaging and leakage of urine per vaginam. Attendants rushed her into the operating room where surgeons reluctantly performed an emergency right nephrectomy and oophorectomy—the removal of the right kidney and ovary. They also evacuated the hematoma and resectioned the torn endometrium.

"I spent about ten days in the hospital after that," she told me as we walked past the Juilliard toward the Hudson River. Those ten days had cost her a place in the school's renowned drama department. "But the worst was still yet to come."

Over the next several weeks, Caroline suffered from recurring abdominal pain, high fever, vaginal discharge, and abnormal bleeding. She was scheduled for both a cystoscopy and a laparoscopy and was once again admitted to the hospital. The exploratory surgeries revealed that a portion of the fetal skull had been imbedded into the resected intra-abdominal tissue. They also revealed a severe pelvic inflammation caused by bacteria from the mangled renal system.

"The doctors said that I had no choice but to undergo a complete hysterectomy." Tears began to well up in her eyes. "I was only twenty-two. My whole life was ahead of me. I was happy. Carefree. And then this . . . well, I just couldn't believe that this was actually happening to me."

The next day, the doctors removed Caroline's remaining ovary, along with her uterus, cervix, fallopian tubes, and lymph glands. She would never again be able to bear children.

"The counselors at Planned Parenthood told me that abortion was the only responsible choice in my situation," she said. "Now look at me. My health is broken. My career is ruined. My emotions are shot. And the only two children I'll ever bear are dead and gone."

By now we were looking out over the dark roiling waters of the Hudson. Angry swells broke over the old stone walls at the river's edge, drenching the sidewalk with a bone-chilling spray. The blaring sounds and glaring lights of the city had receded into the background as the grey turbulent channel before us filled up our senses.

After a long and uncomfortable silence Caroline turned to me, her tears no longer contained. "Why didn't someone tell me? Why didn't *anyone* tell me that abortion wasn't safe? Why?"

Why indeed?

The Medical Risks of Abortion

While Planned Parenthood continues blithely promoting their "safe and legal" abortions,[1] thousands of women just like Caroline Ness all across America and around the world suffer from the "inherent risks"[2] and "complications"[3] that those procedures present.[4] For some that suffering is but a minor and temporary inconvenience. For others, like Caroline, it becomes a permanent disability.

Dr. Horton Dean is a gynecologist with a private practice in a fashionable neighborhood near Los Angeles. Since 1973 he has seen a marked increase in the number of patients with significant complications—both mental and physical—as a result of legal abortions. "I am convinced," he told me, "that the Planned Parenthood programs pose the greatest health hazard in America today."[5] He estimates that as many as fifteen percent of all first trimester, forty percent of all mid-trimester, and ninety percent of all late-trimester abortions result in problems demanding serious medical attention.[6]

A number of studies conducted by some of the finest medical research institutions all around the globe confirm Dean's conclusion that "there is no such thing as a *safe* and legal abortion": in Hungary,[7] Japan,[8] Greece,[9] Great Britain,[10] Czechoslovakia,[11] The Netherlands,[12] Norway,[13] Israel,[14] Yugoslavia,[15] Free China,[16] and in the United States at the Johns Hopkins University Medical School,[17] the Vanderbilt University Medical School,[18] the University of Maryland Medical School,[19] Creighton University Medical School,[20] Cornell University Medical School,[21] the U.C.L.A. Medical School,[22] and the University of North Carolina Medical School.[23] In every case, abortion was found to dangerously risk maternal mortality, perinatal fitness, congenital malformation, and future fertility.[24]

All this evidence flies in the face of what Planned Parenthood has repeatedly maintained over the last several years.[25] According to its statistics, the complication rate for legal abortion is less than one percent and is thus safer than full-term pregnancy and childbirth.[26]

According to renowned obstetrician and gynecologist Matthew Bulfin, the reason that these estimated figures are so skewed is that Planned Parenthood and the various other agencies that measure maternal complication rates are "missing vital input for their mortality and morbidity studies by not seeking information from the physicians who see the complications from legal abortions — emergency room physicians and the obstetricians and gynecologists in private practice. The physicians who do the abortions and the clinics and centers where abortions are done should not be the only sources from which complication statistics are derived."[27]

"There are a lot more complications out there than anyone seems to care to believe," says Dean. "It is a national health disaster."[28]

Although Planned Parenthood stubbornly refuses to admit publicly that such a disaster exists, privately it is quite concerned.

So, in 1986, and again in 1987, it conducted "medical risk reduction seminars."[29] Instead of focusing on the actual abortion procedures and techniques used in their clinics though, the Planned Parenthood professionals gave the bulk of their attention to the question of how to contain sky-rocketing insurance rates and ever increasing malpractice suits.[30] Apparently they knew only too well that it is *impossible* to develop safe abortion procedures or techniques. The best they could hope to do was reduce their legal liability.[31]

The fact is, *every* one of the procedures and techniques that Planned Parenthood utilizes in its booming abortion trade involves two victims: the murdered unborn child[32] and the mutilated, violated, and uninformed mother. It is by Planned Parenthood's own admission a terribly "risky business."[33]

Menstrual extraction. This method of abortion is generally performed immediately following a rape incident. Since a pregnancy cannot be confirmed at this early stage, menstrual extractions are not counted in abortion statistics, but it is estimated that as many as fifteen thousand a year are performed in the United States.[34] The procedure involves the insertion of a vacuum aspirator into the uterus and the extraction of all uterine contents. As innocuous and simple as this may sound, it can result in serious complications: urinary tract infections, cervical trauma, sepsis, peritonitis, endometritis, and salpingitis.[35]

Leslie Thompson was "date raped" in 1985. "When the police were finished taking my statement," she said, "they took me to a Planned Parenthood clinic. The counselor there told me that a doctor was going to treat me with a *rape kit*. I was so upset, I never asked any questions. I didn't have any idea what a *rape kit* was. I figured that the police and the nurses and the doctors were just following procedure."

The clinic personnel performed a menstrual extraction abortion on Leslie and released her an hour later. "For the next several days," she told me, "I had a persistent pain and a low grade fever that I just couldn't knock. I finally went in to see my own doctor." Upon examination he found that she was suffering from endometritis — an inflammation of the uterine lining caused by an infection that had set in following the abortion. He was able to treat Leslie with antibiotics and she quickly recovered. "He told me that if I'd waited even a day or two longer, I'd have been in real trouble. I guess I was fortunate. But it kinda makes me wonder how many women *don't* have that kind of good fortune."

Suction-Aspiration. This first trimester method of abortion is one of the most common techniques used in Planned Parenthood clinics. It may account for as much as eighty-five percent of all abortions now performed in the United States.[36] The procedure involves paralyzing the cervical muscle ring and then inserting a vacuum tube into the uterus and against the body of the child. The suction is almost thirty times more powerful than a home vacuum cleaner, and literally tears the child's body limb from limb. The scraps are then sucked through the tube and into a bottle. The procedure is completed when the abortionist cuts the placenta loose from the inner wall of the uterus and sucks it into the bottle as well. Suction-aspiration abortions share the risks of urinary tract infections, cervical trauma, sepsis, peritonitis, endometritis, and salpingitis that are common to menstrual extraction abortions. But in addition, a number of other complications may also result: uterine laceration, renal trauma, pelvic inflammation, embolism, thrombus, and even sterility.[37]

Martha Tollesk's divorce had been final just three days when she discovered that she was pregnant. "Everybody told me that I should just go out and get an abortion," she said. "I'd just enrolled in night courses at the local community college. I had a great new job. My life was coming together finally. And then this!"

Martha's friends talked her into visiting a Planned Parenthood center where she received a fistful of brochures and tracts on the benefits and blessings of abortion. "It all sounded so simple and so secure. So I went ahead and scheduled an appointment." The doctor performed a suction-aspiration abortion on her three days later. "It was incredibly painful. It was just awful. But they told me all had gone well and they sent me on home."

But all was *not* well. After almost a week, Martha was admitted to the hospital with a number of alarming symptoms: swelling of the abdomen, severe pain, nausea, vomiting, rapid heartbeat, chills and fever, and shortness of breath. Her obstetrician diagnosed her as suffering from peritonitis — an inflammation of the membrane covering the wall of her peritoneum. Caused by a small uterine puncture during the abortion, the bacterial infection had quickly spread throughout her body cavity. "They tell me I'm lucky," she said. "But I'm not sure I call four days in the hospital and a close call with death *lucky.* I call it *irresponsible.*"

Dilatation and Curettage (D&C). This once favored method of abortion now accounts for only about five percent of all abortions performed due to its poor medical track record.[38] The procedure involves the insertion of a curette—a very sharp loop-shaped knife—up into the uterus. The placenta and the child are then dismembered and scraped out into a basin. In addition to all of the complications of menstrual extractions and suction-aspirations, D&C abortions also carry the risk of uterine perforation, hemorrhaging, pelvic abscesses, genital tract infections, bowel lacerations, and thromboembolism.[39]

Jared McCormick took his girlfriend, Susie Glanze, to Planned Parenthood for a pregnancy test late last year. "She was really scared, and so was I," he said. "I told her that we could go ahead and get married. We were planning on it anyway. We'd just have to move things up a little, is all. But she wanted me to finish up with school first. So, there we were. At Planned Parenthood."

The test was positive and Susie made an appointment for an abortion the next Saturday. "I really went berserk," Jared said. "I was dead set against the abortion. I begged her to marry me and keep our baby. But she wouldn't listen."

The doctors performed a D&C. There was profuse bleeding, but since that is quite common with D&C abortions, the clinic personnel didn't think anything of it.

That was a terrible mistake. An hour later, Susie was still hemorrhaging and had to be rushed to the nearest hospital emergency room. There she was given two units of blood and treated for severe lacerations of the cervix and uterus. It would be almost two days later before she would be released.

"It's amazing what can happen between two people in just a couple days' time," Jared said. "Susie was so grieved over what she'd done—over what they'd done—that she just couldn't stand to be with me anymore. Just like that. It was all over between us. I'm convinced that if she'd known how risky the operation was we'd be together today. And our baby would still be alive."

Dilatation and Evacuation (D&E). This particularly brutal method of abortion is commonly used when pregnancies have reached well into the second and third trimesters. Strips of laminaria—a spongy seaweed—are placed in the cervix to stretch it open. A pliers-like pair of forceps is then used to crush the child's skull and snap its spine. The now pliable corpse is wrenched piece by piece out of the womb. Next, the abortionist must reassemble the body parts on the surgical table in order to make certain that nothing was left behind in the uterus. Finally, the raw and empty womb is swabbed with a disinfectant and aspirated with a vaginal vacuum. In addition to the complications common to D&C abortions, the D&E method is especially prone to infections: pelvic, renal, cervical, and peritonital. D&E abortions are also associated with clinically low-birth-weight infants, stillbirths, ectopic implantation, neonatal deaths, and congenital malformations in future pregnancies.[40]

Melinda Davies and Cheryl Cook were best friends all through high school. During the summer following graduation, both girls became pregnant. "We decided to go in to Planned Parenthood together. We didn't want our parents to find out," said Cheryl.

"Yeah, it was kind of scary," Melinda told me, "but we thought we could help each other through it all."

Both girls were given D&E abortions. "Mine went just fine," said Cheryl. "But Melinda really had a lot of trouble." For the rest of the summer, in fact, Melinda fought off one infection after another.

"I had bladder infections, vaginal infections, and cervical infections, and my doctor couldn't understand why. Finally, I had to tell him what I'd done. Thank goodness he was then able to treat the cause." And what was the cause? "Well," Melinda said, "apparently the doctor at Planned Parenthood did the procedure with unsterile instruments. The bacteria just wreaked havoc on my body."

"Nobody told us that something like this could happen," said Cheryl. "I feel like we were deceived."

"We were," agreed Melinda. "We really were. Abortion is a lousy gamble."

Saline Amniocentesis. This once-common method of abortion is now used only when gestation passes the sixteen week mark. During the procedure, a long needle is inserted through the mother's abdomen and directly into the child's amniotic sac. A solution of concentrated salt is then injected into the fluid there. The child breathes in, swallowing the poisonous salt. After about an hour of convulsing and struggling, the child is over-come and the mother goes into labor. About a day later she will deliver a corpse. Not surprisingly, complications are common and include uterine rupture, pulmonary thromboembolism, dis-seminated intravascular coagulation (a dangerous blood clotting disorder), hypernatremia, erosive gastritis, hemolytic anemia, hemoglobinuria, and acute renal failure.[41]

Bethany de Grassi received a saline abortion in 1979. She was nineteen at the time and a freshman at Auburn University. "I was living with a guy at the time," she told me, "and I really thought we were in love. When I got pregnant, I was happy. I thought we'd just settle down, raise a family, and pursue the American dream. But he had other ideas. When I refused to get an abortion he just moved out. Boom. My whole world caved in. I didn't know what to do. I was scared and confused."

Bethany waited almost three months before she did anything at all. Finally, she went to a Planned Parenthood clinic. "They told me that they didn't do the procedure I needed there in the clinic, so they referred me to one of their doctors that had a pri-vate practice on the side for late-term abortions. They gave me all kinds of literature with charts and tables and footnotes and all, telling me that the technique was perfectly safe."

Later, when Bethany was filling out the liability release form, she had a change of heart. "The form had a long, long list of pos-sible complications in tiny print and I started to get really ner-vous. But the nurse came in and sat by me, assuring me that everything was going to be okay. I believed her."

She shouldn't have. Clinic personnel are trained to calm their customers. Sometimes with smiles. Sometimes with lies. Anything, just to get the job done.[42]

Bethany's troubles began with the delivery. "The baby was gasping when it came out," she recalled. "It was awful. I started screaming. The doctor was cursing. And the nurse didn't seem to know what to do. It was a nightmare."

The child expired quickly and the clinic personnel were able, after a few moments of coaxing and consoling, to calm Bethany down. She went into recovery and was released.

Two days later, she suffered a series of seizures and lapsed into a coma. At the hospital, her doctors found that she had hypernatremia—salt poisoning. Her parents were notified and a long six-day struggle for her life ensued. Finally, the medical team at the hospital was able to restore Bethany's electrolyte balance intravenously and she was roused from the coma. "I should have paid attention to my conscience," she now says. "I knew better than to try to come up with some easy fix for my problems. There's just no such thing."

Prostaglandin Abortion. In 1973, the Upjohn Corporation introduced Prostin F2-Alpha, a synthetic hormonal drug, designed to induce violent labor and the premature delivery of an unwanted child. In succeeding years, the company refined its processes and introduced a whole series of new products: Prostin E2, Prostin 15M, suppositories, injections, and urea solutions. For a time it looked as if Upjohn's prostaglandin trade would corner the abortion pharmaceutical market. But then evidence of serious side effects and complications dampened the giant drug maker's hopes. Although the FDA had approved Upjohn's abortion products for widespread consumer use, prostaglandins were quickly shown to commonly cause uterine rupture, sepsis, hemorrhaging, cardio-respiratory arrest, vomiting and aspiration, strokes, and acute kidney failure.[43] The side effects did not occur only occasionally: As many as forty-two percent of all prostaglandin abortions result in one or more of these complications.[44]

Christine Aulen was shocked when her daughter Deana told her one day after school that she was pregnant. "I decided to put on my brave Mom's-your-best-friend-and-confidante act," she told me. "So we sat down together and talked through our options. After much debate and discussion, we realized that we just didn't have enough facts to make a rational decision. As if *rationality* was the issue."

That is when they decided to go to Planned Parenthood. "We thought they could give us the facts so that we could make an objective decision. We were wrong."

The counselor at the clinic immediately recommended abortion. "She seemed to be so sweet and kind. She made the referral for us and set up our appointment."

Sweet and kind or not, what happened was like a script from a horror movie. Once the procedure had begun, there were immediate complications. Deana went into shock and suffered a series of seizures. Frantic, the clinic personnel called for an ambulance. But before it could arrive, Deana died. Christine, sitting out in the waiting room reading magazines, fidgeting, and worrying, never knew what was going on behind closed doors.

That was seven years ago, but for Christine it seems like just yesterday. "Angry? You bet, I'm angry," she says. "No one warned us. No one told us. Tragedies like this shouldn't happen. They don't *have* to happen."

The facts speak for themselves. Abortion is dangerous.

Planned Parenthood officials are not incognizant of the facts. They know that their abortion procedures and techniques are unsafe. They know that tragedies like Christine and Deana Aulen's happen only because they persist in performing those unsafe procedures and techniques. As long ago as 1963, Planned Parenthood published a booklet saying that "an abortion kills the life of a baby after it has begun. It is dangerous to your life and health."[45] Nothing has changed in the intervening years. And they know it.

Late in 1986, pro-life workers in Houston discovered several thousand clinic visit records, medical charts, internal minutes and memorandums, letters, confidential surveys, and financial statements in the trash at a Planned Parenthood abortuary.[46] A comprehensive analysis was made of each document and a data base was developed so that analysis could be tabulated systematically.[47]

Their findings were astonishing.

More than a third of the medical charts recorded "severe" or "very severe pain" for the women during their abortion procedures.[48] Almost five percent of the women were said to have "screamed" during their operations.[49] Another eleven percent "cried," ten percent "overreacted," and five percent "complained."[50] Almost ten percent experienced "nausea" or "vomiting," and another ten percent "fainted" or "fell unconscious."[51]

One chart described blatantly unsterile operating procedures.[52] Another detailed a doctor's brutal and abusive behavior.[53] Still another called into question the racial motivations of the clinic personnel.[54]

The evidence is indisputable.

Planned Parenthood officials know precisely what they are doing. They know full well that abortion is unsafe. They know that women by the thousands are being exploited by the abortion trade. They see it every day.

Even if unborn children were not murdered[55] by abortion, men and women of conscience would still have to stand unwaveringly opposed to it. It is dangerous. Scandalously so.

The Medical Risks of Birth Control

The dangerous propagation of abortion is not the only medical scandal that Planned Parenthood has been involved in over the last several years. Its birth control programs have also been terribly flawed.

All birth control methods are subject to FDA approval, and must be tested on laboratory animals and human subjects before they can be marketed to the public. This process may take anywhere between three and ten years to complete.[56] At first blush, that appears to be a ponderously slow approval process, but in fact, it is far too hasty. It may take as long as fifteen to twenty years for the complications of various birth control methods to become apparent.[57] Planned Parenthood and its birth control allies in the medical-industrial complex[58] have pressured the FDA to rush products to market long before those complications can be known.[59] The result is that women using birth control are little more than guinea pigs—unwitting subjects in prolonged and deathly dangerous experiments.[60] A number of important studies have shown that, indeed, Planned Parenthood's favored contraceptive programs are all unwarranted medical risks.[61]

Dr. Frederick Robbins, a noted figure in population research, justified Planned Parenthood's dependence on unsafe birth control products saying, "The dangers of overpopulation are so great that we may have to use certain techniques of contraception that may entail considerable risk to the individual woman."[62] Once again, "choice" is thrown to the wind.

The Pill. For Margaret Sanger, birth control was not simply a technique, it was a *religion*. And the Pill was the *Holy Grail* of that religion.[63] Beginning in the late twenties and early thirties, she helped fund a number of research projects that she hoped would one day produce a safe and effective chemical contraceptive.[64] In 1950 she met a brilliant biologist named Gregory Pincus. His stunning successes in ovulation research with laboratory animals encouraged Margaret to invest over two million dollars over a ten year span in his work.[65] By 1954 the Pill was ready for human testing. By 1958 Sanger and Pincus had persuaded G. D. Searle, the pharmaceutical giant, to begin test marketing the product in the United States with provisional approval of the FDA. Then finally, after an unprecedented media blitz and political lobbying campaign, the Pill was given full approval in 1960.[66]

Utilizing synthetic hormones—either estrogen or progesterone or a combination of both—the Pill interrupts the regular menstrual cycle, thus preventing ovulation in most cases. If ovulation does occur, the Pill has a number of fail-safe features that help the uterine lining resist implantation, thus aborting any human embryos.[67]

The Pill, on the heels of Planned Parenthood's ecstatic public relations splurge, quickly became the most widely used prescription drug in the world.[68] In the United States more than a million women were using it within two years of its introduction.[69] A decade later, that figure had risen to more than ten million.[70]

And then the trouble began.

Women were reporting a number of minor side effects: migraine headaches, depression, nausea, fatigue, skin rashes, inflammation of the gums, weight gain, breast tenderness, and irregular menstruation.[71]

Although medical research is notorious for contradictory data and inconclusiveness, a number of studies began to pour in indicating that the medical complications did not end there.[72] They showed that women who use the Pill are susceptible to hypertension—abnormally high blood pressure. They have an increased risk of heart attacks, thromboembolism, and strokes. They are significantly more susceptible to various kinds of growths, cysts, and malignancies including ovarian cancer, liver cancer, and skin cancer. In addition, it appears that the Pill can make women more susceptible to diabetes, urinary tract infections, epilepsy, asthma, pleurisy, arthritis, eczema, urticaria, chloasma, and ulcers.[73]

Margaret Sanger's Holy Grail has turned out to be a holy terror.

Since the Pill has an in-use failure rate of as high as eleven percent per annum,[74] the perceived benefits of contraception—whatever they may be—hardly outweigh the risks. And yet Planned Parenthood continues to push this dangerous drug on its clients. Almost eighty percent of those who walk into a Planned Parenthood clinic walk out with the Pill.[75]

Lisa Godet, Patty Manfra, and Barbara Ammunds decided to visit the Planned Parenthood clinic near their school together in order to obtain birth control pills. Lisa and Patty were already sexually active. Barbara was "still just hoping," she said. Their sex education teacher had told them that the clinic would provide them with *free* contraceptives and that their parents wouldn't have to find out. "It sounded almost too good to be true," Lisa told me, "so we decided to check it out."

Sure enough, the staff personnel were very accommodating. The girls were all scheduled for after-school checkups and were given a three month supply of Pills.

Over the next several months, Lisa and Patty noticed no physiological changes to speak of. "Oh, I gained a little bit of weight," Patty said. "But I probably went on a chocolate binge or something."

For Barbara, though, it was a different story. "My blood sugar started to fluctuate really wildly. I'd be really up one minute, and then the next, I'd be totally worn out." Her parents noticed the ups and downs but attributed them to the fickleness of teenage emotions. Then the fluctuations became more dramatic. One evening at the dinner table, Barbara passed out and went into a mild seizure.

A battery of tests over the next several days yielded a diagnosis of diabetes. "My doctor suspected that I might be on the Pill," she said, "because of the unusual way my symptoms suddenly began. He told me that I needed to stop taking it right away. I didn't need any further convincing. I quit."

Lisa and Patty quit, too. After seeing Barbara's trauma and hearing for the first time about the medical risks of birth control pills, they decided that the best way to prevent unwanted pregnancies is abstinence. "I hope we've all learned," Patty said, "that sneaking around and doing the wrong thing can only lead to trouble."

The Intrauterine Device (IUD). Like the Pill, the IUD seemed to be the perfect birth control device when it was introduced in the early sixties. It was said to be nearly ninety percent effective per year and since it did not introduce synthetic hormones into the woman's system or alter her body chemistry, it was supposed to be safe as well. Within just a few years, nearly sixty million women worldwide had begun using the IUD, making it the most popular contraceptive alternative to the Pill.[76]

But, once again, Planned Parenthood and the pharmaceutical industry enthusiastically rushed the product to market and through the approval process long before sufficient research had confirmed its safety.[77] As a result, IUD users were for all intents and purposes the subjects of a vast program of human experimentation.

The device is a small and irregular coil of copper or plastic with several trailing filaments. It is installed in the uterus where it causes an inflammation or chronic low grade infection that inhibits implantation. Thus, the IUD does not prevent conception, it simply dislodges and aborts any human embryos that make their way out of the fallopian tubes. What researchers failed to detect as they were developing the IUD is that the entire obstruction process is terribly risky and terribly dangerous. The product has been directly linked to a high number of cases of Pelvic Inflammatory Disease and spontaneous septic miscarriages.[78] It commonly causes excessive bleeding, cramping, perforation of the uterine wall, ectopic pregnancy, and endometritis.[79] It has even been implicated in dozens of deaths.[80] Currently there are more than a thousand major lawsuits pending against its manufacturers, and several models have been removed from the United States market.[81]

Sandra LaCazio, a mother of four, began using the IUD in 1973. "My next door neighbor was a nurse at Planned Parenthood," she said, "and was constantly urging me to come in and be fitted for an IUD. I'd been having a few problems with the Pill, so I took her up on her offer. That was a big mistake. A *really* big mistake."

Sandra had problems with her IUD right from the start. "It was a constant irritant. I went back several times and my neighbor just told me to be patient—I would get used to it. But I never did."

And no wonder. By the time Sandra finally sought help from her regular obstetrician, the IUD had become embedded in her uterine wall. She was suffering from severe cases of peritonitis, endometritis, and salpingitis. Her fallopian tubes were scarred beyond repair. And her entire uterus was raw and inflamed. The doctor had no choice but to schedule her for a complete hysterectomy.

"I'm so thankful that my doctor knew just what to do," she later told me. "I could very easily have died. My neighbor, of course, keeps insisting that my problems were unusual and isolated. But I know better. Everywhere I go, I hear horror stories from women who have been misled by Planned Parenthood and suffered the consequences."

RU-486. This new drug was developed by the French pharmaceutical company Roussel-Uclaf and financed by the American taxpayer through the National Institutes of Health and the World Health Organization.[82] The fruit of a prolonged search for a post-coital—or "morning after"—pill, RU-486 is actually a self-administered abortifacient.

The drug is an anti-progesterone steroid synthetic that can be administered orally, vaginally, or by injection. Following conception, the drug simply washes the living human embryo out of the womb in an artificially stimulated menses.

Although RU-486 is too new to have undergone a full battery of tests, more than one thousand women have used the drug since its tentative introduction in 1982.[83] And already a number of frightening complications have developed. As many as fifteen percent of the women experienced "incomplete embryonic expulsions," thus requiring surgical abortions to prevent serious infections.[84] Prolonged uterine bleeding—more than thirteen days—was experienced by another six percent of the women.[85] Other complications noted at this early stage include weakness, vomiting, and cervical dilation.[86]

Despite this evidence, Planned Parenthood has been at the forefront of the RU-486 development picture. Etienne-Emile Boulieu, the chief researcher in the project, has publicly acknowledged his debt to the organization and "to the spirit that inspired Margaret Sanger," its founder.[87]

Other Devices. Although the Pill and the IUD are Planned Parenthood's favored contraceptive technologies, several alternative methods are available at its clinics as well.

Ever since Margaret Sanger began smuggling diaphragms into the country—in liquor bottles through rum-runners—

Planned Parenthood has offered the soft rubber barrier devices to its clients.[88] Used alone, the diaphragm's effectiveness is dubious at best. Used in conjunction with spermicidal foams, creams, and jellies, its effectiveness increases significantly, but its safety plummets. Several spermicides have been forced off drugstore shelves due to serious medical complications and a number of multi-million dollar lawsuits.[89]

Vaginal contraceptive sponges and cervical caps may share that same fate.[90] Although both offer some contraceptive protection as a partial barrier within the uterus, their real effectiveness depends on supplementary spermicidal agents. And there is the rub. The spermicides have simply not proven to be safe. They can cause everything from minor allergic reactions to serious vaginal infections, from cervical irritation to serious hormonal imbalances, from a slight genital abscess to chronic endometritis.[91]

Robin Cohen began to use a spermicidal jelly after being fitted for a diaphragm at a Planned Parenthood clinic near her home. Both she and her husband experienced a good deal of irritation during intercourse, so she changed brands. "With the second brand, both Bill and I broke out in a painful genital rash," she said. "So I quickly changed brands again. This time, I tried a cream. And that was even worse. I came down with a serious vaginal infection and had to take antibiotics for almost two weeks."

Still undeterred, Robin's counselor at Planned Parenthood had her try still another spermicide. "I don't know why I couldn't get it through my thick skull that those things just aren't safe. When I got another infection—this time with fever, nausea, headaches, and swollen lymph glands—I knew I'd really blown it."

Indeed she had. The back-to-back infections, though easily treated, caused a good deal of scarring in Robin's fallopian tubes. Two years later when she and Bill decided that they wanted to have children, she found that she couldn't get pregnant. A fertility specialist informed her that if she ever wanted to restore her fertility she would have to undergo reconstructive surgery. "Can you believe it? I have to have surgery now because those people at the clinic are handing out dangerous drugs. It makes you wonder how they can possibly stay in business."

Medicine and the Lost Legacy

The past one hundred years have been called "The Golden Age of Medicine."[92] And for good reason. It has been a period in which mankind has gained "unprecedented insights into diseases that for millennia have held millions of people in a cruel and unrelenting grasp."[93] With a dizzying array of new technologies and treatments at our every beck and call, we are now able to do far more than our grandfathers could have ever imagined. The miracles of organ transplants, software implants, and cybernetic replicants now make it possible for us to help the blind to see, the deaf to hear, and the lame to walk. With the advent of biomedical research, laser surgery, macro-pharmacology, fiber optic scanning, and recombinant DNA engineering, has come new hope. The afflicted are raised up, the broken and distressed are sustained, and those once left for dead are somehow restored. We can now do all this and more.

But sadly, amidst this great hymn of victory, a dissonant chord has sounded. The immoral, barbaric, backward, and scandalously unsafe medical practices of Planned Parenthood have sidled their way into mainstream medicine. And thus the victory celebration has been crashed with the shadowy figures of statistics that do not lie—new diseases, new defects, new ways to die.

Medicine is a tool for the preservation of health and life. Technology is a tool for the enhancement of productivity and fruitfulness. Whenever wicked men try to wield those tools for the dissemination of death and destruction, for broadcasting barrenness and brutality, disaster becomes inevitable.[94]

Fruitfulness is a blessing from God (Genesis 17:20; Exodus 23:6; Deuteronomy 7:14). Life is a glorious gift of grace (John 10:10). And so while fruitfulness and abundant life bring joy and jubilation (Psalm 113:9), barrenness and death bring sadness and sorrow (Job 24:21, 39:6; Jeremiah 4:26).

All men are commanded to be fruitful (Genesis 9:1). We are to be fruitful in all that we set our hands to do (Colossians 1:10). And we are to have *nothing* to do with the works of unfruitfulness (Ephesians 5:11). Now that does not mean that we are not to exercise wise stewardship over our lives, our families, and our environment. On the contrary, we are commanded to "exercise dominion" over these things (Genesis 1:28). But the clear purpose of that stewardship and dominion is to enhance and multiply fruitfulness, not barrenness.

There can be no compromise, no hedging, and no capitulation on this matter: death is the *enemy* that Christ came to destroy (1 Corinthians 15:26; 2 Timothy 1:10). Barrenness is the *curse* that He came to remove (Isaiah 32:15; 2 Peter 1:8). Death and barrenness *never* have been and *never* will be "rest," "relief," "freedom," or "natural." Death and barrenness are the awful, obscene, and wretched results of the fall (Genesis 2:17, 3:16-19). They are the torturous and unnatural shackles of sin (Romans 6:23).

To shun fruitfulness and life for barrenness and death is utterly insane (Romans 1:18-22). It is to invite disaster (Deuteronomy 28:15-68).

One hundred years ago—before the Golden Age—the medical establishment led a valiant crusade to criminalize the flourishing abortion and birth control enterprises of the day.[95] They led that crusade not just because they *thought* they were immoral, but because they *knew* they were unsafe. They fought abortion and birth control because death and barrenness are the antithesis, not the ambitions, of medicine.

As a result of that clear and uncompromising stand, their profession flourished—and the Golden Age dawned.[96]

Today, because the medical establishment has embraced Planned Parenthood's morbid fascination with death and barrenness, the Golden Age is coming to a close, and we are seeing many of the gains of the last century slip out of our grasp: incurable retro-viruses ravaging whole sectors of the population in plague proportions,[97] mutating strains of cancer cutting wide swathes through each new generation,[98] and surprising reversals in undeveloped nations of once-conquered foes like smallpox, malaria, and polio.[99]

But that's not the worst of it.

Horror story after horror story—a veritable litany of abuse—has begun to emerge from the hallowed halls of medicine in our land: fetal harvesting,[100] women serving as breeders in surrogate motherhood programs,[101] euthanasia,[102] genetic manipulation in test tube baby experiments,[103] infanticide,[104] preprogrammed implants and brain-to-computer interfacing for intelligence enhancements,[105] genetic engineering,[106] viral memory manipulation to control psychotic episodes in mental patients,[107] algeny,[108] the development of frighteningly powerful forms of biological warfare,[109] daeliaforcation,[110] the exclusive commercialization of services by health care corporations,[111] biocleatics,[112] poor patients serving as guinea pigs in bizarre particle bombardment experiments,[113] neuroclatology,[114] handicapped patients facing compulsory sterilizations,[115] artificial natalization,[116] and racially motivated Eugenic programs.[117] They are stories that make the Nazi medical atrocities pale in comparison.[118]

How could this come to be? How could modern medicine — fresh on the heels of the Golden Age — have gone so wrong?

The fact is, medicine has always been a special legacy of God's people.

Whenever and wherever Biblical faithfulness has been practiced, the medical arts have flourished. But whenever and wherever Biblical faithfulness has been shunned, medicine has given way to superstition, barbarism, and shamanism.

The earliest medical guild appeared on the Aegean island of Cos, just off the coast of Asia Minor. Around the time that Nehemiah was organizing the post-exilic Jews in Jerusalem to rebuild the walls, another refugee from the Babylonian occupation, Aesculapius, was organizing the post-exilic Jews on Cos into medical specialists — for the first time in history, moving medical healing beyond folk remedies and occultic rituals. It was not long before this elite guild had become the wonder of the Mediterranean world under the leadership of Hippocrates, the son of Panacea, the son of Hygeia, the son of Aesculapius, the son of Hashabia the Hebrew, an exile of fallen Jerusalem.[119]

In other words, the great *Greek* school of healing that gave us the Hippocratic oath, that gave us the scientific standards for hygiene, diagnosis, and systematic treatment that form the basis for modern medicine, wasn't *Greek* at all. It was Hebrew, the fruit of Biblical faith.[120]

And so the story goes, all throughout history.

Medicine always has been and always will be a special legacy of God's people — provoked by Scriptural compassion, fueled by Scriptural conviction, and guided by Scriptural ethics.

When plague and pestilence convulsed the peoples of the past, it was Christians who stood steadfast amidst the terrors, establishing hostels, clinics, and Basileas. It was the *Church* that pioneered the concept of hospitals. For instance, in 372 Basil the Great, bishop of Caesarea in Cappadocia, founded the first non-ambulatory hospital, attended by both nurses and doctors.[121] John Chrysostom opened a similar facility adjacent to his Church in Antioch in 389.[122] And Ambrose, Bishop of Milan, dedicated a hospital modeled on those first two in his diocese in 393.[123] Thereafter, wherever the Good News of Jesus Christ penetrated the darkness of paganism, the light and life of the medical arts were quickly established.[124]

The emergence of medicine's Golden Age came in direct correspondence with the advancement of the Gospel.[125] Christian nations are havens of medical mastery, guarding the sanctity of life. Where the Church of Jesus Christ is weak and faltering, however, medical technology degenerates to crude and barbaric superstition. It becomes just one more bludgeon to exploit the weak, the poor, and the helpless. When Asia Minor and Eastern Europe converted to the faith throughout the first millennium after Christ, a revolution of compassionate and professional care blanketed those regions with a tenacious respect and protection of all human life, from the womb to the tomb.[126] But when successive waves of paganism, first the Ottomans and Tartars and then later the Fascists and Communists, snatched those realms from the fold of Christendom, medicine was reduced to a morbid and medieval malapropism of genocide, triage, atrocity, and perversion.[127]

Where true Christianity is not practiced, true medicine cannot be practiced. Where faith degenerates into faithlessness, healing of necessity degenerates into killing. Where there are no moral or ethical standards, there can be no basis for the nurture and protection of life.

The great lesson of history is that Proverbs 8:35-36 is absolutely and inescapably true: all those who hate God love death, but he who finds God loves life.

Sexual Balance

Sex is good.

In its proper place. And in its proper perspective.

God created it. He endowed it with great value and benefit. He filled it with beauty, dignity, glory, honor — and, of course, *life.* He made it a multi-dimensional blessing, a lavish gift, and a gracious inheritance for all those who have entered into the life-long covenant of marriage.

Sex is good because it affirms and confirms that covenant with intimacy and joy. The marriage bed is rich with pleasure. It is romantic. It is lush with merriment and celebration. And this recreational aspect of marital sex is never to be despised.

Sex is also good because it anoints the covenant with perpetuity. The great blessing of children is a special inheritance bestowed by God's own sovereign hand. This procreational aspect of marital sex is never to be despised.

Sex is good. It is a celebration of life.

Of course, sex can be defiled. When it is ripped out of its covenant context to be used and abused as an end in itself, it is corrupted and polluted. Outside of the marriage covenant, sex becomes a rude and crude parody of itself. It is sullied and putrefied. It becomes a specter of death. The fact that Planned Parenthood's abortion and birth control programs create incentives for premarital sex should be indictment enough.

But not only is sex defiled when it is stolen from the sanctity of marriage, it is also defiled when it loses its delicate balance between recreation and procreation. Any attempt to drive an absolute wedge between those two God-ordained dynamics diminishes the glory of the marriage bed.[128]

Sex is not fruitful just because it's fun—just because it enhances intimacy and communion. Some couples who enjoy extraordinary bedroom exploits never know the fullness of fruitfulness.

Neither is sex fruitful just because it produces babies. Some couples who are never able to have children are nonetheless blessed with abundant fruitfulness.

Fruitfulness is a wholistic concern. It encompasses both recreation and procreation through a careful stewardship of faith, hope, love, time, money, resources, and circumstances. It balances them, like sovereignty and responsibility, in a life of covenant fruitfulness.

But Planned Parenthood is not too terribly interested in balance. Instead, it promotes dangerous drugs and surgical procedures that guarantee—or at least *purport* to guarantee—an absolute division between recreation and procreation. It promotes contraceptive methods that attempt to usurp God's design for sex. It promotes birth control measures that reduce sex to mere sport.

Abortion, then, is nothing but a recreational surgery. A dangerously lethal recreational surgery. Similarly, the Pill—and most of the other forms of prescription birth control—is nothing but a recreational drug. A dangerously toxic recreational drug.

Isn't it about time we told American teens and single adults to "just say no"? Isn't it about time we told them that there is a better way—God's way? Isn't it about time modern medicine stopped toying with the minions of perversion and death and returned to the sanctity of life? Isn't it?

Conclusion

"Abortion in America is a commodity," argues author David Reardon, "bought and sold for the convenience of the buyer and the profit of the seller. Though abortion utilizes medical knowledge, it is not *medical*—that is, abortions are not being prescribed in order to heal the body or cure illnesses. . . . Even in the rare cases where serious medical problems do exist because of the pregnancy, abortion is still not good medicine."[129]

Amazingly, this dangerous and brutal procedure is the *only* surgery which is legally protected from any sort of governmental regulation.[130] There are laws that dictate how tonsils may and may not be removed. There are laws that dictate how broken bones may and may not be set. But there are no laws that dictate how abortions may or may not be performed.[131]

Similarly, prescription birth control has attained the status of a sacred cow. Anyone who questions its viability is instantly vilified as a violator of civil liberties and an imbalanced Victorian snoot. But the fact is that the Pill, the IUD, RU-486, and a large number of spermicidal jellies, creams, and foams are dangerous. They are not *medical*—they are not being prescribed in order to heal bodies or cure illnesses. They are recreational drugs. Dangerous recreational drugs.

Clearly, the medical practices of Planned Parenthood are not *medical* at all. They are scandalous.

I vow before our Sovereign God that I will carry out, according to my ability and judgment, this oath and this indenture: I will use treatment to help the sick according to the best of my ability and godly wisdom, never with a view to injury, wrongdoing, harm, or restraint. I will keep pure and holy before God both my life and my art. In whatsoever houses I enter, I will enter for healing and succor of the sick, regardless of race, color, or creed.

Basil's Hippocratic Oath

A RACE OF THOROUGHBREDS: THE RACIAL LEGACY

homo homini lupus

It was a very good year. America was boisterously happy. With Calvin Coolidge in the White House in Washington, Duke Ellington at the Cotton Club in Harlem, and Babe Ruth at home plate in New York, things could hardly be better. It was 1927, and Cecil B. DeMille was putting the finishing touches on his classic film, *The King of Kings*, Henry Ford was rolling his fifteen millionth Model T off the assembly line, Abe Saperstein was recruiting the razzle-dazzle players that would become the Harlem Globetrotters, Al Jolson was wowing the public in *The Jazz Singer*, and Thornton Wilder was garnering accolades for his newest book, *The Bridge of San Luis Rey*. The Great War was an already distant memory and the Great Depression was still in the distant future. It was a zany, carefree time of zoot suits and flappers, speakeasies and dance-a-thons. It was indeed a very good year.

For most folks, anyway.

It *wasn't* a very good year for Carrie Buck. In a decision written by Justice Oliver Wendell Holmes, the Supreme Court upheld a Virginia State Health Department order to have the nineteen-year-old girl sterilized against her will.

Carrie had recently been committed to a state institution for epileptics, where her mother Emma was also a patient. Upon admission she had been given an I.Q. test and was found to have "a mental age of nine years." Emma was said to have "a mental age of slightly under eight years," and Carrie's seven-month-old baby was said to have "a look" that was "not quite normal."[1] That was evidence enough for the state health officials. They invoked a Virginia Law that required sterilization in families where "hereditary mental deficiency" and "feeblemindedness" could be demonstrated over three successive generations.

Medical experts supplied the court with depositions claiming that Carrie's alleged "feeblemindedness" was "unquestionably hereditary"—without ever having examined Carrie, her mother, or her daughter in person.[2] One of these long distance experts, a renowned genetic biologist, asserted that Carrie's family belonged to "the shiftless, ignorant, and worthless class," that "modern science and beneficent social legislation is obligated to eradicate for the greater good of the White Civilization."[3]

Apparently the court agreed. In his opinion, Justice Holmes wrote, "We have seen more than once that the public welfare may call upon the best citizens for their lives. It would be strange if it could not call upon those who already sap the strength of the State for these lesser sacrifices. . . . in order to prevent our being swamped with incompetence." He concluded, "Three generations of imbeciles are enough."[4]

So, one fine day in 1927, when most of the rest of the world seemed to be celebrating Babe Ruth's record setting sixtieth home run of the season, Carrie Buck entered a hospital in Lynchburg, Virginia, and had her fallopian tubes severed.

Carrie, now seventy-nine, lives near her sister Doris in Charlottesville, Virginia.[5] Doris had been sterilized under the same law, only she never knew it. "They told me," she recalled, "that the operation was for an appendix." Later, when she was married, she and her husband tried to have children. They consulted with a number of specialists at three hospitals throughout her child-bearing years, but none of them detected the tubal ligation. It wasn't until 1980, fifty-two years after the fact, that Doris finally uncovered the cause of her lifelong sadness. It was only then that she was given access to Carrie's medical records, where a cryptic marginal note revealed that she shared her sister's fate.[6] "I broke down and cried," she said. "My husband and me wanted children desperately. We were crazy about them. I never knew what they'd done to me."[7]

The Buck family tragedy has been repeated thousands of times over the years. To this day, twenty-two states have sterilization laws on the books, and young women like Carrie and Doris are subjected to the humiliation of coercive barrenness.[8]

Those laws are the fruit of a philosophical movement called Eugenics—a movement that Planned Parenthood is very much a part of.[9]

White Supremacy

Eugenics—like Darwinism, Marxism, Fascism, Freudianism, and any number of other revolutionary pseudo-sciences—was an offshoot of Malthusianism.[10] Through his writings, Thomas Malthus had convinced an entire generation of scientists, intellectuals, and social reformers that the world was facing an imminent economic crisis caused by unchecked human fertility.[11] Some of those Malthusians believed that the solution to the crisis was political: restrict immigration, reform social welfare, and tighten citizenship requirements.[12] Others thought the solution was technological: increase agricultural production, improve medical proficiency, and promote industrial efficiency.[13] But many of the rest felt that the solution was genetic—restrict or eliminate "bad" racial stocks, and gradually "aid" the evolutionary ascent of man.[14] This last group became known as the Eugenicists. The Eugenicists unashamedly espoused White Supremacy. Or to be more precise, they espoused Northern and Eastern European White Supremacy.[15] This supremacy was to be promoted both positively and negatively.[16]

Through selective breeding, the Eugenicists hoped to purify the blood lines and improve the stock of the Aryan race. The "fit" would be encouraged to reproduce prolifically. This was the positive side of Malthusian Eugenics.[17]

Negative Malthusian Eugenics on the other hand, sought to contain the "inferior" races through segregation, sterilization, birth control, and abortion. The "unfit" would thus be slowly winnowed out of the population as chaff is from wheat.[18]

By the first two decades of this century, according to feminist author Germaine Greer, "the relevance of Eugenic considerations was accepted by all shades of liberal and radical opinion, as well as by conservatives."[19] Some forty states had enacted

restrictive containment measures and established Eugenic asy-
lums.[20] Eugenics departments were endowed at many of the
most prestigious universities in the world.[21] Funding for
Eugenic research was provided by the Rockefeller, Ford, and
Carnegie Foundations.[22] And Eugenic ideas were given free
reign in the literature, theater, music, and press of the day.[23]

The crassest sort of racial and class bigotry was thus embraced
against the bosom of pop culture as readily and enthusiastically
as the latest movie release from Hollywood or the latest hit tune
from Broadway. It became a part of the collective consciousness.
Its assumptions went almost entirely unquestioned. Because it
sprang from the sacrosanct temple of "science"—like Aphrodite
from the sea—it was placed in the modern pantheon of "truth"
and rendered due faith and service by all "reasonable" men.

Of course, not all men are "reasonable," and so Malthusian
Eugenics was not without its critics. The great Christian apologist G. K. Chesterton, for example, fired unrelenting salvos of
biting analysis against the Eugenicists, indicting them for com-
bining "a hardening of the heart with a sympathetic softening of
the head,"[24] and for presuming to turn "common decency" and
"commendable deeds" into "social crimes."[25] If Darwinism was
the doctrine of "the survival of the fittest," then he said, Eugenics
was the doctrine of "the survival of the nastiest."[26] In his
remarkably visionary book *Eugenics and Other Evils*, Chesterton
pointed out, for the first time, the link between Neo-Malthusian
Eugenics and the evolution of Prussian and Volkish Monism
into Fascist Nazism. "It is the same stuffy science," he argued,
"the same bullying bureaucracy, and the same terrorism by
tenth-rate professors, that has led the German Empire to its recent conspicuous triumphs."[27]

But singular voices like Chesterton's were soon drowned out
by the din of acceptance. Long latent biases heretofore held at bay
by moral convention were suddenly liberated by "science." Men
were now justified in indulging their petty prejudices. And they
took perverse pleasure in it, as all fallen men are wont to do.[28]

The Planned Parenthood Connection

Margaret Sanger was especially mesmerized by the scientific
racism of Malthusian Eugenics. Part of the attraction for her
was surely personal: her mentor and lover, Havelock Ellis, was

the beloved disciple of Francis Galton, the brilliant cousin of Charles Darwin who first systemized and popularized Eugenic thought.[29]

Part of the attraction for her was also political: virtually all of her Socialist friends, lovers, and comrades were committed Eugenicists as well — from the followers of Lenin in Revolutionary Socialism, like H. G. Wells, George Bernard Shaw, and Julius Hammer,[30] to the followers of Hitler in National Socialism, like Ernest Rudin, Leon Whitney, and Harry Laughlin.[31]

But it wasn't simply sentiment or politics that drew Margaret into the Eugenic fold. She was thoroughly convinced that the "inferior races" were in fact "human weeds" and a "menace to civilization."[32] She believed that "social regeneration" would only be possible as the "sinister forces of the hordes of irresponsibility and imbecility" were repulsed.[33] She had come to regard organized charity to ethnic minorities and the poor as a "symptom of a malignant social disease" because it encouraged the prolificacy of "defectives, delinquents, and dependents."[34] She yearned for the end of the Christian "reign of benevolence" that the Eugenic Socialists promised, when the "choking human undergrowth" of "morons and imbeciles" would be "segregated" and "sterilized."[35] Her goal was "to create a race of thoroughbreds" by encouraging "more children from the fit, and less from the unfit."[36] And the only way to achieve that goal she realized, was through Malthusian Eugenics.

Thus, as she began to build the work of the American Birth Control League, and ultimately, of Planned Parenthood, Margaret relied heavily on the men, women, ideas, and resources of the Eugenics movement. Virtually all of the organization's board members were Eugenicists.[37] Financing for the early projects — from the opening of the birth control clinics to the publishing of the revolutionary literature — came from Eugenicists.[38] The speakers at the conferences, the authors of the literature and the providers of the services were almost without exception avid Eugenicists.[39]

The Birth Control Review — Margaret's magazine and the immediate predecessor to the *Planned Parenthood Review* — regularly and openly published the racist articles of Malthusian Eugenicists.[40] In 1920, it published a favorable review of Lothrop Stoddard's frightening book, *The Rising Tide of Color Against White World Supremacy.*[41] In 1923, the *Review* editorialized in favor of restricting immigration on a racial basis.[42] In 1932, it outlined Margaret's "Plan for Peace," calling for coercive sterilization, mandatory segregation, and rehabilative concentration camps for all "dysgenic stocks."[43] In 1933, the *Review* published "Eugenic Sterilization: An Urgent Need" by Ernst Rudin, who was Hitler's director of genetic sterilization and a founder of the Nazi Society for Racial Hygiene.[44] And later that same year, it published an article by Leon Whitney entitled, "Selective Sterilization," which adamantly praised and defended the Third Reich's racial programs.[45]

The bottom line is that Planned Parenthood was self-consciously organized, in part, to promote and enforce White Supremacy. Like the Ku Klux Klan, the Nazi Party, and the Mensheviks, it has been from its inception implicitly and explicitly racist. And this racist orientation is all too evident in its various programs and initiatives: birth control clinics, the abortion crusade, and sterilization initiatives.

Racism and Birth Control Clinics

Margaret Sanger's first birth control clinic was opened in 1916. It was located in the impoverished and densely populated Brownsville section of Brooklyn. The ramshackle two-room storefront was a far cry from Margaret's plush Greenwich Village haunts. But since the clientele she wished to attract—"immigrant Southern Europeans, Slavs, Latins, and Jews"—could only be found "in the coarser neighborhoods and tenements," she was forced to venture out of her comfortable confines.[46]

As her organization grew in power and prestige, she began to target several other "dysgenic races"—including Blacks, Hispanics, Amerinds, and Catholics—and set up clinics in their respective communities as well.[47] Margaret and the Malthusian Eugenicists she had gathered about her were not partial; every non-Aryan—Red, Yellow, Black, or White—they were all noxious in their sight. They sought to place new clinics wherever those "feeble-minded, syphilitic, irresponsible, and defective" stocks "bred unhindered."[48] Since by their estimation as much as seventy percent of the population fell into this "undesirable" category, Margaret and her cohorts really had their work cut out for them.[49]

They wasted no time in getting started.

In 1939, they designed a "Negro Project" in response to "south-ern state public health officials" — men not generally known for their racial equanimity.[50] "The mass of Negroes," the project proposal asserted, "particularly in the South, still breed carelessly and disastrously, with the result that the increase among Negroes, even more than among Whites, is from that portion of the population least intelligent and fit."[51] The proposal went on to say that "Public Health statistics merely hint at the primitive state of civilization in which most Negroes in the South live."[52]

In order to remedy this "dysgenic horror story," the project aimed to hire three or four "Colored Ministers, preferably with social-service backgrounds, and with engaging personalities" to travel to various Black enclaves and propagandize for birth con-trol.[53] "The most successful educational approach to the Negro," Margaret wrote sometime later, "is through a religious appeal. We do not want word to go out that we want to exterminate the Negro population and the Minister is the man who can straighten out that idea if it ever occurs to any of their more re-bellious members."[54] Of course, those Black ministers were to be carefully controlled — mere figureheads. "There is a great danger that we will fail," one of the project directors wrote, "because the Negroes think it a plan for extermination. Hence, let's *appear* to let the colored run it."[55] Another project director lamented, "I wonder if Southern Darkies can ever be entrusted with . . . a clinic. Our experience causes us to doubt their ability to work except under White supervision."[56] The entire operation then was a ruse — a manipulative attempt to get Blacks to cooperate in their own elimination.

The project was quite successful. Its genocidal intentions were carefully camouflaged beneath several layers of condescend-ing social service rhetoric and organizational expertise. Like the citizens of Hamelin, lured into captivity by the sweet serenades of the Pied Piper, all too many Blacks all across the country hap-pily fell into step behind Margaret and the Eugenic racists she had placed on her Negro Advisory Council. Soon clinics throughout the South were distributing contraceptives to Blacks and Margaret's dream of discouraging "the defective and dis-eased elements of humanity" from their "reckless and irresponsi-ble swarming and spawning" was at last being fulfilled.[57]

The strategy was of course racial and not geographical. The Southern states were picked simply because of the high proportion of Blacks in their populations.[58] In the 1970s, expansion to the North and West occurred. But the basic guidelines remained: the proportion of minorities in a community was closely related to the density of birth control clinics.[59]

During the 1980s when Planned Parenthood shifted its focus from community-based clinics to school-based clinics, it again targeted inner-city minority neighborhoods.[60] Of the more than one hundred school-based clinics that have opened nationwide in the last decade, *none* have been at substantially all-White schools.[61] *None* have been at suburban middle-class schools. *All* have been at Black, minority, or ethnic schools.[62]

Fortunately, a number of Black leaders have seen through these Eugenic machinations and have begun a counterattack.[63] In 1987, for instance, a group of Black ministers, parents, and educators filed suit against the Chicago Board of Education. The plaintiffs charged that the city's school-based clinics not only violated state fornication laws, but that they also were a form of discrimination against Blacks. The clinics are a "calculated, pernicious effort to destroy the very fabric of family life among Black parents and their children," the suit alleged. They are "designed to control the Black population" and are "sponsored by the very governmental agency charged with the responsibility of reaching and promoting family life values."[64]

Tanya Crawford, one of the parents in the group, was shocked when her daughter Dedrea came home from school with several pieces of Planned Parenthood literature. "I never realized how racist those people were until I read the things they were giving Dedrea at the school clinic. They're as bad as the Klan. Maybe worse, because they're so slick and sophisticated. Their bigotry is all dolled up with statistics and surveys, but just beneath the surface it's as ugly as apartheid. It's as ugly as anything I can imagine."

Racism and Abortion

Again and again Planned Parenthood has asserted that its birth control programs and initiatives are designed to "prevent the need for abortion."[65] Its claim that contraceptive services lower unwanted pregnancy rates is entirely unfounded, however. A number of studies have demonstrated that as contraception becomes more accessible, the number of unwanted pregnancies actually rises, thus *increasing* the demand for abortion.[66] And since minority communities are the primary targets for contraceptive services, Blacks and Hispanics inevitably must bear the brunt of the abortion holocaust.

A racial analysis of abortion statistics is quite revealing. According to a Health and Human Services Administration report, as many as forty-three percent of all abortions are performed on Blacks and another ten percent on Hispanics.[67] This, despite the fact that Blacks only make up eleven percent of the total U.S. population and Hispanics only about eight percent.[68] A National Academy of Sciences investigation released more conservative—but no less telling—figures: thirty-two percent of all abortions are performed on minority mothers.[69]

Planned Parenthood's crusade to eliminate all those "dysgenic stocks" that Margaret Sanger believed were a "dead weight of human waste" and a "menace to the race" has precipitated a wholesale slaughter.[70] By 1975, a little more than one percent of the Black population had been aborted.[71] By 1980 that figure had increased to nearly two and a half percent.[72] And by 1985, it had reached three percent.[73] In most Black communities today abortions outstrip births by as much as three-to-one.[74]

Milly Washington, Lanita Garza, and Denise Rashad attended high school together in Minneapolis. Two years ago, the district installed an experimental school-based clinic on their high school campus. "At first I thought it was a real good idea," Denise told me.

"Yeah. Me too" Lanita chimed in.

"I mean, there's been lotsa girls that's left school 'cause they got in trouble," said Denise, "and I believed this might help some."

"But it hasn't," Milly said. "All it's done is make it so gettin' in trouble is *normal* now."

"And with an easy out," Denise added.

"Yeah. Abortion. It's weird, but you know, a couple of years ago I didn't know *anybody* who'd had an abortion," said Milly. "Now it's like *everybody's* had at least one. Lots have had two. Or even more than that."

"I get scared sometimes," Lanita said "It's like we've opened up this Pandora's Box or something, you know?"

"Really, man, that's it," Milly agreed. "Pandora's Box. One giant mess."

Racism and Sterilization

In order to realize Margaret Sanger's Eugenic ideal of eliminating the "masses of degenerate" and "good-for-nothing" races, Planned Parenthood has not only emphasized contraception and abortion, it has also carried the banner of sterilization.[75] And, of course, that sterilization vendetta has been primarily leveled against minorities.

The sterilization rate among Blacks is forty-five percent higher than among whites.[76] Among Hispanics the rate is thirty percent higher.[77] As many as forty-two percent of all American Indian women and thirty-five percent of all Puerto Rican women have been sterilized.[78]

As was the case with Carrie and Doris Buck, many of these sterilizations have been performed coercively. "Women in the United States are often pressured to accept sterilization in order to keep getting welfare payments," says feminist writer Linda Gordon.[79] And non-White welfare recipients are apparently pressured at a significantly higher level than Whites, resulting in a disproportionate number of sterilizations.[80]

The Association for Voluntary Sterilization has estimated that between one and two million Americans a year are surgically sterilized.[81] But there may be another two hundred fifty thousand coercive sterilizations disguised in hospital records as hysterectomies.[82]

A hysterectomy—the removal of the female reproductive system—should only be performed when its organs and tissues become severely damaged, diseased, or malignant. *Never* should it be performed to achieve sexual sterilization, says Dr. Charles McLaughlin, president of the American College of Surgeons. That would be "like killing a mouse with a cannon."[83] It is also much more lethal than simple tubal ligation sterilization operations. Currently, some twelve thousand women a year die receiving hysterectomies.[84]

Nevertheless, since Planned Parenthood's Eugenic hysteria was unleashed, the annual number of hysterectomies has skyrocketed, so that the operation now ranks with abortion, appendectomy, and tonsillectomy as one of the most frequently performed surgical procedures in the land.[85]

Predictably, the chief victims of these medically needless hysterectomies are poor and minority women. Over a decade ago, the *New York Times* reported that "a hysterectomy which renders a patient sterile costs up to eight hundred dollars, while a tubal ligation, which does the same thing, pays only two hundred fifty dollars to the surgeon, increasing the motivation to do the more expensive operation.

"Medicare, Medicaid, and other health plans—for the poor and the affluent both—will reimburse a surgeon up to ninety percent for the costs of any sterilization procedure, and sometimes will allow nothing for abortion. As a consequence, *hyster-sterilizations*—so common among some groups of indigent Blacks that they are referred to as *Mississippi Appendectomies*—are increasingly popular among surgeons, despite the risks."[86]

Lydia Jones, a Title X and Medicaid eligible welfare mother of four went to the Planned Parenthood clinic near her home and discovered that "free" government programs can be a good news-bad news proposition. "They told me that if I wanted to take advantage of their medical services I would have to undergo sterilization," she said. "The counselor just kept lecturing me about how I needed to do this, and that I should have done it a long time ago. She told me that my children were a burden to society. Well, let me tell you, I love my children. And they're a burden to no one. My two oldest are in college, working their way through. The other two are straight-A students and bound for scholarships. I may be poor, and I may be Black, but I'm not gonna be bullied by these people into despising the heritage God has given me." Lydia walked out—a rare exception.

In Houston, Planned Parenthood distributes discount coupons to minority women in order to lure them into their clinics.[87] In Fort Wayne, it distributes pop records and sponsors dances.[88] In other cities, clients are bribed with cash or prizes.[89] Almost every gimmick in the book has been tried to keep the Eugenic designs of Margaret Sanger on track.

"I really don't know how Planned Parenthood ever got the reputation for being an advocate for poor and minority women" says Marla Cefuentes, a social worker in Albuquerque. "Every chance they get, the clinic personnel here remind poor and Hispanic women that they can't raise a family, that to have children is irresponsible, and that they aren't capable of deciding for themselves. They are constantly pushing for sterilization, even for very young girls. It's reprehensible to see that kind of racism go unchallenged."

"There is no way you can escape the implications," argues Black financial analyst William L. Davis. "When an organization has a history of racism, when its literature is openly racist, when its goals are self-consciously racial, and when its programs invariably revolve around race, it doesn't take an expert to realize that the organization is indeed *racist*. Really now, how can anyone believe anything about Planned Parenthood except that it is a hive of elitist bigotry, prejudice, and bias? Just because the organization has a smattering of minority staffers in key positions does nothing to dispel the plain facts."

Scientific Racism

Fact: Blacks, Jews, Hispanics, and other ethnic minorities are well represented in the upper echelons of the Planned Parenthood organization.

Fact: Even the president of the national association is Black.

Fact: Aggressive minority hiring practices have been standard operating procedure for Planned Parenthood at every level for more than two decades.

Fact: The vast majority of our nation's ethnic leadership solidly and actively supports the work of Planned Parenthood.

Therefore: The charge of racism in the organization is anecdotal at best, entirely ludicrous at worst.

Right?

Wrong.

Because Planned Parenthood's peculiar brand of prejudice is rooted in *Scientific Racism*, the issue is not "color of skin" or "dialect of tongue" but "quality of genes."[90] As long as Blacks, Jews, and Hispanics demonstrate "a good quality gene pool"[91] — as long as they "act white and think white"[92] — then they are esteemed equally with Aryans. As long as they are, as Margaret Sanger said, "the best of their race,"[93] then they can be accounted as valuable citizens. If, on the other hand, individual Whites demonstrate "dysgenic traits," then their fertility must be curbed right along with the other "inferiors and undesirables."94

Scientific Racism is an equal opportunity discriminator. In other words, *anyone* with a "defective gene pool" is suspect. And *anyone* who shows promise may be admitted to the ranks of the elite.

The Theology of Racism

Racism is a vile and detestable sin (Deuteronomy 23:7). According to the Bible, bigots are "wicked" and "proud" (Psalm 94:1-6). They are accursed (Deuteronomy 27:19). They are under the judgment of God (Ezekiel 22:7, 29-31). And they face His stern indignation (Malachi 3:5).

The stranger, the alien, and the sojourner are to be cared for and sustained (Deuteronomy 24:20), not vexed and oppressed (Exodus 22:21). They are to be loved (Deuteronomy 10:19) and protected (Exodus 23:9). They are to be relieved (Leviticus 25:35) and satisfied (Deuteronomy 14:29). They are to receive equal protection under the law (Exodus 12:49, Leviticus 24:22, Numbers 15:16) and special attention in times of need (Leviticus 23:22, Deuteronomy 24:17-19). They are to share fully in the blessings that God has graciously poured out on us all (Deuteronomy 14:29, 16:11-14).

When Jesus was asked what men must do to inherit eternal life, He responded by guiding his interrogator to the Scriptures (Luke 10:26). On the question of eternal life the Scriptures are quite explicit: "You shall love the Lord your God with all your heart, and with all your soul, and with all your strength, and with all your mind; and you shall love your *neighbor* as yourself" (Luke 10:27).

"Do this," Jesus said, "and you will live" (Luke 10:28).

Not satisfied with this answer, the interrogator pressed the Lord to clarify: "And who *is* my neighbor?" he asked. "No sense in loving someone I don't have to" he must have thought (Luke 10:29).

Ever patient, ever wise, Jesus responded with a parable — the beloved parable of the Good Samaritan:

A certain man was going down from Jerusalem to Jericho; and he fell among robbers, and they stripped him and beat him, and went off leaving him half dead. And by chance a certain priest was going down on that road, and when he saw him, he passed by on the other side. And likewise a Levite also, when he came to the place and saw him, passed by on the other side. But a certain Samaritan, who was on a journey, came upon him; and when he saw him, he felt compassion, and came to him, and bandaged up his wounds, pouring oil and wine on them; and he put him on his own beast, and brought him to an inn, and took care of him. And on the next day he took out two denarii and gave them to the innkeeper and said, "Take care of him; and whatever more you spend, when I return, I will repay you" (Luke 10:30-35).

Jesus then concluded his lesson saying: "Go and do likewise" (Luke 10:37).

Certainly this was not what the interrogator was expecting. A Samaritan! How odd!

Seven hundred years earlier, Assyria had overrun and depopulated the northern kingdom of Israel, including Samaria. The conquerors had a cruel policy of population-transfer that scattered the inhabitants of the land to the four winds. Then, the empty countryside was repopulated with a ragtag collection of vagabonds and scalawags from the dregs of the Empire (2 Kings 17:24-41). Instead of regarding these newcomers as prospects for Jewish evangelism, the people of Judah, who continued in independence for another full century, turned away in contempt, and the racial division between Samaritan and Jew began its bitter course.

Samaritans were universally despised by good Jews. They were racial "half-breeds" who observed a "half-breed" religious cultus. Worse than the pagan Greeks, worse even than the barbarian Romans, the Samaritans were singled out by Jews as a perfect example of despicable depravity.

And now, Jesus was elevating a *Samaritan*, of all things, to a position of great respect and honor. A *Samaritan* was the good neighbor, the hero of the parable.

Jesus was slapping the religious leaders of Israel in their collective faces.

After demanding a clarification of Christ's textbook answer, the interrogator might have expected a parable that encouraged him to show condescending justice to all men, *even* to Samaritans. But never in a thousand years would he have guessed that Christ would show how such a despised one could actually be his neighbor — to be loved even as he loved himself! Even for eternal life, this surely was asking too much!

Jesus shattered the pretense of pious prejudice once and for all. "God is no respecter of persons" (Acts 10:34) and so, neither should men be (1 Timothy 5:21, James 3:17). He breaks the barriers between "Jew and Greek, bond and free, male and female" (Galatians 3:28). In Him there is neither "circumcision nor uncircumcision, Barbarian nor Scythian" (Colossians 3:11).

There are no "bad stocks," no "dysgenic races," and no "choking human undergrowth." No matter what Planned Parenthood says or does, "all men are created equal," and are endowed "with certain inalienable rights."[95]

> Behold, how good and how pleasant it is for brothers to dwell together in unity! It is like the precious oil upon the head, coming down upon the beard, even Aaron's beard, coming down upon the edge of his robes. It is like the dew of Hermon, coming down upon the mountains of Zion; for there the Lord commanded the blessing — life forever (Psalm 133:1-3).

Conclusion

During the 1988 Presidential primary season, Republican contender Pat Robertson caused a nationwide stir when he charged that the long range goal of Planned Parenthood is the creation of a "master race."[96] He also asserted that Margaret Sanger was an advocate of Eugenics and various coercive sterilization programs.[97]

Planned Parenthood's response was immediate. And vehement. Faye Wattleton, the stunningly attractive black president of Planned Parenthood Federation of America said that "All the charges are unfounded and, frankly, ridiculous."[98] She said that Robertson's contentions were "without any basis, any substance, or even any remnants of facts."[99] Margaret Sanger's "philosophies were not based on Eugenics," she argued. "Her philosophy was based on people being allowed to choose for themselves."[100] She then dismissed the charges of racism as "the same rhetoric we've heard from televangelists for ten years."[101]

Interestingly, just four years earlier in an interview with *Washington Times* journalist John Lofton, Wattleton admitted that Sanger did indeed advocate "Eugenics and the advancement of the perfect race."[102] And though she tried to distance herself and her organization from those views, she was forced to confess that Planned Parenthood had never *officially* repudiated them.

It appears that Robertson was right after all. The cloud of rhetoric from Planned Parenthood notwithstanding.

Who, committed to the flames,
    goes without burning?
Who, ensconced in Paria,
    seeks a chaste sojourning?
Where Venus with come-hither eyes
    and cheeks adorned for rapture,
Crooks a finger to secure
    another youthful capture.

                    Carmina Burana

SELLING SEX: THE EDUCATIONAL SCANDAL

alere flaminam

Set into the midst of an urban Negev, the school backed up to an old weather-stained overpass in a grimy tangle of narrow streets and alleyways. It was a preposterous oasis of quiet, surrounded by the garish cacophony of the inner city. Parents, pupils, and would-be visitors had to turn sharply just at the base of the overpass, and then carefully negotiate their fat Pontiacs past dilapidated apartments and convenience stores to reach the crumbling asphalt drive that circled the flagpole and swept up toward the grand red brick facade.

Four successive generations had sent their children through that ill-tempered neighborhood, around the turn, up the drive, past the flagpole, and into the school *to learn*. Catherine Toleson reflected on that long unbroken lineage as she stood at her locker between classes. The crowded halls reverberated with the wheedling jive of the eighties. But it smelled of powerful floor wax and disinfectant — the age-old smell of tradition. And there were inscriptions scratched into the small metal door of the locker that several layers of repainting over the years had failed to erase: "John L. loves Gaye Lynn," "Go Raiders, beat Jefferson!" "Seniors '57," "Jesus saves, Moses invests," and "Frodo Lives." Catherine had always before felt that she was participating in a sacred and undisturbed continuity when she heard those sounds, smelled those smells, and saw those sights. It was as if she had been in the topmost branches of the deeply planted tree of time, resting on its gigantic girth and reveling in its unobstructed vantage. Knowing that fathers and forbearers had walked the same dim and dingy halls she did, that they had sat in the same marred and wobbly desks, and that they had stared out the same tall, double-glazed windows, had given her a sense of security and stability.

But that was before.

Now, Catherine was terribly unsettled. She was confused. She was embarrassed. She felt isolated and alone. Connected to nothing—past, present, or future—she had been torn from the free and easy continuum she had known. The school's ancient reminders had suddenly become mocking, deceiving ghosts.

Second period on Tuesdays and Thursdays was her "Health" class. Her teacher, a matronly woman in her late fifties, often brought in outside speakers to discuss various topics of interest with the students. This week, a representative from Planned Parenthood had come to talk about sex, contraception, pregnancy, and abortion.

"I was shocked," Catherine told me later. "Not by the *facts of life*, but by the way those *facts* were presented. My parents had already had plenty of discussions with me about the *birds and bees* stuff. I figured I knew just about all a fifteen-year-old should *need* to know."

Apparently, Catherine's "Health" teacher and the Planned Parenthood speaker disagreed. Their brazen disregard of decorum was unconscionably unctuous.

"The woman from Planned Parenthood was so sleek and sophisticated," Catherine recalled. "She was beautiful and soft-spoken. Her clothes were gorgeous. Like a model almost, only really professional looking. And she was kinda funny and *very* articulate. When she walked in, she had our attention immediately—I mean, she was so confident and assured and relaxed, the whole class just fell under her spell."

With her disarming presence, she stripped away the youngsters' inhibitions. Sitting on the edge of the teacher's desk, she joked, kidded, winked, and bandied with them.

"At first, I couldn't tell where all this was leading," Catherine said. "But then it became *really* obvious. She started asking us personal questions. *Very* personal questions. Like about our feelings. About sex. And even about . . . well, about . . . masturbation! It was *so* disgusting. All the boys were kinda giggling. But you could tell, even *they* were embarrassed."

If that had been all, it would have been bad enough. But the speaker didn't stop with mere titillating and perverse conversation. She pulled a stained and mottled screen down over the old dusty blackboard, closed the long-tattered shades over the windows, turned off the bright, humming fluorescent lights, and put a short film on the school's wheezing, rattling projector.

"I've never seen pornography before," Catherine admitted. "But this film was worse than what I could have ever imagined hard-core pornography to be."

The film was extremely explicit. An unashamedly brash couple fondled each other in preparation for intercourse. At appropriately prurient moments of interest, the camera zoomed in for close-up shots — sweaty body parts rubbing, caressing, kissing, stroking, clasping, petting, and embracing. At the height of passion, the camera fixed on the woman's hands, trembling with ecstasy, as she tore open a condom package and began to slowly unroll its contents onto her partner.

"I wanted to look away or cover my eyes, but I couldn't," Catherine said. "I just stared at the screen — in horror."

When the lights came back on, the entire class was visibly shaken. With eyes as wide as saucers, the youngsters sat speechless and amazed.

But their guest was entirely unperturbed.

"She began to tell us that everything that we'd just seen was totally normal and *totally* good," Catherine remembered. "She said that the couple obviously had a *caring, loving,* and *responsible* relationship — because they took proper precautions against conception and disease."

At that, the speaker passed several packages of condoms around the room — one for each of the girls. She instructed the boys to hold up a finger so that the girls could *practice* contraceptive application.

Already shell-shocked, the students did as they were told.

Afterwards, several of the girls began quietly sobbing, another ran out of the room and threw up, still another fainted. Mercifully, the class ended just a moment later.

"I have never been more humiliated in all my life," Catherine said. "I felt dirty and defiled after seeing the film. But then, when I had to put *that thing* on Billy's finger — well, that was just awful. It was horrible. It was like I'd been *raped*. Raped in my mind. Raped by my school. Raped by Planned Parenthood. I think I was—that we all have been—betrayed."[1]

The Shocking Betrayal

Planned Parenthood-style sex education is shocking. It seems to be designed to break down sexual inhibitions, invalidate sexual taboos, and undermine sexual values.[2] It is almost as if it purposefully betrays parental and community trust, inciting youngsters to an emotional and sensual frenzy.[3]

Spawned out of the psycho-sexual morass—the bastard child of Havelock Ellis,[4] Sigmund Freud,[5] Bertrand Russell,[6] Alfred Kinsey,[7] William Masters,[8] Virginia Johnson,[9] Alex Comfort,[10] Alan Guttmacher,[11] Wardell Pomeroy,[12] Mary Calderone,[13] Shere Hite,[14] Ruth Westheimer,[15] Sol Gordon,[16] Sheri Tepper,[17] and, of course, Margaret Sanger[18]—Planned Parenthood's sex education programs and materials are brazenly perverse. They are frequently accentuated with crudely obscene four-letter words[19] and illustrated by explicitly ribald nudity.[20] They openly endorse aberrant behavior—homosexuality, masturbation, fornication, incest, and even bestiality—and then they describe that behavior in excruciating detail.[21]

Catherine Toleson's dreadful classroom experience was by no means an isolated incident.[22] This, the crassest brand of moral hedonism and sexual relativism, is *consistently* presented to millions of teens *every day* in the guise of academic objectivity and cosmopolitan neutrality.[23] Any resistance their consciences may offer at first is, thus, slowly but surely overwhelmed.

"Our goal," one Planned Parenthood staffer wrote, "is to be ready as educators and parents to help young people obtain sex satisfaction before marriage. By sanctioning sex before marriage, we will prevent fear and guilt."[24]

According to a Planned Parenthood pamphlet for teens: "Sex is too important to glop up with sentiment. If you feel sexy, for heaven's sake, admit it to yourself. If the feeling and the tension bother you, you can masturbate. Masturbation cannot hurt you and it will make you feel more relaxed."[25]

Another Planned Parenthood publication for teens asserts: "There are only two kinds of sex: sex with victims and sex without. Sex with victims is always wrong. Sex without is always right."[26]

"Relax about loving," admonishes still another Planned Parenthood booklet, "sex is fun and joyful, and courting is fun and joyful, and it comes in all types and styles, all of which are Okay. Do what gives pleasure, and enjoy what gives pleasure, and ask for what gives pleasure. Don't rob yourself of joy by focusing on old-fashioned ideas about what's *normal* or *nice*. Just communicate and enjoy!"[27]

That is a far cry from dispelling childish myths about storks and cabbage patches. But that is what Planned Parenthood's sex education programs and materials are like. They are *not* designed to simply provide accurate biological information. Instead, they are designed to *change* the minds, morals, and motivations of an entire generation. They are designed to completely *reshape* the positions, perspectives, and personalities of children everywhere—including yours and mine. One former Planned Parenthood medical director, Mary Calderone, has forthrightly admitted that, in sex education, "Mere facts and discussion are not enough. They need to be undergirded by a set of values."[28]

But *whose* values? Why, Planned Parenthood's, of course: the values of Margaret Sanger; the values of Revolutionary Socialism; the values of Eugenic Racism; and the values of unfettered sensuality. Thus, according to Calderone, curriculums need to, first, *separate* kids from their parents; second, *establish* a new sexual identity for them; third, help them *determine* new value systems; and, finally, help them *confirm* vocational decisions.[29]

In addition to utilizing traditional inductive and deductive teaching techniques, Planned Parenthood utilizes several different experimental methodologies in its sex education programs in order to accomplish these four aims: Values Clarification, Peer Facilitation, Sensitivity Training, Role Playing, and Positive Imaging.

Values Clarification. Based on the notion that everyone should "do what is right in his own eyes,"[30] Values Clarification is a strategy designed to help children "choose" their own value system from a wide variety of alternatives.[31] The idea, according to Values Clarification pioneer Sidney Simon, is to *stop* parents and teachers from defining for children "their emotional and sexual identities" and to keep them from "fostering the immorality of morality."[32]

In Values Clarification, "decision making scenarios" are placed before the children and they are asked to make a series of "life and death decisions" where the "only absolute" is that "there are *no* absolutes."[33]

Missy Gallagher and Tom Blatten are "high school sweet-hearts" who recently endured a Planned Parenthood Values Clarification course in Los Angeles. In one exercise, Missy and Tom were brought to the front of the class and given a "decision making scenario" that they, and the rest of the class, were supposed to respond to.

"The way the teacher set it up," Missy explained, "was that Tom was supposed to have gotten me pregnant. On top of that, we both were supposed to have been kicked out of our homes by our parents, threatened with the loss of college scholarships, and facing the possibility of serious physical problems due to venereal disease. On that basis, we were supposed to decide, with the help of the rest of the class, whether or not we should have an abortion."

"Of course, everyone in the class got a big kick out of all this," Tom said. "They knew that Missy and I are both Christians and that the whole premise of the silly charade was an insult to us."

"When Tom explained right off that we'd have to accept the consequences of our sin, if we ever *did* fall into such rebellion, well the teacher got really mad at us, made fun of us, and then had the gall to give us a failing grade for the exercise," Missy recalled.

"The whole thing was a real eye-opener for me," Tom said. "It seems there is room in Planned Parenthood's pluralism for anyone and everyone *except* Christians."

Peer Facilitation. If word of mouth is the best advertising and satisfied customers are the best endorsement, then it only stands to reason that the best propaganda is peer propaganda. That is the idea behind Planned Parenthood's Peer Facilitation strategy. Teens who display "leadership qualities" are recruited to be "sex educators of their peers" and even of "younger children with whom they may come into contact."[34] These leaders are given "intensive personalized training" so that they will later be able to "facilitate healthy sexual messages and behaviors" among other teens.[35] In one "learning activity" for these "leaders-in-training," Planned Parenthood recommends "Brainstorming all the terms used for penis, breast, intercourse, vagina, homosexuality, and VD. . . . This will familiarize group members with all forms of sexual terms they might hear from their peers and should lower their shock value. This exercise also helps set an atmosphere for questions in training sessions, in effect giving students permission to discuss sexuality in whatever terms they are most familiar."[36]

Walt Maxwell was a teen trainee in a Peer Facilitator program sponsored by Planned Parenthood in Northern Virginia. Briefly. "I only lasted a week in the program," he told me. "I just couldn't handle it. Watching porno films and talking dirty is not exactly my idea of a healthy extra-curricular activity."

After he dropped out of the program, he was called in to talk to his school counselor and two assistant principals. "They wanted to know why I had such a *bad attitude* about the class, and why I was being so *uncooperative*. I told them that I thought the whole program was *disgusting*. They just looked at me like I was from another planet or something."

Sensitivity Training. Planned Parenthood often uses small, informal discussion groups to "raise the sexuality awareness of children."[37] Using the "social pressure" of carefully designed classroom situations, teachers are able to break down "home training" and then to instill the precepts of "the new morality"—the amoral morality of Margaret Sanger's sexual revolution.[38]

In one Sensitivity Training program, the "teacher-change agent" is instructed to divide students into small groups, giving each an envelope containing cards with topics to be discussed: "Virginity, Oral-Genital Sex, Intercourse, Masturbation, Sterility, Group Sex, Homosexuality, Extra-Marital Relations, Abortion, and Nudity—with acquaintances, with family, with the opposite sex, with the same sex, and with close friends."[39]

The students are "to *identify* and *express* their present *attitudes* and *feelings* about these matters and to practice *active listening* and *honest self-disclosure*."[40] Once this "self-disclosure" process is complete, the group is to "bring consensus by *winning* over other members."[41] Those members of the group who refuse to change "are *considered* non-conformists or deviants."[42]

Gloria Frankel was recently suspended from her high school near Dallas because she refused to participate in a Planned Parenthood-sponsored Sensitivity Training class.

"After I was ridiculed for my Christian stance on abortion and pre-marital sex, I just couldn't continue going to the class," Gloria said. "I asked for an exemption. I asked to be placed in a study hall. I asked for anything but the sex class. But the teachers and administration refused. They said the class was mandatory. So I talked to my parents, and they agreed that I would just skip the class. That's when I got in trouble and finally was suspended."

Outraged, Gloria's parents took the issue up with school administrators and with the school board. "They were told," Gloria said, "that *the law is the law* and everyone has to obey it whether they like it or not." The family's only recourse was to sue. That is an awfully high price to pay for moral purity and familial liberty.

Role Playing. Another psycho-therapeutic technique Planned Parenthood uses to effect "personality changes" in students is role playing. According to one psycho-educator: "Role playing is a natural method of learning and unlearning various reactions to complex life problems. . . . It seems to have some advantages . . . over other methods of psychotherapy since it simultaneously attacks modes of thinking, feeling, and behavior — the entire province of psychotherapy."[43]

Thus, sex education expert Sandalyn McKasson says that role playing "is an indirect, manipulative method of transforming attitudes and behavior. Hence, it is a *method of coercion*, not instruction."[44]

In fact, she argues that it is a methodology that "has its roots in the occultic manipulation. It by-passes the will and relies on spontaneous reactons."[45] To illustrate, she cites a typical sex ed role playing exercise from *Values in Sexuality*, a widely recommended resource for Planned Parenthood teachers and counselors.[46] In the exercise, seven students are asked to act out a particular pre-determined role:

Roommate 1: You have invited a *lover* to spend the weekend with you in your room. You tell your roommates.

Roommate 2: You are a devout Catholic and feel homosexuality is a serious *sin*.

Roommate 3: You feel whatever anyone does sexually is their business, but you feel very *sad* that your friend has closed off lots of options.

Roommate 4: You're a psychology major, and try to *help* by giving advice and diagnosing why your roommate might be gay.

Roommate 5: You feel threatened by the knowledge that your roommate is gay. You try to reason with him and *argue* him into heterosexual good sense.

Roommate 6: You are shocked by the announcement and outraged that a *fag* will be on your dorm floor.

Roommate 7: You already know about your *friend's* gay lifestyle. The two of you have talked some about it. You have no serious difficulties with this and still feel comfortable with him.[47]

After playing their roles, the seven students are then asked to "come to a consensus" about which of the roommates' attitudes is "the most constructive."

Martin Campbell was forced to participate in that very scenario in a Planned Parenthood-sponsored class at his high school near Chicago. "After we played our parts," he told me, "we had to de-role and then analyze our feelings in a group discussion. The teacher asked us what stereotypes of homosexuality had emerged in the skit. And then we were supposed to talk about why those stereotypes were wrong and based on ignorance and fear. Well, I was really hacked off by the whole deal. I felt like I was being set up."

When the teacher found that Martin was acting a bit recalcitrant, she began to lecture him about being *open, tolerant, accepting, mature, respectful,* and *honest.* "I just kept telling her that I didn't agree, and *wouldn't* agree, but she wouldn't let up on me," Martin said. "It's pretty bad when a teacher isolates one kid like that. I felt like I was getting ganged up on. It wasn't at all *fair.*"

Positive Imaging. Very similar to role playing techniques is Planned Parenthood's fantasy, or Positive Imaging, methodology. According to one school "mental health" proponent: "The concept of educational imagery is used to approximate a described behavior, decision or outcome through guided imagination or fantasy in the conscious mind of the individual. In theory, educational imagery can bridge the gap between making the decision and behaviorally incorporating the decision. The theory is that if the decision is clearly imagined and acted out repeatedly, then when the opportunity comes to enact the decision, the process will be facilitated."[48]

And what fantasies and decisions are the curriculums facilitating? One government-sponsored program used widely by Planned Parenthood educators told teens that they could have fantasies which involved "sexual feelings about people of the same or opposite sex, parents, brothers and sisters, old people, animals, nature, inanimate objects, and almost anything you can imagine. It is *unusual* for a person not to have some strange sexual fantasies."[49]

Carrie Lipscombe and Laura Gibbs participated in a Positive Imaging exercise in a Planned Parenthood-sponsored class at their neighborhood YWCA. "The teacher told us to close our eyes," Carrie remembered. "We were to imagine ourselves standing on the end of a diving board."

"She went into a lot of detail, helping us to imagine the crystal clear water, the bright blue sky, and the warm, dry sunshine on our skin," Laura said. "She asked us to *feel* ourselves bouncing off the board and splashing into the cool, refreshing pool."

"Then she told us that that feeling was very much like an orgasm," Carrie said. "After that, we were supposed to imagine all kinds of situations where we could *relive* that feeling of going off the diving board *sexually*."

"I was pretty shook up by that," admitted Laura.

"Me, too," Carrie said. "The whole deal was pretty manipulative. I didn't like it. Not a bit."

"The objectionable feature of these programs now being promoted by Planned Parenthood," says economist and social analyst Jacqueline Kasun, "is not that they teach sex, but that they do it so badly, replacing good biological education with ten to twelve years of compulsory *consciousness raising* and *psycho-sexual therapy*, and using the public schools to advance their own *peculiar worldview*."[50]

Like Catherine Toleson, Carrie Lipscombe, and the others, Rhonda Williams was shocked by the foul and indecent materials Planned Parenthood was distributing in her junior high school. She was especially distressed by one brochure that openly *attacked* Christian morality and the institutional Church. "I can't believe that they can get away with this kind of thing," she told me. "You'd think that someone — a teacher, a principal, a counselor, an administrator, a parent, or *someone* — would put a stop to it."

Rhonda showed me the brochure. Illustrated with grotesque cartoon caricatures of Christian leaders, it said: "Some religious and semi-religious groups dominated by elderly men, simply cannot deal rationally with sex. They can't talk about it rationally, can't think about it rationally, and, above all, can't give up the power which controlling other people gives them. They control other people through sex."[51]

"Did you know that they were handing stuff like this out in the schools?" Rhonda asked me.

"Yes," I had to admit. "I did."

"Then why don't you *do* something?"

"I'll try," I told her.

"I'm not sure that just *trying* is good enough. A whole generation is at risk here."

Indeed, it is.

The Business of Revolution

Planned Parenthood *sells sex*.[52] Its *business* is to assault youngsters like Catherine Toleson, Carrie Lipscombe, and Rhonda Williams with an unholy barrage of vulgar and licentious temptation.[53] Its *avocation* is to lure them into dependence on its lucrative contraception and abortion services.[54]

And it does what it does very well.

With a passionate, evangelistic zeal and a shrewd entrepreneurial effectiveness, Planned Parenthood has translated its sordid sex business into a multi-million dollar monopoly: it publishes sex ed books, pamphlets, and curriculum;[55] it develops model sex ed programs for communities, schools, and affiliates;[56] it creates pre-service, in-service, and enrichment programs for sex ed trainers;[57] it provides a national resource clearinghouse as a conduit for the dissemination of sex ed information and materials;[58] it distributes journals, magazines, and newsletters to sex ed professionals;[59] it catalogues and evaluates all available sex ed materials and publications;[60] it produces films, videos, and advertisements that broadcast sex ed themes far and wide;[61] it advocates unrestricted sex ed propagation—kindergarten through twelfth grade—through political lobbying and the courts;[62] and it sends an army of sex ed speakers into schools, Churches, and public forums every day—day in and day out.[63]

Planned Parenthood has not gone unrewarded for all its efforts. With all the hype of a wild West miracle medicine show—claiming that sex education would *cure* virtually every societal ailment: from child abuse to teen pregnancy, from juvenile delinquency to infant mortality, from birth defects to welfare dependency, from drug abuse to venereal disease, and from sexual abuse to academic decline—Planned Parenthood has hawked its wares to a ready market of concerned parents, educators, and civic leaders.[64] And they have proved to be ready buyers.

As a result, virtually every man, woman, and child in America has been exposed to Planned Parenthood's luridly immoral notions of love, sex, and intimacy. Almost seventy-five percent of the nation's school districts have institutionalized sex ed programs.[65] And untold millions of tax dollars have been poured into Planned Parenthood's already overstuffed coffers.[66] It has done such a convincing job of selling its obscene services and products that, now, anyone who *dares* to question the value of Planned Parenthood's sex ed monopoly is immediately castigated as "some sort of unenlightened crank."[67]

But, like the old medicine show potions, elixirs, and tonics, Planned Parenthood's programs don't actually do what they are *advertised* to do.[68] They don't solve the problems posed by the teen sexuality crisis.[69] If anything, they aggravate them—stirring up unhealthy passions, inspiring unnatural affections, suggesting untamed concupiscence, and defiling naive innocence.[70] The fact is, the proliferation of Planned Parenthood-style sex education all across the country has coincided with an unprecedented increase in teen promiscuity.[71] For nearly two decades, the nation's schools have faithfully followed Planned Parenthood's prescriptions only to see the number of teen pregnancies swell to more than a million each year[72]—an increase of almost ninety percent.[73] The number of teen abortions has risen to nearly half a million each year[74] — an increase of more than 230 percent.[75] And the number of reported cases of venereal disease has sky-rocketed to almost fourteen million each year[76] — an increase of nearly 140 percent.[77] Study after study has shown that sex education is *anything but* an effective remedy for the teen sex epidemic.[78]

As a result, a number of voices have begun to cry out in the wilderness. Scott Thompson, executive director of the National Association of Secondary School Principals, has said that such programs are a "charade," bordering on "educational fraud."[79] William Leatherton, president of the American Bureau of Educational Research, has called them "a scandal of immense proportions."[80] They are simply a "failure," according to Jackie Manley, a program associate at the Center for Population Options.[81] And Senator Jesse Helms has argued: "One and a half billion dollars in the hands of terrorists could not have inflicted the long-term harm to our society that [these programs'] expenditures have. . . . No one can deny the fact that [they do] indeed subsidize teenage sexual activity. It is on the basis of this fact that some argue [that the programs] directly and positively increase the incidence of venereal disease, teenage pregnancy, and abortion. At a minimum, [they] tend to create an atmosphere in which teenage promiscuity is viewed as normal and acceptable conduct and which in turn fosters the very problems we are trying to solve."[82]

Despite this, Planned Parenthood remains unconcerned.[83] As long as it can keep its customers lining up with don't-confuse-me-with-the-facts grins spread across their faces, it can blithely ignore the negative figures and fulminations. *Business* is its business. And business couldn't be better. Sex sells.

From its inception, Planned Parenthood's goal has been to *change the world*. And to do it at a substantial profit. To foment the revolution is good. To do it at a forty percent mark-up is even better. So forget the statistics, the studies, and the statements — from Planned Parenthood's perspective, the "failure" of its sex education programs has been its greatest "success."[84]

This Phoenix-like ability of Planned Parenthood — to not only survive, but thrive, in the face of its programs' impotence and incompetence — is due almost entirely to its skill in controlling and defining the terms of the debate.

Defining the Terms

The irrepressible John Selden once quipped that "syllables govern the world."[85] If that is true, then the definers of words are the most powerful of men.

George Orwell explored that notion, with chilling effect, in his classic *1984*.[86] The book tells the story of a society where a repressive bureaucratic elite attempts to manipulate the very thoughts of men by controlling their language. Old words, with comfortable, familiar meanings, are either scuttled into disuse, or are redefined to fit the elite's pernicious perspective. They are either slyly sidled, or are emptied of their common significance, only to be filled with some alien denotation. Thus, according to this *Newspeak*, words like *honor, justice, morality, science*, and *religion* cease to exist altogether, while words like *war, peace, freedom, slavery*, and *ignorance* have their meanings completely transposed.[87]

Orwell meant the book to be a *warning*.[88] Like Rudyard Kipling, he believed that "words are the most powerful drugs used by mankind."[89] Like Tristram Gylberd, he believed that "whoever controls the language controls the culture."[90] And, like John Locke, he believed that "whoever defines the words defines the world."[91] Thus, he implored his readers to beware of logogogues — word tyrants. He warned *us* to resist the seductive allure of lexographic molesters.

Sadly, we have failed to heed that warning. It seems that we are presently witnessing the emergence of our own *Newspeak*. Allan Bloom, author of the phenomenal blockbuster *The Closing of the American Mind*, argues that we have begun to develop "an entirely new language of good and evil, originating in an attempt to *get beyond* good and evil, and preventing us from talking with any conviction *about* good and evil."[92]

Not surprisingly, Planned Parenthood has been one of the primary practitioners of this *Newspeak*.[93] By manipulating certain words, Planned Parenthood has attempted — and, in all too many cases, succeeded — in manipulating reality.

The word *responsibility* was once synonymous with *trustworthy*. A responsible person could be counted on to uphold his commitments and fulfill his obligations.[94] Now, though, according to Planned Parenthood's *Newspeak*, *responsible* simply means "to use birth control" during illicit sexual liaisons.[95]

The word *chastity* was once synonymous with *purity*. A person who practiced chastity could generally be considered virtuous and modest.[96] Now, though, according to Planned Parenthood's *Newspeak*, *chastity* is just "a *stage* in life," a temporary "immaturity."[97]

The word *neutral* was once synonymous with *objective*. A person who took a neutral position on a subject could be counted on to be impartial and teachable.[98] Now, though, according to Planned Parenthood's *Newspeak*, *neutral* refers to an "open-minded," and "amoral" *relativism*.[99]

The word *choice* was once synonymous with *freedom*. The right to choose protected men from every assault of life and limb.[100] Now, though, according to Planned Parenthood's *Newspeak*, *choice* is "the right" of one person "to prevail" over another — even to the point of *death* — whenever the fancy strikes.[101]

The word *fetus* was once synonymous with *unborn child*. A fetus was universally recognized as a *baby*, a *blessing* from Almighty God.[102] Now, though, according to Planned Parenthood's *Newspeak*, *fetus* is nothing more than "*disposable tissue*," or, worse, a unique form of "*venereal disease*."[103]

The word *gay* was once synonymous with *happy*. If someone was gay, he was *cheerful*, *jolly*, and *content*.[104] Now, though, according to Planned Parenthood's *Newspeak*, *gay* is a noun, not an adjective, meaning a sodomizing *homosexual*.[105]

The word *morality* was once synonymous with *virtue*. A moral person could be counted on to act *uprightly* and with all *integrity*.[106] Now, though, according to Planned Parenthood's *Newspeak*, *morality* is an "outdated" and "judgmental" value system rooted in "fear," "prejudice," and "ignorance."[107]

The word *relationship* was once synonymous with *friendship*. A person who had a relationship with another simply had a *rapport* with them.[108] Now, though, according to Planned Parenthood's *Newspeak*, a *relationship* is an *adulterous affair*, or an occasional opportunity for *fornication*.[109]

This is the vocabulary that Planned Parenthood has grafted into their sex education programs and literature.[110] Even if those books, pamphlets, films, and curriculums did not openly endorse perversion, promiscuity, and prurience, they would *still* be damningly destructive just because of the way they use and control the language.

According to Orwell, the original purpose of *Newspeak* was "to make all other modes of thought impossible."[111] Certainly, Planned Parenthood's sex ed *Newspeak* has accomplished *that*.[112] What teenager wouldn't rather be *responsible* and *open-minded* than *immature* and *ignorant*? How do you tell your son or daughter *not* to be *fulfilled*? Does the Bible ever say "Thou shalt not evacuate uterine *tissue*?"[113] The fact is, the language of sex education — the language that has been systematically taught to our children — makes it impossible to entertain any other mode of thought than Planned Parenthood's mode of thought.

Mark Twain once asserted that "the difference between the right word and the *almost* right word is like the difference between lightning and the lightning bug."[114] There can be little doubt that Planned Parenthood has chosen its words very carefully and, as a result, it has struck an entire generation dumb, like a bolt from the blue. Not content to rake and strafe our children's bodies with dangerous drugs, devices, and procedures,[115] Planned Parenthood has launched a *blitzkrieg* against their minds as well.[116]

Backwards Deal

Lucy Lommers, Deborah Sullivan, Sarah Bakker, and Jackie Landry were all chosen to participate in a unique educational experiment at their school in the nation's capitol. Sponsored by Planned Parenthood, the "Peer Education in Human Sexuality" program was designed to train teens to become "peer facilitators" and "responsible information givers."[117]

"The idea," Lucy told me, "was to take a few of us and *really* teach us everything that a sex education teacher knows. All the techniques, all the methods, all the ideas, all the strategies: we got all of it. And then we were supposed to lead group discussions with our friends so that we could *influence* them."

"The training was mostly just discussion between ourselves," Sarah said. "And they were usually pretty *wild* discussions."

"Wild is right," Jackie interjected.

"Yea, see, the Planned Parenthood counselors who worked with us would open up a topic and get us to share our personal experiences and feelings about it," Deborah explained. "Sometimes we'd see a film — man, were they ever explicit — and then we'd talk about our reactions." "I always felt a tremendous amount of *pressure* in those sessions," Jackie said. "I thought that maybe I was the only one in the group that wasn't hopping into the sack with some guy every weekend. Listening to the stories my friends started telling made me wonder if I really knew them at all. And if I really fit in with them."

"Course, what none of us realized at the time," Lucy said, "was that we were *all* feeling the same things. We were just too scared to admit it. I mean, who wants to come right out and say that they're really not all that keen on *sex*! That's just not *normal*. Nobody wants people to think that they've got some sort of weird *hang-ups* or that they're some sorta *prude*."

"So we all just *lied*," Sarah said. "We made up all these kinky stories about wild sex parties and stuff."

"Well," admitted Lucy, "we didn't *just* lie. We also started fooling around some. I got on birth control. Most of us did. But we were doing it mostly to be *normal* and *accepted*."

"And to live up to the reputations we were creating for our-selves in the training session," added Sarah.

"Yea, that, too," Deborah piped in.

"The thing was, the *dirtier* our discussions got, the more *bizarre* our stories were, the *better* the Planned Parenthood coun-selors seemed to like it," Jackie said.

"I *know*! Isn't it weird?" Lucy said. "They would say stuff like, 'Now we're really getting somewhere,' or 'It's very impor-tant to be able to communicate like this.' I'd always think to myself, Yea. Right. What a pile of crock. But then, of course, I wouldn't say *anything*."

"The whole mess began to fall apart, though, when one of the other girls in our group got pregnant and had to have an abortion," Deborah said.

"She was probably the quietest person in the program," Lucy explained. "Real pretty. Got great grades. But she kinda just kept to herself. Tina was her name. Anyway, she was on the Pill. She told me that she was pretty freaked out that she could do something as *radical* as take birth control without her parents *ever* finding out. I mean, we have to call home and get permission to get an *aspirin* from the school nurse, but we can get an IUD, or birth control pills, or even an abortion, without *anybody* knowing about it. Kinda crazy, isn't it? Well, the point is, Tina was a little amazed by the whole deal."

"When she found out she was pregnant, she seemed to take it real well. All in stride," Sarah noted. "She even talked about it in our group meeting. The Planned Parenthood counselors set up an appointment for her to get an abortion and that was that."

"Only that wasn't the end of the story," Jackie said.

"Not by a long shot," agreed Lucy.

"No, after the abortion, we all got together for our regular meeting. And Tina was there. She'd had the abortion three days earlier," Lucy said.

"She really looked awful," commented Jackie.

"The counselor asked her to talk about it," Lucy went on. "But she just sat there not saying anything at all. The counselor then went into this *long* lecture about how important it is to get all your feelings out, to communicate, to be honest — you know, all that *psycho-therapy* stuff. Well, before any of us knew what was happening, Tina just went berserk."

"Yea, she started screaming and crying and throwing stuff around," Jackie said.

"She said that the 'peer' training project had pushed her into sex, filled her mind with all sorts of obscene ideas, and then forced her into an abortion," Deborah remembered. "She said she'd learned *everything* except the *right* things and that she *hated* what she'd become."

"After a while, she was just sobbing uncontrollably," Lucy said. "And none of us knew what to do."

"I think we were all pretty confused," agreed Jackie.

"And, what was worse, for *me* anyway," Sarah said, "was that I *knew* she was right. We'd been sold a bill of goods. None of us *wanted* to learn all that stuff about lesbianism and masturbation and orgies and abortion and birth control and kinky fetishes and stuff. And the things we *did* need to know we never even talked about — things like a baby's development, guilt, venereal diseases, the health hazards of birth control, alternatives to abortion, PMS, and depression. None of that."

"After a minute or two, Tina left," Jackie continued with the story. "We were pretty stunned. But one of the Planned Parenthood counselors, well, she just started rattling on about how *good* it was that Tina was 'able to *ventilate* her frustrations,' and how the group was 'obviously growing in honesty toward one another,' and all that stuff."

"That night, Tina committed suicide," Lucy concluded.

The girls were all quiet now. Heads bowed in sadness and shame.

"When that happened, we all got together," Deborah said finally, "*without* anybody from Planned Parenthood to look over our shoulders. And we just talked."

"And cried," added Lucy.

"For all that hype about *honesty*," Jackie admitted, "that was the *first* time we actually *were* honest."

After another long pause, Deborah noted, "I think we learned a *lot* of lessons out of this, but two really kinda stand out. First, Planned Parenthood was trying to *force* us to learn about—and think about, talk about, and experiment about—things *none* of us *wanted* to. And, second, Planned Parenthood skipped over the stuff that we *did* want—and *need*—to know."

"Yea, the whole deal was really *backwards*, wasn't it?" Lucy said.

"I'm just *glad* it's over, and I'm glad that I'm out of it—that we're *all* out of it," Deborah sighed.

"Really!" the other girls nodded. "Really!"

According to Planned Parenthood's own national survey, conducted by the Louis Harris pollsters, *most* teens agree with Lucy, Deborah, Sarah, and Jackie.[118] More than eighty-seven percent said that they did *not* want comprehensive sexuality services in their schools.[119] Sixty percent said they didn't even want such services *near* their schools.[120] Only twenty-eight percent of the teens had actually become involved in sexual activities,[121] but ninety percent of those admitted that they had become promiscuous simply because of a *perceived* peer pressure.[122] Nearly eighty percent of them felt that they had been drawn into sexual activity *far* too soon.[123]

The teens in the poll admitted that their comprehensive sex education courses *had* affected their behavior. There was a fifty percent *higher* rate of sexual activity for them *after* the classes.[124] Sadly, their understanding of the consequences of such activity was not correspondingly enhanced.

According to another national study, no less than ninety percent of all women who receive abortions experience moderate to severe emotional and psychiatric stress following the procedures.[125] Up to ten percent require psychiatric hospitalization or other treatment.[126] Teens are not told that.

Almost eighty percent felt that their teachers and counselors discouraged, avoided, or trivialized their questions about *important* issues — the *hard* issues — especially the *truth* about abortion.[127] Eighty-nine percent confessed that their Planned Parenthood contacts were "strongly biased."[128] The organization's claim to offer girls "good, non-directive counseling and education"[129] was overwhelmingly *denied* by the girls who actually used those services.[130] Ninety-five percent said that the counselors gave them "little or no biological information" and over eighty percent said that they gave "little or no information about the potential health risks" inherent in birth control and abortion products and procedures.[131] Over sixty percent said they had yearned for an alternative to the Planned Parenthood programs, but did not know where to turn.[132]

It appears that Planned Parenthood's sex education programs are, as Lucy Lommers and the other girls from Washington put it, "a backwards deal." Wicked ideas, couched in wicked terms, to achieve wicked ends — that is the educational scandal of Planned Parenthood. That is how Planned Parenthood sells sex.

Brazen Lips

The wicked are not only unsavory, they are unreliable as well.

> There is nothing reliable in what they say; their inward part is destruction itself; their throat is an open grave; they flatter with their tongue (Psalm 5:9).

Perversity and deceit go hand in hand (Proverbs 17:4). You can't have one without the other (Proverbs 6:12; Isaiah 59:3).

That is why men are warned again and again to avoid at all costs froward speech and obscene lips (Job 27:4; Proverbs 4:24; Psalm 34:13; Ephesians 4:2; Colossians 3:8; 1 Peter 3:10).

> There are six things which the Lord hates, yes, seven which are an abomination to Him: haughty eyes, a lying tongue, and hands that shed innocent blood, a heart that devises wicked plans, feet that run rapidly to evil, a false witness who utters lies, and one who spreads strife among brothers (Proverbs 6:16-19).

Although indiscreet talk is "sweet in the mouths" of fallen men (Job 20:12), it is terribly destructive (James 3:6). It *defiles* the flesh (Jude 1:8). It invites corruption, untowardness, crookedness, and perversity (Deuteronomy 32:5). It contributes to the delinquency of minors (Proverbs 7:6-23). It creates strife and dissension (Proverbs 16:28). It devises *evil* in the midst of innocence (Proverbs 16:30). It unleashes mischievous destruction (Proverbs 17:20). It perverts justice (Deuteronomy 16:19). And it wreaks *havoc*, "like a sharp razor, working deceitfully" (Psalm 52:2), even to the point of overthrowing an entire culture (Proverbs 11:11). "A soothing tongue is a tree of life, but perversion in it crushes the spirit" (Proverbs 15:4).

Foul speech is inescapably *fraudulent* (Psalm 10:7), just as it is inescapably *violent* (Proverbs 10:11; 12:6).

Because such *brazenness* is an *abomination* to both God and man (Psalm 109:2; Proverbs 4:24; 8:7), all men who indulge in it, of necessity "have their consciences *seared* as with a hot brand" (1 Timothy 4:2). Their hearts are hardened (Proverbs 28:14). Their necks are stiffened (Proverbs 29:1). Their souls are impoverished (Matthew 16:26). And, their lives are cheapened (Proverbs 6:26).

Planned Parenthood claims to teach our children the "*facts* of life."[133] But details about unspeakable perversions, concealed horrors, and obscene titillations are *not* the "*facts* of life."[134]

The "*facts* of life" can only be found in the Word of Life. And that is one source of inspiration that Planned Parenthood studiously avoids.

> With the fruit of a man's mouth his stomach will be satisfied; he will be satisfied with the product of his lips. Death and life are in the power of the tongue, and those who love it will eat its fruit (Proverbs 18:20-21).

Conclusion

In his remarkable article entitled "The Fraud of Educational Reform," Samuel L. Blumenfeld has stated, "The more I read what secular educators write these days, the more convinced I become that their grasp of reality has slipped beyond retrieval."[135] The schools have failed so miserably in accomplishing their basic tasks — teaching our children how to read and write and compute and complete and compete — that Blumenfeld says those educators *know* that they will have to reform their precious system. But what will that reform be like? Blumenfeld tells us that we should "expect the next phase of educational reform to be dominated by radical ideas disguised in *pedagogic clothes*. Such phrases as *critical thinking*, *emancipatory pedagogy*, and *master teachers* will sound benign to the public but will convey the right message to the radicals."[136]

In other words, reforming the present educational system is *not* the answer. Planned Parenthood and the other radical educational activists are so deeply entrenched in the public school machinery that reform can only mean *more* of the same: more debauchery, more brazenness, more humanism, and more wickedness.

The early promoters of public, state-controlled education rallied around the slogan "It costs less money to build schoolhouses than jails."[137] The great patriot-theologian of the South, Robert L. Dabney, responded to this in 1876 saying, "But what if it turns out that the state's expenditure in school-houses is one of the things which necessitates the expenditures in jails?"[138] To which we might add: *What if that expenditure also necessitates the expenditure in AIDS hospitals, nationalized child care, and an ever-burgeoning abortion industry?*

The only hope for our children — and their children, and their children's children — to escape these horrendous hazards are uncompromising, unwavering, unmitigating Christian schools: Christian day schools and Christian home schools.[139] Christian educator Robert Thoburn has argued, "Salvation is by grace, not by education."[140] Even so, he says we have a "moral obligation"[141] to work hard, building up Christian schools[142] and restoring moral sanity to our nation.[143]

Certainly, we need to battle the blazing concupiscence of Planned Parenthood's sex education programs by sounding the alarms in PTA meetings, community forums, and school board hearings. But, in the meantime, it is essential that we rescue our own children from the flickering flames of promiscuity and perdition. At all costs.

It is the algebra of need.
Get place and wealth,
If possible with grace;
If not,
By any means,
Get place and wealth.

Alexander Pope

SEVEN

ROBBER BARONS: THE FINANCIAL SCANDAL

argumentum ad crumenam

Skimming the streets on a razor sharp high of adrenaline and paranoia, Roxanne Robertson circled the clinic's concrete fortress half a dozen times before she finally screwed up enough courage to pull into the parking lot. An acid rain, the sins of her fathers, blew down hard and cold, etching obscure messages into the surface of the graceless asphalt. As she stepped out of the car and moved toward the building, a scrap of rubbish, plucked up by the wind, did a careless pirouette before being carried away.

She stepped quickly under the parapet, around the corner, through glass doors, along a carpet mapped with stains shaped like dark continents amid a sienna sea, and into a long narrow lobby. Hunched behind the reception desk sat a gnomish and disheveled woman with a beaked nose and tufts of frowzy brown hair reminiscent of a lark's nest. It seemed that upon her forehead the engraved word *finality* would not have been at all inappropriate.

The room was close and warm. From within, drifted the smell of bodies pressed together, cigarette smoke, disinfectant, perfume, and something else — the almost metallic scent of fear.

"I believe I have an appointment," Roxanne said.

The woman handed her a clipboard. "You'll need to fill this out." She smiled a ragged smile. It was a hollow haunting gesture — a feeble attempt to veil her intentions with an unspoken cant of compassion.

Roxanne took a seat next to a petite teen — a girl about her own age she guessed — and across from an older woman — an unsettling vision of frustrated resignation. Neither of them seemed to notice her as Roxanne sat on the edge of her seat scratching bits of biographical information onto the form on her lap—life, love, and hope hemorrhaging from her soul with each completed line.

Saturday morning at Planned Parenthood. Day of decision. Valley of decision.

Roxanne handed the completed form to the haggard receptionist and returned to her seat. Tossed to and fro on waves of doubt, weak from resisting swells of guilt, and helpless in the face of a flood of loneliness, she felt as if she were drowning.

But then the tide rolled out and resolve rushed in when she heard her name called.

She followed a tall and elegant woman down a dimly lit hall to a small office cubicle. Spare and unfurnished, save for a small round table and two straight-backed chairs, the room bore the unmistakable mark of bureaucratic impersonalism. And the woman's expressionless features did little to dispel that institutional gloom. A shiver ran up and down Roxanne's spine.

After a brief exchange of rote pleasantries the woman turned her attentions to a small folder of paperwork. "Tell me Ms. Robertson," she intoned without looking up, "what is your actual monthly income?"

"Well, I'm going to school full time right now," Roxanne replied. "I work at the Student Union about fifteen hours a week— or whenever they need me. That comes out to about $50.00. And then my parents send me about $150.00 a month for other expenses, clothes, supplies, gas for the car, and stuff. Course, they pay tuition, books, and my room and board at the dorm."

"So then, the only money that actually passes through your hands is the $50.00 a week from your part-time job and the $150.00 a month from your parents?" the woman asked.

"Yea, I guess so."

"Well, then according to state guidelines, you qualify for government subsidy for your care today. You will only be responsible for co-pay of twenty percent."

"Oh well, I don't need to do that. My parents have sent me the money I need."

"You qualify. You might as well take advantage of your benefits."

"Gee, I don't know. I'd feel kinda dishonest doing that."

"Oh don't be silly, hon. It's for just this kind of thing we all pay our taxes."

"Hmmm. Well . . ."

"Besides, from the looks of your chart here, you're going to need a full battery of tests and services. That can get to be quite expensive."

"But . . . all I need is a pregnancy test. And a uh . . . uh . . ."

"I know hon. Don't worry about it."

"But . . ."

The conversation went back and forth like that for almost ten minutes: the Planned Parenthood counselor doing everything she could to sign on Roxanne as a government subsidy client, Roxanne weakly resisting the offer of "charity." In the end though, the counselor prevailed.

"Alright then. What do I have to do?" Roxanne finally said in surrender.

"Just sign here." The woman handed a sheet across the table. Her eyes quickly took in the two rings that adorned Roxanne's hands — one with rubies and diamonds, the other with a large fire opal set in an ornate gold band. As those hands took the sheet and signed, the woman smiled for the first time. The deed was as good as done.

Hours later, Roxanne stepped out into a still damp, brownish haze that made a ghost of the horizon, and began rushing after an ever receding destination — her child now dead, her conscience now seared, and her worth now reduced to a jingle in the till.

"I never could understand," she recently told me, "why the counselor was so insistent. She refused to take *no* for an answer. It was almost like I was gonna sign up for Title XX benefits whether I wanted to or not. I only wish that I'd resisted her arguments and walked out the door. I'd have saved myself a lot of grief. And of course, I'd have saved a lot of money — tax money — that went to pay for my foolish sin."

Soaking the Taxpayer

Roxanne Robertson is just the kind of customer that Planned Parenthood is looking for: young, Black, uninformed, frightened, unmarried, pregnant, and best of all, government subsidy eligible.[1]

Nearly thirty-five years ago Congress began pouring millions of dollars into Planned Parenthood's draconian programs in a desperate attempt to hold down the burgeoning costs of welfare dependency.[2] Lobbyists for Planned Parenthood argued that without a comprehensive, nationwide, tax funded abortion and birth control network, thousands, if not millions of girls like Roxanne would be abandoned to an irrevocable spiral of poverty.[3] They would become a chronic strain and drain on the system. "Every dollar invested in *family planning*," they argued, "would save two to three dollars in health and welfare costs."[4]

That logic — you've got to spend money in order to save money — sounded logical enough to Congress. So, anxious to demonstrate a fiscal responsibility heretofore inimicable to its character, it authorized several well-heeled *family planning* measures.

In 1964, the Economic Opportunity Act was passed which included a number of birth control and maternal health and hygiene provisions for the very poor.[5] For the first time the federal government became involved in regulating families and policing their bedroom behavior.

In 1968, the Center for Population Research was established in order to coordinate federal activities in "population-related matters."[6] A significant appropriations commitment was passed at that time to provide for contraceptive and abortifacient research, placement, and service.[7]

In 1970, President Richard Nixon signed into law the Tydings Act, consolidating the funding base for the Center, and granting service contracts and subsidy support for independent providers.[8] The bill created Title X of the Public Health Service Act and set funding precedents for Title V, Title XIX, Title XX, and a whole host of other *family planning* and social welfare spending programs that came along in later years.[9]

Interestingly, Section 1008 of the Tydings legislation stipulated that "none of the funds appropriated under this title shall be used in programs where abortion is a method of *family planning*."[10] The strong wording of this provision indicates that Congress not only wished to prohibit the use of tax dollars for abortion procedures, but to exclude the funding of programs and organizations that counseled or referred for abortion as well.[11]

Other provisions made it clear that the grants, investments, awards, gifts, and service contracts provided by the act were to be spent exclusively on programs for low and marginal-income adults.[12]

Planned Parenthood quickly discovered that those restrictive provisions were virtually unenforceable.[13]

It also discovered that dipping into the deep well of public funding could be phenomenally profitable. The mind boggling growth of Planned Parenthood since the heady days when *the Great Society* was just being launched is a lesson on how to exploit appropriations for personal and institutional gain—or how to turn the hard-earned tax dollars of the average American into what the Bible calls *filthy lucre*.[14]

A comprehensive statistical, clinical, and demographic analysis of several thousand randomly selected Planned Parenthood client records recently provided evidence that the organization was not only sidestepping the Tydings provisions as a matter of policy, but that it was deliberately inflating government charges.[15] The fact is, "Planned Parenthood bills more services and charges more fees when taxpayers are footing the bill than when a client pays cash."[16] As demographer Robert Ruff has said, "To put it bluntly, Planned Parenthood is soaking the taxpayer."[17]

For example, if a young girl goes to a Planned Parenthood affiliate for a simple pregnancy test and pays cash, her bill will total, on the average, just over sixteen dollars.[18] If, however, she qualifies for a government subsidy, her bill will total, on the average, just over fifty-seven dollars.[19] For the very same service! In the very same clinic! At Planned Parenthood, a procedure that is *free* at most crisis pregnancy centers and community health clinics, and which can be done at home for less than ten dollars, has become a remarkably profitable enterprise, thanks to government funding.

But it is not just subsidized pregnancy tests that Planned Parenthood has inflated beyond the stratosphere. It bills more services and charges higher fees for government paid clients than for cash clients in every area of its repertoire. The average cost of an initial cash paid birth control visit is just over thirty-two dollars.[20] But when the taxpayer foots the bill, Planned Parenthood charges an average of just over seventy-seven dollars.[21] An annual birth control check-up costs a cash client approximately forty dollars.[22] But when the government pays, Planned Parenthood charges more than eighty-five dollars.[23] A repeat visit costs a cash client just over twenty-five dollars.[24] For the same service, the taxpayer is charged almost thirty-six dollars.[25] A birth control supply visit costs an average of under eleven dollars cash.[26] But when that same visit is paid for out of public funds, the cost averages more than thirty-five dollars.[27] When public hospitals, local communities, school districts, county health departments, and state governments contract with Planned Parenthood to perform abortions the same pattern of price inflation holds true.[28] The cost of *family planning* services at Planned Parenthood is directly related to who pays the bill — the client or the taxpayer. When the taxpayer pays, the services are between two and four times more expensive.[29]

If a defense contractor can get two hundred dollars out of the Pentagon for a common ball peen hammer, then by golly it will — all moral compunction aside.[30] It is simply a matter of supply and demand. Likewise, if Planned Parenthood can get sixty dollars out of the welfare establishment for a cheap little rabbit test, be assured, it will.[31] And just as the defense contractor robs the treasury in the name of patriotism, so Planned Parenthood soaks the taxpayer in the name of philanthropy.

Is it any wonder then that Planned Parenthood is so intent on qualifying girls like Roxanne Robertson for government grants and subsidies?

Highway Robbery Made Easy

Prior to 1981, states and organizations that wanted to participate in the various federal *family planning* programs provided by the Tydings legislation and its prolific progeny were required to submit a detailed spending proposal to the Department of Health and Human Services. Only if and when they could demonstrate legitimate need were funds approved. In addition, they were obligated to report back to the department on a regular basis how they spent the funds and how effective those expenditures were.[32]

A number of conservative spending watchdog groups fought those strict accountability requirements on the basis that they were fiscally counterproductive. They argued that the states and organizations were only using the restrictions as an annual excuse to request ever higher funding levels. Providers like Planned Parenthood would report that they spent two hundred million on *family planning* but that teen pregnancy rose another ten percent. And thus, according to their convoluted logic, *more* federal funding was needed to combat the teen sexuality crisis.[33] Such pleas became an inescapable hurdle at the annual budget negotiations. Not surprisingly program costs began to skyrocket.

The solution proposed by the watchdog groups was to eliminate accountability altogether. The funds would be dispensed as no-strings-attached gifts known as block grants.[34] There would be no federal supervision. No federal control. No federal evaluation. There would not even be federal requirements to establish eligibility guidelines: the states and organizations would be free to dispense the funds to anyone—rich or poor—for any purpose, however they saw fit.[35] The Department of Health and Human Services would only be able to *recommend* that the funds be used in a particular fashion.[36]

Remember, *family planning* programs began as a "money savings" strategy for the welfare system. Now, in order to save the economy from that "money saving" strategy, a *new* "money saving" strategy had to be devised. Congress couldn't resist.

Deficit conscious, it rushed to implement the new measures. And in so doing, it gave Planned Parenthood what was for all intents and purposes a blank check.[37]

Now, thoroughly obscured within the belly folds of Washington's ponderous social services bureaucracy, Planned Parenthood quickly transformed Congress' new "money saving" strategy into a tax dollar black hole. Its metabolism was such that it was constantly in search of new kingdoms to consume, and Washington was only too happy to comply. In just two years' time Title X funding for *family planning* services rose from about one hundred thirty million dollars to almost one hundred forty-three million dollars.[38] Maternal and child health funding programs rose from about sixty-eight million dollars to nearly seventy-two million dollars.[39] Social Services Block Grant funding rose from just over two and one half billion dollars to nearly three billion dollars.[40] Population Research funding rose from about eighty-seven million dollars to more than one hundred four million dollars.[41] And Community Services Block Grant funding rose from three hundred twenty million dollars to three hundred thirty-five million dollars.[42] Without exception, Planned Parenthood has pressed for, and won increases in each of its federal tax entitlements including Title V, Title XIX, and Title XX.[43]

Planned Parenthood has been able to have its cake and eat it too.

A reputation for conscientious economy and humanitarian philanthropy—however well deserved or undeserved—is a most effective means of overcoming resistance to the use of vast unchecked power for looting the public treasury.[44]

To this day, Planned Parenthood's spending juggernaut remains unchecked.[45]

And to this day, it has a free hand in determining how that spending is to be misappropriated.

Program eligibility is determined at the clinic level, by clinic personnel, according to clinic standards, at clinic prices, governed by clinic guidelines.[46] Thus, almost *anyone* can qualify for the subsidies.[47] If Planned Parenthood says you are *poor*, then you *are* poor. If Planned Parenthood says you qualify, then you really *do* qualify. And Uncle Samuel *has to* ante up—at a premium rate. No questions asked. No verification process required. No accountability necessary. No checks. No balances. No rules. No regulations.

It's a perfect con game.

Just ask Roxanne Robertson.

If At First You Don't Succeed . . . Sue

Admittedly, Planned Parenthood's path to bureaucratic *Nirvana* has not been without its trials, tribulations, and temporary *Bodhisattvahs*. Despite its tenured place on the liberal legislative agenda of Congress, pro-life and pro-family forces have not yielded the ideals of "life, liberty, and the pursuit of happiness" without a fight. In 1976, the *Hyde Amendment* prohibited Planned Parenthood's use of Medicaid funds for abortions.[48] In 1981, a comprehensive federal audit revealed that the organization had misused public funds and engaged in illegal activities jeopardizing its tax exempt charitable status.[49] In 1982, the National Eligibility Committee for the Combined Federal Campaign, which solicits charitable contributions from federal employees, was able to temporarily remove Planned Parenthood from its list of beneficiaries.[50] In 1983, the *Hatch Amendment* was introduced in the Senate and came within eighteen votes of overturning *Roe v. Wade's* legalized abortion.[51] In 1984, funding for international abortion programs in developing countries was temporarily curtailed by President Ronald Reagan's *Mexico City Policy.*[52] In 1986, conservatives nearly ambushed Planned Parenthood's IRS non-profit exemption with the *Tax Exemption Equity Act.*[53] In 1987 and again in 1988, Title X regulations were temporarily stiffened to exclude any and all programs that performed, counseled for, or referred for abortion.[54]

In almost every instance, however, Planned Parenthood was able to reverse its setbacks through a masterful use of the courts. It filed innumerable lawsuits, restraining orders, briefs, tactical delays, and judicial ploys, and, as a result, was able to emerge victorious time after time after time.[55] Regardless of what executive order the President handed down, or what administrative decisions the program managers made, Planned Parenthood was able to control the outcome through the courts.

George Will has said that "when political movements become anemic, they abandon legislation for litigation, using courts as shortcuts around democratic processes. . . . As liberalism became lazy and arrogant, and then weak and unpopular, it retreated from political arenas to courts."[56]

In any case, the combination of flabby and unrestricted *family planning* appropriations and brilliant judicial maneuvering has enabled Planned Parenthood to hold the American taxpayer hostage and to indulge its every whim and fancy. The combination of legislative and litigal *manipulation* has enabled it to continue and even expand its medical, racial, and educational *malpractice*. The combination of Congressional and Court contumacy has, very simply, made it rich. And that is a financial scandal that makes Charles Ponzi's famous "Roaring Twenties Securities Sting" pale by comparison.[57]

At Mammon's Shrine

From its earliest days, the Planned Parenthood movement has been involved in financial scandal. Despite the fact that she received generous donations from some of the richest philanthropies in the world, Margaret Sanger kept her organization on the brink of bankruptcy for years, failing to pay her bills and refusing to give an account of her mismanagement.[58]

Financial disclosure would have brought disaster upon Margaret and her fledgling operation. She often spent Planned Parenthood money for her own extravagant pleasures.[59] She invested organizational funds in the black market.[60] She squandered hard-won bequests on frivolities.[61] And she wasted the money she'd gotten "by hook or by crook"[62] on unrestrained vanities.[63]

Because of her wastrel indiscretions, she was removed from the Planned Parenthood board several times,[64] but the organization found that it simply could not survive without her.[65] In the end, Planned Parenthood was forced to take on the character and attributes of its founder. "The love of money is the root of all evil" (1 Timothy 6:10). Violence and greed are inseparable (Proverbs 1:8-19). Thus, Planned Parenthood's evil agenda of violence to women and children cannot be cut loose from the deep tap root of avarice and material lust that Margaret planted.

Sexual immorality, theft, adultery, covetousness, greed, malice, wickedness, deceit, lewdness, lasciviousness, arrogance, blasphemy, pride, ruthlessness, and folly are all related sins (Mark 7:21-22). They commonly coexist (Romans 1:29-31). Certainly they did in the tortured concupiscence of Margaret Sanger. And they still do, in the organization that honors her as pioneer,[66] champion,[67] and patron saint.[68]

For example, in 1981, the Congressional auditing agency, the General Accounting Office, investigated the financial records of Planned Parenthood and uncovered numerous glaring discrepancies.[69] Following in the footsteps of its founder, the organization had abused the public trust, spending tax dollars with a total disregard for decorum, discretion, or legality. It had used public funds to engage in partisan politics.[70] It had misappropriated federal money to pay dues to lobbying organizations.[71] And it had diverted tax dollars to advocate its legislative and judicial programs.[72] All this on top of its price fixing, eligibility tinkering, and appropriations manipulation.

It appears that graft and corruption are endemic to the Planned Parenthood movement. They always have been. Apparently, they always will be.

Today, government funding provides the majority of revenues at more than half of Planned Parenthood's affiliates.[73] Nineteen different federal appropriations measures pour millions of dollars into its cankered coffers every year through dozens of agencies, programs, and projects.[74] And as a result several of those affiliates have accumulated vast holdings in stocks and real estate, and bank accounts with ready cash reserves in excess of a million dollars each.[75] Not bad for a "privately funded," "social services charity organization."[76]

Still, that isn't even the half of it. The real financial legacy of Planned Parenthood becomes evident only as its establishment, expansion, and recruitment scheme is exposed.

Money Laundering: Establishment

Tax dollars are not supposed to be spent for abortions.[77] They can pay for the building where abortions are done.[78] They can pay for the personnel that counsel, refer, and perform those abortions.[79] And they can pay for the programs that teach, protect, encourage, and support those abortions.[80] But, they cannot actually provide for the abortions themselves.

Supposedly.

In reality, however, tax dollars are used all the time to brutalize women and butcher their children.

Planned Parenthood not only fleeces the American taxpayer for its educational and birth control services, it has cleverly ferreted out ways to fleece them for abortion as well. Dozens of ways.

You see, many of the federal *family planning* programs are administered through the states and through local communities.[81] Sometimes Washington offers matching funds to those lower magistrates.[82] Sometimes its bequests are simple grants.[83] But either way, how the funds are to be spent is determined locally.

In effect, Planned Parenthood is able to funnel federal appropriations through state bureaucracies, county health departments, community school districts, and city council administrations for its abortion programs.

In eleven states the use of tax dollars for abortion is quite open and up front.[84] In others it is rather clandestine.[85] In only a very few is it completely outlawed.[86] But in all, Planned Parenthood is actively involved in funneling new tax income sources into its bank accounts.

Mac Lawton lives in North Carolina where state matching funds and service provider grants to Planned Parenthood have been cut off. Despite innumerable lawsuits brought by the five affiliates in the state, lawmakers have stood firm in denying access to state-controlled tax dollars.

But last year when Mac was elected to a county commissioners seat he made a startling discovery. His county had been coerced into a revenue sharing program that benefited Planned Parenthood to the tune of eighty-five thousand dollars a year.

"I just couldn't believe it when I first saw those figures," he told me. "Here we are in the middle of the most conservative section of the most conservative state in the whole country. Who'd have ever guessed that we'd be pouring *any* money into that abortion business? Much less *that much* money? Frankly, I was shocked. And outraged."

Mac went to work right away to defund the county's *family planning* program. "The more I got into it the more I realized that the whole thing was a wicked perversion of the law," he said. "Deals had been struck. Favors had been called in. Heads had been turned. Money had been exchanged under the table. It was a mess."

Needless to say, when Mac began to turn over a few stones and ask a few questions, he began to feel a good deal of political heat. "Several of my colleagues were up to their eyeballs in graft, and my investigations were a real threat to them," he explained. "Their political survival was on the line. They were afraid that I was going to blow the whistle on them. Then all their dirty little deeds would be exposed and the public would discover that their taxes were being used to support Planned Parenthood and to skirt the law."

When he began to receive threatening phone calls and letters, Mac only stepped up his efforts. "If they wanted to play hardball I was ready," he said. "Or at least I thought I was."

A coalition of pro-abortion groups began a public smear campaign designed as much to stymie Mac's efforts as to mire his character in controversy and conflict. In less than three months he decided to resign rather than to subject his family to any further harassment. "I hated to back out of the fight," he admitted, "but I was out there practically on my own. The thing is, they've got so much money and so many people on the abortion side that it just doesn't seem to matter any more what is right, what is true, what is legal, or what is moral. Money is power. Of course, the maddening thing is, that the money they used to drive me out of office was *my own money*. It was tax money."

Two months after Mac resigned, the other county commissioners voted to increase their funding of the program.

Sadly, Mac Lawton's experience is all too typical.

That is the financial legacy of Planned Parenthood.

Planned Parenthood and Parents: Expansion

As many as one third of Planned Parenthood's clients are youngsters living at home.[87] Most of them are not the least bit *needy*, but because they do not have incomes independent of their parents, they are classified as needy by clinic personnel.[88] Verification is verbal only, so the matter is left entirely to the discretion of Planned Parenthood.[89] Not surprisingly then, ninety-seven percent of them are approved for government subsidies, thus providing a massive infusion of new income for the clinics.

By funneling federal money through state and local governments behind the taxpayers' backs, Planned Parenthood is able to *establish* its programs. By applying it to teens behind their parents' backs, it is able to *expand* those programs.

That is why over the years, Planned Parenthood has been the single most vigorous opponent of parental consent laws for birth control and abortion services.[90] It has fought the right of parents to know in the courts[91] and in the media,[92] through lobbying[93] and through legislation,[94] with curriculum in the schools[95] and with campaigns in the communities.[96]

This despite the fact that again and again, parental consent laws have been shown to be an effective deterrent to teen promiscuity, pregnancy, abortion, and venereal infection.[97]

After it enacted a parental notification law, Minnesota saw a twenty-three percent decline in the number of teen births.[98] It saw a forty percent decrease in the number of abortions.[99]

In Rhode Island the abortion rate dropped forty-four percent and the number of teen pregnancies declined thirty percent after the state enacted a parental consent law.[100]

Massachusetts saw a fifteen percent decline in both its total teen pregnancy rate and its total teen abortion rate following the enactment of a parental consent statute.[101]

Planned Parenthood's opposition to parental consent then is purely selfish. As demographer Robert Ruff has argued, "Planned Parenthood simply cannot afford to have parents interfere with its secretive provision of birth control and abortion to their children. To allow such parental intrusion upon its fundamental right to profit from teen promiscuity would cripple it financially."[102]

Only seven states have been able to pass parental consent laws that have effectively stood the test of Planned Parenthood's judicial barrage.[103] But as Leslie Forrester recently discovered, even those "victories" may ring hollow.

Leslie fought hard to get the parental consent law passed in her home state, Rhode Island. Pro-lifers there, anxious to just get *anything* on the books, compromised the bill to include a *judicial bypass* clause. "Our lawyers and lobbyists told us that without the clause, the bill simply couldn't pass, much less stand judicial inspection," Leslie told me. "So we put it in as an *exception*. Basically it said that teens had to get their parents' permission to receive birth control or abortion services *unless* a judge signed a hardship waiver for her."

When the bill passed and then succeeded in getting through the courts unscathed, most pro-lifers, including Leslie, were ecstatic. "We all felt like we'd won a tremendous victory," she said.

Then about three months later, Leslie received a disturbing phone call. "It was my neighbor down the street," she told me. "Her thirteen-year-old daughter had gotten a three month supply of birth control pills at Planned Parenthood without her permission, consent, or knowledge. The girl had gotten her judicial bypass with a simple phone call in less than fifteen minutes. It is almost as if law doesn't matter any more. Groups like Planned

Parenthood always seem to find a way to do whatever they jolly well please. And to make a buck while doing it."

Sadly, Leslie Forrester's experience is all too typical.

And *that* is the financial legacy of Planned Parenthood.

Through the Back Door: Recruitment

Planned Parenthood does not offer *comprehensive* health care at *any* of its eight hundred clinics, two hundred affiliates, or fifty chapters in this country.[104] It is in the sex business. It does not treat the flu, or give hearing tests, or perform vaccinations, or set broken bones, or clean teeth, or check for heart murmurs, or assuage coughs. If a treatment, or procedure, or prescription, or therapy, or examination, or remedy, or medication, or regimen, or cure is unrelated to sex, then Planned Parenthood doesn't offer it. It wants nothing to do with it.[105]

Which makes its latest strategy to place sex clinics in high schools all the more intriguing.[106]

Since it is tough to sell parents at the local PTA or school board meeting on confidential birth control and abortion services for their children, Planned Parenthood has resorted to other tactics.[107] Instead of asking those parents to ante up several hundred thousand additional tax dollars every year to corrupt community standards and teen morals, it simply asks them to provide "good *comprehensive* health care."[108] Then later, when no one is looking, it slips its sex services in on the sly.[109]

One school-based sex clinic supporter writing in Planned Parenthood's journal reported, "Most school-based clinics begin by offering comprehensive health care, then add *family planning* services later, at least partly in order to avoid local controversy. . . . A clinic limited to providing *family planning* services, pregnancy testing, prenatal, and post-partum care, and testing for and treatment of sexually transmitted diseases will be unacceptable even to many of the students."[110]

Another clinic advocate wrote, "The most common strategy adopted to avoid controversy is to maintain a low profile — generally by keeping programs out of sight . . . by relying on word of mouth for recruitment, and by giving names to programs that obscured their functions."[111]

Thus, to the students, to the parents, and to the taxpaying community at large, the "clinics generally are presented as comprehensive, multi-service units that emphasize physical examinations and treatment of minor illnesses."[112]

But that is hardly their real purpose. Planned Parenthood remember, isn't interested in scrapes and bruises or sniffles and sneezes. It is interested in sex.

That is why Planned Parenthood advises that "when a student comes to the clinic ostensibly for other reasons, the clinic staff can take that opportunity to see if the student wants to discuss sexual behavior and birth control."[113]

Planned Parenthood Vice President Louise Tryer urges that, "every medical contact should be utilized as an opportunity to offer the option of contraception."[114]

The plan is to encourage the clinic personnel "to become aggressive counselors to young women. If, for example, a young patient comes in for *tennis elbow*, the physician should manage to introduce birth control. . . . The conversation should then be directed to use of abortion in the first trimester if traditional methods fail."[115]

This kind of deception is the third prong of Planned Parenthood's scheme to scalp the American taxpayer. By funneling federal money through state and local governments behind the taxpayers' backs, it is able to *establish* its programs. By applying the money to teens behind their parents' backs, it is able to *expand* those programs. And by planting covert clinics in the schools behind *everybody's* back, it is able to *recruit* for those programs.

Without the school-based clinic network, Planned Parenthood's ambitious plan to achieve "the perfect contracepting society" becomes little more than a pipe dream.[116] Without that recruitment program, the financial foundations that the organization has laid over the years through arduous injustice would be washed away by the tides of time.

So the deception is essential. For both the short run and the long run.

Kelley Frias and Roma Ratiglia are classmates in the ninth grade at a large high school in the up-scale Orange County suburbs of Los Angeles. When they both decided to try out for the school's swim team, they went together to the health clinic for a mandatory physical exam.

"One of the first things the nurse asked me," Kelley related "was whether I was on birth control. When I told her I wasn't she proceeded to lecture me about *responsibility* and *health* and *hygiene* and all that."

"It was really embarrassing," Roma agreed. "I mean, here I was, just trying to get an okay to swim, and this lady I've never even seen before starts to talk about all this really *private* stuff."

"Yea, and then it was like we were some kinda *bad* kids if we didn't get on the Pill," Kelly said.

"I went ahead and took a whole bunch of Planned Parenthood brochures and stuff, just to get her off my back," Roma said. "Man, you shoulda seen my parents' reaction when I showed it all to 'em. They hit the roof."

"Mine did too," Kelly said.

"But then when they went to talk to the principal," Roma said, "they just got the run-around."

"Yea, well that's pretty typical," Kelly interjected.

"Its pretty weird to think we had to go through all that mess just to get a physical for the swim team," Roma said. "Remind me never to do *that* again."

Sadly, the experience of Kelly Frias and Roma Ratiglia is all too typical.

And *that* is the financial legacy of Planned Parenthood.

The Day Draws Nigh

Planned Parenthood has plotted its course carefully. It has developed foolproof strategies. It has put together an iron clad get-rich-quick scheme. It has made every contingency. It has covered every base.

But like the rich fool who built ever larger storehouses to contain his wealth only to discover afterward that his soul was required of him that very night, Planned Parenthood's day is quickly coming to an end (Luke 12:15-21). In one hour their riches will come to nought (Revelation 18:17). For their judgment shall not long linger, nor will their damnation slumber (2 Peter 2:3).

The Bible makes it clear that the wicked are "greedy dogs," they "never have enough" (Isaiah 56:11). They are "like wolves ravaging their prey to shed blood, and destroying souls to get dishonest gain" (Ezekiel 22:27). They oppress the poor (Proverbs 22:16) and exploit the weak (Proverbs 22:22) choking out the truth (Matthew 13:22) and trusting in a lie (Mark 4:19). And yet their gold and silver quickly becomes cankered, the rust of them becomes a witness against their unrighteousness (James 5:3). For God Himself will smite them (Ezekiel 22:13). He Himself will avenge all those who have been defrauded (1 Thessalonians 4:6).

"Riches profit not in the day of wrath" (Proverbs 11:4). And "He that trusts in riches shall fall" (Proverbs 11:28).

The best laid plans at Planned Parenthood will come to ruin simply because ill gotten gain cannot, will not, and does not last. The organization may attempt to fix prices, manipulate legislation, initiate litigation, launder money, expand markets, and develop recruitment, but in the end, the whole scandalous affair will be exposed. And the people of God will arise and be exalted in their stead.

> Give to them according to their deeds, and according to the wickedness of their endeavors; give to them according to their hands; render to them what they deserve. Because they do not regard the works of the Lord, nor the operation of His hands, He shall destroy them and not build them up (Psalm 28:4-5).

Conclusion

Honore de Balzac once quipped that "behind every great fortune there is a crime."[117] That is certainly true of Planned Parenthood's great fortune. Its vast wealth has been built not only on the broken bodies of its unborn victims and the ghoulish tortures of its unsuspecting clients, but on the perverse manipulation of the American family and the American taxpayer as well. In short, it has committed unspeakable crimes.[118]

Exposed to the light of day, these crimes would surely elicit a public outcry—a cry for justice, a cry for restitution, and a cry for repentance. Exposed to the light of day, these crimes would surely provoke a groundswell of indignation against Margaret Sanger's cause.

The only question is, will we demonstrate the courage necessary to actually expose Planned Parenthood's crimes? Will we bring its financial legacy to the light of day? Or will we continue to allow it to cower under the dark shade of the forbidden tree?

Hark! He heard the horns hooting loudly, no ghostly laughter of grim phantom, no wraithlike feet rustling dimly, the Orcs were up; their ears had hearkened the cries of Turin; their camp was tumult, their lust was alight ere the last shadows of night were lifted. Then, numb with fear, in hoarse whisper to unhearing ears he told his terror; for Turin now with limbs loosened, leaden-eyed was bent crouching crumpled by the corpse, moveless; nor sight, nor sound his senses knew, and wavering words he witless murmured, "Ah, Beleg," he whispered, "my brother-in-arms."

J. R. R. Tolkien

EIGHT

STRANGE BEDFELLOWS: THE INSTITUTIONAL SCANDAL

asinus asinum fricat

Beyond the tall, eighth-floor windows, the Houston city-scape darkened to a drab December twilight, then blossomed into the glittering and sparkling gem that is the city's trademark. Below, the crowds had begun thinning along Milam Street. The light changed at Rusk and headlights began moving again, poking through the thin, slanting winter rain. Across the street, a long, weary line of pedestrians dodged puddles and potholes—some straggling home after a full day's grind, some catching a bite to eat before taking on the snarled freeways, others going to assignations over cocktails in boisterous corner bistros. They moved past the endless upward thrust of new, grimly skeletal constructions that seemed to punctuate each block. Stopping, even in the rain, to peer through holes cut into the wooden walkways, they stared at now-quiet earthmovers and watched the arcs, pink and orange, of the helmeted welders up among the girders.

Dana Meier squinted into the night. Rain blew streaks against the window. The nervous glare of neon and halogen refracted a pulsing nimbus of come-on colors.

It was a familiar scene—a daily ritual for her. Over the last several months, Dana had watched the Republic Bank complex, directly across from her window, rise magnificently from the deep square excavation pit, foot by foot, taking its shape—a guild hall rakishness in fire-flecked Italian granite. Fascinated by the odd mix of Old World appointments and space-age technology, she noted each day's progress on the building with a cat-like curiosity and a child-like ardor.

"It's an architectural icon," she whispered to herself, breath frosting on the cold, damp glass. "A contradiction in terms. A post-modern anomaly. Beautiful, but frightening. Confusing. Like me."

"That's the first sign of the onset of senility, you know — talking to yourself into the wee hours of the night." Bill Maxwell, from accounting, had poked his head through the doorway of her office. "Positively foreboding."

"Senility!" she chuckled, taking off her smart, horn-rimmed glasses and turning slowly away from the window. "Thanks a lot, Bill. You know, you have an unfailing ability to inflict a venial wound in passing whenever I least expect it. Charming."

"Well, you know what Wodehouse used to say. When he was past ninety?"

"I'm not sure I'm in the mood. I doubt I'll find this too terribly amusing."

"Oh, sure you will. He said that as long as you're going to get old . . . you might as well get as old as you can."

"Very funny."

"I thought so."

She turned toward her desk. A drilling lease and several contracts lay there, lounging in a puddle of soft light.

"Come on," Bill beckoned. "Enough already. You've been at it all day. Let's go grab some supper at Ninfa's. Maybe see if we can get tickets for the theater after. What do you say?"

"Thanks, but no thanks, Bill. I've got a couple of things to tie together and then I've got to get home. I'm utterly bushed."

"Oh, baloney. Come on. Loosen up a little, will ya?"

"Really, I'm sorry, Bill. Another time."

"Okay, okay. Try not to make it a late one." He pulled on his trench coat. "Good night. And don't forget to lock up." He went away whistling.

She heard the door close out in the reception area and breathed a deep sigh of relief. She just wanted to be alone. To think.

She shoved the contracts and the lease aside and pulled out the memo she'd received just before lunch. "One hundred percent participation this year," it read. "No exceptions."

Apparently, the battle that she'd been waging for the past year was lost. Corporate management had handed down a decree from on high. No ifs, ands, or buts about it.

She wandered through the empty rooms. The small gas pipeline subsidiary that she supervised occupied most of one floor in a handsomely decorated Shell Oil property. And she loved it. The comfortable jumble of rooms, the winking computer terminals, the sagging, over-burdened bookcases on tatty Oriental carpets—it was home away from home. Work was her life. Life was her work.

That memo put a kink in all that, though.

Five years ago, Dana had had an abortion. At Planned Parenthood. A botched abortion. For half a decade, she'd struggled with the physiological effects of a torn cervix. But worse, she'd struggled with the psychological effects of a seared conscience.

Her therapy had been her work. It was all she'd had left. Pro-abortion rhetoric had driven her out of her Church. Pro-abortion sentiment had cooled most of her relationships. And pro-abortion politics had dampened her enthusiasm for social activism. So, she had invested everything in her work—her hopes, her dreams, and her passions.

But, now, even her work was threatened—haunted by the morbid and spectral shade of abortion. Company policy dictated that every employee be "strongly encouraged" to participate in the annual donation drive for United Way. And since in many states United Way donations directly benefit Planned Parenthood affiliates as member agencies, those employees were being subtly coerced into financing its birth control and abortion activities.

That was something that Dana just couldn't tolerate.

At first, she'd tried to simply ignore the policy. She'd explained her personal position to her superiors. But since she was in senior management, they felt that she simply *had* to set an example for the other employees.

She had fought the policy then. For a year. All the way to the highest corporate level. All the way to the Board of Directors.

The memo was their answer.

"And this is *my* answer," she said aloud, reaching across the desk to scan once more, for the thousandth time that day, her letter of resignation. As much as she loved her job, as much as

she depended on it, she would not sacrifice her integrity for it.
She would not sacrifice the children for it.

She walked out into the night. The Houston streets glistened
like blood on gold.

Looking a Gift Horse in the Mouth

It is bad enough that Americans *unwillingly* give millions of
dollars every year to Planned Parenthood with our taxes. But
that we *unknowingly* give millions more with our charitable giving is tragic.

We are a generous people. Every year we give almost fifty
billion dollars to various private charities.[1] And that doesn't
even count the nearly forty billion dollars in support we lend to
our local Churches and synagogues,[2] and the additional five billion dollars we ante up in foundation and corporate giving.[3]

We give to schools, to hospitals, to relief agencies, to research
institutes, to social service providers, and to community projects. No people has ever given more freely to the needy, the
suffering, or the oppressed.[4] Of course, we give out of great
wealth and comfort.[5] And, often, we give foolishly, hastily, and
unthinkingly.[6] Still, we give. And we give freely.

When thousands and even millions languished in hunger
and desperation in Communist Ethiopia, we responded with
more than three hundred million dollars in emergency aid.[7]
When the Soviet-occupied Ukraine faced calamity and disaster
following the Chernobyl nuclear accident, we dispatched teams
of medical workers and nearly twelve million dollars in relief.[8]
When the oppressive regimes of Nicaragua, Viet Nam, Cam-
bodia, Zimbabwe, Cuba, and Angola slaughtered thousands of
their citizens and drove thousands of others into exile, we fed
them, clothed them, housed them, nursed them, and trained
them, spending millions of dollars in refugee camps and immigration centers all around the globe.[9]

We support everything from the March of Dimes to the
PTA, from the United Way to the YMCA, from Hands Across
America to UNICEF, simply because we want to help.

And that is good.[10]

Unfortunately, we are *so* willing to give, that we fail to ask
enough questions. Or we fail to ask the *right* questions.

And that is bad.[11]

The fact is, huge sums of the money we faithfully donate every year to those charitable organizations wind up in the hands of Planned Parenthood.[12] To the tune of seventy million dollars.[13] About one-third of that comes from United Way and other community chest combined charities.[14] Another one-third comes from corporate grants and foundation bequests.[15] And the final one-third comes from miscellaneous endowments, matching gifts, individual donations, and direct-mail solicitation.[16]

Most people simply don't realize that when they give they are actually aiding and abetting Planned Parenthood's Eugenic agenda. Only occasionally does someone—like Dana Meier—ask questions, raise objections, and voice concerns. Only occasionally is the conventional wisdom—that donations will be applied *where most needed*—actually challenged. And, thus, only occasionally do charitable contributions end up going where they were originally intended.[17]

Program Sweepstakes

From its earliest days, Planned Parenthood wooed corporations, foundations, celebrities, and charities in the hopes of securing operating capital.

Margaret Sanger rubbed shoulders and shared beds with the radical chic in the roaring twenties—the artists, actors, writers, musicians, and activists in New York's Village and London's Fabian Enclave.[18] She shrewdly used her proximity to them to promote her revolutionary ideas.[19] And she carefully networked with them to gain contacts in the political and financial world.[20]

Single-minded in her commitment to the cause, her persistence and unflagging enthusiasm began to open doors. She was tireless and driven. Some even said she was "possessed"[21]—which, no doubt, she was.[22] At any rate, her crusade quickly became a *cause célèbre*. By the thirties, corporation grants and foundation bequests began to pour the money into her coffers.[23] By the forties, she had won the endorsements of such notables as Eleanor Roosevelt[24] and Katherine Hepburn.[25] By the fifties, she had attained international renown and counted among her supporters Julian Huxley,[26] Albert Einstein,[27] Nehru,[28] John D. Rockefeller,[29] Emperor Hirohito,[30] and Henry Ford.[31] The sixties brought her tremendous fame and acceptance. Before her death, she received the enthusiastic endorsements of former Presidents Harry Truman and Dwight Eisenhower.[32] She won over arch-conservatives like Mrs. Barry Goldwater,[33] and arch-liberals like Margaret Mead[34] — ideology didn't seem to matter.

In addition, Margaret Sanger was a tenacious organizer. Her days with the Socialist Party[35] and the Communist Labor movement[36] not only trained her in effective propaganda techniques, they taught her how to solicit, train, and activate volunteers.[37] Using these skills, Margaret literally combed the country, and ultimately the world, searching for donors.[38] She left no stone unturned. She applied for every grant, appealed to every foundation, made presentations to every corporation, and appealed to every charity.[39] She wanted a piece of every philanthropic pie, and she would go to great pains to make her case to any who would listen.[40] She was a dogged promoter. And, like the persistent widow in Christ's parable, she was so unrelenting, she prevailed more times than not (Luke 18:1-8).

Perhaps Margaret's greatest coup came when she was able to gain for her organization an IRS charitable tax-exempt status.[41] That move put Planned Parenthood in the same legal category as a local Church or a philanthropic society.[42] All donations became tax-deductible, and that made solicitation and donor development all too easy.[43]

The fund-raising apparatus that she set in place has only grown in size and sophistication in the years since she died. It has garnered hundreds of celebrity endorsements.[44] It has affiliated with every major national and international professional and educational association even remotely related to Planned Parenthood's work.[45] And it has tapped into the fiscal lifeblood of virtually every major charitable resource available.[46]

The United Way

Founded in 1918, United Way of America is the world's largest cooperative coalition of charity organizations in the world.[47] Its multi-million dollar annual effort not only distributes much needed cash to local private sector service providers, but it provides program support and consultation in the areas of "fund-raising, budgeting, management, fund distribution, planning, and communications."[48] It conducts major national media campaigns, produces films and audio-visual presentations, administers staff and volunteer development training, and publishes dozens of booklets, pamphlets, and directories every year.[49] It assists local service groups by conducting company-wide and community-wide campaigns and cultivating increased corporate giving through donor development programs.[50] United Way funds help organizations like the Salvation Army, Goodwill, the Red Cross, and Big Brothers do what they do best: care for the needy.[51] Millions of dollars every year are used to strengthen the work of drug rehabilitation, medical research, emergency food relief, sheltering the homeless, crisis counseling referrals, legal services to the poor, and job re-training for the unemployed.[52]

But they also go to Planned Parenthood — millions of dollars worth every year.[53] Even those few local United Way groups that have yielded to pro-life pressure over the years, and removed Planned Parenthood as a *direct* recipient of funds, continue to support hot lines, family counseling centers, health service agencies, and community associations that *counsel* for abortion and *refer* clients to the organization's abortuaries.[54]

Nationally, United Way, over the years, has strongly defended its commitment to Planned Parenthood and has consistently upped its share of the annual fund-raising bounty.[55] It has even gone so far as to entangle itself in Planned Parenthood's political spats,[56] even to the point of risking its own tax-exempt status.[57]

Jim Singleton is an executive with an international oil tool manufacturing company based in Oklahoma City. Always active in civic affairs and community development, he has long been an enthusiastic sponsor for United Way's corporate program. "I would personally go to each of our employees," he said, "and encourage them to give. I would help executives in other companies set up incentive programs. I even did some volunteer work at the regional United Way office."

Jim's enthusiasm was dampened significantly when he discovered that the funds he had worked so hard to raise were being used for Planned Parenthood's abortion and birth control crusade. "I went to several of the directors and board members to see if there was any possibility of dropping that support," he said. "But they were all thoroughly committed to maintaining the status quo. The thing is, they were *very* defensive. It was like this subject had already been driven into the ground and they weren't even willing to discuss it anymore."

Of course, they didn't want to lose Jim altogether, so they proposed an alternative. "They told me that if I didn't want my donation to go to Planned Parenthood," he remembered, "all I had to do was to ask for a *negative designation*. They really wanted me to stay with the program. The trouble with *negative designations*, though, is that Planned Parenthood gets a set percentage of the United Way total. That is pre-arranged. So, no matter *how* I designate or don't designate, the very fact that I've made a United Way contribution raises the total that Planned Parenthood gets. Negative designations are, thus, a sham. My protest would be irrelevant."

Frustrated, Jim pulled his company out of the program. "The whole reason I worked so hard for years to raise money was to help people. To learn that my efforts were actually having the *opposite* effect was terribly sobering. Now, every time I see one of those United Way ads during football games, I have to wonder how many other folks there are in the same boat — wanting to help, but doing it in a completely misbegotten fashion. It is tragic."

The March of Dimes

Founded in 1938 by President Franklin D. Roosevelt, the March of Dimes is one of the world's premier private sector health and medical associations.[58] Dedicated to the prevention of birth defects, it raises nearly millions of dollars each year for education, research, and service. It works to improve maternal and newborn health.[59] It makes basic clinical grants to hospitals and universities for perinatal and genetic study programs.[60] It sponsors medical conferences, coordinates symposia, and publishes literature.[61] Since it successfully led the fight to cure polio during the early fifties, the March of Dimes has become a symbol of hope for millions of parents all around the globe.[62]

But it has also placed itself at the forefront of the Planned Parenthood movement.[63]

Since the early sixties, it has increasingly turned its attentions away from *curing* genetic disorders and birth defects to *detecting* and *eliminating* them.[64] And, as a result, amniocentesis and abortion have become its chief concerns, consuming a vast majority of its funding.[65] Instead of trying to *solve* the problem of birth defects, the March of Dimes now disposes of those problems by funding "search and destroy" missions.

Eighty-eight percent of all March of Dimes geneticists favor abortion-on-demand.[66] Seventy-one percent argue that if amniocentesis diagnostic tests prove a child to be defective, he should be terminated regardless of the stage of pregnancy.[67] A large number even revealed that they were involved in live fetal experimentation and fetal harvesting.[68] This despite the persistent claims of the organization that it is "abortion neutral."[69]

The connection between the March of Dimes and Planned Parenthood is not just philosophical. Many faithful donors would be shocked to discover that the money they have given over the years to "help fight birth defects" has actually wound up in Planned Parenthood coffers.

In 1980, for instance, the March of Dimes gave more than one-half million dollars to a Planned Parenthood abortionist for a major research project.[70] The results of the study, published in *Obstetrics and Gynecology*, has been widely heralded in pro-abortion circles and selectively circulated by Planned Parenthood affiliates all around the country.[71]

In response to pro-life criticism of its close relationship with Planned Parenthood, the national office of the March of Dimes called its critics "ideological zealots eager to invent new enemies."[72]

Today, the kinship between the two groups is friendlier than ever. They display and distribute each other's literature.[73] They refer clients back and forth to each other's programs.[74] They cooperate in sponsoring genetic research and perinatal medical conferences.[75] And they support each other in their political lobbying efforts.[76]

Joseph Resnick for years was a dedicated March of Dimes fund-raiser. And for good reason. "I felt that I owed a deep, personal debt to the March of Dimes," he told me. "See, in 1954, when I was fourteen-years-old, an epidemic of polio myelitis was sweeping across America. My mother and my younger sister both were stricken. For weeks, both of them lingered near death.

Then they were both confined to an iron lung for months on end. Today, though, thanks to the March of Dimes, they are both healthy, productive citizens. My mother uses a cane to walk, but my sister shows no effects of the disease at all."

Joseph's mother and sister were both a part of a March of Dimes therapy program for almost a year and a half. "Without the March of Dimes, neither of them would have had a chance of recovery," he said.

Not surprisingly, Joseph tried to show his gratitude to the organization by working hard every year in its fund-raising drive. "My wife and I ran our local campaign six out of seven years in the seventies," he said. "But then, around 1978 or 1979, I began to detect a major shift in the organization's interest and concern. Then, in 1981, my pastor showed me a number of surveys and studies that implicated the March of Dimes in major abortion and amniocentesis research, in cooperation with groups like Planned Parenthood. Well, I was *outraged*. Not at the March of Dimes. But *at my pastor*! I was angry that he would even entertain the thought that the organization I'd worked so hard to support was compromised morally."

Joseph immediately set out to vindicate the organization and prove his pastor wrong. "The next couple of weeks were very painful for me. I made a number of calls. I wrote letters. I read articles. I made inquiries. And, in the end, I was forced to admit that my pastor was right. I was devastated. Here was an organization committed to life, promoting death. It broke my heart. I felt ashamed, embarrassed, and humiliated."

For some time, Joseph tried to work within the organization to change the Planned Parenthood orientation. But all to no avail. "I finally had to come to the conclusion that the March of Dimes was just not going to change. That it was unchangeable and unredeemable."

Fortunately, Joseph's commitment to fighting birth defects did not end with his break with the March of Dimes. Today, he is actively involved with The Michael Fund, an internationally respected pro-life genetic research foundation.[77] "Now, I feel like I'm actually accomplishing what I'd been trying to do all those years," he said. "Now, I'm actually helping kids *live* and live *better*."

Corporate Philanthropy

For some time, America's biggest companies have been involved in an almost suicidal mission to underwrite radical and leftist causes.[78] Overseas, their trade support is virtually the only thing that has kept the Communist dictators in the Soviet bloc afloat economically.[79] Their diplomatic meddling has toppled Western Alliance regimes on four continents.[80] And, at home, their charitable giving has bankrolled the febrile militants in innumerable anti-business, anti-family, and anti-life groups.[81]

In a remarkable study of the *Forbes* 100 companies, a University of Texas professor, Marvin Olasky, found that seven of every ten corporate dollars contributed for public policy purposes go to such liberal groups.[82] For instance, he reported that grants from Aetna, Allied Stores, AT&T, Atlantic Richfield, Dayton Hudson, Exxon, General Motors, RCA, and Westinghouse help support "social and recreational events" for lesbians, and programs designed to "eradicate homophobia."[83]

Chevron, Travelers, Standard Oil, Cigna, U.S. West, Bell Atlantic, Ford, and the Sun Company all have made major grants to groups "teaching aggressive use of federal regulatory agencies to extort concessions from business."[84] Defense contractors like Honeywell support leftist peace organizations that disseminate false propaganda against itself and its industry.[85]

Although virtually all of the organizations of the left—from the Urban League to Peace Child, and from the NAACP to Kinheart—benefit from free enterprise's generosity, pro-abortion feminist groups seem to be the big winners. Nineteen of the top twenty-five companies support radical feminist organizations.[86] The revolutionary National Organization for Women, with fewer than 250,000 members nationwide, received large bequests from American Express, Ameritech, Bell South, Burlington Northern, Chrysler, Coca-Cola, Dart & Kraft, Eastman Kodak, Goodyear, Johnson & Johnson, Manufacturers Hanover, Merrill Lynch, J. C. Penney, Philip Morris, R. J. Reynolds, and Xerox.[87]

Of course, amidst this morass of confusion and corruption, Planned Parenthood has found a way to profit, and profit handsomely. Companies such as AT&T, Citicorp, Dayton Hudson,

Morgan Guaranty Trust, Standard Oil, and Union Pacific gave more than one hundred thousand to the organization's abortion and birth control crusade.[88] Corporate giving has proven to be so lucrative over the last several years that several Planned Parenthood affiliates have full-time corporate development staffs that do nothing but wine and dine executives in the hopes of wooing more dollars into its Midasized vaults.[89]

Ruth Demmik is a systems engineer for a large Silicon Valley manufacturing company. She is also very active in the pro-life movement, donating ten hours a week to counsel battered women and abused children at her Church's crisis outreach center. Last year, she was instrumental in helping her pastor organize a community-wide protest of Planned Parenthood.

To her dismay, she discovered just two weeks before the march that her company was actively cooperating with a National Organization for Women and Planned Parenthood effort to diffuse the effects of the picket. "The pro-abortion people went around to business and civic leaders soliciting donations," she said. "But they didn't just ask for donations straight out; instead they asked contributors to pledge a certain amount for every pro-lifer that turned out for the picket. In other words, the bigger *our* turnout, the greater *their* gain. When they came to our company, they asked for a corporate matching grant: however much they could raise out in the community, matched dollar for dollar by the company. Double or nothing. Well, our board said yes. I was flabbergasted."

Ruth went from boss to boss all the way up the corporate ladder, trying to get the board to reverse their decision. "They had their minds made up, though," she said. "They didn't want me to confuse them with the facts. I don't think I've ever been more frustrated in all my life. Here I was, working *for* a company that was working *against* everything that I believe in. That's a tension that will have to be resolved soon. One way or another."

Family Foundations

During the first three decades of this century, a number of family-controlled philanthropic foundations were established.[90] The era of the industrial tycoon and the manufacturing monopoly was also the era of graduated taxes and heavy governmental regulation.[91] Family foundations were, thus, not merely altruistic, they were very pragmatic hedges against high tax rates and magisterial interference.[92] In other words, they provided the rich with exemptions and loopholes.[93]

That is not to say, of course, that the foundations did not accomplish great things that contributed to the public good. They did, and often still do.

The Carnegie Foundation, established in 1911 by Andrew Carnegie, almost single-handedly endowed the public library movement in the United States.[94] With assets of nearly half a billion dollars at work every year funding universities, hospitals, and community development projects, it has been a remarkable institution of help and hope.[95]

The Rockefeller Foundation, established in 1913 by John D. Rockefeller, likewise has endowed, over the years, innumerable worthy philanthropic projects.[96] It has endowed hunger relief projects worldwide.[97] It has established hospitals and health care facilities on every continent.[98] And its support of educational progress has led to the development of research centers, the publication of academic advances, and the subsidizing of private institutes and universities.[99] With assets of almost a billion dollars at work every year, it has been a powerful force for good.[100]

The Ford Foundation, established in 1936 by Henry Ford, has greatly advanced the public welfare by trying to identify and contribute to the solution of significant national and international problems.[101] Interested primarily in improvement of educational quality and opportunity in schools, colleges, and universities, it has endowed alternative learning projects, scholarship programs, and research management seminars.[102] With assets of nearly three billion dollars at work every year, it, too, has wrought tremendous grace around the world.[103] Dozens of other family foundations—established by the Mellons, the Astors, the Morgans, the Johnsons, the Roosevelts, the Kennedys, the Vanderbilts, and many lesser known clans, like the Kelloggs, the Dukes, the Watumulls, the Motts, and the Kaufmans—have similarly exercised considerable charitable effect.

Sadly, though, much of the good work that these foundations have done has been, at best minimized, at worst nullified, by their counterproductive contributions to organizations like Planned

Parenthood. Instead of supporting organizations, institutions, services, charities, and ministries that strengthen the family, lower taxes, produce individual initiative, and promote health and justice, they tend to endow the narrow, sectarian, and destructive programs and pogroms of the Left.[104]

The Rockefellers began funding Planned Parenthood in 1952 when Margaret Sanger charmed John D. Rockefeller at a lavish *tête-à-tête* in her Tucson mansion.[105] In 1959, the Fords began giving and, before long, virtually all the others had followed suit.[106] Since then, millions of dollars have been pumped into the organization by their foundations. As nimble as a dry leaf in the whirlwind, Planned Parenthood has been able to sidestep its ideological commitment to Revolutionary Socialism long enough to stretch a supplicating hand toward America's greatest capitalists. And, often enough, to make it as rich as they.

Gerald Wilson is an heir to a multi-million dollar privately held business. For years, he fought the patronage of the Left, generally, and Planned Parenthood specifically, in his family's philanthropic foundation. But the task turned out to be both thankless and fruitless. In the end, he was forced to endow his own foundation, one that he could control. "It is terribly frustrating," he told me, "to see so much opportunity for good translated into so much opportunity for evil."

He especially bemoaned the vanity, graft, and manipulation that is almost inherent in the endowment process. "In many ways," he said, "the system is just a series of unholy alliances, meant for right, destined for wrong."

Unholy Alliances

Throughout the Bible, warnings against entering into unholy alliances are abundant and clear.

"Woe to the rebellious children," declares the Lord, "who execute a plan, but not Mine. And make an alliance, but not of My Spirit, in order to add sin to sin" (Isaiah 30:1).

Do not enter the path of the wicked, and do not proceed in the way of evil men. Avoid it, do not pass by it; turn away from it and pass on. For they cannot sleep unless they do evil; and they are robbed of sleep unless they make someone stumble. For they eat the bread of wickedness, and drink the wine of violence. But the path of the righteous is like the light of dawn, that shines brighter and brighter until the full day. The way of the wicked is like darkness; they do not know over what they stumble (Proverbs 4:14-19).

How blessed is the man who does not walk in the counsel of the wicked, nor stand in the path of sinners, nor sit in the seat of scoffers! But his delight is in the Law of the Lord, and in His Law he meditates day and night (Psalm 1:1-2).

Whenever men have violated this basic principle, catastrophe has resulted. What was originally intended for good, for security, and for justice, ended in evil, destruction, and oppression.

Lot entered into an unholy alliance with Bera, king of Sodom and, as a result, lost all his wealth, his position, his home, and, finally, his family (Genesis 19:1-26).

Asa entered into an unholy alliance with Ben-Hadad, king of Aram and, as a result, emptied both the royal and the temple treasuries, virtually bankrupting the kingdom (1 Kings 15:16-19).

Jehoshaphat entered into an unholy alliance with Ahab the apostate king of Israel and, as a result, nearly lost his life to deception and intrigue (1 Kings 22:24-33).

Having failed to learn his lesson, Jehoshaphat entered into still another unholy alliance, this time with Ahab's son, Ahaziah, and, as a result, the entire royal fleet was lost in Ezion-geber (2 Chronicles 20:35-37).

Ahaz entered into an unholy alliance with the kings of Assyria despite the dire warnings of the prophet Isaiah and, as a result, the nation became impoverished and subject to pagan pilfering and perfidy (2 Chronicles 28:1-19).

The first-century Church at Thyatira entered into an unholy alliance with the wanton prophetess Jezebel and, as a result, sickness, tribulation, and pestilence befell the people in great waves of judgment and retribution (Revelation 2:18-29).

Again and again, this truth is driven home. When men ally themselves with the wicked and their causes and their institutions, heartache and calamity are the only possible outcomes.

All the good that the United Way or the March of Dimes or corporate benevolences or family foundations attempt is completely subsumed in impotence and failure due to their unholy alliance with Planned Parenthood. One bad apple spoils the whole batch. One bad recipient spoils the whole fund.

> Do not be bound together with unbelievers; for what partnership have righteousness and lawlessness, or what fellowship has light with darkness? Or what harmony has Christ with Belial, or what has a believer in common with an unbeliever? Or what agreement has the temple of God with idols? For we are the temple of the living God; just as God said, "I will dwell in them and walk among them; and I will be their God, and they shall be My people. Therefore, come out from their midst and be separate," says the Lord. "And do not touch what is unclean; and I will welcome you. And I will be a father to you, and you shall be sons and daughters to Me," says the Lord Almighty. Therefore, having these promises, beloved, let us cleanse ourselves from all defilement of flesh and spirit, perfecting holiness in the fear of God (2 Corinthians 6:14-7:1).

Conclusion

Katharine Hepburn usually does not attend gala fundraisers, but when Planned Parenthood recently decided to honor the actress and her late mother for their outspoken support of the organization, she was more than willing. Proceeds from the star-studded dinner, priced at five hundred to one thousand dollars a ticket, benefited Planned Parenthood's abortion and birth control programs.[107]

With all the rich and famous, the chic and sophisticated, the high and the mighty, and the best and brightest in tow, Planned Parenthood once again demonstrated its ability to attract the support of the very people who should know better. The very people who should be using their power, privilege, and prestige to impact the world for good, side instead with the minions of darkness.

But Planned Parenthood likes them all the better for it.

It's the law of the jungle here fellows. But even here you can live. The first to go is the guy who licks out bowls, puts his faith in the infirmary, or squeals to the screws.

Aleksandr Solzhenitsyn

NINE

THE CAMERA BLINKED: THE MEDIA LEGACY

ad captandum vulgus

Always in wanton pursuit of the new, the costly, and the conspicuous, New York City is a paragon of haute. Ironically, though, a stroll through its streets always yields a king's ransom of Proustian memories as well.

Like Venice and Genoa, it is a sea city. And like the Venetians and Genoans of old, its leaders have always been eager to display their wealth, puissance, and aplomb by building the avante — grand polazzi and campanili — as monuments to themselves. But, they — again, like the Venetians and Genoans — also have a fine eye for preserving the ephemera that define bygone eras. It is almost as if, seeking connections in an "insecure country," they clutch at the relics of a stable and secure nostalgia. It is almost as if, still groping for the ever-elusive "radiant way," they belay against the rock solid certainty of the past.

And so the view of Central Park is shared equally by the Citicorp Center, the Seagram Building, and the Waldorf-Astoria. The crooked little streets of Greenwich Village are shared equally by the Bobst Library, the Provincetown Playhouse, and the Washington Mews. The grand promenade down Fifth Avenue is shared equally by the Empire State Building, the Trump Tower, and St. Patrick's Cathedral.

The city's gestalt of raw tension and hungry ambition calves its persona like an Arctic berg — splinters drifting away. The eclecticism is everywhere evident. It is a bright matrix of contradiction unfolding across a tantrum of logic and illogic, of antiquity and modernity, of substance and illusion, of objectivity and bias, of bondage and freedom, and of honesty and deception.

That odd juxtaposition, that almost schizophrenic New York yin-yang, is nowhere more evident than in its mid-town information agribusiness. With a proud legacy dangling like a medallion upon its chest, the New York media—which is the national media—simultaneously belies that legacy with a brash bravado of contemporaneity.

In other words, it *ain't* what it seems to be.

Why Don't We Know

"This kind of country can't work," says television journalist Charles Kuralt, "unless people have a reliable way of finding out what's going on."[1]

The news media is supposed to be that reliable source of information.

But it's not.

And, perhaps, that is part of the reason why this country *doesn't* work very well right now.[2]

Much of the information in this book is probably surprising, even shocking, to you. "Could this possibly be true?" you may be asking yourself. "If it is, then why haven't I heard it before? Why don't I already know about it?"

The answer is that the media has acted as a filter, screening out most of the information that could "damage" groups like Planned Parenthood "in the public view."[3] Instead of helping people *find out* what is going on, it is insuring that they don't. And won't. And can't.

The media has an agenda. It imposes its values on its audience. As Herbert Gans, renowned media analyst, has argued, "Journalism is, like sociology, an empirical discipline. As a result, the news consists not only of the findings of empirical inquiry, but also of the concepts and methods which go into that inquiry, the assumptions that underlie those concepts and methods, and even a further set of assumptions, which could then be tested empirically if journalists had the time."[4]

In other words, the media operates according to its own perspectives and presuppositions. It retells the news according to its bias, according to its worldview.

That, in and of itself, is not necessarily bad. That, in and of itself, does not make the media "unreliable." All of us have inescapable presuppositions that make genuine objectivity impossible. We all have worldviews.

Our worldview is simply the way we look at things. It is our perspective of reality. It is the means by which we interpret the situations and circumstances around us. Whether we know it or not, we have a worldview. Everyone does. Alvin Toffler, in his landmark book *Future Shock*, said, "Every person carries in his head a mental model of the world, a subjective representation of external reality."[5] This mental model is, he says, like a giant filing cabinet. It contains a slot for every item of information coming to us. It organizes our knowledge and gives us a grid from which to think. Our mind is not open and our viewpoint is not impartial. "When we think, we can only do so because our mind is already filled with all sorts of ideas *with which* to think," says economic philosopher E. F. Schumacher.[6] These more or less fixed ideas we think with make up our mental model of the world, our frame of reference, our presuppositions — in other words, our worldview.

"A worldview is a map of reality," author James Sire tells us. "And, like any map, it may fit what is really there or it may be grossly misleading. The map is not the world itself, of course, only an image of it, more or less accurate in some places, distorted in others. Still, all of us carry around such a map in our mental make-up, and we act on it. All of our thinking presupposes it. Most of our experience fits into it."[7]

When writers write, when journalists report, and when broadcasters go on the air, they communicate from the peculiar perspective of their own worldview. From the stories they select, to the way they present them, from the evidence they show, to the time they afford them, newsmen not only slant the news, they *make* the news. They decide what we know. And what we don't know.

Investigative reporter Geraldo Rivera has said that objectivity "was invented by journalism schools. It has very little to do with real life."[8]

Robert Bazell, of NBC, proclaims that "objectivity is a fallacy. Journalism almost always is about a point of view."[9]

Ace reporter Linda Ellerbee agrees: "We report news, not truth. There is no such thing as objectivity. Any reporter who tells you he's objective is lying to you."[10]

And NBC's senior analyst, Irving R. Levine, asserts that it is "the reporter who has to determine ultimately what is valid and what is not, whose arguments are the most persuasive and whose are not."[11]

There is no such thing as news free of editorial comment.[12]

Again, that, in and of itself, is not necessarily bad. What *is* bad is the *way* that the media slants the news. What *is* bad is *how* the media decides what news becomes the news. What *is* bad is the "unreliable" perspective that the media has. What *is* bad is its worldview.

God's condemnation of ancient Israel came because "their ways were not His ways, and their thoughts were not His thoughts" (Isaiah 55:8). They did not have a worldview shaped and informed by God's Truth. Instead, they "did what was right in their own eyes" (Judges 21:25).

Similarly, the news media today is driven by a worldview that is entirely alien to the Biblical standards of truth, justice, mercy, and integrity. Its ways are not His ways, and its thoughts are not His thoughts. Instead, it does what is right in its own eyes. And, having eaten from the forbidden tree, it has become like a god in its own sight, knowing good and evil (Genesis 3:5, 22).

According to the now famous study of the media conducted by three political scientists, Linda Lichter, Robert Lichter, and Stanley Rothman, the overwhelming majority of newsmen in major media outlets are hostile to Biblical values.[13] Only eight percent are regular Church-goers.[14] Eighty percent believe that homosexuality is a perfectly acceptable alternative lifestyle.[15] Eighty-four percent said that they did not have strong aversions to adultery.[16] Ninety-two percent oppose traditional family structures.[17] And a full ninety-seven percent take a clear pro-abortion stand.[18]

Meanwhile, nearly seventy percent endorse the idea that the media should actively promote its ideas, values, and perspectives.[19]

As Franky Schaeffer has argued, "With such widespread agreement about basic issues, which can only stem from the same philosophic outlook, it hardly takes a conspiracy for the media machine to speak with one smothering voice."[20] Is it any wonder, then, that the truth about Planned Parenthood has been systematically buried beneath the prodigious New York scatology that now passes for news?

The Seven Deadly Sinners

Along with the "corporatization" of American culture in general has come the "corporatization" of the media in particular.[21] Amazingly, almost half of the national news and information outlets are concentrated in the hands of just seven corporate monoliths: CBS, RCA, CapCities, The New York Times, The Washington Post, Gannett, and Time-Life.[22] And this despite the explosive growth in recent years of alternative networks, cable systems, and satellite technology.[23]

All seven of these communications monopolies have maintained a consistent pro-abortion editorial policy over the years.[24] Their strict advocacy of Planned Parenthood's agenda has become as much a hallmark of their profile as their slick promotions and high-tech imagery.

CBS. Founded in 1928 by William Paley, the Columbia Broadcasting System operates one of the country's three major commercial television and radio networks.[25] With two hundred-sixteen affiliated television stations and four hundred twenty-eight affiliated radio stations, it is able to spread its message to all fifty states, reaching as much as ninety-six percent of the United states population.[26]

In addition to that, CBS is the world's largest producer, manufacturer, and marketer of recorded music.[27] It makes and distributes computer software and on-line data bases.[28] It publishes magazines and books for educational, consumer, and professional markets.[29] It publishes music, produces music videos, develops and produces motion pictures, makes and distributes videocassettes, programs cable television, and develops video-text services.[30] If it has to do with communications, CBS is in it. And it is in it with a vengeance.

Sadly, this vast power and influence has been marshalled to Planned Parenthood's cause.[31] Besides the consistently slanted newscasts by the likes of Walter Cronkite and Daniel Rather, and documentaries by Mike Wallace and Ed Bradley, CBS has used prime-time entertainment programming, like the sitcom *Maude* and the action-drama *Cagney and Lacey*, to bolster its propaganda predilection.[32]

RCA. One of the great electronics pioneers, RCA is, today, a formidable global communications giant. Besides engaging in the research, manufacture, distribution, sale, lease, and servicing of everything from television receivers to electro-optic devices, from video-cassette equipment to audio records, tapes, and CDs, and from commercial communications satellites to military electronic hardware, the company operates the NBC network, with two hundred affiliated television stations and more than five hundred radio stations.[33] In addition to that, the company operates a system of satellite and submarine cable circuits linking the continental United States directly with numerous foreign countries and overseas points.[34] It offers telex services, data transmission programs, telegram transmissals, teleprinter circuits, and high speed multi-point line data communications services for terminal communication and point-to-point lines to host computers.[35]

For years, the NBC network has dominated radio and television broadcasting.[36] It has more often than not controlled the airwaves and dictated programming fashions.[37] And, not surprisingly, it has imposed its leftist perspective on virtually everything that it broadcasts.[38] News reporting by Chet Huntley and David Brinkley, documentaries by Roger Mudd and Tom Brokaw have constantly reinforced the Planned Parenthood party line.[39] Its entertainment programming has fallen in line as well with rabid pro-abortion pieces profiled on prime-time shows like the drama *St. Elsewhere* and the sitcom *Valerie*.[40]

CapCities. For many years, ABC was the stepchild of national radio and television broadcasting.[41] A distant third in ratings, earnings, and affiliates throughout the sixties and seventies, the network perpetually lagged behind CBS and NBC, exerting little influence in either news or entertainment. But, then, a series of dramatic events in the eighties, including a merger with the vast Capital Cities Communications Group and a bold and innovative programming twist, catapulted the network into the number one position.[42] It grew to more than two hundred affiliated television stations and nearly two thousand affiliated radio stations.[43]

With its new-found strength, the company began to build its own communications empire. It invested in cable and subscription television programming, buying ESPN, the Arts and Entertainment Network, and Lifetime.[44] It began publishing nine big-city daily newspapers and forty smaller community papers.[45] It branched out into home video markets, magazine publishing, institutional investing, and music recording, distribution, and sales.[46] It even bought the second largest Christian publishing company, Word, Inc., in an attempt to cash in on that market as well.[47]

Like the other networks, though, ABC has used its position to catechize its audiences with the Planned Parenthood message.[48] In news reports by Harry Reasoner and Peter Jennings, and documentaries by Hugh Downs and Barbara Walters, the pro-abortion message has been driven home again and again.[49] And although its entertainment programming has tended to be unconscious of social obligations, political ideologies, or moral consequences—focusing almost exclusively on the Nielsen ratings—several shows, such as the sitcoms *Soap* and *The Love Boat*, have often portrayed a pro-abortion spirit.[50]

The New York Times. Although not even the *best selling* paper in New York City, *The Times* is far and away the *most influential* newspaper in the country, perhaps in the world.[51] Founded in 1851, the venerable old publishing concern now reaches more than a million homes a day, with a worldwide distribution system.[52]

In addition, it owns and operates eighteen other daily and weekly papers throughout the United States.[53] It publishes five major magazines, including *Family Circle*, the largest-selling women's magazine in the country.[54] It runs three television stations and is a major force in radio broadcasting.[55] It operates its own news service which has grown to be the leading supplemental news wire in the country, distributing material from *The Times* to more than five hundred dependent publications around the globe.[56] It owns two publishing companies, an information bank, an editorial syndicate, two companies that manufacture audiovisual materials for schools, colleges, and universities, a microfilm processor and distributor, and four of the world's largest paper mills.[57] As Bernard Nathanson has said, "This is not exactly your average Mom 'n Pop country weekly that James Stewart takes over when he resigns in a sanctimonious huff from the corrupt *Big City Daily* and turns the weekly into the rural equivalent of the *Manchester Guardian* after three weeks of Herculean effort and the devoted and adoring efforts of June Allyson."[58]

Over the years, *The New York Times* and its various ancillary organs, has been the primary forum used by Planned Parenthood to spread its merciless message.[59] Virtually every new campaign, every new strategy, every new rhetorical ploy, and every new emphasis has been launched in its pages.[60] Full-page advertisements, op-ed articles, feature stories, editorial cartoons, literature reviews, public service announcements, and opinion page commentary have been scrupulously exploited for the cause.[61]

The Washington Post. Like *The New York Times*, the privately-held *Washington Post* is a communications giant, with annual sales of almost $600 million and more than five thousand employees.[62] Besides its Capitol Hill flagship, it owns three newspapers, including the *International Herald Tribune*.[63] It operates television stations in several major markets.[64] It owns its own paper mill and a newsprint manufacturing company.[65] Most importantly, though, it publishes one of the two most influential news magazines in the world: *Newsweek*.

Both *The Post* and *Newsweek* steered fairly clear of the abortion issue throughout the sixties.[66] With only a few obligatory reports on various court cases and medical developments, the issue was otherwise ignored.[67] But, then, with the dawning of the seventies, they allied themselves unreservedly with Planned Parenthood.[68] They began to laud the heroics of pro-abortion advocates as "humane and compassionate" and to denigrate pro-lifers as rabid "missionaries" and "crusaders."[69]

Gannett. The nation's largest newspaper chain, with some eighty-eight daily newspapers, was founded in 1906 by an upstate New York entrepreneur, Frank Gannett.[70] By the time he died in 1957, he had acquired twenty-three very profitable small-town papers in five states.[71] His successors built the company from that small base into an international phenomenon. Today, the company's local newspapers have a combined circulation of more than six million copies a day.[72] Its shareholders have enjoyed eighty-two consecutive quarterly earnings gains—more than twenty years of uninterrupted growth in profits.[73] It owns thirty-two print sites besides its eighty-eight local news facilities, including one in Switzerland and another in Singapore.[74] It has seven television stations and twelve radio stations.[75] And it runs the largest outdoor advertising and billboard company in North America.[76] But its greatest asset is *USA Today*, the phenomenally popular national newspaper known for its bright colors, short articles, breezy, upbeat style, and TV-shaped dispensers. Since it was launched on September 15, 1982, *USA Today* has exploded onto the American scene, attracting nearly five million readers a day, more than any other newspaper in history.[77]

Even though Gannett has become a new and powerful presence in worldwide communications, it has not carved for itself a unique editorial niche. Thus, despite its attempt to produce news with "an unrelenting cheerfulness" and a "journalism of hope," *USA Today*, and the other Gannett outlets, have toed the Planned Parenthood line.[78] The militant pro-abortion tack of Gannett's papers have, at times, even surprised Planned Parenthood with their vehemence and intolerance.[79]

Time-Life. With annual sales of nearly three billion dollars, and more than 25,000 employees, Time-Life is the biggest, richest, and most powerful of all the communications monoliths.[80]

It owns and operates six magazines, including *Life, Fortune, Money, People, Sports Illustrated*, and its flagship, *Time*.[81] It runs the Book-of-the-Month Club and the Quality Paperback Book Club.[82] Its other publishing ventures include the Little, Brown, and Company, the New York Graphics Society, the St. Paul Pioneer Press, and the Angelina Free Press.[83] It operates the Home Box Office cable network, as well as forty-one local cable TV companies.[84] It has a controlling interest in several transportation businesses, mortgage companies, insurance concerns, steel mills, music publishers, real estate agencies, hotel chains, and computer software manufacturers.[85]

Time first covered the abortion issue in 1965 with an openly sympathetic article in the medicine section.[86] But that was only a hint of things to come. By 1967, it had burst out of the closet and declared itself "unequivocally in favor of the repeal of restrictive abortion laws."[87] From that day forward, *Time* has remained resolutely in the Planned Parenthood vanguard with the rest of the mega-press.[88]

Franky Schaeffer has said, "Given the concentration of the media's power in relatively few hands, and their shared values, it's nearly impossible to avoid the conclusion that the media represents a monolithic, unelected force in public life: a self-assured, self-perpetuating elite that relishes its power and would have more."[89]

On the Offensive

The cooperation between the seven major media monopolies and Planned Parenthood was vividly illustrated in a series of coordinated stories during the eighteen months between October, 1985 and March, 1987.[90]

Concerned that the grassroots pro-life movement was at last gaining an upper hand in the abortion battle, Planned Parenthood put together a well-orchestrated, heavily-financed, no-holds-barred, negative public relations campaign.[91] The campaign was aimed at the more than three thousand counseling centers established by pro-lifers in order to offer women, in the midst of crisis pregnancies, abortion alternatives and genuine help.[92] The centers, which were typically small, poorly financed, and run by volunteers, apparently had begun to substantially cut into the abortion trade.[93] But, perhaps more importantly, they had also begun to steal Planned Parenthood's thunder. The centers were receiving favorable publicity from many quarters for their "helpful contributions to the process of developing informed choice on abortion."[94]

Planned Parenthood argued that many women were making appointments at the alternative centers thinking that they were actually abortion clinics. From time to time the volunteers at a few of the centers would allow that illusion to persist in the hopes of gaining a fair hearing on the facts of fetal development and the risks of abortion procedures. Although such tactics were extremely few and far between, Planned Parenthood saw in them a golden opportunity.[95]

Amy Sutnick, a public information associate for Planned Parenthood of New York City, wrote several news releases and put together a press packet labeling the alternative centers as "bogus" and "deceptive," luring" clients in by "masquerading" as abortion clinics and then "terrorizing" them with "horror stories," "gory photographs," and "brainwashing techniques."[96]

Sutnick approached a sympathetic reporter at the New York tabloid, *The Daily News*, with her packet and a proposal for a story. The reporter took the assignment and published a piece written along the lines of Sutnick's news releases, often even using the same wording.[97]

With *The Daily News* article now in hand, Sutnick began to call on other pro-abortion journalists in the city. Before long, she was able to place similar stories on virtually every New York television station, including the network affiliates, and in the other New York newspapers.[98]

Soon the strategy began to snowball. Sutnick sent her growing pile of clippings along with her press packet to Planned Parenthood affiliates, clinics, and chapters around the country so that they could contact their local media outlets. Meanwhile, she also contacted all the various women's magazines.

Hundreds of articles, stories, editorials, profiles, and news features resulted.[99] From *Vogue, Glamour,* and *Cosmopolitan* to *The Detroit Free Press, The Houston Chronicle,* and *The New York Times,* Planned Parenthood's smear campaign confronted consumer audiences everywhere.[100]

But the big break came when both *Newsweek* and *USA Today* translated Sutnick's now-stuffed portfolio into major stories.[101]

The author of the two *USA Today* pieces, entitled "Bogus Abortion Clinics Draw Legal Fire" and "Anti-Abortionists Masquerade as Clinics," later admitted that she had not even visited any of the alternative centers.[102] The only women she talked to were provided by Planned Parenthood.[103] And a full quarter of the material was direct quotation and paraphrase from Sutnick.[104]

The *Newsweek* story was built around dozens of independently verified news reports from all across the country — actually, the incestual progeny of Sutnick's diligent labors.[105] It described the pro-life volunteers working in the alternative centers as "radical" and "militant," but "clever" "fundamentalists" who used "scare tactics" in order to "jolt" women out of the abortion decision.[106] Entitled "Clinics of Deception: Pro-Lifers Set Up Shop," the article's synergism with Planned Parenthood's campaign was perfectly choreographed.

Sutnick's sleight-of-hand trick triggered an avalanche of concern, stimulated a bevy of lawsuits, and manufactured a major news event.

News and Truth

The damage inflicted by Amy Sutnick's stories was tremendous.[107] The momentum that pro-life forces had gained over several years of diligent work and compassionate care was almost immediately undermined. Planned Parenthood, feigning ethical outrage, was able to embezzle the moral high ground. Even the pro-lifers themselves began to waver here and there, throwing the movement into confusion and disarray.[108]

The reason for this is that the media, by the sheer force of its smothering dominance, has successfully erased the distinction between *news* and *truth*.

More than half a century ago, Walter Lippman, the godfather of modern journalism, argued that "the function of *news* is to signalize an event; the function of *truth* is to bring to light hidden facts, to set them into relation with each other and make a picture of reality on which men can act."[109] He concluded that if the public required "a more truthful interpretation of the world they lived in, they would have to depend on institutions other than the press."[110]

But we have *not* depended on other institutions. We have accepted the media's *news* as *truth*. Thus, it has ceased to function as a news *reporter* and has become, instead, a news *maker*, or, more to the point, a *truth* maker. In a very real sense, the media actually defines our reality.

James Hitchcock, Professor of History at St. Louis University, has said, "What is presented in the media, and the way in which it is presented, are for many people the equivalent of what is real. By determining what ideas will be discussed in public, the media determines which ideas are to be considered respectable, rational, and true. Those excluded from discussion, or treated only in a negative way, are conversely defined as disreputable, irrational, and false. The media has the power almost to confer existence itself. Unless a belief or an institution receives some recognition, it does not exist. Even those who know that the media is fundamentally hostile to their values nonetheless court media recognition as a way of achieving status in the public eye."[111]

From the media we discover what is important and what is not. We learn what is tragic and what is heroic, what is commendable and what is dishonorable, what is sober and what is humorous.[112] We learn how to dress, what to eat and drink, and what kind of car to drive. And, of course, we learn how we should think about public issues, how we should react to personal crises, and how we should live our lives.[113]

In his scathing critique of ethics in journalism, *The News At Any Cost*, Tom Goldstein suggests that not only are reporters the "kingmakers" and "kingbreakers" of our day, they are the "unacknowledged legislators" of our none too pluralistic society.[114] They shape cultural mores, he says, affect political contests, create the parameters of public issues, unveil hidden truths — whether true or not — and dictate the social agenda, all on a two-hour deadline! They function not only as the judge, jury, and executioner in the courtroom drama of life, but also as both public defender and criminal prosecutor.[115]

Such power should not be taken lightly. It colors everything it touches.

When Karen Denney first began to see the news reports and the articles denigrating the pro-life cause, she simply shrugged them off as just one more series of pro-abortion attacks on the truth. As a volunteer counselor at an alternative center, she had seen any number of media distortions and moral tirades aimed at her work. "At the start, it seemed like it was just the same old propaganda," she said.

But when the reports persisted and even intensified, Karen began to have serious doubts. When she saw the article in *Newsweek*, those doubts became a full-fledged crisis of confidence. "I just began to wonder if I'd gotten myself all involved in some sort of fringe group," she said. "I began to think that we were all just a bunch of kooks or something. I began to question all my presuppositions. I was depressed for days. It was like there was an emotional and theological and intellectual tug-of-war going on inside me. I didn't want last night's newscast or last week's news magazine to determine truth and error for me, but it was hard to overcome the feeling that we pro-lifers were flying in the face of everything reasonable, sensible, sane, and *normal*."

Fortunately, Karen had the emotional stamina and the intellectual honesty to weather the storm of confusion and examine the facts rationally. "I finally settled down and reconciled the whole thing," she said. "In the end, I was thankful that I'd gone through it all. I came away with a new understanding of the power and influence of the media. And I came away with a whole new commitment to stand for the truth that sets us all free."

Sadly, very few people have the inclination or the determination to wrestle with the issues like Karen Denney did. And so they take the media's version of reality at face value.

Very few people have the time, the resources, or the ability to ferret out the facts that challenge the media's version of reality.

Dozens of issues could be cited to illustrate this:

The Birth Dearth. The media has incessantly harped on the dangers of the "population explosion" for more than a quarter-century.[116] Somehow, though, it has failed to report that all of its earlier estimates have proven to be utterly erroneous.[117] Somehow it has failed to report that, instead of facing a "population explosion," we are now facing a "birth dearth."[118] There is, indeed, a "population crisis," but, instead of having "too many people," the crisis is that we don't have enough.[119]

If the media refuses to report the facts, if it continues to bolster its alternate "reality," how can people *ever* know the truth?

The Chinese Holocaust. Wowed and enamored with the "new" China, the media has somehow overlooked one of the most insidious massacres in man's long and turbulent history.[120] In its few obligatory passing mentions of the Communist government's coercive abortion and infanticide programs, the media has, at best, mumbled incoherently about the "harsh necessities" of reducing the country's burgeoning birth rate.[121] Hardly the kind of reporting you'd expect of a genocide that claims as many as fifty million lives every year, is it?[122]

If the media refuses to report the facts, if it continues to bolster its alternate "reality," how can people *ever* know the truth?

Post-Abortion Syndrome. The media has posed itself as a champion of women's rights, as an advocate of women's issues.[123] Somehow, though, it has failed to report the fact that a *majority* of women who undergo abortions suffer significant psychological distress.[124] One study showed that sixty-two percent had become "suicidal" following the procedure, twenty percent had actually made attempts, thirty percent began drinking heavily, forty percent experienced nightmares, and twenty percent had undergone a "nervous breakdown."[125] And yet, the most we hear from the media is that women are "ambivalent" towards abortion.[126]

If the media refuses to report the facts, if it continues to bolster its alternate "reality," how can people *ever* know the truth?

Fetal Harvesting. The horrors of Nazi Germany are consistently vilified by the media, even today.[127] Somehow, though, it has failed to report that the very kinds of atrocities we roundly condemn Hitler's doctors for are today practiced routinely by upstanding physicians and researchers in America's hospitals and universities.[128] Babies that survive abortions are subjected to bizarre and barbaric live experiments.[129] Human tissue is bought and sold on the open market for everything from cosmetics to pharmacology.[130] Fetal organs are often artificially sustained and then later "harvested" for commercial consumption.[131] Somehow we are led to believe that abortion only involves the woman's body, that the "product of conception" is little more than a "blob of tissue."[132]

If the media refuses to report the facts, if it continues to bolster its alternate "reality," how can people *ever* know the truth?

For all intents and purposes, they can't.

The Press As a Moral Force

The media scene has not always been a scythe of unrighteousness. Once upon a time, long ago and far away, the press actually took a vital role in quashing the first abortion movement in America.[133] It took a strident stand against the racist and Eugenic programs of Margaret Sanger.[134]

During most of the nineteenth century, abortion was an open commercial enterprise.[135] In fact, between 1830 and 1880, abortionists advertised their services quite freely.[136] And they did a booming trade.[137]

One woman, Ann Lohman, built her abortion business into an incredibly profitable enterprise with clinics in Newark, Providence, Boston, Philadelphia, and five more in New York.[138] She operated a mail-order business that ranged across the continent, with dozens of salesmen up and down the East Coast peddling her abortifacient pills.[139] Known professionally as Madame Restell, Lohman spent as much as sixty thousand dollars a year on advertising — an incredible amount in that day — to support her empire.[140] By the 1870s, she was living in the lap of luxury, with an opulent mansion on Fifth Avenue, a magnificent horse-drawn coach, and a social standing of the highest order.[141]

Lohman was not alone in her prosperity. Abortion was big business.[142] Any number of opportunists cashed in. The dogma of Mammon leaked into the whole land, touching the air with benediction.[143]

At the time, there was not even a semblance of a unified Christian opposition to the trade which claimed as many as a million young lives a year.[144] A number of doctors complained that the public was apathetic and unaware, and that even the "clergy, with very few exceptions, have thus far hesitated to enter an open crusade against criminal abortions."[145] One pro-life leader of the day contended that ministers "have been very derelict in handling this subject too delicately and speaking of it too seldom."[146] He wondered if anyone would ever take leadership in alerting and arousing the public.[147]

The New York Times — then owned and edited by committed Christians — stood in the gap, grasped the ring, and took the leadership. In 1870, it published an editorial entitled "The Least of These Little Ones." Filled with Biblical references, editor Louis Jennings complained that the "perpetration of infant murder . . . is rank and smells to heaven. Why is there no limit of punishment?"[148] Again, in 1871, he wrote that abortionists "have openly carried on their infamous practice . . . to a frightful extent, and have laughed at the defeat of respectable citizens who have vainly attempted to prosecute them."[149]

Late that year, he gave one of his top-flight reporters an undercover assignment in order to expose the most prosperous abortuaries and their medical malpractice. The explosive story that resulted, "The Evil of the Age," by Augustus St. Clair, launched *The Times* into a moral crusade that would not end until pro-life legislation, outlawing abortion and protecting women, was passed in every state in the Union.[150] Not only that, it triggered a wave of support that engulfed much of the rest of the media, and saw to the prosecution of the most offensive abortionists, including Lohman.[151]

Clearly, the media has come a long, long way on the downgrade in the last one hundred years.

The Cloak of Conspiracy

Absalom was the passionate third son of David, King of Israel. His personal comeliness and charisma was matched in greatness only by his undisciplined ego and ambition. Thus, he was forever getting himself into trouble and embroiling the palace in controversy and scandal (2 Samuel 13:38-39; 14:28). When finally his father received him back into favor, the old king was repaid by a plot against his throne.

> And Absalom used to rise early and stand beside the way to the gate; and it happened that when any man had a suit to come to the king for judgment, Absalom would call to him and say, "From what city are you?" And he would say, "Your servant is from one of the tribes of Israel." Then Absalom would say to him, "See, your claims are good and right, but no man listens to you on the part of the king." Moreover, Absalom would say, "Oh, that one would appoint me judge in the land, then every man who has any suit or cause could come to me, and I would give him justice." And it happened that when a man came near to prostrate himself before him, he would put out his hand and take hold of him and kiss him. And in this manner Absalom dealt with all Israel who came to the king for judgment; so Absalom stole away the hearts of the men of Israel (2 Samuel 15:2-6).

Playing the part of the people's advocate, Absalom stole away their hearts. With delicious whisperings and twisted murmurings he plied circumstances in his favor. With great skill and evident adroitness he slanted the facts, edited the truth, and filtered the news, always with an eye toward the ratings.

Then, at the peak of the game, he upped the ante.

> Now it came about at the end of forty years that Absalom said to the king, "Please let me go and pay my vow which I have vowed to the Lord, in Hebron. For your servant vowed a vow while I was living at Geshur in Aram, saying, 'If the Lord shall indeed bring me back to Jerusalem, then I will serve the

Lord.'" And the king said to him, "Go in peace." So he arose
and went to Hebron. But Absalom sent spies throughout all the
tribes of Israel, saying, "As soon as you hear the sound of the
trumpet, then you shall say, 'Absalom is king in Hebron.'"
Then a messenger came to David, saying, "The hearts of the
men of Israel are with Absalom" (2 Samuel 15:7-10, 13).

Absalom covered his conspiracy with a cloak of righteousness. His conniving, malignant intentions were obscured by a
thoroughly benevolent, pious exterior.

And the king, taken as he was by that exterior, didn't know
what was happening until it was too late. By then he was too
compromised to arrest the crisis. He was forced to flee (2 Samuel
15:14). He had to learn the hard way—as Eve had before him—
that just because someone or something looks "good," "desirable,"
or even "delightful," is assurance of precious little (Genesis 3:6).
He had to learn the hard way, as Paul would after him, that just
because someone or something comes disguised as an "angel of
light" or a "servant of righteousness," is no guarantee of anything
(2 Corinthians 11:14-15).

What Absalom did was to take very real concerns and issues
and blow them out of proportion, twisting the situation to serve
his own ends: the overthrow of the reigning administration. He
took facts, figures, and anecdotes and molded them and shaped
them to fit his own predisposition. He called on all his skill, all
his charisma, all his personal attractiveness, and all his inside
contacts. He played on the emotions of the people. He showed
an impeccable sense of timing. In short, he manipulated the situation masterfully. He exploited an aged king, a complacent administration, and latent discontent, making news and making
truth by the sheer force of his proficient willfulness—not at all
unlike the modern news media and its masterful manipulation of
the facts to give credence to its particular socio-political causes.

Absalom wreaked a lot of havoc. So has the media. But there
is one thing that neither of them counted on: The good guys
always win in the end. There may be defeats along the way.
There may be major setbacks from time to time. Tranquility
may be dashed. The faithful may be sent into flight. But only for
a time. In the end, the cause of the righteous will be upheld (Job
27:16-17). The true truth will come out (Ezekiel 36:33-36). God's

people will prevail (Matthew 6:10; 16:8). If—and that is a big "if"—if they will only do right, cling to the blessed hope, and stand steadfast on the very great and precious promises of God (Joshua 1:7-9).

Absalom abandoned the good legacy of his past, shielding his wickedness with a cover of sophistication and moral indignation. Similarly, the media has abandoned the good legacy of its past, shielding its tainted advocacy of Planned Parenthood with a smothering cover of professional objectivism and market manipulation.

In the end, though, it *will* have its due.

> A fool's lips bring strife, and his mouth calls for blows. A fool's mouth is his ruin, and his lips are the snare of his soul. The words of a whisperer are like dainty morsels, and they go down into the innermost parts of the body (Proverbs 18:6-8).

Conclusion

Nat Hentoff was at one time a card-carrying establishment media spokesman. He was a board member of the ACLU. He was a renowned advocate of civil liberties and radical liberal causes. And he was a tenured journalist with the left-of-gauche newspaper, *The Village Voice.*

But then he began to cover several widely publicized infanticide and abortion cases. And he did the unthinkable: he began to deviate from "the orthodox liberal position that women cannot achieve their basic rights without the right to kill inconvenient fetuses."[152]

Hentoff's colleagues were shocked.[153] He was quickly dropped off the board of the ACLU.[154] And pressure from the left beckoned for him to return to the fold. To conform.

It seems that freedom of the press in this country is little more than theoretical these days.

And about that, Planned Parenthood couldn't be happier.

But see the angry Victor hath recalled His ministers of vengeance and pursuit back to the gates of Heaven; the sulfureous hail shot after us in storm, o'er blown hath laid the fiery surge, that from the precipice of Heaven received us falling, and the thunder, winged with red lightening and impetuous rage, perhaps hath spent his shafts, and ceases now to bellow through the vast and boundless deep. Let us not slip the occasion, whether scorn or satiate fury yield it from our foe.

John Milton

TEN

A DIVINE TRAGEDY: THE RELIGIOUS LEGACY

anguis in herba

Easter is the greatest of all the Christian festivals. It is the day when every Believer rejoices in the knowledge of His Redeemer's resurrection. Even so, there was precious little joy in the hearts of the people of Constantinople on Easter Sunday, 1453. It fell that year on April the first. After a long and stormy winter, spring was coming at last to the Thracian peninsula. In the lush orchards throughout the venerable city the fruit trees were bursting into flower. The nightingales had returned to sing in the Lycus thickets and the storks were already rebuilding their nests on the peaked rooftops all along the Mese. The sky was mottled with long thick lines of migratory birds flying to their summer havens way away in the north. But the Bosphorus was rumbling with the sounds of war: the men, armaments, and accoutrements of a great and dreaded army.

Hagia Sophia was thronged with the faithful, as were the hundreds of other Churches throughout the city. They culminated Holy Week surrounded by a millennium of glory and majesty. Within eight weeks all of them would be exiled, captive, or dead. The infidel Turks that began gathering outside the great Theodosian Walls that day would soon be upon them. The glory and majesty was doomed. And everyone knew it.

The fall of the greatest city in all of Christendom would send devastating quakes throughout the West, shaking the foundations of life and hope and truth. The civilized world would never be the same.

Back in the days when historians were but simple men, the catastrophic conquest of Constantinople was believed to mark the end of the Middle Ages. In these more complex and cosmopolitan times we know only too well that "the stream of history flows on relentlessly and there is never a barrier across it."[1] As discontinuous as the events in 1453 were, we must say that there is no sudden or precise point at which the medieval world was transformed into the modern world. Long before 1453, the Renaissance had begun in Florence, Venice, Genoa, and Paris. Long after 1453, the feudal life persisted in Flanders, Bavaria, and Russia. Long before 1453, the great navigators and discoverers had begun to explore the ocean routes that would ultimately alter the economy of the whole world. Long after 1453, vast, vast uncharted realms were still left for the stout of heart to claim.

As calamitous as the events in 1453 were, they were largely symbolic. They were neither the beginning nor the end.

Since Calvary there have been no absolute divisions in history, only benchmarks.

Thus in 1973, when another citadel of majesty fell, the stream of history, though disturbed, continued to flow ever onward. As in the sack of Constantinople, this modern assault on life and hope and truth would reverberate throughout the civilized world, shaking the foundations of every institution: family, Church, and state. And yet, long before the Supreme Court's *Roe v. Wade* decision legalizing abortion that year, liberty and security had already been seriously jeopardized. Several states had already liberalized their abortion laws.[2] Tax funding for Planned Parenthood had already been appropriated.[3] And epidemic promiscuity had already begun to ravage the land.[4] Long after 1973 strong and righteous resistance challenged the seductive tyranny of death on demand.[5] The Church arose from its cultural slumber and began to reassert its disciplining role in society.[6] Pro-lifers developed creative alternatives for women and children in crisis.[7] And serious legal challenges continued to threaten Planned Parenthood's death grip on the nation's purse strings.[8]

As calamitous as the decision in 1973 was, like the Fall of Constantinople, it was largely symbolic. It was neither the beginning nor the end.

Abortion, promiscuity, racism, greed, and deception are as ancient as mankind.[9] They did not spring up full blown in 1973 with Justice Blackmun and the Supreme Court or even in 1917 with Margaret Sanger and Planned Parenthood.[10] And sadly, they will probably continue to plague us even after *Roe v. Wade* is overturned and Planned Parenthood's aims are vanquished.[11]

In The Beginning

Exposure, abortion, child sacrifice, and other forms of infanticide more often than not were both legal and respectable in pagan societies from the earliest times.[12] Unwanted children in ancient Rome were abandoned outside the city walls to die from exposure to the elements or from the attacks of wild forging beasts.[13] The Greeks often gave pregnant women heavy doses of herbal or medicinal abortifacients.[14] The Persians developed highly sophisticated surgical curette procedures.[15] Ancient Hindus and Arabs concocted chemical pessaries—abortifacients pushed or pumped directly into the womb through the birth canal.[16] The primitive Canaanites threw their children onto great flaming pyres as a sacrifice to their god Molech.[17] The Polynesians subjected their pregnant women to onerous tortures, their abdomens beaten with large stones or hot coals heaped upon their bodies.[18] The Egyptians disposed of their unwanted children, especially girls, by disemboweling and dismembering them. Their collagen was then ritually harvested for the manufacture of cosmetic creams.[19] The more things change the more they stay the same.

Plato and Aristotle both recommended infanticide and abortion for Eugenic purposes.[20] Juvenal and Chrysostom revealed that many abortions were performed in order to conceal illicit or illegal sexual activity.[21] Soranos argued that some women killed their children out of sheer convenience or self-indulgent vanity.[22] Ambrose and Hippolytus said that some families resorted to these drastic measures for economic reasons.[23] Others, according to Justinian, did so for religious, ideological, or sectarian reasons.[24] But most women, reported Calaetus, simply were coerced by oppressive cultural norms, values, and structures to despise and reject their progeny.[25]

Indeed, "there is nothing new under the sun" (Ecclesiastes 1:9).

From time to time voices were raised against the slaughter of the innocent and helpless.[26] But they were like voices crying in the desert: hauntingly prophetic but scornfully spurned.

It was not until the rapid spread of Christianity throughout the Mediterranean world in the second and third centuries that a consistent and convincing pro-life message began to sound. But when it did, the whole civilized world stopped to listen.[27] It was not long until laws were passed and a cultural consensus was reached to protect both women and children.[28] The Church's pro-life message was arresting.

The reason Christianity commanded such attention and compelled such action was not just that the sanctity of life was a new and novel notion. The pro-life emphasis was provocative because the Church affirmed it universally and without dissent, because it was undeniably rooted in Scriptural Revelation, and because it was coupled with complementary action on the part of the faithful.[29]

Affirmation. The wholehearted consensus of the early Church was that abortion and infanticide were in fact *murder.*[30] No ifs, ands, or buts about it. On that, all of the patristics absolutely agreed.

The *Didache* was a compilation of Apostolic moral teachings that appeared at the end of the first century. Among its many admonitions, it asserted an unwavering reverence for the sanctity of life: "Do not murder a child by abortion or kill a newborn infant."[31]

The *Epistle of Barnabas* was an early second-century theological tract that was highly regarded by the first Christian communities. Like the *Didache*, it laid down absolute strictures against abortion and infanticide: "You shall love your neighbor more than your own life. You shall not slay a child by abortion. You shall not kill that which has already been generated."[32]

The second-century apologist Athenagoras in a letter to Emperor Marcus Aurelius wrote, "We say that women who induce abortions are murderers, and will have to give account of it to God. . . . The fetus in the womb is a living being and therefore the object of God's care."[33]

In the third century, Clement of Alexandria asserted that "our whole life can proceed according to God's perfect plan only if we gain dominion over our desires, practicing continence from the beginning instead of destroying through perverse and pernicious arts human offspring, who are given birth by Divine Providence. Those who use abortifacient medicines to hide their fornication cause not only the outright murder of the fetus, but of the whole human race as well."[34]

At about the same time Tertullian wrote in his *Apology* that "murder is forbidden once and for all. We may not destroy even the fetus in the womb. . . . To hinder a birth is merely a speedier man-killing. Thus, it does not matter whether you take away a life that is born, or destroy one that is coming to the birth. In both instances, destruction is murder."[35]

In the fourth century, Basil the Great argued, "She who has deliberately destroyed a fetus must bear the penalty for murder. . . . Moreover, those who give abortifacients for the destruction of a child conceived in the womb are murderers themselves, along with those receiving the poisons."[36]

Ambrose, bishop of Milan, condemned those who "deny in the very womb their own progeny. By use of paricidal mixtures they snuff out the fruit of their wombs. In this way life is taken before it is given. . . . Who except man himself has taught us ways of repudiating our own children?"[37]

Likewise, Jerome wrote that those who "drink potions to ensure sterility are guilty of rebuffing God's own blessings. Some, when they learn that the potions have failed and thus are with child through sin, practice abortion by the use of still other potions. They are then guilty of three crimes: self-mutilation, adultery, and the murder of an unborn child."[38]

Augustine condemned those whose "lustful cruelty" provoked women "to such extravagant methods as to use poisonous drugs to secure barrenness; or else, if unsuccessful in this, to murder the unborn child."[39]

Origen,[40], Hippolytus,[41] Cyprian,[42] Methodius of Olympus,[43] Chrysostom,[44] Minucius Felix,[45] and Gregory Nazianzus[46] all added their voices of affirmation as well. Again and again they decried the wickedness of abortion and infanticide. Together they affirmed the sanctity of life.

Revelation. The potency of the Church's pro-life message was not simply due to a subjective unanimity, as important as ecumenical agreement was. The Patristics did not pull their view of the sanctity of life out of thin air. Their common affirmation was but an obedient response to God's Revelation, the Bible.

It was abundantly clear to those faithful early Christians that the Scriptures commanded a reverence for life. Embedded in every book and interwoven into every doctrine was the un-wavering standard of justice and mercy for all: the weak and the strong, the great and the small, the rich and the poor, the lame and the whole, the young and the old, the unborn and the born.

The Bible declares the sanctity of life in its account of God's creation (Genesis 1:26-28; 1 Timothy 6:13; Psalm 36:9, Psalm 104:24-30; John 1:34; Acts 17:25).

> Woe to him who strives with his Maker! Let the potsherd strive with the potsherds of the earth. Shall the clay say to him who forms it, "What are you making?" Or shall your handiwork say, "He has no hands?" Woe to him who says to his father, "What are you begetting?" or to the woman, "What have you brought forth?" Thus says the Lord, the Holy One of Israel, and his Maker: "Ask Me of things to come concerning My sons; and concerning the work of My hands, you command Me. I have made the earth, and created man on it. It was My hands that stretched out the heavens, and all their host I have commanded (Isaiah 45:9-12).

The Bible declares the sanctity of life in its description of God's sovereignty (Deuteronomy 32:39; Psalm 22:9-10; Job 10:12; John 5:21; Romans 11:36; Colossians 1:16-17).

> For You have formed my inward parts; You have covered me in my mother's womb. I will praise You, for I am fearfully and wonderfully made; marvelous are Your works, and that my soul knows very well. My frame was not hidden from You, when I was made in secret, and skillfully wrought in the lowest parts of the earth. Your eyes saw my substance, being yet unformed. And in Your book they all were written, the days fashioned for me, when as yet there were none of them (Psalm 139:13-16).

The Bible declares the sanctity of life in its discussion of Christ's incarnation (John 3:16; John 11:25; John 14:6; Acts 2:22-28; Colossians 3:4; Romans 5:21).

The thief does not come except to steal, and to kill, and to destroy. I have come that they may have life, and that they may have it more abundantly (John 10:10).

The Bible declares the sanctity of life in its explanation of Christ's redemption (Matthew 18:10-11; Mark 10:45; Romans 8:11; 1 Corinthians 15:26, 54-56; 2 Corinthians 2:16; 1 John 5:11-12).

But has now been revealed by the appearing of our Savior Jesus Christ, who has abolished death and brought life and immortality to light through the Gospel (2 Timothy 1:10).

The Bible declares the sanctity of life in its exposition of judicial ethics (Genesis 9:6; Exodus 20:13; Exodus 21:22-25; Leviticus 24:17; Isaiah 1:15; 1 Peter 3:7).

I call heaven and earth as witnesses today against you, that I have set before you life and death, blessing and cursing; therefore choose life, that both you and your descendants may live (Deuteronomy 30:19).

The Bible declares the sanctity of life in its exhortation to covenantal mercy (Deuteronomy 10:18; Isaiah 1:17; Isaiah 58:6-7; Acts 5:20; James 1:27; Titus 2:11-14).

If you faint in the day of adversity, your strength is small. Deliver those who are drawn toward death, and hold back those stumbling to the slaughter. If you say, "Surely we did not know this," does not He who weighs the hearts consider it? He who keeps your soul, does He not know it? (Proverbs 24:10-12).

From Genesis to Revelation (Genesis 2:7; Revelation 22:17), in the Books of the Law (Exodus 4:12; Leviticus 19:16), in the Books of History (Judges 13:2-24; 1 Samuel 16:7), in the Books of Wisdom (Psalm 68:5-6; Proverbs 29:7), in the Prophetic Books (Amos 1:13; Jeremiah 1:5), in the Gospels (Matthew 10:31; Luke 1:15, 41-44), and in the Epistles (Galatians 1:15; 1 Corinthians 15:22), the pro-life message of the Bible is absolutely inescapable. It is indeed "the Word of Life" (Philippians 2:16).

Thus, when Christians spoke to their culture in defense of life and liberty, they spoke with great authority. Theirs was a message rooted in precept *not* mere prejudice or preference.

Application. The early Christians dramatically redirected the civilized world's attitude toward and treatment of the helpless. But it was not just on the strength of their common affirmation and Biblical Revelation that they were able to win the day. Those faithful pioneers *proclaimed* a pro-life message and *believed* a pro-life message, so they *lived* a pro-life message.

In Rome, Christians rescued babies that had been abandoned on the exposure walls outside the city.[47] These "foundlings" would then be adopted and raised up in the nurture and admonition of the Lord.[48]

In Corinth, Christians offered charity, mercy, and refuge to temple prostitutes who had become pregnant.[49] These despised, rejected, abused, and exploited women were taken into homes where they could safely have their children and then get a fresh start on life.[50]

In Caesarea, Christians cared for the poor, the sick, the suffering, the lame, and the aged in clinics and hostels.[51] The Church protected and provided for these unwanted and dispossessed souls without partiality.[52]

Whenever and wherever the Gospel went out, Believers emphasized the priority of good works,[53] especially works of compassion toward the needy.[54] For the first time in history, hospitals were founded,[55] orphanages were established,[56] rescue missions were started,[57] almshouses were built,[58] soup kitchens were begun,[59] shelters were endowed,[60] charitable societies were incorporated,[61] and relief agencies were commissioned.[62] The hungry were fed, the naked clothed, the homeless sheltered, the sick nursed, the aged honored, the unborn protected, and the handicapped cherished.[63]

The pro-life message of the Church was not mere rhetoric. It was a commitment. It was a lifestyle. And as a result, it made a deep and lasting impression on the whole civilized world.[64] Even in those regions where the Christian faith never predominated, or where the Gospel took root only to be supplanted later, the sanctity of life was grafted into the cultural conscience.[65]

The idea that infanticide and abortion are wrong, then, is a distinctly Christian idea. And it is an idea that the Church has *always* held to.[66] At no time in its vaunted two thousand year history has it ever wavered. Its witness, rooted in common affirmation, Scriptural Revelation, and selfless application has never been repudiated.

At least, not until now.

The Betrayal

All of the Church's forefathers, fathers, patriarchs, prophets, apostles, preachers, evangelists, martyrs, confessors, ascetics, theologians, and every righteous spirit made perfect in faith have tenaciously defended the sanctity of life. In times of persecution and times of triumph, in times of adversity and times of prosperity, in times of conflict and times of peace they have remained stalwart and steadfast. None of them ever even considered dissenting from the common affirmation of the faithful. None of them ever even considered denying the clear Revelation of the Bible. And none of them ever even considered departing from the practical application of compassion. After all, these are the very things that make Christianity what it is: *orthodoxy*,[67] *orthopraxy*,[68] and *orthotraditio*.[69]

Today though, there are men and women in the Church who not only *consider* abandoning these things, they *do* it. And with relish.[70]

Sadly, those men and women now actually control most of the large mainline denominations in the American Church. As a result, the American Baptist Church, the Disciples of Christ, the Episcopal Church, the Evangelical Lutheran Church in America, the United Methodist Church, the Presbyterian Church U.S., and the United Church of Christ have all jettisoned their pro-life commitments to officially embrace the old pagan consensus about abortion and infanticide.[71]

They have also successfully diverted millions of dollars, intended by parishioners for missions, into radical causes and militant organizations like Planned Parenthood.[72] Additionally, many of them have even developed organizational ties,[73] recruited staff volunteers,[74] pioneered cooperative programs,[75] sponsored seminars and conferences,[76] co-published educational literature,[77] filed amicus briefs,[78] lent the use of Church properties,[79] and established public testimony[80] for Planned Parenthood.

In less than a generation they were able to whisk away the two thousand year old voice of ecumenical affirmation, the eternal witness of Divine Revelation, and the spiritual service of charitable application. In less than a generation they were able to betray the most basic principles of the Christian faith.

The Balak Strategy

When Balak, King of Moab, was confronted with the advancing armies of Israel immediately following the Exodus sojourn, he began to cast about for a strategy to stop them (Numbers 22:2-3). Military confrontation seemed hopeless. Diplomatic appeasement seemed suicidal. And defensive alliances seemed delinquent (Numbers 22:4). So in desperation he sent for Balaam, a diviner, who was thought to have the power to bless and bind through spells and incantations (Numbers 22:5-6).

At first the magician was reluctant to take part in Balak's ploy despite his generous offer (Numbers 22:15-35). But eventually he gave in and delivered four oracles (Numbers 22:36-24:25). Much to Balak's chagrin, however, each of the oracles predicted that Israel was invincible from without. No army, no king, no nation, and no empire would be able to stand against it. The only way God's Chosen People could be defeated was if they defeated themselves through moral defilement.

That was all Balak needed to know. He didn't need an army. He didn't need diplomats. He didn't need allies. And he didn't even need diviners. He would rely on wolves in sheep's clothing (2 Timothy 3:6).

The next time the curtains of history draw back, the women of Moab have gone down into Israel's camp at Peor. Enticing the people to play the harlot, those women were able to do what no warrior or general possibly could: trap and defeat Israel. And not a sword was drawn. Not an arrow was unsheathed. Not a javelin was hurled.

It would be several hundred years before Moab would be able to consummate their victory and actually sack the capital of Israel. But that future conquest in Jerusalem was insured by the moral defeat wrought by Balak's women at Peor.

Early on, Planned Parenthood adopted a similar strategy against the Church. Margaret Sanger recognized that the Church was "the enemy" of her crusade.[81] But she also recognized that an all out frontal assault on God's People was suicidal.[82] And so she put together a "Balak strategy." She relied on wolves in sheep's clothing (2 Timothy 3:6).

Margaret began by wooing young and ambitious ministers with the trinkets and baubles of power, prestige, privilege, and position. She doted on them, feeding their sense of self-importance.[83] She enticed them with honors.[84] She invited them to sit on her boards.[85] She patronized their pet projects.[86] She wined them and dined them.[87] She rewarded them with trips, junkets, and tours.[88] She knew just how to tantalize them with attention and appreciation.[89] Her winsomeness was irresistible and her thoroughness was incomparable.[90]

But even without all that alluring charm, Margaret's campaign to seduce Christians would probably have won support in three broad sectors of the Church.

Racists. Especially during the Great Depression when tensions were high and jobs were scarce, racists saw Margaret's Eugenic plans and programs as an open opportunity to eliminate whole "undesired" races and "dysgenic" classes.[91] Tragically many of them carried out their vendetta in the name of Christ.[92]

Lettie Perkins grew up in a small sharecropper's cabin deep in the heart of rural South Carolina. When she was just a youngster she remembers a countywide tent revival meeting cosponsored by several large all White Baptist Churches and several social service agencies including Planned Parenthood. "We were all excited," she said. "The revival was always the social event of the year. And that year was to be the first time Blacks were allowed to attend. We could hardly contain ourselves. Most of the women bought or made new dresses. We got hats and gloves. We really were going to do things right. It was like debutante's coming-out for us."

The pastor of one of the sponsoring Churches spent a good deal of his time for nearly a month before the revival making sure that black pastors in the area turned their people out. "I don't know why we were so naive at the time," Lettie told me. "It was so obvious that he was setting us up for something."

Indeed, he was. On the day that the revival was to begin, Planned Parenthood set up several tents. Blacks were herded into them and "counseled" on the "benefits" of sterilization and birth limitation. "We weren't even allowed to go into the revival meeting itself until we'd listened to their whole spiel," Lettie said. "And even then, they segregated us off to one side. Like usual."

Most of the Black families were outraged. The blatantly racist collusion between Planned Parenthood and the all-White Churches was shocking to them, even in that day of raw and festering prejudice. "I can still remember my Mamma just shaking with anger and humiliation," Lettie said. "Our family *never* went to Church again. Not any Church, Black or White. Mamma didn't want to have anything to do with a faith that could sanction things like that."

Liberals. But it wasn't just racists that were attracted to Margaret Sanger's cause. During the first three decades of this century, the great Modernist-Fundamentalist controversy erupted onto the American Church scene.[93] More disruptive than even the eleventh-century Schism[94] or the sixteenth-century Reformation,[95] the controversy forever changed the face of Christianity in this country.[96] In reaction to the Modernists' emphasis on the "Social Gospel," most Fundamentalists withdrew from all cultural involvement to focus on "spiritual things."[97] Meanwhile the Modernists pursued cultural involvement with a vengeance, uncritically embracing every fringe Liberal cause, issue, and organization including Planned Parenthood.[98] Since the conservative Fundamentalists no longer actively opposed them, the Liberals were able to capture the seats of power and influence.[99]

Men who no longer believed the Bible and who were committed to a radical social agenda were easy prey for Margaret.[100] She exploited the Liberal coup brilliantly.[101]

Richard L. Ford was the young idealistic pastor of a large Methodist Church on the West Coast during World War II. Already thoroughly infected with Liberalism even then, his congregation sponsored several cooperative programs with Planned Parenthood. "At the time we were giddy with excitement," he told me recently. "We felt that we'd been sequestered in a religious ghetto. That we'd been irrelevant for years. Now at last we were doing things that made a *difference* in the world. Unshackled of every encumbrance—tradition, the Bible, everything—we loyally followed every new fad and fashion."

A funny thing happened on the way to relevance, however. "I found that I didn't have answers anymore," Richard said.

"When people are facing a crisis in their lives they don't need their pastor to experiment on their souls and minds with whatever the latest pop therapy is. They need answers. When teens are facing a barrage of temptation you just can't turn them over to Planned Parenthood. That's like throwing gas on a fire. They need standards. Solid and sure."

No longer able to provide his congregation with decisive guidance Richard was left helpless in the face of a rapidly deteriorating moral climate. "There wasn't any such thing as *sin* anymore for us," he said. "So, not surprisingly, we began to indulge ourselves. Illegitimate pregnancies skyrocketed. Divorce rates soared. And the worse things got, the more we turned to the very organizations that prompted our demise in the first place. Imagine! Going to Planned Parenthood to solve the teen pregnancy epidemic! That makes about as much sense as going to a pusher to stop drug abuse or to a pimp to stop prostitution. But, that's exactly what we did."

Compromisers. Margaret Sanger was able to successfully recruit large numbers of Fundamentalist, Evangelical, Catholic, and Orthodox Christians into her fold as well. Unlike the racists and liberals who were converts of conscience, these men and women were converts of convenience.[102] They were fine upstanding Christians who opposed Planned Parenthood's promiscuous sex education programs. They stood firmly against abortion. Until . . .

Charles Boothe is a respected and admired Christian leader. A former pastor and now the chairman of his Church's deacon board, he runs a community wide youth ministry. From the expression on his face I could tell that he was deeply disturbed when he walked into my office. "Jeanie, my youngest daughter, is pregnant," he told me. "She's just seventeen, a senior in high school. What am I going to do? She has her whole life ahead of her. Why this? Why now?"

We briefly talked through the Biblical options: maternity homes, adoption agencies, alternative centers, and marriage to the father. We consoled one another. We wept together. We prayed together. And we talked long into the afternoon. We embraced warmly when he left.

He then promptly took Jeanie to Planned Parenthood and had his grandchild killed.

I was shocked.

Why? Why would he do such a thing? Why would he resort to that which he *knew* was wrong?

"I've always been against abortion," he told me later. "Always. And I still believe that it's wrong. It's murder. But . . . I tell ya. When it's your own daughter. . . . Well, I just couldn't see ruining her life by making her go through the humiliation of an illegitimate pregnancy. And besides, our reputation . . . my reputation. . . . Well, I uh . . . I just. . . . Well, you know."

Margaret Sanger's "Balak Strategy" proved to be a phenomenal success. Enticing Christians to "play the harlot," she was able to do what no activist or ideologue possibly could: trap and defeat the Church (Numbers 25:19).

It would be several decades before Planned Parenthood would be able to consummate its victory and actually sack the citadel of Christian consensus.[103] But that future conquest in the Supreme Court was insured by the moral defeat wrought by Margaret's minions in the Church.[104]

Reaping the Whirlwind

Margaret Sanger's "Balak Strategy" and the Church's capitulation have had devastating results. Even Bible-believing Evangelicals, traditional Catholics, and faithful Orthodox Christians have been caught in a maelstrom of destruction.

In a recent survey conducted for Josh McDowell's *Why Wait?* campaign it was revealed that as many as forty-three percent of all Christian teens have experienced intercourse, with another twelve percent reporting sexual activity just shy of that.[105] Eighty percent of those teens confessed Christ as their "personal Savior."[106] And sixty-seven percent agreed that "the Bible is a totally reliable guide for all situations."[107]

What the survey seems to indicate is that the moral and behavioral distinctions between Believers and unbelievers have almost completely disappeared.

Moab was able to prevail over Israel only when that nation lost its distinctiveness and became assimilated into Moabite culture.

Planned Parenthood has been able to prevail over the Church simply because Believers have allowed themselves to become assimilated into a corrupt and promiscuous culture.

An analysis of Planned Parenthood's clinic visit records highlights that dismal truth.[108] A random sample of nearly thirty-five thousand medical charts from fourteen affiliates coast-to-coast revealed that sixty-two percent of the girls receiving abortions identified themselves as Evangelical Christians.[109] Another twenty percent professed to be either Catholic or Orthodox.[110] Of those eighty-two percent, a full seventy-six percent not only specified their religious preference, they identified their local Church membership and pastor.[111]

The notion that it is primarily "rank heathens" or "flaming liberals" who are aborting their future away simply doesn't hold up under the facts. The scandal of Planned Parenthood has become the scandal of the Church. Sowing the wind, it has reaped the whirlwind (Hosea 8:7).

Achan in the Camp

Flushed with confidence following their spectacular victory at Jericho, the people of Israel advanced to the much smaller, much weaker city of Ai. So certain were they of another victory that they sent up only a very small contingent to take the city (Joshua 7:2-3).

Much to their surprise, however, the men of Ai routed their vastly superior forces (Joshua 7:4-5).

Joshua and the leaders of the nation fell on their faces in fear and trembling before God. Trying to make rhyme or reason out of the lopsided battle they begged for an explanation (Joshua 7:6-9). And what was God's reply?

The Lord said to Joshua: "Get up! Why do you lie thus on your face? Israel has sinned, and they have also transgressed My covenant which I commanded them. For they have even taken some of the accursed things, and have both stolen and deceived; and they have also put it among their own stuff" (Joshua 7:10-11).

It seems that one man, Achan, had violated God's specific commands, hiding his sin in his tent, and thus had brought judgment and condemnation upon the entire nation.

Ai was lost, and lives were lost. All because Achan was in the camp. All because sin was in the tent.

There are any number of Christians today who are dumbfounded in the face of our impotence against Planned Parenthood. They cannot understand why we are so constantly and consistently defeated when we contend with its forces in our schools, our courts, and our assemblies. But the reason is abundantly clear. We cannot effectively assault the gates of Planned Parenthood until we cast Achan out of the camp. We cannot successfully vanquish Planned Parenthood until we repent of the sin hidden in our own tent.

> Judge not, that you be not judged. For with what judgment you judge, you will be judged; and with the same measure you use, it will be measured back to you. And why do you look at the speck in your brother's eye, but do not consider the plank in your own eye? Or how can you say to your brother, "Let me remove the speck out of your eye;" and look, a plank is in your own eye? Hypocrite! First remove the plank from your own eye, and then you will see clearly to remove the speck out of your brother's eye (Matthew 7:1-5).

Conclusion

Citing the modern American Church's ambivalence to life, mercy, justice, and truth, Federal Judge John F. Dooling, Jr. ruled in 1984 that the Supreme Court's pro-abortion stand was "in the mainstream of the nation's religious tradition."[112]

By all indications, he was right.

Abortion is still legal in America because American Christians still want it legal.

Running in the face of Scripture and tradition, truth and experience, wisdom and discretion, and sanctity and justice, the Church has bolstered the sordid killing business of Planned Parenthood by both its complacency and complicity, for both its convenience and its continuance.

We can point our condemning fingers at Planned Parent-hood, but until we turn our gaze toward home, we will never be able to give a convincing rendition of indignation.

And we will never be able to remove the stigma of death and destruction from our land.

Judgment begins with the house of God.[113]
Well it should.

PART THREE

THE TRUTH

This day,
   in sadness borne,
   we must confess:
The Spirit of the Age
   has crushed
   the infant in the cradle.
Yet,
O glorious, yet.
One day,
   in gladness shown,
   we must profess:
   the Infant from the manger
Has crushed
   the Spirit of the Age.

Tristram Gylberd

The end of learning is to repair the ruins of our first parents by regaining to know God aright, and out of that knowledge to love Him, to imitate Him, to be like Him, as we may the nearest by possessing our souls of true virtue, which, being united to the heavenly grace of faith, makes up the highest perfection.

John Milton

SLAYING DRAGONS: THE CHARACTER TO CONFRONT

cum tacent clamant

By the thirteenth-century, medieval civilization had reached its height. It had also plunged to its depth.

The Christian faith mingled with speculative philosophy, humanist sociology, and recalcitrant theology in urbane amity. The arts flourished. Trade was prosperous and abundant. The woes and cares of the Dark Ages were past. Merriment abounded.

At the same time, morality deteriorated. Troubadours spread liberal and lascivious notions from town to town. Women were imperiously beautiful and impiously immodest. Greed, avarice, and materialism dominated the people's lives.

Into this volatile mix of old and new, good and bad, virtue and vice, came a profusion of new cults and sects. Moving with returning Crusaders, waves of Oriental mysticism and occultism assaulted Christian truth remorselessly. From the Persians, they brought echoes of Manichean dualism and Mazdakian communism. From the Turks, they brought an ascetic iconoclasm and resigned fatalism. From the Hindus, they brought a libertine gnosticism and a lust for the obscene.

A bevy of religious communities sprang up around these odd heresies and the men who proclaimed them. The Paulicians and Bogomiles gained wide followings in the Balkans, along the edge of Byzantium. The Beguines and Beghards gained wideranging popularity in the Low Countries of Flanders and Lothier.

The Waldensian and the Albigensians won devotees throughout Toulouse, Lyons, and all of Southern France. Before long, the thriving towns along the Mediterranean were honeycombed with apostates zealously proselytizing for their cause. "The cities," one Bishop exclaimed, "are *filled* with these false prophets."[1] Indeed, Milan alone had seventeen new religions. Cults outnumbered Churches in Viterbo, Ferrara, and Rimini. And defections in Orleans, Avignon, Sardica, and Nicomedia had become terribly alarming.

Most of the sects had an amazing uniformity of dogma. They all shared an Arian conception of Christ and a Manichean notion of creation. They were pacifistic and ascetic. They were communistic and anarchistic. They exalted individual autonomy, liberty, and equality. They were generally sexually indulgent, opposed to traditional family life, and rejected childbearing and rearing as oppressive. They revived the popularity of abortion, infanticide, and euthanasia. Because they abandoned vocations and work, they often resorted to theft, confiscation, looting, deception, conspiracy, and divisiveness. They indulged in drunkenness, carousing, and all manner of sensuality. They dabbled in sorcery, witchcraft, alchemy, astrology, divining, and idolatry. Of course, these tendencies and practices varied somewhat from time to time, from place to place, and from cult to cult, but their general conformity was such that Churchmen often referred to them all by the name of the largest and best-organized group: the Cathari.

At first, the Church was tolerant and indulgent. But, as the cults became more and more extreme, and as their excesses wreaked more and more havoc, it saw the necessity of confronting and exposing them.

The Apostle Paul had warned believers not to tolerate the evil and unfruitful "deeds of darkness," but, rather, to "expose them." The question was, were the cults actually *evil*, or were they simply *misguided*?

Bernard of Clairveaux, the greatest Western preacher of the day, answered by saying that evil was "not a matter of opinion."[2] The Scriptures had afforded men, he said, with an objective, measurable, and tangible definition of evil:

Now the deeds of the flesh are evident, which are: immorality, impurity, sensuality, idolatry, sorcery, enmities, strife, jealousy, outbursts of anger, disputes, dissensions, factions, envying, drunkenness, carousing, and things like these, of which I forewarn you just as I have forewarned you that those who practice such things shall not inherit the kingdom of God (Galatians 5:19-21).

Gregory Palamas, the greatest Eastern theologian of the day, likewise answered, saying, "The Church has no option," but to "apply the unerring, unwavering Standard" against all "concepts and notions that challenge the Truth."[3] Evil was not a matter of degree, he argued, it was "knowable and definable":[4]

There are six things which the Lord hates, yes, seven which are an abomination to Him: haughty eyes, a lying tongue, and hands that shed innocent blood, a heart that devises wicked plans, feet that run rapidly to evil, a false witness who utters lies, and one who spreads strife among brothers (Proverbs 6:16-19).

Both Bernard and Gregory determined to expose these Scripturally-defined evils, and before long were met with great success. The cults quickly lost momentum and popularity. Because they did not hesitate to objectively identify evil, and because they earnestly contended for the faith, Bernard and Gregory not only were able to turn back the rising tide of error in their day, they were able to usher in an era of spiritual revival and cultural renaissance as well.[5]

The cults did not disappear, however. They simply went underground, waiting for a better day, a moment in the sun. That moment seemed to come in the seventeenth and eighteenth centuries. The old Cathari cults resurfaced among Vienna's literati, in Paris' Palais Royale, and at London's Fabiata. Variously called Rosicrucianism, Free Masonry, Unity, and Theosophy, the old sects found ready acceptance with social revolutionaries and activists.

By the nineteenth and twentieth centuries, the cults held an honored and tenured place among Liberals on the cutting edge of anti-Christian crusades. Hitler, Lenin, and Stalin were all fascinated and enamored by their rituals and philosophies.[6]

H. G. Wells, Bertrand Russell, and George Bernard Shaw all dabbled in their eclectic esoterica.[7] And, not surprisingly, Margaret Sanger accepted their tenents and practiced their ethics as well.[8] She was an avid Rosicrucian and a dues-paying member of Unity.[9]

The Light of Day

It is no coincidence that the extremism, brutality, excessiveness, and promiscuity of Planned Parenthood and its various programs so directly matches that of the Cathari. Planned Parenthood is little more than an institutional incarnation of Margaret's faith.

It is also no coincidence that the objective standard that Bernard and Gregory applied to the cults is just as relevant today as it was then. Virtually every major dogma of those heretical sects is a plank in the Planned Parenthood philosophical platform: promiscuity, greed, deception, revolution, socialism, abortion, sorcery,[10] birth limitation, and materialism.

Bernard and Gregory knew that such things were *evil* in the thirteenth-century. They are no less *evil* in the twentieth.

To expose such evil is a Christian duty (Luke 17:3). To rebuke sin and admonish error is never an option (2 Timothy 2:4). Instead, it is an obligation (Titus 2:15). Modeled by Christ before His disciples (Luke 9:41), and before the world (John 6:26), it is like bearing testimony, an essential aspect of true discipleship (Hebrews 12:5). It was openly practiced by the Apostles Paul (Romans 15:14), James (James 5:1-6), Peter (2 Peter 2:1-22), John (3 John 9-12), and Jude (Jude 4-23). And it has been responsible for many of the Church's great revivals throughout history.[11]

Evil must be exposed.

Planned Parenthood must be exposed.

But exposing evil is not a thing to be taken lightly. It is a serious matter.

When the Apostle Paul was hounded day in and day out by a demonic medium, he refrained from acting hastily or rashly (Acts 16:16-17). Finally, after "many days" had passed, he confronted the evil, exorcising the woman (Acts 16:18).

Why had he waited so long? Because he knew that evil was nothing to be trifled with (Ephesians 6:10-18). To bring consummate darkness to the light of day is no mean feat (Matthew 17:21).

Confronting evil is not the least bit trivial. It is not a matter of persuasion. It is not best left to education. It is not, after all, a dispassionate discussion of concepts, ideas, and philosophies. It is war. It is real. It is serious. And it is deadly.

It is a war in which opponents are disarmed (Colossians 2:15), captives are taken (2 Corinthians 10:5), and casualties are exacted (1 Peter 5:8). It is a war in which commissions are extended (Mark 6:15), ambassadors are engaged (2 Corinthians 5:20), weapons are dispensed (2 Corinthians 10:4), strategies are formulated (Revelation 5:1-8), espionage is exposed (Acts 20:29-30), battle cries are sounded (1 Corinthians 14:8), and victories are won (1 John 5:4). It is a war more devastating than any other war, where strongholds are demolished and fortresses are destroyed (2 Corinthians 10:4-5). It demands special precautions (2 Corinthians 10:7), special provisions (2 Corinthians 10:3), and special prescriptions (Ephesians 6:11).

Both Bernard and Gregory understood this only too well. Bernard argued that men should not even *think* about confronting "the crafty, impure, vile, loathsome, and alien spirit of evil" without first "clothing themselves in the holy illumination of righteous *character*."[12]

Gregory asserted that "to oppose wickedness while yet unconsecrated is the fool's bane."[13] Spiritual warfare demands "spiritual armor," he said, "an armor bestowed from above by grace, appropriated from below by faith, secured from within by *character*."[14]

Like the evil they opposed, the *character* that Bernard and Gregory esteemed was objective, measurable, and tangible. It was "knowable and definable."[15]

Again, it was not coincidence that both Bernard and Gregory challenged their followers with the same exhortation from Scripture,[16] echoing the Apostle Paul: "Be on the alert, stand firm in the faith, act like men, be strong. Let all that you do be done in love" (1 Corinthians 16:13-14).

Alertness, steadfastness, courage, strength, and love: these are the character traits that Bernard and Gregory believed were essential to successfully confront the Cathari in the thirteenth-century. No doubt they are the same character traits essential to successfully confront the Cathari's progeny, Planned Parenthood, in our own day.

Alertness

If we are to expose the evil of Planned Parenthood, we must be sober, watchful, alert, and informed. This is a cornerstone of Christian character.

We are all called to watch over ourselves (Revelation 3:2-3). We are to watch over our relationships (Exodus 34:12), watch over our hearts (Proverbs 4:23), watch over our lips (Psalm 141:3), watch over the paths of our feet (Proverbs 4:26), and watch over our moral conduct. We are to be alert to the call of Christ (Ephesians 5:14), the judgment of Christ (Micah 7:7), and the coming of Christ (Matthew 24:42-43).

We are to be sober in spiritual warfare (Ephesians 6:18) and sober in prayer (Colossians 4:2).

We are to be sober, watchful, and alert in all things, at all times, and in all places so that we can be wise to the snares of our enemies and so that we can avoid the near occasion of temptation and sin (1 Peter 5:8).

> So then let us not sleep as others do, but let us be alert and sober (1 Thessalonians 5:6).

> Awake, awake, put on strength, O arm of the Lord; awake as in the days of old, the generations of long ago. Was it not Thou Who cut Rahab in pieces, Who pierced the dragon? (Isaiah 51:9).

> Take heed, keep on the alert; for you do not know when the appointed time is. It is like a man, away on a journey, who upon leaving his house and putting his slaves in charge, assigning to each one his task, also commanded the doorkeeper to stay on the alert. Therefore, be on the alert—for you do not know when the master of the house is coming, whether in the evening, at midnight, at cockcrowing, or in the morning—lest he come suddenly and find you asleep. And what I say to you I say to all, "Be on the alert!" (Mark 13:33-37).

Christians need to be aware of what is going on. They need to be informed.

Aimee Kuiper is a volunteer at an abortion alternatives center sponsored by her Church. But just two years ago, she was an avid supporter of Planned Parenthood. "I donated money, volunteered my time, and used my influence to spread their programs in the schools," she told me. "As stupid as this may sound, I was just ignorant of the facts. I didn't know what was going on. Most people don't. I'm convinced that most people would be shocked beyond belief if they could ever find out what's really going on in our schools and at Planned Parenthood's clinics. I guess, in a way, it's a character flaw that they aren't more alert. I know it was for me."

"Through knowledge the righteous are delivered" (Proverbs 11:9), but they are "exiled for the lack of knowledge" (Isaiah 5:13).

If knowledge of the truth does not proliferate, a society is doomed (Hosea 4:6). The educational system cannot convey that knowledge. And the established media will not. The fact is, "the senseless have no knowledge" (Psalm 92:6), "fools shun knowledge" (Proverbs 1:29), and "the ungodly hate knowledge" (Proverbs 1:29). If Christians are not sober, watchful, and alert, actively disseminating accurate information about Planned Parenthood, *no one* will.

It is crucial, then, that we nurture this character trait in our lives. We are to seek knowledge (Proverbs 8:10). We are to store it up (Proverbs 10:14). And we are to preserve it (Malachi 2:7).

We are to apply our minds to know the truth (Proverbs 22:17). We are to apply our hearts to receive it (Proverbs 23:12). And we are to apply our lives to spread it (Proverbs 15:7).

But how are we supposed to obtain that knowledge?

First, and foremost, we need to study the wellspring of knowledge, the treasure-trove of knowledge, the Bible. We need to understand its statutes, commands, and decrees. We need to grasp its dictates, mandates, and commissions. We need its insight, its wisdom, and its inspiration. We cannot hope to nurture Christian character in our lives if we do not daily read it, study it, meditate on it, memorize it, and cherish it.

Second, we need to discover the wealth of knowledge handed down from generation to generation in Church History. There is no need for us to reinvent the wheel. The righteous men and women who have gone before us faced virtually every situation that we will ever face. They fought virtually every fight. They confronted virtually every evil. Amazingly, their wisdom, their insight, and their understanding is still available. (Ephesians 4:17) Through their letters, books, tracts, confessions, treatises, dogmas, liturgies, prayers, apologies, and commentaries, they can speak to us today. Athanasius, Basil, Chrysostom, Augustine, Cabasilas, Cyril Lucarius, Calvin, Spurgeon, Chesterton, Schmemann, and Schaeffer: they can all equip us for alertness if only we will take the effort to seek their counsel by reading their works.

Third, we need to pass along to others the knowledge we've obtained. With knowledge comes responsibility. We need to teach Sunday School classes in our Churches. We need to print up small circulation newsletters for our neighborhoods. We need to teach extension classes at local schools, colleges, and universities. We need to write letters to the editor. We need to inform our magistrates and leaders. We need to conduct home Bible studies and issue-oriented discussions. In other words, we need to get the word out. Once we've learned the facts, we need to get those facts widely disseminated.

Fourth, we need to develop local information networks. Whenever a development occurs in the legislature, or in the schools, or in the media, a local network needs to spring into action. Telephone trees, photocopied notices, computer bulletins, cable TV flashes, radio announcements, newsletter distribution, and direct mail drops can all be utilized if a network has been set up ahead of time. We can then build a grassroots response. A number of "pro-life hotlines" have been established around the country, but we need many, many more.[17] There are also more than two thousand *Right to Life* organizations and committees scattered across the nation, but again, we need more. Planned Parenthood's howitzers are very effective against the slow and cumbersome tanks of the federal bureaucracy and the pro-life institutions. But they are useless against a swarm of mosquitoes.

Fifth, we need to develop national information networks. This is the information age. We have been blessed with a proliferation of information technologies. There is no need for us to depend on the national media any longer. Sadly, Christians have, by and large, failed to realize that. We have not yet capitalized on those technologies. But, of course, one or two brave pioneers could quickly and easily turn things around. For instance, *Conservative Digest* and the *Free Congress Foundation* have recently combined their efforts to produce a high-tech data distribution system. With their *American Press International* wire service, daily updates of executive, legislative, judicial, and bureaucratic actions can be downloaded onto any IBM compatible computer using existing modern technology.[18] *National Right to Life* also has an extensive information network utilizing both print and electronic media around the country in all fifty states.

Knowledge produces endurance (Proverbs 28:2). It multiplies resources (Proverbs 24:4). It provides encouragement (Proverbs 2:10). It releases power (Proverbs 24:5), joy (Ecclesiastes 2:26), prudence (Proverbs 13:16), protection (Acts 20:31), and security (Ecclesiastes 7:12).

Confronting the evil of Planned Parenthood demands the sturdy advantage of Christian watchfulness. It requires the informed stamina of Christian soberness. It necessitates the righteous character of Christian alertness.

> Therefore, gird your minds for action, keep sober in spirit, fix your hope completely on the grace to be brought to you at the revelation of Jesus Christ. As obedient children, do not be conformed to the former lusts which were yours in your ignorance, but like the Holy One Who called you, be holy yourselves also in all your behavior . . . (1 Peter 1:13-15).

Steadfastness

If we are to expose the evil of Planned Parenthood, we must also be faithful, steadfast, and unwavering. Like alertness, this is a cornerstone of Christian character.

We are all called to stand firm in the faith (2 Thessalonians 2:25). We are to be steadfast in the midst of suffering (1 Peter 5:9), in the midst of strange teaching (Hebrews 13:9), and in times of trying circumstances (James 1:12).

We are to be steadfast in good works (Galatians 6:9), in enduring love (Hosea 6:4), in conduct (Philippians 1:27), in decision-making (1 Kings 18:21), and in absolute loyalty to the Lord God (Proverbs 24:21).

> Therefore, my beloved brethren, be steadfast, immovable, always abounding in the work of the Lord, knowing that your toil is not in vain in the Lord (1 Corinthians 15:58).

It was for freedom that Christ set us free; therefore keep standing firm and do not be subject again to a yoke of slavery (Galatians 5:1).

Nevertheless, the righteous shall hold to his way, and he who
has clean hands shall grow stronger and stronger (Job 17:9).

Steadfastness is not an attribute that we can simply conjure
up by sheer force of will. It demands a long-term *commitment*.

Marsha Gatlin is a member of her local school board and has
been for more than a decade. She first ran for the seat when her
teenage daughter brought home several Planned Parenthood
booklets from school one day.

"I made up my mind then and there," she told me, "that I was
going to do something about the moral plague that was infecting
our children. My children. Well, I'll tell you, it's not been easy.
It's been one fight after another. Ten years of conflict. But I'm
confident that I've been able to make a difference. So, I'm gonna
continue to hang in there. I'm not about to back down on my
commitment now."

That kind of commitment is what the Bible calls *vision*. It is
the willingness to sacrifice unceasingly for the Gospel's sake. It is
the willingness to bypass immediate gratification, instant satisfaction, and momentary recognition for the good of the future.
For the good of Christ's Kingdom. Where *faith* is "the assurance
of things hoped for" (Hebrews 11:1), *vision* is "the hope of things
assured of." Where *faith* is "the conviction of things not seen"
(Hebrews 11:1), *vision* is "the seeing of those convictions."

Visionary men and women are confident, assured, and undaunted even in the face of calamity and catastrophe, because
they can see beyond the present. They can remain sure, secure,
and steadfast, because they have a broader perspective. They
can look past petty defeats and setbacks. They can plot and plan
far in advance of the day of vindication and victory. They have a
future-orientation. They believe in the idea of progress.

Though that progress may come in very small stages over
very long epochs, visionary men know that it eventually *will*
come. They believe in its inevitability.

And so they remain faithful. Toiling day in and day out, year
in and year out. Never despising "the day of small beginnings"
(Zechariah 4:10).

This is a special legacy of Christianity in modern civilization. It was this Biblical conception of hope, promise, patience, assurance, victory, steadfastness, advancement, dominion, confidence, faith, conviction, and commitment that set the modern world on its course of cultural, technological, and sociological progress.

Vision catalyzes and empowers faith. It is vision that releases faith from the safety zone of irrelevancy to the war zone of cultural transformation.

It was only by exercising visionary faith that believers in past ages were able to "conquer kingdoms, perform acts of righteousness, obtain promises, shut the mouths of lions, quench the power of fire, escape the edge of the sword, and from weakness be made strong" (Hebrews 11:33-34).

Just as Josiah remained steadfast (2 Kings 22:2), just as David remained steadfast (1 Samuel 17:45-49), just as Daniel remained steadfast (Daniel 6:5-11), and just as Job (Job 23:11), Joseph (Genesis 39:7-16), John (Acts 4:19-20), and Paul (Acts 20:24) all remained steadfast, so we are to remain undaunted and immovable in our devotion to truth, justice, and righteousness (Psalm 119:105-112). Theirs was the visionary determination to adhere to God's standards, to uphold God's statutes, to apply God's principles, and to enforce God's decrees. If we are to have any success whatsoever in confronting the evil of Planned Parenthood, we must develop that same kind of vision.

But how? How are we supposed to inculcate that kind of unswerving faith?

First, we need to feed our faith. Vision demands nurture. Commitment necessitates growth. And the only way we can obtain these things is through a dynamic and vital spiritual life. Through worship, personal devotion, and fellowship, we must strengthen and bolster our steadfastness. We must draw vitality and confidence from the "very great and precious promises" of the Word (2 Peter 1:4). We must draw encouragement and stamina from the "assembling together" of the saints (Hebrews 10:25). We must draw life and hope from the glorious presence of the royal throne room (Revelation 5:1-14).

Second, we need to develop habits of personal evangelism and discipleship. The best way to "keep the faith" is to *share* it. Christ commissioned *all* His followers to become "fishers of men" (Matthew 4:19). We should constantly share the Gospel with the lost (Colossians 4:5). We should constantly build up the saved (Colossians 3:16-17). And we should constantly spur on the inactive (Hebrews 10:24-25). At work, at home, at Church, at school, around the neighborhood, with family members, with friends, and with casual acquaintances, we should be incessantly enlisting men for the Kingdom and for the work of the Kingdom. We should build our faith by sharing our faith.

Third, we should undertake one or two projects and see them through to completion. Christians are notorious for never finishing what they begin. And there is nothing that stymies and stultifies vision more than that. We should pick out one or two long-term projects that we know we can remain faithful to, and then actually go the whole distance. Tackle the school board, or close down the school-based clinic, or defund Planned Parenthood's local tax-paid abortion clinic, or boycott businesses that support affiliate programs, or maintain a regular picket vigil, or volunteer at an alternative center, or pledge financial support to a pro-life ministry, or distribute appropriate literature, or install a speakers bureau at the local high school: We need to choose a battle and fight it to the end. That is vision made practical. That is steadfastness made tangible.

Confronting the evil of Planned Parenthood demands the undaunted vision of Christian faithfulness. It requires the unwavering commitment of Christian vigilance. It necessitates the righteous character of Christian steadfastness.

> Therefore, my beloved brethren whom I long to see, my joy and crown, so stand firm in the Lord, my beloved (Philippians 4:1).

Courage

If we are to expose the evil of Planned Parenthood, we must also be valiant, courageous, and brave. Like alertness and steadfastness, this is a cornerstone of Christian character.

We are all called to be fearless in the Lord (Isaiah 12:2). We are to be brave in the face of our enemies (Deuteronomy 31:6), and brave in the midst of chastisement (Job 5:17-24).

We are to demonstrate valor in our obedience to the Word of God (Joshua 23:6), for the sake of His people (2 Samuel 10:12), and in all our service (1 Chronicles 28:20). Because we know that God is sovereign, we are to be courageous (2 Chronicles 32:7). Because we know that God is ever present, we are to be courageous (Psalm 118:6). Because we know that God comprehends all things, we are to be courageous (Psalm 139:13-19). We are to take heart and remain certain even in the face of terrifying circumstances (Psalm 91:5) or utter dismay (Joshua 10:25).

> The wicked flee when no one is pursuing, but the righteous are bold as a lion (Proverbs 28:1).
>
> God is our refuge and strength, a very present help in trouble. Therefore we will not fear, though the earth should change, and though the mountains slip into the heart of the sea; though its waters roar and foam, though the mountains quake at its swelling pride (Psalm 46:1-3).
>
> For God has not given us a spirit of timidity, but of power and love and discipline (2 Timothy 1:7).

Courage means standing against the tide, struggling for right to the bitter end, and investing our all-in-all for the cause of the Kingdom.

Mark Dury is a high school senior who has had to learn about courage the hard way. "I had a teacher that constantly tried to bait me," he said. "She desperately wanted to shake my faith. The thing was, she was a really popular teacher, so whenever I tried to oppose some of the stuff she was doing—like showing our class hard-core porn and stuff—I caught a lot of grief from the other kids. When I found out that she was counseling girls to go to Planned Parenthood for birth control, well, that was just too much. I went to the administration about it. That only made the persecution increase. But, hey, that's inevitable. I've gotta stand up for what is right. There's no way I can compromise."

The fact is, "all those who desire to live godly lives *will* be persecuted" (2 Timothy 3:12). There is no way around it. Persecution is inevitable.

Jesus explained this fact to His disciples saying:

> If the world hates you, you know that it has hated Me before it hated you. If you were of the world, the world would love its

own; but because you are not of the world, but I chose you out of the world, therefore the world hates you. Remember the word that I said to you, "A slave is not greater than his master." If they persecuted Me, they will also persecute you; if they kept My word, they will keep yours also (John 15:18-20).

We need not be disheartened by this. Persecution does not just bring with it pain and privation; it also brings great purpose and promise. It brings with it the hope of *resurrection*.

"God causes all things to work together for good to those who love God, to those who are called according to His purpose" (Romans 8:28). When we refuse to compromise, we may risk rejection or rebuke. But we know all the while that rejection and rebuke become *opportunities* under the sovereign direction of God Almighty.

Joseph risked everything he had by refusing to compromise his obedience to God (Genesis 39:7-16). As a result, he was thrown into prison (Genesis 39:19-20). But God used his prison experience for good. It became the first stage of dominion for him. It was not long before Joseph was raised up out of the depths to rule over the whole land (Genesis 41:37-45). Because he remained courageous and uncompromising, he emerged victorious.

David, too, risked all that he had by refusing to compromise his obedience to God (1 Samuel 18:1-6). As a result, he was cast into exile (1 Samuel 19:11-18). But God used his exile experience for good. It became the first stage of dominion for him. It was not long before David was raised up out of the depths to rule over the whole land (2 Samuel 2:4). Because he remained courageous and uncompromising, he emerged victorious.

Similarly, Daniel risked all that he had by refusing to compromise his obedience to God (Daniel 6:10). As a result, he was thrown into the lions' den (Daniel 6:16-17). But God used his lions' den experience for good. It became the first stage of dominion for him. It was not long before Daniel was raised up out of the depths to rule over the whole land (Daniel 6:23-28). Because he remained courageous and uncompromising, he emerged victorious.

The early Christians also risked all that they had by refusing to compromise their obedience to God (Acts 4:19-20). As a result, they were thrown into prison (Acts 5:19). But God used their prison experience for good. It became the first stage of dominion for them. It was not long before they were raised up out of the depths to rule over the whole land (Acts 19:26). Because they remained courageous and uncompromising, they emerged victorious.

This same pattern runs all throughout the Bible. It underlies the stories of Abraham (Genesis 12:10-20), Esther (Esther 3:6-15; 8:1-7), Job (Job 1:13-22; 42:10-15), Jeremiah (Jeremiah 37:11-16; 39:11-12), Elijah (1 Kings 17:1-16; 18:20-46), Hosea (Hosea 1:2-9; 3:1-5), Micaiah (1 Kings 22:7-12, 24-40), and the Apostle Paul (Philippians 1:7; 3:8-16). Each of these heroes of the faith witnessed the *resurrection* power of Almighty God. Each of them saw the most difficult and oppressive circumstances transformed into glorious victory. Each of them went from death to life, from bondage to liberty, and from prison to promise. Each of them mirrored and illumined the Gospel by their great courage:

> For I delivered to you as of first importance what I also received, that Christ died for our sins according to the Scriptures, and that He was buried, and that He was raised on the third day according to the Scriptures . . . (1 Corinthians 15:3-4).

Jesus refused to compromise (Luke 22:42; Philippians 2:5-8). As a result, He was abandoned to the shame of the cross and the prison of the grave (Matthew 16:21). But God used both the cross and the grave, the shame and the prison, for good. They became the first stage of dominion for Him. On the third day, Jesus arose out of the depths to rule and reign over the whole land (Philippians 2:9-11). That is the very essence of the Gospel.

When we remain courageous, facing persecution head on, walking "by faith and not by sight" (2 Corinthians 5:7), we affirm the very essence of the Gospel. We are also invincible.

So, how are we to nurture such courage?

First, we need to develop a personal program of obedience. We need to demonstrate courage in the smaller arenas of life before we attempt to conquer the world—or Planned Parenthood. We need to show an individual willingness to implement God's plan for marriage, childrearing, financial responsibility, business integrity, interpersonal ethics, and moral uprightness. We need to show ourselves faithful in the small things before God can give us responsibility over the big things (Luke 16:10).

Second, we need to develop leadership recruitment and training programs. We must find the willing, train the eager, and encourage the hesitant. We need to scour the hedgerows and beat the bushes (Luke 14:21-23). Courage is both taught and caught. It is, thus, our responsibility to gather the next wave of Christian warriors, training them for valor while, at the same time, modeling valor for them.

Third, we need to transform our Churches into both hives of activity and havens of rest. We should be equipped to do the *whole* work of the ministry at Church (Ephesians 4:12). That means that picketers for the local Planned Parenthood should be enlisted, trained, and mobilized there. That means that volunteers for the local alternatives center should be encouraged and commissioned there. But the Church should also be a place where the courageous can find sanctuary and take refuge. It should be a place where we can find refreshment. That kind of balance can only be found in true worship.

Confronting the evil of Planned Parenthood demands the unflinching confidence of Christian valor. It requires the uncompromising commitment of Christian bravery. It necessitates the righteous character of Christian courage.

> Be very firm, then, to keep and do all that is written in the book
> of the law of Moses, so that you may not turn aside from it to
> the right or to the left. . . . But you are to cling to the Lord
> your God, as you have done to this day (Joshua 23:6, 8).

Strength
If we are to expose the evil of Planned Parenthood, we must also be mighty, stalwart, dynamic, and strong. Like alertness, steadfastness, and courage, this is a cornerstone of Christian character.

We are all called to be strong in Christ (2 Corinthians 10:3-6). God has not given us a spirit of weakness, but of power (2 Timothy 1:7).

The Gospel comes in power (1 Thessalonians 1:5). The Kingdom comes in power (1 Corinthians 4:19). And salvation comes in power (Romans 1:16). It is a power that the wicked can never know (Matthew 22:29). But every Believer is already anointed with it (Luke 24:49).

We have been endowed with the strength to witness (Acts 1:8), to labor (Colossians 1:29), and to do every good thing (Philippians 4:13).

Christ has given us all the strength of His might (Ephesians 1:9) and the strength of His grace (2 Timothy 2:1).

> He gives strength to the weary, and to him who lacks might He increases power. Though youths grow weary and tired, and vigorous young men stumble badly, yet those who wait for the Lord will gain new strength; they will mount up with wings like eagles, they will run and not get tired, they will walk and not become weary (Isaiah 40:29-31).

> And He has said to me, "My grace is sufficient for you, for power is perfected in weakness." Most gladly, therefore, I will rather boast about my weaknesses, that the power of Christ may dwell in me. Therefore I am well content with weaknesses, with insults, with distresses, with persecutions, with difficulties, for Christ's sake; for when I am weak, then I am strong (2 Corinthians 12:9-10).

> Finally, be strong in the Lord, and in the strength of His might. Put on the full armor of God, that you may be able to stand firm against the schemes of the devil (Ephesians 6:10-11).

Strength means harnessing the excellent power of Christ to confront and captivate the powers and the principalities and the rulers of this poor, fallen world.

Nicholas Brooks is a lobbyist for a pro-life network in a state noted for its very liberal stance toward abortion. "Planned Parenthood has an easy time of it in this state, I'm afraid," he told me. "Their funding levels are actually higher than some state agencies. I suppose I could let that get me down. But I believe strongly that, despite the fact that we've got the deck almost completely stacked against us here, we've put together an excellent statewide organization. We're here to demonstrate the power of the Living God, to testify boldly of His great mercies. We do that, not by taking over, necessarily, but by demonstrating excellence and ability and skillfulness day in and day out. God's power is made perfect in our weakness when we display that weakness with precision and excellence."

As God's representatives before men (2 Corinthians 5:20), we are to "proclaim His excellencies" (1 Peter 2:9). But our proclamation must not merely be "in word or with tongue, but in deed and with truth" (1 John 3:18). We proclaim His mighty excellence by *our* mighty excellence. In everything we do and in everything we say, we are to manifest Him Who has "called us by His own glory and excellence" (2 Peter 1:3). As we follow after Him (Matthew 4:19), as we walk in His footsteps (1 Peter 2:21), and as we imitate His attributes (1 Peter 1:16), *excellence* is to be the hallmark of our strength.

God expects nothing less.

He Who long ago demanded excellent sacrifices (Malachi 1:8-10), excellent artistry (Exodus 28:2), and excellent service (Proverbs 12:4), has in no way altered His standards of discipleship. We are to live lives marked by moral excellence (2 Peter 1:5). We are to keep our behavior excellent at all times (1 Peter 1:1-2). Our minds are to dwell constantly on excellence (Philippians 4:8). We are to walk in the way of excellence (1 Corinthians 12:31), manifesting cultural excellence (Genesis 1:28), economic excellence (Proverbs 31:10-31), spiritual excellence (Philippians 1:10), and evangelistic excellence (Matthew 28:18-20). The power of God cannot be expressed through mediocrity and triviality.

The great God of excellence and power has called us to be men and women of excellence and power (1 Thessalonians 4:1, 10).

And how is this excellence to be nurtured and manifested?

First, we need to determine just what our gifts and talents are. We need to discipline and harness those abilities for the Kingdom. Focusing our energies on those things that we are qualified to handle enables us to do those things with excellence. We are able to accomplish more. We are able to attain fulfillment. And we are able to manifest our strength in Christ. God's power is made manifest.

Second, we need to make sure that whatever tasks we determine to undertake, we take pains to perform to the *best* of our abilities. Sloppy, shoddy work does nothing to advance the cause of Christ. There is really no excuse for it. Each of us has areas of expertise that we can consecrate for the Kingdom. Whatever those areas are, we need to concentrate on heightening our skillfulness and perfecting our abilities.

Third, we need to support the causes and ministries that are really accomplishing something.[19]

The scandalous goings on in TV evangelism have only served to underscore the need to carefully target our giving and to support the works of genuine excellence. Ministries that are little more than fundraising operations or personality cults should be avoided at all costs. Causes that do little more than stoke the star-maker machinery are worse than worthless. Time, resources, and money are in precious short supply. They should be distributed only to those ministries that actually manifest the excellent power of God.

Fourth, we need to promote and support youngsters that show genuine promise. Scholarships must be secured for Christian students in journalism, medicine, economics, political science, philosophy, history, education, fine arts, biology, and business. And support must be developed for those few institutions that are actually taking those young, impressionable students and turning them into excellent champions for Christ, dynamic activists for the Kingdom, and mighty workers for life and truth.

Confronting the evil of Planned Parenthood demands the unbending fortitude of Christian might. It requires the excellent dynamic of Christian power. It necessitates the righteous character of Christian strength.

> For this reason, I bow my knees before the Father, from whom every family in heaven and on earth derives its name, that He would grant you, according to the riches of His glory, to be strengthened with power through His Spirit in the inner man; so that Christ may dwell in your hearts through faith; and that you, being rooted and grounded in love, may be able to comprehend with all the saints what is the breadth and length and height and depth, and to know the love of Christ which surpasses knowledge, that you may be filled up to all the fullness of God. Now to Him who is able to do exceeding abundantly beyond all that we ask or think, according to the power that works within us, to Him be the glory in the church and in Christ Jesus to all generations forever and ever. Amen (Ephesians 3:14-21).

Love

If we are to expose the evil of Planned Parenthood, we must be respectful, affectionate, loving, and tenderhearted. Like alertness, steadfastness, courage, and strength, it is a cornerstone of Christian character.

We are all called to be long-suffering in love and tenderness (Philippians 1:3-11). We are to show love to strangers (Deuteronomy 10:19), as well as neighbors (Leviticus 19:18). We are to show love to enemies (Matthew 5:44), as well as brethren (1 Peter 3:8).

In all things, at all times, we are to be examples of love (1 Timothy 4:12). We are to abound in love (Philippians 1:9). We are to walk in love (Ephesians 5:2). We are to comfort one another in love (Titus 3:5), provoke one another in love (Hebrews 10:24), and labor with one another in love (1 Thessalonians 1:3). For love is the Royal Law (James 2:8).

> And so, as those who have been chosen of God, holy and beloved, put on a heart of compassion, kindness, humility, gentleness and patience; bearing with one another, and forgiving each other, whoever has a complaint against anyone; just as the Lord forgave you, so also should you. And beyond all these things put on love, which is the perfect bond of unity (Colossians 3:12-14).

Behold, how good and how pleasant it is for brothers to dwell together in unity! It is like the precious oil upon the head, coming down upon the beard, even Aaron's beard, coming down upon the edge of his robes. It is like the dew of Hermon, coming down upon the mountains of Zion; for there the Lord commanded the blessing — life forever (Psalm 133:1-3).

> A new commandment I give to you, that you love one another, even as I have loved you, that you also love one another. By this all men will know that you are My disciples, if you have love for one another (John 13:34-35).

Jan Oberholtzer is a sidewalk counselor. Every Saturday, she spends about five hours talking with girls outside a Planned Parenthood abortuary, providing them with information that they would never receive inside the clinic.

"Most of the girls have never been given *any* information about fetal development or fetal pain," she told me. "They know absolutely nothing about the medical risks of abortion. They are totally misinformed about everything from payment schedules to liability release forms. So, I'm out here to try to bring a little balance to the situation. Sometimes it's really frustrating. I go home and just weep for the girls that get sucked in and believe the lies. I have to keep reminding myself that I'm here out of obedience. Otherwise, I don't think I could do this week after week. I'm here out of obedience. And that is the highest love of all."

Love is not just a feeling. It is not a warm and fuzzy affection deep inside our hearts. Love is something we *do*.

Jesus said that if anyone loves Him, he will keep His commandments (John 14:23). Whoever does not keep the commandments, then, does not have love (John 14:24). Love and obedience are inseparable.

Genuine love can only occur when we do what is right in the sight of the Lord, not turning aside to the right or to the left (2 Kings 22:2). It can only flourish in lives that are forthright in the condemnation of sin (Daniel 4:27), unguarded in the pronouncement of truth (Daniel 5:13-28), and single-minded in adherence to the Word of God (Daniel 6:5).

Love means to hold fast to Scripture (Joshua 23:8), to be immovable from it (1 Corinthians 15:58), and to serve the truth with all our hearts (1 Samuel 12:21-22, 24-25).

So how are we to develop and demonstrate such love?

First, we need to *serve* others. Service is a visible manifestation of obedient love. But it is also a hothouse for the development of obedient love. As we serve, as we obey, our feelings, affections, and desires are brought into line. When we serve girls with crisis pregnancies by providing them with a home and medical care and nurture and sustenance, our love is stirred and substantiated. When we give our time to the local high school, or to the city government, or to the county jury to oppose the encroachment of Planned Parenthood, our love is developed and demonstrated.

Second, we need to pray for the perpetrators of the Planned Parenthood scandal. When we pray for our enemies, our hearts are changed. God answers our prayers by working in our lives as well as theirs. We must pray for the doctors, the lawyers, the administrators, the nurses, the security guards, the receptionists, the secretaries, the bureaucrats, the judges, and the legislators that make the Planned Parenthood juggernaut possible. We must pray both imprecatorily and approbatively. Then, and only then, will a genuine, obedient love permeate our work.

Third, we must work hard at integrating obedient love into our families. Parents are charged by God with the awesome and fearsome responsibility of raising their children up "in the nurture and admonition of the Lord" (Ephesians 6:4). That is not the job of the pastor, the Sunday School teacher, the youth director, the summer camp counselor, the TV evangelist, or the Christian school educator. It is, first and foremost, the job of parents. Thus, it is our job to inculcate prayer habits in our children by actually praying with them. It is our job to establish Bible study disciplines in our children by actually studying with them. It is our job to nurture a commitment to Body life by actually fellowshiping with them. It is our job to confirm a respect for the throne of God by actually worshiping with them. And it is our job to teach them about their bodies and their feelings by not only talking with them but by actually fasting with them, feasting with them, and displaying self-control in their midst.[20] *That* is obedient love.

Confronting the evil of Planned Parenthood demands the respectful commitment of Christian tenderness. It requires the obedient long-suffering of Christian tenderness. It necessitates the righteous character of Christian love.

> If I speak with the tongues of men and of angels, but do not have love, I have become a noisy gong or a clanging cymbal. And if I have the gift of prophecy, and know all mysteries and all knowledge; and if I have all faith, so as to remove mountains, but do not have love, I am nothing. And if I give all my possessions to feed the poor, and if I deliver my body to be burned, but do not have love, it profits me nothing. Love is patient, love is kind, and is not jealous; love does not brag and is not arrogant, does not act unbecomingly; it does not seek its own, is not provoked, does not take into account a wrong suffered, does not rejoice in unrighteousness, but rejoices with the truth; bears all things, believes all things, hopes all things, endures all things. Love never fails . . . (1 Corinthians 13:1-8).

Character in Context

Christian character traits are essential. Alertness, stead-fastness, courage, strength, and love are indispensable. Confronting the evil of Planned Parenthood would be impossible without them.

But, by themselves, even those character traits are not enough. They must be placed in their proper context. And that context is the Church.

The Church has become the spurned and neglected step-child of the modern era. It is perceived as being moss-backed and archaic. Or awkward and irrelevant. It is regarded as little more than a water-boy to the game of life.

Part of the reason for this horribly low estimation of the Church is due to the fact that the Church has always *limped* through history.[21] Men look at the all too evident, all too apparent, sometimes even glaring, weaknesses of Christ's Bride and just assume that its lame and crippled state is ample justification for dismissing its importance.

The fact is, though, the Church's limp is actually a *confirmation* of its power, relevance, and significance.

After the Fall, God told Satan that the Righteous Deliverer, Jesus Christ, would crush his head. But God also said that, in the process, the heel of the Lord would be bruised (Genesis 3:15). The limp, then, that Christ's Body displays is actually a sign of great victory, not a sign of defeat or incompetence. It is an emblem of triumph.

This reality is portrayed all throughout the Bible. For instance, when Jacob, the father of Israel's twelve tribes, wrestled through the night at Penial, he limped ever after as a sign that he had prevailed (Genesis 32:31).

The Apostle Paul, father of the Gentile Church, was given a thorn in the flesh. Since thorns grow along the ground, Paul was pricked—at least symbolically—in the foot. It kept him limping in the eyes of men (2 Corinthians 12:7). Even so, it was in this weakness that Christ's power was affirmed and perfected (2 Corinthians 12:9).

Thus, when the Church limps through history, as believers we need not be frustrated or discouraged. On the contrary, we should be encouraged that God's Word is sure and true. For victory has, indeed, already been won.

The reality is that whatever the Church does or doesn't do directly affects the course of civilization. It determines the flow of historical events (Revelation 5-6).

The Church has the keys to the Kingdom (Matthew 16:19). It has the power to bind and to loose (Matthew 18:18). It has the authority to prevail over the very gates of hell (Matthew 16:18). It is, thus, the Church—not governments or movements or causes or organizations—that will determine our destiny and the destiny of our world.

Thus, all our efforts to confront the evil of Planned Parenthood must be placed in the context of the Church. Even if we are alert, steadfast, brave, strong, and loving, if we separate ourselves from the Church, we are doomed to frustration. There simply cannot be any "Lone Rangers."

The reason for this is three-fold:

First, it is the Church that offers us the source of life. It offers the Waters of Life (Revelation 22:17), the Bread of Life (John 6:31, 1 Corinthians 11:24), and the Word of Life (1 John 1:1). The sacramental ministry of the Church is our *only* source for these grace provisions. There is nowhere else that we can turn for these "medicines of immortality."[22] They effect a tangible offering *to* God, a consecration *before* God, a communion *with* God, and a transformation *in* God. Thus, they actually readjust us to the ultimate reality, making our alertness, steadfastness, courage, strength, and love forces to be reckoned with.

Second, the Church offers us accountability and discipline. Sin cripples any work. Whenever sin is casually tolerated, all our efforts are defiled (1 Corinthians 5:6-13), evangelism is stifled (1 Corinthians 5:1-5), and victory is denied (Joshua 7:1-15). Only the Church has the authority to discipline heinous sin (Matthew 18:15-20). The purpose of this kind of accountability is, of course, protective and restorative, not defensive or punitive. It is to erect a hedge of responsibility and respectability around our efforts to confront the evil of Planned Parenthood.

Third, the Church offers us a place of rest. When, as God's people, we assemble ourselves together, we are at last able to lie down in green pastures, beside still waters (Psalm 23:2). As we gather around the throne of grace, we are at last able to take refuge and find sanctuary (Psalm 61:1-4). We are able to enter His gates with thanksgiving and His courts with praise (Psalm 100:4). In other words, in the Church, we are able to find rest (Hebrews 4:1-13), restoration (Psalm 19:7), reconciliation (Psalm 32:3-6), and recompense (Psalm 73:15-24).

Without the context of the Church, even the most dynamic Christian character is exposed to atrophy and entropy. But, within that context, our alertness, steadfastness, courage, strength, and love become powerful weapons in our desperate confrontation with the evil of Planned Parenthood.

Conclusion

Nothing can compensate for a lack of integrity and a deficiency of character. Not great wealth. Not access to the masses. Not wild-eyed popularity. Not superb organization. And not mind-boggling power. Just ask the kingpins of the once proud empire of television evangelism.

The collapse of televangelism was not due to the unpopularity of its message, but to the impiety of its messengers. It was not due to the opposition of its enemies, but to the opulence of its allies.

Our efforts for life, liberty, and truth face similar jeopardy.

Without Christian character, all our scheming and dreaming inevitably comes to naught. Without it, we are impotent in the face of wickedness and evil. Without it, we are helpless before the Planned Parenthood juggernaut.

Our picketing is essential. Our lobbying is crucial. Our education is vital. Our voting is imperative. Our activism is momentous. But if we are ever to effectively expose and confront evil, we must develop and demonstrate Godly character.

The worker must one day seize power, in order to erect the new organization of labor; he must push to one side the old politics which uphold the old institutions, if he does not want to suffer the loss of heaven on earth, even as the old Christians did by despising and neglecting it.

Karl Marx

IDOLS FOR DESTRUCTION: A STRATEGY FOR PROPHETS AND PRIESTS

in hoc signo vinces

Sand was blowing in off the desert, carried into the city by freak Santa Ana winds. Carbon arcs, mounted on the roofs of several police cars, threw the cracked roadbed into stark relief and made the sand look like static on a video screen.

Reba Elvin stared at the surreal scene, blinking back her tears. Her husband, her son, her pastor, and her Sunday School teacher had all just been arrested. For praying outside a Planned Parenthood clinic.

"I was in shock," she told me later. "To think that in America you can be handcuffed and dragged off to jail for praying on a sidewalk! It's frightening. Where will all this end?"

Unfortunately for Reba and the members of her small Presbyterian Church, it didn't end that day with a trip to jail. Three days later, several pro-abortion groups, including Planned Parenthood, asked a federal judge to revoke the Church's tax-exempt status, to force the pastor to hand over the Church's files and financial records, and to restrain the Church's members "and all those acting in concert with them" from any further public protests against abortion.[1]

Planned Parenthood's spokeswoman told the press the Church was "in violation of IRS restrictions on political activity by non-profit organizations. So, besides the fact that the pastor and the membership were trespassing on private property and attempting to restrict the constitutional rights of others, they were also transgressing the time-honored . . . wall of separation between Church and State."[2]

But that is not exactly how eye witnesses of the incident reported it. "First of all," Reba told me, "no one was on Planned Parenthood's property. Everyone was on the public sidewalk in front of their building. No one even stepped on the grass. Secondly, no one was attempting to restrict anybody's constitutional rights. The people from the Church were just there to pray — quietly, peaceably, and in order. No one blocked ingress or egress. No one stopped clients from entering if they wanted to. Now really, since when is praying an attempt to restrict somebody's rights? Thirdly, this wall of separation business is nothing more than an attempt to keep Christians out of public life. If we're ever going to adequately deal with groups like Planned Parenthood, we're going to have to put that myth to rest."

Church and State

According to the design for society outlined in the Bible, Church and state are separate institutions.[3] They have separate jurisdictions. They have separate authorities. And they have separate functions.

A balanced social order depends on that kind of institutional differentiation. When any one institution begins to encroach upon another, anarchy and tyranny inevitably result. Checks and balances begin to break down.

Thus, it is important that the state not meddle in the affairs of the Church. That is simply not its concern. The Church is outside of the state's jurisdiction. The framers of the American Constitution recognized this fundamental plank of liberty and, thus, the first article in the Bill of Rights states, "Congress shall make no law respecting an establishment of religion, or prohibiting the free exercise thereof."[4] The state has no authority over the Church and, therefore, must not regulate or interfere in the work of the Church. Local municipalities, and even individual commonwealths, might render support to the Church — as they often did — but never were they to control the Church.[5] Church and state are separate.

Likewise, the Church must not meddle in the affairs of the state. That is simply not its concern. The state is outside of the

Church's jurisdiction. Again, the framers of the American Constitution wanted to protect their fledgling republic from any and all tyrannies: both *statism* — in the form of imperialism, socialism, or democracy; and *oligarchy* — in the form of ecclesiocracy, agathism, or caesaro-papism. The Church has no authority over the state and, therefore, must not regulate or interfere in the work of the state.[6] They are separate.

This, of course, does not mean that Church and state are to have nothing to do with each other. On the contrary, it is essential that they interact and cooperate with each other. They are to balance each other. They are to serve each other. They are to check each other. So, even though they are institutionally separate, their separation is not absolute and exclusive. There is no *wall of separation*. Rather, Church and state are distinct but cooperative. They are separate but interdependent.

The *wall* is a myth.

Joseph Story, perhaps America's foremost nineteenth-century legal historian, underscored this truth in his book on the Constitution saying, "The First Amendment was not intended to withdraw the Christian religion as a whole from the protection of Congress. . . . At the time, the general, if not universal, sentiment in America was that Christianity ought to receive encouragement from the state so far as was compatible with the private rights of conscience and the freedom of worship. . . . Any attempt to level all religions, and to make it a matter of state policy to hold all in utter indifference would have created . . . universal indignation."[7]

The state was to encourage the Church.

At the same time, the Church was to cooperate with and encourage the state. For instance, the Church was to teach the citizenry the Bible, the common standard of law for both Church and state.[8] The Church was to instruct all men and women in the basic principles of godly citizenship and righteous cultural action.[9] The Church was to mobilize the forces of mercy, truth, and justice in times of difficulty or crisis.[10] The Church was to recruit from the ranks of the congregation able men and women for the work of civil service.[11] The Church was to confront evil, expose sin, and denounce injustice whenever and wherever it might be found, public and private, civil and congregational.[12]

The Church was to encourage the magistrates, pray for them, support them, instruct them, and advise them.[13] In other words, the Church was to serve as society's prophet and priest.

The American system was, thus, set up as a decentralized, confederated, and republican social structure.[14] It followed the Biblical order of multiple jurisdictions, separate but cooperating, under the sovereignty of God and the rule of His Law.[15]

The current notion of the *wall of separation* between Church and state is, thus, a far cry from what our Founding Fathers intended.[16] It is, in fact, a denial of the multiplicity of institutions and jurisdictions. It cripples the Church and exalts the state.[17] It asserts the absolute authority of the state and excludes Believers from participation in the cultural, social, and political processes.[18]

The *wall of separation* idea was slow to catch on in our nation. Until the War Between the States erupted, Christianity was universally encouraged at every level of the civil government.[19] Then, in 1861, under the influence of the radical Unitarians, the Northern Union ruled in the courts that the civil sphere should remain "indifferent" to the Church.[20] After the war, that judgment was imposed on the Southern Confederation as well.[21] One hundred years later, in 1961, the erosion of the American system of checks and balances continued with the judicial declaration that all faiths were to be "leveled" by the state.[22] By 1963, the courts were protecting and favoring a new religion — *humanism* had been declared a religion by the Supreme Court in 1940 — while persecuting and limiting Christianity.[23] The government in Washington, much to the delight of groups like Planned Parenthood, began to make laws "respecting an establishment of religion" and "prohibiting the free exercise thereof."[24] It banned posting the Ten Commandments in school rooms, allowed the Bible to be read in tax-supported institutions only as an historical document, forbade prayer in the public domain, censored seasonal displays at Christmas, Easter, and Thanksgiving, regulated Church schools and outreach missions, demanded IRS registration of religious institutions, and denied equal access to the media for Christian spokesmen.[25] In short, it has stripped the Church of its jurisdiction and dismantled the institutional differentiation the Founding Fathers were so careful to construct.[26] It has robbed the Church of its prophetic and priestly functions.[27]

If our society is ever to return to the balance and integrity that the Founders intended, then the Church will have to reclaim its legacy. And that won't be easy. Unpleasant incidents, like the one Reba Elvin and her Church had outside Planned Parenthood, demonstrate that.[28] Even so, such sacrifices may be necessary.

> When the righteous increase, the people rejoice, but when a wicked man rules, people groan (Proverbs 29:2).

For the sake of life and liberty in our land, the Church must reassert its prophetic and priestly roles.

The Prophetic Church

Part of the reason the Church is in such bondage today is that it has failed to teach the truth. Instead of nurturing God's People with the rich truths of practical Biblical instruction, we have indulged in theological junk food, sectarian arcania, and intellectual irrelevancies. Instead of cultivating commitment on the unwavering foundation of God's Word, we have humored ourselves with ecclesiastical white elephants.

> Therefore My people go into exile for their lack of knowledge; and their honorable men are famished, and their multitude is parched with thirst (Isaiah 5:13).

> "Behold, days are coming," declares the Lord God, "when I will send a famine on the land, not a famine for bread or a thirst for water, but rather for hearing the words of the Lord. And people will stagger from sea to sea, and from the north even to the east; they will go to and fro to seek the word of the Lord, but they will not find it . . ." (Amos 8:11-12).

When Sava of Trnova visited the Kievan Christian republic in 1202, he was struck by the glorious architecture of the Churches, by their magnificent music, by their extravagant art, and by their elaborate liturgies. But it was the preaching that impressed him the most. "The vaunted greatness of this land," he wrote, "is surely rooted in the vaunted greatness of its Church. The

vaunted greatness of its Church, though steeped in the mighty
weigh of orthodoxy, is surely rooted in the power and suasion of
its prophetic proclamation from the pulpit."[29] The Church *taught*
its people then. And, as a result, those people had built a marvelous culture with liberty and justice for all.

When Alexis de Tocqueville visited the United States in
1830, he had a similar experience. He attributed much of the
greatness he observed in the land to the vibrancy and relevancy
of the Church's prophetic role. He noted that virtually every
community in the vast new republic was indelibly marked by
"pulpits aflame with righteousness."[30] The Church *taught* its people then. And, as a result, those people had built a marvelous
culture with liberty and justice for all.

The prophetic Church applies the Bible to every sphere of
life: art, music, ideas, government, education, medicine, history, economics, agriculture, and science.[31] It believes that "the
Bible is authoritative on everything of which it speaks."[32] And it
believes that "it speaks of everything."[33] It believes that "all Scripture is God-breathed, and is useful for teaching, rebuking, correcting, and training in righteousness, so that the man of God
may be thoroughly equipped for every good work" (2 Timothy
3:16-17). It believes that "not one jot or tittle" has in any wise
passed from it (Matthew 5:18). It believes that it is "settled in
heaven" (Psalm 119:89), and "established on earth" (Psalm
119:90). It believes the Bible, and it teaches it systematically at all
times, "in season and out of season" (2 Timothy 4:2).

> Jesus therefore was saying to those Jews who had believed
> Him, "If you abide in My word, then you are truly disciples of
> Mine; and you shall know the truth, and the truth shall make
> you free" (John 8:31-32).

The prophetic Church does not just *teach* the Bible though. It
also *applies* it. The word *prophet* literally means *guide*. Whenever
and wherever sin exists, the prophetic Church is there: exposing, rebuking, reproving, correcting—and guiding.

> Let no one deceive you with empty words, for because of these
> things the wrath of God comes upon the sons of disobedience.
> Therefore do not be partakers with them; for you were for-

merly darkness, but now you are light in the Lord; walk as children of light (for the fruit of the light consists in all goodness and righteousness and truth), trying to learn what is pleasing to the Lord. And do not participate in the unfruitful deeds of darkness, but instead even expose them (Ephesians 5:6-11).

When Planned Parenthood, and its allies in government and the media, rattle their sabers against the poor, the helpless, and the uninformed, the Church must arise and expose them. The Church must *guide*.

"Son of man, speak to the sons of your people, and say to them, 'If I bring a sword upon a land, and the people of the land take one man from among them and make him their watchman; and he sees the sword coming upon the land, and he blows on the trumpet and warns the people, then he who hears the sound of the trumpet and does not take warning, and a sword comes and takes him away, his blood will be on his own head. He heard the sound of the trumpet, but did not take warning; his blood will be on himself. But had he taken warning, he would have delivered his life. But if the watchman sees the sword coming and does not blow the trumpet, and the people are not warned, and a sword comes and takes a person from them, he is taken away in his iniquity; but his blood I will require from the watchman's hand' " (Ezekiel 33:2-6).

If the Church refuses the prophetic mantle of John the Baptist (Matthew 4:3-12), of Elijah (1 Kings 21:1-25), and of Nathan (2 Samuel 12:1-13) in exposing the evil deeds of darkness and guiding the people into all truth then the innocent are sure to perish, and God's vast army will slumber through one Megiddo after another.

For if the bugle produces an indistinct sound, who will prepare himself for battle? (1 Corinthians 14:8).

The Priestly Task

Man's chief end "is to glorify God and enjoy Him forever."[34] We are supposed to glorify and enjoy Him in every area of life and with every activity. But we are to do it particularly in worship.[35]

Man is not merely one species among many. He is not a naked ape. He is not simply *homo sapiens* — or thinking man. Instead, he is *homo adorans* — or worshiping man as well. It is his ability to know and serve God that sets man apart from all the rest of creation.[36]

When Moses went before Pharaoh to lobby for Israel's liberty, he did not say, "Let my people go that they may start a new political movement." Nor did he say, "Let my people go that they may establish a Christian nation." No, instead, he said, "Let my people go that they may hold a feast to Me in the wilderness" (Exodus 5:1). And, again, "Let my people go that they may serve Me in the wilderness" (Exodus 7:16).

As author David Chilton has written, "We know the story of Israel. God forces Pharaoh to release them and they went on to inherit the Promised Land. But the really crucial aspect of the whole Exodus event, as far as the people's activity was concerned, was *worship*."[37] And so it continues to be today. Chilton concludes, "The orthodox Christian faith cannot be reduced to personal experiences, academic discussions, or culture-building activity — as important as all these are in varying degrees. The essence of Biblical religion is the worship of God. . . . True Christian reconstruction of culture is far from being simply a matter of passing Law X and electing Congressman Y. Christianity is not a political cult. It is the divinely ordained worship of the Most High God."[38]

Notice what happens when God's people — *homo adorans* — forget this very fundamental truth:

> In the second year of Darius the king, on the first day of the sixth month, the word of the Lord came by the prophet Haggai to Zerubbabel the son of Shealtiel, governor of Judah, and to Joshua the son of Jehozadak, the high priest saying, "Thus says the Lord of hosts, 'this people says, "The time has not yet come, even the time for the house of the Lord to be rebuilt."' "
>
> Then the word of the Lord came by Haggai the prophet saying, "Is it time for you yourselves to dwell in your paneled houses while this house lies desolate?" Now therefore, thus says the Lord of hosts, "Consider your ways! You have sown much, but harvest little; you eat, but there is not enough to be satisfied;

you drink, but there is not enough to become drunk; you put on clothing, but no one is warm enough; and he who earns, earns wages to put into a purse with holes." Thus says the Lord of hosts, "Consider your ways! Go up to the mountains, bring wood and rebuild the temple, that I may be pleased with it and be glorified," says the Lord. "You look for much, but behold, it comes to little; when you bring it home, I blow it away. Why?" declares the Lord of hosts, "Because of My house which lies desolate, while each of you runs to his own house" (Haggai 1:1-9).

When we neglect the priestly role of the Church, when we neglect worship, all else goes to seed.

If our first response to Planned Parenthood—or any other evil, for that matter—is political, or social, or organizational, or litgal, or judicial, we are no better than they, for we have put our trust in *human action* as the ultimate determiner of history.

The priestly Church believes in the power of worship (Revelation 8:1-8). It believes in the primacy of worship (John 4:23-24). It believes in the preeminence of worship (Matthew 16:19). It believes that worship reorients us to God's plan, God's purpose, and God's program (Psalm 73:1-28). It believes that worship is the starting point for cultural transformation (1 Timothy 2:1-4), for it is worship that ultimately brings about the demise of the wicked and the exaltation of the righteous (Psalm 83:1-18).

O come, let us sing for joy to the Lord; let us shout joyfully to the rock of our salvation. Let us come before His presence with thanksgiving; let us shout joyfully to Him with psalms. For the Lord is a great God, and a great King above all gods, in whose hand are the depths of the earth; the peaks of the mountains are His also. The sea is His, for it was He who made it; and His hands formed the dry land. Come, let us worship and bow down; let us kneel before the Lord our Maker. For He is our God, and we are the people of His pasture, and the sheep of His hand (Psalm 95:1-7).

The priestly Church does not just *perform* worship though. It also *applies* it. The word *priest* literally means *guardian*. Thus, a priest is someone who guards. He protects. He preserves. He stays the hand of destruction and defilement.

Adam was called to be a priest. He was to "cultivate and *guard* the garden" (Genesis 2:15). When he failed to do his duty, the Fall resulted and judgment fell on the land (Genesis 3:1-20).

Aaron was called to be a priest. He was to *guard* the people from sin and shame (Exodus 32:25). When he failed to do his duty, the people began to worship and revel before a golden calf and judgment fell on the land (Exodus 32:1-6).

The Levites were called to be priests. They were given that honor and privilege because they *guarded* the integrity of God when all the rest of Israel was consumed with idolatry (Exodus 32:26-29). It was not until they completely failed to do their duty that condemnation and judgment befell the land (Jeremiah 6:13-15).

Jesus commissioned the Church to take up the priestly task (Matthew 28:19-20; 1 Peter 2:5). It was to preserve, protect, and guard the nations.

> "You are the salt of the earth; but if the salt has become tasteless, how will it be made salty again? It is good for nothing anymore, except to be thrown out and trampled under foot by men" (Matthew 5:13).

If the Church refuses the priestly mantle of Adam, Aaron, and the Levites, the poor and helpless will, indeed, be trampled under foot by men. They will be crushed by the likes of Planned Parenthood.

So now, in practical terms, just exactly how is the Church to manifest its *prophetic* and *priestly* roles in the struggle for life? Once believers have been taught, exhorted, equipped, and commissioned, what then? Once they have worshiped, prayed, and proclaimed, what then? What do Christians do once they leave the four walls of the Church?

Very simply, we go out and change the world.[39] We serve the whole of society guiding and guarding the land: in the schools, in the media, in local government, in the legislature, in the courts, and in the bureaucracy.

The Schools

"A nation at risk."[40] That is how the United States Department of Education describes the state of the Union, as viewed from the classroom.

Public education in this country is a dismal failure. Johnny can't read and Susie can't spell. Willie can't write and Alice can't add. Teacher competency is down. Administrative effectiveness is down. Student advancement is down. Test scores are down. Everything to do with our public school system is down — everything, that is, except crime, drug abuse, illicit sex, and the cost to tax-payers.[41]

As many as twenty-three million adults in this country are functionally illiterate.[42] An additional thirty-five million are alliterate — they can read a few basics with difficulty, but that is about all.[43] SAT score comparisons reveal an unbroken decline from 1963 to the present.[44] Average verbal scores have fallen over fifty points and mathematics scores have dropped nearly forty points.[45] Among the one hundred fifty-eight member nations of the United Nations, the United States now ranks forty-ninth in its literacy levels.[46] And this despite one of the most extensive and expensive school systems the world has ever seen.[47] Education is, in fact, the second largest industry in the nation, spending more than a quarter trillion dollars every year, with nearly three million teachers and administrators, and the largest union in the world.[48] Despite that, more than forty-five percent of all the products of that system cannot even read the front page of the morning newspaper.[49]

Into the morass of mediocrity, Planned Parenthood has stepped, wreaking havoc. As if things weren't bad enough already. With guest speakers, information bureaus, sex education, curriculums, films, literature distribution, and school-based clinics, Planned Parenthood has launched a full-scale invasion of our schools.[50]

If we are going to serve society as prophets and priests, guiding and guarding the land, we are going to have to reach out to our schools.

There are several things that each of us can do to do just that.

First, we can go to local PTA meetings. Believe it or not, a great deal can be accomplished at this grassroots level. Why not gather a small packet of Planned Parenthood materials, quotes, and statistics, and pass it around to the parents at a monthly meeting? Or volunteer to speak on the subject of sex education? Or, perhaps, form a task force group to investigate the school's programs and procedures? The PTA has a tremendous amount of influence on the school administration and even the School Board. If we can catalyze a bottom-up surge of concern, or even outrage, we may be able to turn things around yet.

Second, we can go to School Board meetings. Mandates are often developed on the national level. Programs are formulated on the state level. But all the implementation and spending decisions ultimately pass through the School Board. Because Board members are elected officials, they are generally responsive to those who attend their meetings. Of course, that is the catch. Hardly anyone ever actually makes it to those meetings. Why not commit to attending just a couple of meetings a year? Or maybe we could get a group from our Church to switch off so that each of the meetings is monitored. A few well-phrased proposals, a few well-timed testimonies, a few well-thought-out comments, a few wisely-placed books, and a few attended meetings could mean the difference between Planned Parenthood's receiving another School District contract, or some responsible social service provider's receiving it.

Third, we can volunteer to put together an alternative speakers bureau for the schools. Why not contact several local pro-life doctors and nurses and educators and get them into the schools instead of the Planned Parenthood staffers? Why not get a list of speakers and suggested assembly ideas to every health teacher, school nurse, gym teacher, coach, counselor, and principal in our school district? A little time, a little effort, and a little creativity can make all the difference in the world.

Fourth, we can buy good books, films, videos, and curriculum and donate them to our school libraries.[51] The schools often operate on a very tight budget so they are not likely to buy much more than the required items. So, why not stock the shelves of the library with good, wholesome, and helpful items? Perhaps we could even sponsor a book fair so that Christians from throughout the community can participate in your project. A school can't very well use what it doesn't have.

Fifth, we can get involved with the students ourselves. Why not start a youth Bible study after school? Or maybe volunteer with an existing *Youth for Christ* or *Navigator* or *Young Life* or *Campus Crusade* or *Fellowship of Christian Athletes* or *Chi Alpha* program? Building relationships with the students and discipling them for Christ will do more to stymie Planned Parenthood than almost anything else.

One way or another, we need to reach out to our schools. We need to serve them as prophets and priests, guiding and guarding the land.

The Media

Planned Parenthood, for all intents and purposes, has the media in its pocket. It has accomplished that feat in part by shrewdly developing and craftily implementing a comprehensive system of news releases, news contacts, media spokesmen, data retrieval, source procurement, public relations campaigns, expert analysis, advertising, and interview leads.[52] As a result, it has been able to nurture stories, do lead generation, time breaking events, create desirable publicity, snowball feature items, and shape public opinion.[53]

Why has the Church failed to develop that kind of media acumen? Why have pro-life groups not been able to exploit the media as a wedge against public policy the way Planned Parenthood has? Certainly, it is not because the opportunities are lacking. It is not because the technology is unavailable. Nor is it because the resources are inaccessible. But, for some reason, we have yet to make the long-term commitments necessary to turn the media around.

That must change. If we are going to serve our society as prophets and priests, guiding and guarding the land, we are going to have to recapture the media.

There are several things that each of us can do to do just that.

First, we can write letters to the editor. If we have something to say, we ought to say it. Instead of constantly murmuring and complaining about the biased coverage in our local newspapers and magazines, we can voice our opinion. Why not offer an alternative perspective of the latest Planned Parenthood initiative? Or, perhaps, we can gain publicity for the positive programs that our local Church or alternative center is offering? A brief, polite, respectful, and well-phrased letter may be able to spark a community-wide dialogue where the facts about Planned Parenthood can actually come to light.

Second, we can put together press packets and media contact networks ourselves. It is hard to dispute facts. And it is hard to ignore facts that are *constantly* presented in an amiable and professional manner. Why not begin to circulate to local reporters and newsmen a few selected fact sheets, statistical surveys, financial charts, pamphlets, and books on Planned Parenthood? Or, perhaps, develop a series of press releases that we hand deliver to one or two sympathetic broadcasters? If we plan ahead and prepare properly, we can, at the very least, let the media know that we're here and that we mean business.

Third, we can hold press conferences. If we regularly recover the broken bodies of children from the dumpsters behind a Planned Parenthood clinic, there is no reason in the world why we shouldn't let the world know. Why not call out the camera crews, contact the newspapers, and notify the radio stations? If we can consistently deliver hard news, controversial stories, and substantial interviews, they will keep coming back to us. We can then begin to use them instead of the other way around.

Fourth, even if every avenue is closed in our community, we can still get the word out. Why not start a radio program? Or even a TV show?[54] Many stations around the country sell air time at very reasonable rates. If we can put together a crisp, professional, responsible, and informative program, we can go straight to the community. Then, instead of constantly having to fight with the media, we *become* the media. If radio is out of the question, why not try a newsletter? Even a small, little mimeographed neighborhood information sheet can cause Planned Parenthood all kinds of headaches if it presents accurate, up-to-date, hard-hitting information.

Fifth, we can sway advertisers and sponsors to press for more objective coverage. A boycott is not the only kind of leverage that we can use with businesses to get them to spend their publicity dollars more responsibly. A clear presentation of the facts can do wonders. Why not include major advertisers and public relations firms in our press release list? Or, perhaps, we could develop a relationship with the decision-makers, helping them to realize what kind of impact they have on the community. The media will not continue to support Planned Parenthood if they see their advertising space dropping off significantly.

One way or another, we need to recapture the media. We need to serve it as prophets and priests, guiding and guarding the land.

Local Governments

Local governments are truly the nuts and bolts of the American system. Without the administration of cities, counties, parishes, districts, precincts, zones, commissions, municipalities, and states, civil stability would surely disintegrate. The Founding Fathers of our nation recognized that, and the system of government that they designed was purposefully decentralized and localized.[55] They wanted to make certain that the villages, townships, communities, and states shaped the policies of the nation and the priorities in Washington, not vice versa.

Napoleon once asserted that the way to capture a nation is not to "storm the palaces," but to "capture the countryside." He was right.

The impact of Planned Parenthood has been enhanced as much by local zoning ordinances, health codes, and funding appraisals as it has by court rulings and legislative packages. There is a basic principle at work here — not just a constitutional principle, but a Biblical principle: whoever will be faithful with "few things" and "small things," will be made master over "many things" and "great things" (Matthew 25:14-30).

If we are going to serve society as prophets and priests, we are going to have to participate in, and influence, our local governments.

There are several things that each of us can do to do just that.

First, we can attend meetings. Again, it is the small meeting that determines the course of community life: city council meetings, county health board meetings, utility district meetings, tax appraisal meetings, county development meetings, and environmental impact meetings. Only a tiny handful of people — about one tenth of one percent of the registered voters — attend those meetings on a regular basis. Only about two percent of the electorate *ever* attend such meetings. Needless to say, that minuscule minority has an inordinate amount of influence over the day to day administration of their local governing bodies. So why not be a party to that powerful minority? Why not sit on a few committees, put together a few budget proposals, and develop alternatives to the present programs? If we would, Planned Parenthood would surely be exposed for what it is.

Second, we can participate in precinct caucuses. The precinct is the lowest common denominator in the American political process. Basically, it is an election district. It is the place where votes are cast and counted. But it is also the hub of party organization. It is there in the precinct that our political parties receive their direction, support, continuity, platform, and purpose. What a party is, who it nominates, and where it is going is determined in those small meetings all across the country, in schools, American Legion halls, and polling booths, not under the bright lights of the national convention. And the thing is, anyone who votes in a party's primary is eligible to participate in the precinct caucus. Only about three percent ever actually do.[56] So, why not let that three percent be us? Why not submit resolutions that hit hard on Planned Parenthood's programs of lust and greed? Why not elect pro-life activists as precinct chairmen, election marshals, poll watchers, and convention delegates? We can actually make a difference if only we will.

Third, we can participate in local campaigns and elections. Every vote really matters. Since only about sixty percent of the citizens of this country are registered to vote, and only about thirty-five percent actually bother to go to the polls, a candidate only needs the support of a small elite group of people to win.[57] It only takes about fourteen percent of the electorate to gain a seat in the Senate.[58] It takes about eleven percent to gain a seat in the House.[59] Only about nine percent is needed to win a governorship.[60] And it takes a mere seven percent to take an average mayoral or city council post.[61] Any race is winnable. Why not get involved in a worthy campaign? Why not work to get magistrates in office who will defund Planned Parenthood? Why not give up a few weekends to stuff some envelopes, post some yard signs, man a phone bank, host a candidate forum, distribute bumper stickers, or mount a voter registration drive? We truly can make every vote count.

One way or another, we need to participate in, and influence, our local governments. We need to serve them as prophets and priests, guiding and guarding the land.

The Legislature

Ostensibly, Congress is the source of all federal law in this country. The President cannot make law, he only administers it. The courts cannot make law, they only adjudicate it. Only the combined efforts of the two branches of Congress—the House and the Senate—can make law.

The House of Representatives has four hundred thirty-five members apportioned on the basis of population, and elected every two years from among the fifty states. The Senate has one hundred members, two from each state, elected to staggered six-year terms. Together those five hundred thirty-five magistrates have the power to stop abortion, defund Planned Parenthood, clean up our schools, regulate the profligate birth control drug trade, revoke tax-exempt status for aborturaries, enforce parental consent, and increase legal and medical liabilities.[62] If only they would.

And they would if we could only bring the right kind of pressure to bear.

If we are going to serve our society as prophets and priests, guiding and guarding the land, we are going to have to influence the legislature.

There are several things that each of us can do to do just that.

First, we can initiate correspondence with our legislators. Only one out of every twenty Americans has *ever* written to their Congressmen.[63] Only one out of every two hundred has written more than once.[64] And only one out of every ten thousand has written more than five times.[65] So while the mail room on Capitol Hill may receive several thousand letters every day, only a few hundred actually address specific policy issues—the rest are trivial or intercessory. Because the congressional staff tabulates these letters and then surveys them in the manner of a poll, any one letter can leave a tremendous impact on the policy-making process. And a regular, consistent correspondence may mean the difference between a pro or con vote on something as important as Title XX appropriations for Planned Parenthood or Hyde Amendment restrictions. So why not invest the price of a stamp and fifteen minutes time and write a letter? But not just *one* letter. Why not develop a habit of correspondence? Informative, cordial, fact-laden, action-oriented, positive, and helpful letters launched the first American Revolution.[66] Perhaps they can launch a second.

Second, we can attend our legislator's home district meetings. Most Congressmen come home for town meetings, or issues seminars or fundraisers or social events or campaign stops or holiday celebrations. Only a very small part of the constituency regularly attends these meetings. Why not take it upon ourselves to make as many of those appearances as we possibly can? Or delegate various meetings out to several people in the Church who can report back to the whole group? If our legislator knows that a very informed, very active, very vocal core of his constituency is unalterably opposed to Planned Parenthood funding and contracting and coddling, he is much more likely to examine the issues with some degree of care. And if we have the opportunity at those personal appearances to hand him fact sheets, press kits, tracts, or books, then all the better.

Third, we can respond to our legislator's polls. Most Congressmen use the mails to gauge constituency concerns. Why not make the most of those prime opportunities? Why not answer his polls thoughtfully and carefully with hand-written comments in the margins? A personal, neat, well-composed comment shows Congressional staffers that we *really* care about an issue, and they are more likely to consider our thoughts.

Fourth, we can testify before Congressional committee and sub-committee hearings. There are at least sixteen different stages that a bill must pass through before it actually becomes law. It must be introduced. It must be referred to committee. It must proceed through the appropriate sub-committees within that committee. It must then be subjected to hearings and mark-up. Next, the bill must be reported to the full House. Then it is put on the calendar. When the date for discussion on the floor finally comes up, consideration must be obtained. Then discussion, amendment, and debate occurs. Next comes the voting stage. If the bill passes the House it is referred to the Senate where a similar, albeit shorter, consideration, committee, and floor process is followed. Once the Senate passes its version, the bill goes before a joint committee of both branches to consolidate any differences. The completed bill then goes to the President for signing. Only then does the bill become law. The thing is, anywhere along the way, the bill can be altered, adjusted, or scrapped altogether. That is why committee and sub-committee hearings are so crucial. Debate, discussion, and expert testimony in those early stages of a bill can decide whether it will be a strong moral and ethical piece of legislation or one more capitulation to the powers that be at Planned Parenthood. Why not get the doctors, lawyers, teachers, and counselors we know to go to Washington and testify for the several committees and sub-committees considering family planning legislation? Why should Planned Parenthood's experts be the only ones called on? We can just as easily make the calls and write the letters and pull the strings to get our people in as they can.

One way or another we need to influence the legislature. We need to serve it as prophets and priests, guiding and guarding the land.

The Courts

The judiciary has become a virtual playground for Planned Parenthood. Besides the infamous *Roe v. Wade* decision, at least nine other decisions have been handed down by the Supreme Court that violate the sanctity of life and undermine the viability of the Constitution.[67] In most of them, Planned Parenthood played a central role, as either the plaintiff or as a "friend of the court."[68]

In *Doe v. Bolton*, in 1973, the Court invalidated a Georgia statute limiting abortions to "accredited medical facilities." The decision also broadened the definition of "maternal health" to include a broad range of factors including "general maternal well-being" as a justification for last trimester abortions.

In *Bigelow v. Virginia*, in 1975, the Court struck down a state law restricting abortion clinic advertising policies.

In *Singleton v. Wulff*, in 1976, the Court gave abortionists the right to challenge government abortion funding restrictions "on behalf of their patients." Thus, the industry was given free reign to act as plaintiffs and lobby for themselves through the courts. In *Planned Parenthood of Missouri v. Danforth*, also in 1976, the Court struck down provisions in the state law requiring abortionists to save the life of the aborted child when possible. It also invalidated a spousal consent statute.

In *Colautti v. Franklin*, in 1979, the Court struck down a Pennsylvania statute creating a standard for the determination of the viability of unborn children.

In *Bellotti v. Baird*, also in 1979, the Court invalidated a Massachusetts statute requiring parental consent for minor children receiving abortions.

In *Akron v. Akron Center for Reproductive Health*, in 1983, the Court struck down a city ordinance requiring all second and third trimester abortions to be performed in hospitals. It also invalidated a statute requiring abortionists to inform their patients of the medical risks of abortion and of possible alternatives to abortion. It argued, in essence, that the "pro-choice movement" need *not* provide women with choices.

In *Planned Parenthood of Kansas City v. Ashcroft*, also in 1983, the Court invalidated a state statute requiring second trimester abortions be performed in hospitals.

In *Thornburgh v. American College of Obstetricians and Gynecologists*, in 1986, the Court struck down all mild forms of abortion regulation, including restrictions for informed consent, informational reporting requirements, and performance of abortions after viability. The decision, for all intents and purposes, made abortion the *only* completely unregulated surgical procedure in the United States.

The lower courts have proven to be equally hostile to life and liberty. Repeatedly stiff sentences have been handed down to abortion protesters, alternative service providers, and pro-life organizers, often on trumped up charges.

Clearly, if we are going to serve society as prophets and priests, guiding and guarding the land, we are going to have to help turn the courts around.

There are several things we can do to do just that.

First, we can utilize our vote. Many of the judges that wreaked havoc on life and liberty in our land are *elected* to the bench and they must stand for re-election. So, why not mount a campaign to replace pro-abortion, anti-family judges? Why not spend as much time and energy on those obscure judicial races as we do on legislative campaigns? In that way we can cut right to the heart of the matter.

Second, we can begin to exercise the principle of jury nullification. The purpose of a jury is to put a check on the power of the magistrates by putting ultimate power in the hands of individual citizens. In a very real sense, the Founding Fathers gave each citizen three votes: the first was the free elections vote in order to choose their representatives; the second was the Grand Jury vote in order to prevent overzealous prosecutors from harassing the citizenry; and the third was the jury vote in order to restrain the courts from unjustly applying legitimate laws or from legitimately applying unjust laws. Thus, the true function of the jury is to try not only the actions and the motives of the defendant, but the actions and the motives of the prosecution, the court, and the law as well.

According to the 1972 decision of *U.S. v. Dougherty*, juries have the "unreviewable and irreversible power . . . to acquit in disregard of the instruction on the law given by the trial judge." In other words, the jury can ignore the prosecutor, ignore the judge, and even ignore the law if the courts and the law seem to be out of line with Biblical directives. This is the cherished doctrine of jury nullification that men like John Adams, James Madison, John Jay, Alexander Hamilton, and John C. Calhoun struggled for so long.[69]

Sadly, it is an almost forgotten doctrine. That is why it is so essential that we become informed jurors, to hold the courts in check. Thus, we need to *aspire* to jury duty, not *avoid* it. We need to apply ourselves diligently so that we can be selected. We need to be certain never to disqualify ourselves in pro-life cases just because we hold moral convictions on those matters. Moral conviction is just *exactly* what the courts need right now.

So, why not take the opportunity next time jury duty comes up and serve willingly? Why not exercise jury nullification and throw a legal wrench in the judicial works? It can only help matters.

Third, we can begin to go on the offensive. Why should we always be on the defensive? Why should Planned Parenthood be the only organization to take cases before the courts as a means of policy advocacy?

Although a few Christian pro-life groups, like the Rutherford Institute[70] and the Christian Legal Society,[71] have begun to scratch the surface in these areas, much more needs to be done.

Litigation needs to pour forth from the Christian community in torrents. Parents need to sue school districts over the debauched curriculum programs. Women abused by abortion need to sue Planned Parenthood and other abortuaries for medical malpractice.[72] Pro-life leaders need to sue the various media outlets for slander and deliberate misrepresentation of the facts. And Churches need to sue zoning commissions for discriminatory regulation. In the same way that Planned Parenthood has smothered Believers over the last thirty years with their lawsuits, we need to take to the courts, fighting fire with fire. We need to stop waiting until we are sued to utilize the system to save the system. Why not initiate a few lawsuits? Or, perhaps, sponsor some of our friends in a court fight? Planned Parenthood has had the courts to themselves for long enough now.

Fourth, we can begin to utilize the defense of necessity. The *defense of necessity* is a legal maneuver that argues that "lesser laws may be broken so that a greater good might be done." So, for instance, breaking and entering a burning house to save a victim from the flames is not a crime. Likewise, assault and battery on a rapist in order to free his victim is a justified act. The *defense of necessity* may also be utilized to test laws that protect abortionists. Sit-ins in the Planned Parenthood clinics where the unborn children are butchered in wholesale slaughter are not simple cases of civil disobedience, but are opportunities to bring the *defense of necessity* into the courts, thereby testing the validity of the laws. Planned Parenthood has been utilizing the various legal tests to throw out Christian laws for years. Isn't it about time to turn the tables? Why not begin to set some legal precedents in a few minor trials so that the *defense of necessity* is available for us to use in the major cases? It is crucial that we plan ahead, gain a foothold, and forge some victories.

One way or another we need to help turn the courts around. We need to serve them as prophets and priests, guiding and guarding the land.

The Bureaucracy

The bureaucracy is, perhaps, the most powerful "branch" of the American governmental system. It is certainly the largest and the most expensive. Yet it is nowhere mentioned in the Constitution. It was in no way envisioned by the Founding Fathers.

That makes for a very dangerous situation. Who monitors the bureaucracy? Who checks and balances its administration? Who even knows what it does?

When section 1008 of the Title X appropriations bill for population control went into effect, the bureaucratic minions simply ignored it and did whatever they jolly well pleased. Section 1008 stated that no funds could be issued to "any program or agency where abortion is utilized as a method of family planning." Despite that clear injunction, the Department of Health and Human Services has poured millions of dollars into the coffers of Planned Parenthood. Thus, the bureaucracy has illegally provided more than half of the budget for Planned Parenthood's program of death, deception, and perversion, out of *our* tax dollars.

Because the bureaucracy is unmonitored and unchecked, it is above the law. Quite literally.

If we are going to serve society as prophets and priests, guiding and guarding the land, we are going to have to bring the bureaucracy back under control.

There are several things we can do to do just that.

First, we can call for the enforcement of existing laws. Every day, the bureaucracy publishes several hundred new pages of rules, regulations, statutes, policies, orders, directives, and restrictions that carry the force of law. But, all too often, these new ordinances in the *Federal Register* are contrary to existing law. They are nothing but an attempt to anonymously end-run the legislature and the courts.

If we could monitor both the *Federal Register* and the policy programs that go unpublished, holding the various civil servants accountable to existing law, the humanistic loopholes would be virtually closed. Planned Parenthood would lose its tax funding. The administration would, at long last, be returned to the sanity of a standard of law. Why not specialize in a particular area of the law and then hold the bureaucracy accountable to it? Why not turn the screws and actually make the system work the way it is *supposed* to work? If we don't make it work, no one will.

Second, we can hold bureaucrats accountable for their actions. The great advantage of most civil servants over elected magistrates is the cover of anonymity. No one knows who they are. They are nameless and faceless. Thus, they are able to wield power and influence without fear of exposure or public reprisal. Often they can work for years behind the scenes, doing damage to life and liberty without any notoriety whatsoever. They are buried beneath a thick insulation of red tape, well-disguised from the penetrating gaze of public and media.

But what if these well-protected, long-anonymous civil servants were exposed? What if they were held accountable for their actions? What if their names and faces and actions and activities were published for all to see? What if we began to put them under the same kind of scrutiny that elected officials must undergo?

Why not make the bureaucracy accountable for its policies and programs? Why not call individual administrators to task for their behind-the-scenes activities? We need to do the research necessary to catalog the names, computerize the lists, and monitor the decisions so that wayward civil servants can be made to *serve* the citizenry once again.

Third, we can clog the machinery of the bureaucracy with delays, requests, and inquiries, buying time for more permanent measures. The bureaucracy is a lumbering, bumbling monolith. It is a vast Goliath. A monstrous giant. But a few Christians properly prepared can walk in David's footsteps and become giant-killers.

When Planned Parenthood's cohorts in the bureaucracy begin to lay waste to justice, mercy, and liberty, we need to swarm into the fray, slowing, stalling, deterring, frustrating, distracting, and annoying. With speed, flexibility, and commitment, a few insignificant mosquito-like maneuvers can clog the bureaucratic machinery for months. Why not ask for an official inquiry or, a hearing? Or, maybe demand all the files on a given subject for the last decade under the Freedom of Information Act? We can make phone calls. Or write letters. Or ask questions. Or visit offices. Or talk to supervisors. Or make appeals. By buying time, perhaps we can sway the process in a more sane and sensible directive.

One way or another, we need to bring the bureaucracy back under control. We need to serve it as prophets and priests, guiding and guarding the land.

Paying the Piper

Serving society as prophets and priests is all too often a thankless task. And, at times, quite dangerous. You can be sure that Planned Parenthood is none too thrilled to see Christians guiding and guarding this nation's cultural and political affairs. The fact is, there simply isn't enough room in its pluralism for us.

As a result, it — and a number of other groups — has pressed for, and won, a number of restrictions on Christian activity in the society at large. Various IRS regulations, Federal Election Commission regulations, and Federal statutes constrain Christians, and especially ministers and Church congregations, from engaging in particular political actions.

If a Church is registered with the government as a 501(c)(3) organization, the minister and the membership must pay close attention to the details of these restrictions. Not all of them are fair, or just, or right, but they do exist, and Churches should at the very least know what the boundaries and risks are.

According to the IRS and the FEC, a Church or minister "may not directly or indirectly participate in, intervene in (including the publishing or distributing of statements) any political campaign on behalf of or in opposition to any candidates for public office."[73]

Even so, the regulations do have loopholes.

For instance, the courts have ruled that a minister may allow his name to be used in political ads in support of particular *issues*. He may be identified in the ad as the minister of a particular Church. He may even work with other individuals to establish a political action committee, though that committee must operate and "be viewed" as separate from the Church. He may also engage in lobbying activities, circulate petitions, conduct voter registration drives, loan mailing lists, and introduce candidates at services. And, of course, the courts have ruled that he may speak from the pulpit to encourage the members of the congregation to become active in every aspect of the political process. He may preach on the importance of political activism and may pray for elected officials as often as he chooses. He may even lead public prayers for the election of candidates who support a particular philosophy or cause as long as the prayer "cannot be construed as a direct endorsement of a candidate or candidates."

At times, it seems that the loopholes in the system are open so wide that our prophetic and priestly duties are entirely unencumbered.

Sadly, there are other times when the loopholes built into the system close up tighter than a drum. Reba Elvin and the members of her Church found that out the hard way.

There are times, in fact, when the system seems only to work against the cause of life and liberty.

Church historians for years have pondered with inquisitive awe the uncharacteristically ferocious persecution that the New Testament era Believers faced. In a day of tolerance, prosperity, and governmental stability, why did the intense public outrage break forth?

Was there something about the early Church rituals that particularly irked the Romans?

Almost unquestionably not. The Empire sheltered within its folds all manner of esoterica and erratica. In comparison, the Church was tame to say the least.

Was there something about the early Church doctrine that particularly irked the Romans?

Again, that's highly unlikely. Mystery cults, occultic covens, and theosophic sects of the wildest order thrived under the tolerant wings of the Empire.[74]

So what was it that singled Christianity out to be so awfully *despised* by the civil magistrates and the populace at large?

According to Francis Schaeffer, "The early Christians died because they would not obey the state in a civil matter . . . they were *civil rebels*. The Roman State did not care what anybody believed religiously; you could believe anything or you could be an atheist. But you had to pay homage to Caesar as a sign of your loyalty to the state."[75]

The Christians said "no." That is why they were thrown to the lions. They were civil rebels. They were not imprisoned, beaten, reviled, stoned, exiled, and executed because of their peculiar dogmas. They met with persecution because they refused to obey the government.

An excerpt from the first-century *Law of the Twelve Tables* states that no Roman citizen was to "have gods on his own, neither new ones nor strange ones, but only those instituted by the state."[76] A statute in the second-century *Celsus Tables*, aimed specifically at the Christians, stated that "they form among themselves secret societies that exist *outside* the *system of laws . . .* an obscure and mysterious community founded on *revolt* and on the advantage that accrues from it."[77] And, according to the great second-century Christian defense attorney, Athenagoras, prosecution against Believers proceeded on two points: "That we do not sacrifice and that we do not believe in the same gods as the state."[78]

The historian, Dio Cassius, confirmed this emphasis in Roman law during the reign of Domitian. He stated that the Emperor "had executed, among many others, the consul Flavius Clemens, even though he was a cousin of his, and his wife, Flavia Domitilla, who was also related to Domitian. The accusation against both was that of *treason*. On the basis of this accusation, many others who had adopted the customs of the Jewish Christians were also condemned. Others were, at the very least, deprived of their property or suffered banishment."[79]

Clearly, the Roman government saw the Christians not simply as an arcane religious group, but as a band of civil insurrectionists. They were undermining the authority of the state by claiming a higher allegiance. Christianity knocked the state from its messianic pedestal. Thus, it was anarchy in the eyes of the imperial protectors.

Any time the state attempts to make itself "the center of all human loyalties, the goal of all human aspirations, the source of all human values, and the final arbiter of all human destiny," says John W. Whitehead, "conflict becomes inevitable."[80]

Such was the case in Rome.

And, all too often, such is the case in our own day.

Why was there such severe persecution against Christians in the days of Imperial Rome? For the same reasons that Christians are being harassed today so brutishly by Planned Parenthood: the Law of God is higher than the law of men. And in the monolithic modern federalism, the law of men unavoidably contravenes the precepts of Scripture. Christians, thus, are branded as subversives to the welfare of the society.

If so — so be it!

Peter, James, and John had to work outside the system for a time in order to get the message of the Gospel out (Acts 4:19-20).

Ultimately, the Gospel won and the Roman Empire was converted. But, until that had occurred, the disciples of Christ had to find other means to affect the ministry of cultural action.

At the present time, the laws of many states and municipalities hinder us from fulfilling our God-ordained responsibilities: rescuing the perishing (Proverbs 24:10-12), educating our children in the Law of God (Deuteronomy 6:1-9), and caring for the poor and homeless (Isaiah 58:6-12). What are we to do when such civil tyranny actually *excludes* us from the system? Do we have to resort immediately to civil disobedience?

Not at all.

In the Scriptures, God's people, at various times and in various situations, demonstrate a number of different reactions to civil tyranny that involve working within the system. When the state oversteps its bounds and begins to violate God's immutable Law, Believers have several models of tactical action from which to choose.

For instance, Daniel, when asked to violate Scripture, simply utilized the tactic of the wise appeal. Instead of instantly indulging belligerent rebellion against divinely instituted authority, he proposed an alternative course of action, which ultimately gained for him the favor of the court (Daniel 1:8-16).

Similarly, the Apostle Paul, when faced with an ungodly and unscrupulous jury, exercised the tactic of lawyer delay. Instead of reviling the authorities, instead of outright rebellion, and instead of sullen submission, Paul upheld the integrity of God's law through the appellate process (Acts 25:1-27).

Moses, when faced with the awful oppression of God's people, began a very forthright lobbying initiative. Rather than advocating an armed rebellion, he sought a change in Pharaoh's tyrannical policy. His whole approach, though from without, was to force the evil system of Egypt to change from within (Exodus 5:1-21).

Obadiah was the chief counsel to King Ahab, perhaps the most corrupt and tyrannical of all the kings in Israel's history. As a devout Believer in the Lord, Obadiah was able to instigate a program of reform and renewal right under the haughty noses of Jezebel and her dastardly Baalic courtiers. Instead of actively rebuking the evil monarchs and their consorts, he worked *around* the system to promote Scriptural resistance and positive reclamation (1 Kings 18:3-16).

Jeremiah counseled the people of Israel to submit to the totalitarian rule of Nebuchadnezzar. Many commentators have taken this to be an example of humility and subservience, but Jeremiah actually exercised a tactic of Scriptural resistance. It is what we might call the *wounded lamb* approach. In contrast to the *wounded water buffalo* strategy so articulately advocated by his contemporary Hananiah, Jeremiah's plan was to humiliate the invaders through the Godly goading of their own consciences (Jeremiah 44:1-30). Ezekiel, too, avoided civil disobedience in his struggle against tyranny. His resistance tactic involved graphic public protest. He took his prophetic message to the streets and therein garnered both public and divine favor (Ezekiel 4:1-5:17).

Each of these heroes of the faith was forced by circumstance to work for cultural reform. But they all understood that when the messianic state begins to violate its divine trust, there are still a wide variety of tactical options available to them short of civil disobedience. Like them, we can work within the system with the wise appeal, lawyer delay, lobbying, legislative reform, suffering servanthood, and public protest. Even when faced with awful debilitating oppression, Believers should draw on these alternative avenues of resistance before resorting to more dire strategies. A veritable arsenal of Scriptural tactics has been supplied to the Believer in order to stay him from the last resort of rebellious confrontation.

Scriptural respect for divine institutions must forever remain foremost in our minds (Romans 13:1-7; 1 Peter 2:13-25). Though tyranny may incline us toward libertarian activism, though godlessness may provoke grief in our bowels of compassion, though the barbarism of Planned Parenthood may rankle our wrathful ire, Believers have a Scriptural mandate to do God's work, God's way, in God's time. Until the tactics of the wise appeal, lawyer delay, lobbying, legislative reform, suffering servanthood, and public protest have been exhausted and entirely frustrated, civil disobedience is not a live option. Again, we must say civil disobedience is a *last resort*. There is no ground whatsoever in the Biblical narrative for skipping ahead to the drastic when the mundane might just as well do. To advocate civil disobedience before the exhaustion of alternative resistance is to thwart God's redemptive program and the rule of Law.

Of course, once every alternative has been exhausted — and in many cases they already have been — then we may have to go the way of Peter, James, and John, and stand for the truth of God regardless of the costs: rescuing the perishing, protecting the innocent, defending the defenseless, exposing injustice. Notice, for instance, that Daniel, Paul, Moses, Obadiah, Jeremiah, and Ezekiel all eventually *had* to exercise civil disobedience in order to protect the integrity of their faith.

In this day of humanistic tyranny and the unrelenting barbarism of Planned Parenthood, these kinds of issues are, once again, prominent for the ministry of prophets and priests. It would stand us in good stead to pay heed to the procedural agenda as set forth in Scripture — and Scripture alone. Witness for instance, the careful Biblical parameters set for civil disobedience by the participants in abortion clinic rescues.[81]

Tearing Down the High Places

In his remarkable book, *Idols for Destruction*, Herbert Schlossberg asserted, "When a civilization turns idolatrous, its people are profoundly changed by that experience. In a kind of reverse sanctification, the idolater is transformed into the likeness of the object of his worship."[82]

As the Psalmist put it:

> Those who make idols are like them and thus are all who put their trust in them (Psalm 115:8).

"Blood-thirsty gods produce blood-thirsty people," Schlossberg continues. "If someone thinks that chance rules the universe, his actions are likely to appear random. If people increasingly think that malevolence rules . . . we can expect more human sacrifice. If there is a decline in the number of people who believe that God is love, we can expect fewer who think that actions of love are moral imperatives. For any individual or society, therefore, the religious questions are the ultimate ones that govern human conduct, whether they believe it or not."[83]

This is why it is so crucial for us, as prophets and priests guiding and guarding the land, to do more than point out the dangerous idolatries of Planned Parenthood. We must destroy every idol and we must tear down the high places. Whatever the cost.

Asa was a good king who ruled over the kingdom of Judah for forty-one years. "He did what was right in the sight of the Lord," and he walked in the steps of "David, his father" (1 Kings 15:11). He instituted a number of crucial reforms, including the removal of male cult prostitutes and the destruction of Asherah images (1 Kings 15:12-13). But, despite all the good that he did, he is remembered most for what he did *not* do. His final epitaph was simply that he had failed to remove the high places (1 Kings 15:14). He was good. He was moral. But he just did not go far enough.

Asa's son, Jehoshaphat, was also a good king. He reigned in Jerusalem for twenty-five years, "doing right in the sight of the Lord" (1 Kings 22:42-43). He, too, instituted important reforms but, like his father, he just did not go far enough. "The high places were not taken away, and the people still sacrificed and burnt incense there" (1 Kings 22:43).

Similarly, Jehoash was a good and moral king. He reigned in Jerusalem for forty years (2 Kings 12:1). And he "did right in the sight of the Lord all his days" (2 Kings 12:2). But he did not go far enough: "the high places were not taken away" (2 Kings 12:3).

Amaziah was a good and moral king for twenty-nine years in Jerusalem (2 Kings 14:2). He, too, "did right in the sight of the Lord" (2 Kings 14:3). And, yet, "the high places were not taken away" (2 Kings 14:4). He simply did not go far enough.

Azariah, son of Amaziah, reigned fifty-two years in Jerusalem (2 Kings 15:2). Like his father, "he did right in the sight of the Lord" (2 Kings 15:3). And, yet, he, too, is remembered for the epitaph: "the high places were not taken away" (2 Kings 15:4). He was good. He was moral. But he just did not go far enough.

Jotham was another of the good kings of Judah. He reigned sixteen years in Jerusalem (2 Kings 15:33), "and he did what was right in the sight of the Lord" (2 Kings 15:34). Sadly, though, "the high places were not taken away" (2 Kings 15:35). He was good and moral, but he did not go far enough.

Each of these kings ultimately failed, despite their good works and good intentions, because they did not utterly destroy the idols of the land. And, bit by bit, the idolatry eroded their culture until one day it completely destroyed it (2 Kings 25:8-21). Each of the kings failed to serve their society as prophets and priests, guiding and guarding the land.

May we not make the same terrible mistake. May we stir up within ourselves the courage to remove all the high places and to destroy all the idols.

Conclusion

On January 22, 1988 while more than fifty thousand pro-life workers assembled on Capitol Hill, President Reagan issued an historic proclamation establishing the sanctity of all human life, including unborn children. In that proclamation he wrote, "I, Ronald Reagan, President of the United States, by virtue of the authority vested in me by the Constitution and laws of the United States, do hereby proclaim and declare the unalienable personhood of every American from the moment of conception until natural death, and I do proclaim, ordain, and declare that I will take care that the Constitution and the laws of the United States are faithfully executed for the protection of America's unborn children. Upon this act, sincerely believed to be an act of justice, warranted by the Constitution, I invoke the considerate judgment of mankind, and the gracious favor of Almighty God."[84]

Despite this, abortion proceeds apace. Despite this, Planned Parenthood proceeds apace. Apparently a lot has changed since the days when Presidential proclamations actually *meant* something—since the days of Abraham Lincoln.[85]

There is an important lesson for us in this: Presidential politics, Presidential policies, and Presidential personalities cannot and will not effect the kinds of changes we need in order to protect the helpless, the disenfranchised, the poor, the despised, and the neglected. There is more to confronting and exposing systematic injustice than electing a "good, pro-life President." There is more to toppling idols than obtaining "good, pro-life proclamations." Symbolic gestures simply are *not* sufficient.

The Church must reassert its priestly and prophetic roles, guarding and guiding the land in the schools, in the media, in local government, in the legislature, in the courts, and in the bureaucracy. Anything less is just not enough.

Signs are taken for wonders.
"We would see a sign!"
The word within a word,
unable to speak a word.
Swaddled with darkness.
In the juvenescence of the year.
Come Christ the tiger.

T. S. Elliot

ALTARS FOR CONSTRUCTION: AN AGENDA FOR THE FUTURE

Adeste Fideles

We can't fight *something* with *nothing*.

That is a basic truth that the Church has always understood.[1] Its great struggles *against* darkness, defilement, death, and deception through the ages have simultaneously been struggles *for* light, loveliness, life, and liberty. Wickedness was always met with righteousness, not just righteous indignation.

Thus, in our efforts to defend the helpless, the hopeless, and the harassed in our own day, it is important that we not simply say "no" to Planned Parenthood; we must say "yes" to the fullness of the Christian faith and its disciplines.

John Chrysostom knew only too well that you can't fight something with nothing. The great fourth-century saint was renowned far and wide for his scintillating and prophetic oratory. His sermons, first in the city of Antioch and then in Constantinople itself, attracted throngs of rapt listeners. He was known as the "golden tongued" preacher and glorious revival followed him wherever he went. This despite the fact that he readily denounced sin in high places, he unhesitatingly confronted vice and corruption, and he fearlessly exposed the powers and the principalities.

Why was he so popular? He seemed to break every homiletical rule in the book. His messages were too long. His arguments were too complex. His rhetoric was too harsh. And his counsel was too demanding. How then was he able to so mesmerize the crowds and to catalyze repentance?

According to Thrasymachos of Trace, a fifth-century Church historian, Chrysostom's sermons were almost entirely Biblical and thus had "all the vibrancy and authority and suasion of Holy Writ itself."[2] He believed that "the dispensation of the Word to the people was sacramental" and thus necessitated "a careful exegesis of Scripture" as well as "a practical exposition of Scripture every time he took to the pulpit."[3] Unlike many of the preachers in his day, he refused to indulge in either "philosophical speculation or recreational pleasantry."[4] He avoided "pastoral mundania and communal absurdia" serving his listeners instead "the pure meat of the Gospel, turning neither to the right nor the left, distracted from his Holy Duty by neither clamoring urgency nor beckoning tyranny."[5]

Chrysostom was a Biblical preacher. And no doubt that alone set him apart from many, if not most, of his contemporaries.

Even so, that still does not adequately explain his great power and popularity. And Thyrasymachos admits as much. "As important as his Biblio-centricity was," noted the historian, "it was his spiritual estate that lent Chrysostom such anointing and favor. . . . It was his personal commitment to the basic disciplines of the faith . . . almsgiving, prayer, and fasting."[6]

John Chrysostom did not simply say "no" to sin and malevolence; he said "yes" to the fullness of the Christian faith and its disciplines.

Jan Hus also knew that you can't fight something with nothing. The great fourteenth-century reformer was, like Chrysostom, renowned far and wide for his scintillating and prophetic preaching. His sermons, first in the city of Prague and then in the countryside surrounding Bohemia attracted enthusiastic and rapturous crowds. He was known as the "firebrand of the Czechs" and renewal broke out spontaneously wherever he went. This despite the fact that he openly challenged papal exclusivity, he courageously condemned the selling of indulgences, simony, and ecclesiastical larceny, and he forthrightly demanded uncompromising discipleship from every Believer.

Why was he so popular? Again, he seemed to break every homiletical rule in the book. He exploded popular beliefs. He condemned common practices. And he stood against the tide of his entire generation. How then was he able to become a passionately lauded national hero?

According to Herve Kotasek, a sixteenth-century Czech historian, it was Hus who first gave currency to the notion of *Sola Scriptura* — Scripture only — a doctrinal cornerstone of the Reformation. "The Bible was his all-in-all," Kotosek asserted."[7] He adhered to the faith of the Englishman, John Wyclif, affirming the supremacy of the Holy Ordinances."[8] Preaching expositorily through the Gospels, he emphasized a "precept upon precept, line upon line, verse upon verse ministration, taking full upon himself the necessity to feed his flock."[9] Unlike many of the preachers in his day, "he refused to pander to the rich and esteemed."[10] He remained "entirely uninterested in the most popular of intrigues, sacred or secular, holy or profane."[11] Instead, he studiously maintained the "sacramental office of preaching the Word of Life, unadorned and unadulterated with trivial concerns."[12]

Hus was a Biblical preacher. And no doubt that alone set him apart from many, if not most, of his contemporaries.

Even so, that still does not explain his great power and popularity. And Kotasek admits as much. "Though thoroughly compelling in the pulpit," the historian commented, "his allure was assured by as much in what he was, as what he said . . . for indeed the holiness of Hus was great. He gave of himself unto the poor. . . . He gave of himself unto the prayers, and. . . . He gave of himself unto the fasts of the year . . . holding sway o'er unrighteousness with an anointing that may delight upon only those who walk in the footsteps of the Master."[13] Jan Hus did not simply say "no" to sin and malevolence; he said "yes" to the fullness of the Christian faith and its disciplines.

Charles Haddon Spurgeon also knew that you can't fight something with nothing. The great nineteenth-century pastor and evangelist was, like Chrysostom and Hus, renowned far and wide for his scintillating and prophetic preaching. His sermons, first in Victorian London, and then all around the globe, drew unprecedented crowds week after week, year after year, and decade after decade. He was known as the "prince of preachers" and enthusiastic revival followed him wherever he went. This despite the fact that he was uncompromising in his doctrinal fidelity, he was forthright in his non-conformity, and he was unflinching in his opposition to vice and corruption.

Why was he so popular? He seemed to break every homiletical rule in the book. His sermons were too coarse. His theology was too rigid. His passion was unbridled. And his temperament was colloquial. How then was he able to attract such a loyal following?

According to Spurgeon's contemporary W. C. Wilkinson, the great preacher's sermons were a "steady unfailing river of Biblical utterance."[14] During his remarkable ministry, he held to "an absolute, simple, single fidelity, maintained by him throughout, maintained unintermittingly, from the juvenile beginning to the culminating maturity of his work — the serene, unperturbed, untempted fidelity of mind, of heart, of conscience, of will, of all that was in him, and all that was of him, to the mere and pure and unchanged and unaccommodated Gospel of Jesus Christ, the same yesterday, today, and forever. That stands up and out in his sermons, that lifts itself and is eminent, like a peak of the Himalayas, high regnant over all the subjected high table-land of this noble Church."[15] What his preaching did "was to present to his hearers the one unchanging Gospel in countless changes of form, each perfectly level to the comprehension of all. He turned and turned the kaleidoscope of the sermon, and exhibited to his hearers, never weary of beholding, the same precious Biblical truths, over and over again."[16] Unlike many preachers in his day, he was never tempted to entertain "the little waves of scientific guess, of new theologic shift, or of filial culture seeking to replace Biblical ethics with pagan aesthetics."[17] He never "stood before his hearers like a reed shaken with the wind."[18] Instead, "he stood solid on the Rock of Scripture, with the whole balanced weight of his great persona."[19] Wilkinson concluded saying, "Spurgeon was one of the greatest preachers of all times and of all climes. Such is the indefeasible heritage of anointed exposition."[20]

Spurgeon was a Biblical preacher. And there is no doubt that his pulpit prowess set him apart from most, if not all, of his contemporaries.

Even so, that still fails to adequately explain his phenomenal, worldwide, multigenerational, long lasting popularity, influence, and power. And Wilkinson admits as much. "His remarkable greatness was not simply due to his magnificent gift of eloquence, that steady unfailing river of Scriptural utterance, that winning, manly, pathetic voice, like a silver trumpet, like a flute, like an organ. Nay, it was his inexhaustible holiness of mind and body and discipline. It was his commitment to the poorest of the poor. . . . It was his commitment to prayer and fasting. . . . It was his nobility of Christian discipline and character."[21]

Like John Chrysostom and Jan Hus before him, Charles Haddon Spurgeon did not simply say "no" to sin and malevolence; he said "yes" to the fullness of the Christian faith and its disciplines.

The Brass Tacks

At the heart of his great Sermon on the Mount, Jesus details for his followers three essential disciplines: almsgiving, prayer, and fasting. (Matthew 6:2-18). Notice that in His discussion about these things He never said, "*If* you give," or "*If* you pray" or "*If* you fast." These disciplines were not options to Him. He unequivocally said, "*When* you give" (Matthew 6:3), and "*When* you pray" (Matthew 6:5), and "*When* you fast" (Matthew 6:17). Genuine faith in Christ will *always* be expressed in these ways.

Throughout the history of the Church, these three practices have been the recognized and recognizable marks of true spirituality. Godly character ultimately manifests them. Priestly compassion necessarily embraces them. Prophetic fervor inevitably relies on them.

Adeimantos of Thessily, the great seventh-century liturgist often asserted that "upon these three hang the whole of our faith, the whole of our hope, and the whole of our love."[22]

Cephalos of Chalcedon, a famed eighth-century philanthropist and physician, argued that "the care of our Christian culture would surely disintegrate, should we ever abandon our three Beatific Disciplines: alms, intercessions, and fastings."[23]

Otto Blumhardt, the great seventeenth-century Lutheran missionary to Africa, claimed that "on the day the Church abandons its care of the poor, its fervent ministry of supplication, and its intently chosen fast, we will undoubtedly see its clergy dragged off in wickedness and promiscuity, its parishes awhoring after greed and avarice, and its congregants awash in every vain imagination and unspeakable perversion. On that day the Church will no longer be the Church. May it never be. May it never be. Stay the day with the hand of faithful diligence, I pray."[24]

Like Chrysostom, Hus, and Spurgeon, each of these men, and thousands, or even millions of others recognized that Christ's three essential disciplines were the dynamic upon which genuine grace turned. Impeccable character without faith-provoked deeds — alms, prayer, and fasting — is lifeless (James 2:14-26). Eloquent expository preaching without faith-provoked works — alms, prayer, and fasting — is impotent (James 1:22-27).

Almsgiving

Jesus was a servant. He came to serve, not to be served (Matthew 20:20). And He called His disciples to similar lives of selflessness. He called them to be servants (Matthew 19:30).

Oddly, servanthood is a much neglected and largely forgotten Christian vocation today. Most of us who bear the banner of Christ are obsessed with leading. We want headship. We want prominence. We want power, privilege, and prestige. We want dominion, not servitude.

But Jesus made it plain that if we want to help transform the world — doing God's will on earth as it is done in heaven — we must not grasp at the reins of power and influence. We must serve. We must give. We must sacrifice. Only then will we be fit for leadership. Jesus said, "Whoever wishes to be chief among you, let him be your servant," (Matthew 20:27). Our attitude, in fact, "should be the same as Christ's, who, being in very nature God did not consider equality with God something to be grasped, but made Himself nothing, taking the very nature of a servant, being made in human likeness. And being found in appearance as a man, He humbled Himself and became obedient to death, even death on a cross. Therefore God exalted him to the highest place and gave Him the name that is above every name" (Philippians 2:5-9).

This basic principle is reiterated throughout Scripture. The theme of the suffering servant who later triumphs, who serves faithfully and then succeeds, is one of the most common Biblical paradigms. We see it in the lives of Jacob (Genesis 31:1; 36-42), Joseph (Genesis 39:1,7-20; 41:38-43), David (1 Samuel 16-19; 23; 24:20), Daniel (Daniel 6:3-28), and the Apostle Paul (Galatians 1:10; Romans 1:1).

It is no accident then that those of us who are commissioned by the King of kings and the Lord of lords to be "witnesses in Jerusalem, Judea, Samaria, and to the uttermost parts of the earth" (Acts 1:8), and "to make disciples of all nations" (Matthew 28:19) are commissioned as servants. Not as overlords.

When the Apostle Paul wrote to Titus, the young pastor of Crete's pioneer Church, he pressed home this fundamental truth with impressive persistence and urgency. The task before Titus was not an easy one. Cretan culture was marked by deceit, ungodliness, sloth, and gluttony (Titus 1:12). And he was to provoke a total Christian revival there! He was to introduce peace with God through Christ. Thus, Paul's instructions were strategically precise and to the point. Titus was to preach the Word diligently, but he was also to live out the Word practically. Charity was to be a central priority.

Paul wrote:

"For the grace of God that brings salvation has appeared to all men, teaching us that, denying ungodliness and worldly lusts,we should live soberly, righteously, and godly in the present age, looking for the blessed hope and glorious appearing of our great God and Savior Jesus Christ, who gave Himself for us, that He might redeem us from every lawless deed and purify for Himself His own special people, zealous for good works" (Titus 2:11-14).

Word *and* deed. Biblical preaching and almsgiving.

This was a very familiar theme for Paul. It wasn't exclusively aimed at the troublesome Cretan culture. He returned to it at every opportunity. Earlier, he had written to the Ephesian Church saying:

For by grace you have been saved through faith, and that not of yourselves; it is the gift of God, not of works, lest anyone should boast. For we are His workmanship, created in Christ

Jesus for good works, which God prepared beforehand that we should walk in them (Ephesians 2:8-10).

God saves us by grace. There is nothing we can do to merit His favor. We stand condemned under His judgment. Salvation is completely unearned—except by Christ—and undeserved—except to Christ. But we are not saved capriciously, for no reason and no purpose. On the contrary, "We are His workmanship, created in Christ Jesus for good works." We are "His own possession," set apart and purified to be "zealous for good deeds." Word and deed are inseparable. Judgment is answered with grace. Grace is answered with charity. This is the very essence of the Gospel message.

So, Paul tells Titus he must order his fledgling ministry among the Cretans accordingly. He himself was "to be a pattern of good deeds" (Titus 2:7). He was to teach the people "to be ready for every good work" (Titus 3:1). The older women and the younger women were to be thus instructed, so "that the Word of God might not be dishonored" (Titus 2:5). And the bondslaves, "that they might adorn the doctrine of God our Savior in all things" (Titus 2:10). They were all to "learn to maintain good works, to meet urgent needs, that they might not be unfruitful" (Titus 3:14). There were those within the Church who professed "to know God, but in works they denied Him, being abominable, disobedient, and disqualified for every good work" (Titus 1:16). These, Titus was to "rebuke . . . sharply, that they might be sound in the faith" (Titus 1:13). He was to affirm constantly, "that those who believed in God would be careful to maintain good works" (Titus 3:8).

As a pastor, Titus had innumerable tasks that he was responsible to fulfill. He had administrative duties (Titus 1:5), doctrinal duties (Titus 2:1), discipling duties (Titus 2:2-10), preaching duties (Titus 2:15), counseling duties (Titus 3:12), and arbitrating duties (Titus 3:12-13). But intertwined with them all, fundamental to them all, were his *charitable* duties. Almsgiving was to be central to his task.

What was true for Paul and Titus in the first century is just as true for us today, for "these things are good and profitable for all men" (Titus 3:8).

Chrysostom understood that. So did Hus and Spurgeon. Genuine discipleship always weds Word and deed. It always combines Biblical preaching with almsgiving. It always has. It always will.

The Bible tells us that if we would obey the command to be generous to the poor, we would ourselves be happy (Proverbs 14:21), God would preserve us (Psalm 41:1-2), we would never suffer need (Proverbs 28:27), we would prosper and be satisfied (Proverbs 11:25), and even be raised up from beds of affliction (Psalm 41:3). God would ordain peace for us (Isaiah 26:1-3). He would bless us with peace (Psalm 29:11). He would give us His peace (John 14:27). He would guide our feet into the way of peace (Luke 1:79). He would ever and always speak peace to us (Psalm 85:8). And He would grant peace to the land (Leviticus 26:6).

Therefore let us be "zealous for good works"(Titus 2:14).

"Is this not the fast which I chose, to loosen the bonds of wickedness, to undo the bands of the yoke, and to let the oppressed go free, and break every yoke? Is it not to divide your bread with the hungry, and bring the homeless poor into the house; when you see the naked, to cover him; and not to hide yourself from your own flesh? Then your light will break out like the dawn, and your recovery will speedily spring forth; and your righteousness will go before you; the glory of the Lord will be your rear guard. Then you will call, and the Lord will answer; You will cry, and He will say, 'Here I am.' If you remove the yoke from your midst, the pointing of the finger, and speaking wickedness,and if you give yourself to the hungry,and satisfy the desire of the afflicted,then your light will rise in darkness, and your gloom will become like midday. And the Lord will continually guide you, and satisfy your desire in scorched places, and give strength to your bones; and you will be like a watered garden,and like a spring of water whose waters do not fail. And those from among you will rebuild the ancient ruins; you will raise up the age-old foundations; and you will be called the repairer of the breach, the restorer of the streets in which to dwell" (Isaiah 58:6-12).

We can't fight *something* with *nothing*. We can't simply say "no" to Planned Parenthood; we must say "yes" to the fullness of the Christian faith and its disciplines. We must say "yes" to good works to the needy and neglected. We must say "yes" to girls in crisis pregnancies, and teens caught in the web of immorality, and families trapped in financial difficulty. We must say "yes" to almsgiving and servanthood.

But how do we go about doing that?

First, we must begin to implement effective programs of Biblical charity in our Churches that transform poverty into productivity.[25] In 1950, one in twelve Americans lived below the poverty line.[26] In 1979, that figure had risen to one in nine.[27] Today, one in seven fall below the line — nearly thirty-four million people.[28] More than one-fourth of all American children live in poverty.[29] And for black children under the age of six, the figures are even more dismal: more than fifty percent.[30] Today, eighty-one percent of elderly women, living alone, live in poverty, all too often in abject poverty.[31] As many as two million Americans are homeless, living out of the backs of their cars, under bridges, in abandoned warehouses, atop street-side heating grates, or in lice-infested public shelters.[32] Even at the height of the Great Depression, when dust-bowl refugees met with the "grapes of wrath" on America's highways and byways, there have *never* been so many dispossessed wanderers.[33] The fact is, the Reagan Recovery of the eighties never reached into the cavernous depths of the bottom third of the economy.[34] Shelters are bulging at the seams.[35] And social service agencies are buried under an avalanche of need.[36] And the situation here at home is *nothing* compared to that of the Third World.[37]

Even so, we could make a dramatic difference simply by practicing Biblical charity.[38] If only we would. Not only would the poor be cared for and the oppressed set free, but we would be able to reclaim the moral high ground from groups like Planned Parenthood as well.

Second, we must begin to find ways to encourage, uphold, and support working mothers in our nation. Over the last decade, per capita family income has increased about seven percent.[39] At the same time, however, the consumer price index has inflated more than eleven percent.[40] Add to that the fact that only one out of every five jobs actually pays enough to lift a family of four above the poverty line, the fact that the tax burden falls on poor families especially hard, the fact that home businesses and cottage industries are heavily restricted, that occupational licensing has closed many traditional family trades to the family, and that cultural and societal pressures have tainted the vocation of homemaking, and working mothers become a foregone conclusion.[41] In 1970, only thirty-nine percent of America's mothers had entered the work force.[42] By 1980, fifty-four percent were working.[43] And by 1985, sixty-one percent were.[44] According to the Bureau of Labor Statistics, almost half of those working mothers have children under the age of six.[45] The emotional pressure, the physical fatigue, and the spiritual entropy that working mothers face day in and day out can be utterly debilitating.[46] And with no relief in sight. Ever.

Again, though, we could make a difference.[47] If only we would. Not only would families be strengthened and mothers be protected, but we would be able to reclaim the moral high ground from groups like Planned Parenthood as well.

Third, we must begin to come to the aid of widows and displaced homemakers in our society. The liberalization of divorce laws, the breakdown of family solidarity, and run-away immorality have combined to create a whole new underclass in American society: the abandoned housewife. The number of displaced homemakers rose twenty-eight percent between 1975 and 1983 to more than three million women.[48] Another twenty percent increase from 1983 to 1988 brought that number to more than four million.[49] An astonishing sixty-one percent of those women suddenly left alone had children under the age of ten at home.[50] Often without job skills and stranded without alimony or child support, as many as seventy percent of these women make less than ten thousand dollars a year, and fifty percent are employed at minimum wage or less.[51] It is, thus, readily apparent why a full seventy-five percent of all Americans living below the poverty line in the United States are women and their children.[52] Caught between traditionalism and feminism, these women have no advocate. No matter where they turn, they don't fit in. They know no context.

Once again, though, through a proper and Biblical administration of alms, we could make a real difference.[53] If only we would. Not only would the widows and orphans be cared for, but we would be able to reclaim the moral high ground from groups like Planned Parenthood as well.

Fourth, we must develop compassionate and dignified ministries for and to the handicapped. They are the forgotten and the neglected. And there are millions of them. As many as sixteen percent of all Americans suffer from some sort of crippling disability — congenital or accidental.[54] There are almost seven million mentally retarded Americans, with an additional fifteen million suffering from severe learning disorders.[55] There are at least a million men, women, and children with total hearing loss, and six and a half million with total visual impairment.[56] Still another seven million are restricted by paralysis, atrophy, deformity, amputation, degeneration, or immobility.[57] Abandoned by families, shunned by peers, frustrated by dependency, targeted by Planned Parenthood, United Way, and the March of Dimes, and incapacitated by loneliness and doubt, the handicapped are all too often society's pariah.

But, we could make a difference with ministries of compassion. A *real* difference. If only we would. Not only would the handicapped be able to vouchsafe their dignity and worth, but we would be able to reclaim the moral high ground from groups like Planned Parenthood as well.

Fifth, we must lend full support to existing pro-life ministries: alternative clinics,[58] adoption agencies,[59] shepherding homes,[60] maternal care hospitals,[61] natural family planning centers,[62] *moral* sex education programs,[63] research organizations,[64] and charitable outreaches.[65] And in order to do this, not only are we going to have to open our homes, volunteer our time, and dedicate our talents,we are going to have to loosen our purse strings as well. Planned Parenthood has invested vast sums of money in its dastardly programs. It has marshalled tremendous resource pools. It has funded, subsidized, and capitalized for maximum impact. It has withheld nothing from the cause.

But wealth is a gift from God, set aside for one purpose and one purpose only: to confirm the Covenant and to establish the Kingdom (Deuteronomy 8:18). Even the wealth of the wicked will one day be converted to Kingdom purposes (Proverbs 13:22). That is why the Bible places so much emphasis on stewardship. Every Christian should be a giver (Deuteronomy 16:17). We should give to the Church through tithes (Malachi 3:10). We should give to special projects through offerings

(1 Corinthians 16:1-2). And we should give to those who have ministered to us through gifts (Galatians 6:6). Giving is an aspect of worship (Deuteronomy 16:10-11). Thus it should be done with a cheerful heart (2 Corinthians 9:7), whether out of prosperity (1 Corinthians 16:2), or paucity (2 Corinthians 8:2). After all, giving is an investment in the Kingdom of God (Matthew 6:19-21).

We can't fight *something* with *nothing*. We can't simply say "no" to Planned Parenthood; we must say "yes" to the fullness of the Christian faith and its disciplines. Like Chrysostom, Hus, and Spurgeon, we must say "yes" to good works. We must say "yes" to almsgiving.

Prayer

If we are going to conform ourselves to God's holy and perfect will, we must pay heed to the eternal and established Word of Truth.

> The grass withers, the flower fades, but the Word of our God stands forever (Isaiah 40:8).

> The Law of the Lord is perfect, converting the soul; The testimony of the Lord is sure, making wise the simple (Psalm 19:7).

> The entrance of Your Words gives light; It gives understanding to the simple (Psalm 119:130).

> For the Commandment is a lamp, and the Law is light; Reproofs of instruction are the way of life (Proverbs 6:23).

To ever go *beyond* Scripture would mean to evade the purposes of God (1 Corinthians 4:6). That is why the heroes of the faith were so driven to the discipline of prayer. Diligence in prayer always grounds God's people in a dependence on His Word. Such was the case of David (Psalm 51:1-19), Nehemiah (Nehemiah 1:1; 2:1), Jeremiah (Lamentations 5:1-22), Jonah (Jonah 2:2-9), the disciples of Jesus (Acts 1:8-14), and the first Jerusalem Church (Acts 2:1-47).

A failure to seek God in prayerful fellowship leads invariably to a violation of God's Word and a rejection of His purposes. Such was the case with Cain (Genesis 4:3-8), Korah (Numbers 16:1-35), Balaam (Numbers 22:2-40), and Saul (1 Samuel 13:5-14).

That is why the Bible makes it plain that Christians are to be *constant* in prayer. We are to pray in the morning (Mark 1:35). We are to pray at noon (Psalm 55:17). We are to pray in the evening (Mark 6:46). We are to pray during the night watch (Luke 6:12). In fact, we are to pray unceasingly (1 Thessalonians 5:17). God has given us access to His throne (Hebrews 4:16). He has given us fellowship with Christ (1 Corinthians 1:9) and counsel with the Holy Spirit (John 14:26). Therefore, we are to make use of the glorious privilege of prayer at *every opportunity* (1 Timothy 2:8).

The fact is though, prayer doesn't simply make us more cognizant of God's Word. Prayer changes things. By the grace of God.

No matter how bad things may look, no matter how ominously the odds may be stacked against the cause of truth, justice, and mercy, prayer can transform it all.[66] Planned Parenthood may seem to have a frightening advantage in money and manpower. They may seem to have unending resources and unflagging energy. But Christians have prayer. And prayer is the most potent force in all the cosmos availed to mere mortal men. Prayer binds and it looses (Matthew 18:18). It casts down and it raises up (Mark 11:23-24). It ushers in peace (1 Timothy 2:1-2), forgiveness (Mark 11:25), healing (James 5:14-15), liberty (2 Corinthians 3:17), wisdom (1 Kings 3:3-14), and protection (Psalm 41:2).

We can't fight *something* with *nothing*. We can't simply say "no" to Planned Parenthood; we must say "yes" to the fullness of the Christian faith and its disciplines. Like Chrysostom, Hus, and Spurgeon, we must say "yes" to prayer. We must pray with wholeheartedness (Jeremiah 29:13). We must pray with contrition (2 Chronicles 7:14). And we must pray faithfully (Mark 11:24), fervently (James 5:16a), obediently (1 John 3:22), and confidently (John 15:7).

But how do we go about doing this in a *comprehensive, practical*, and *effective* way?

First, we must develop a deep and abiding commitment to personal and devotional prayer. We must pray for national and cultural revival. We must intercede mightily and persistently for our magistrates and leaders. And we need to be specific: naming names, stating issues, claiming promises, and invoking Scripture. It is crucial that we cry out from our prayer closets for justice and mercy to blanket the land like a sweet morning dew. It is ludicrous for us to picket, lobby, and labor against Planned Parenthood if we have not first honed our principle weapons.

> For though we walk in the flesh, we do not war according to the flesh, for the weapons of our warfare are not of the flesh, but divinely powerful for the destruction of fortresses. We are destroying speculations and every lofty thing raised up against the knowledge of God, and we are taking every thought captive to the obedience of Christ, and we are ready to punish all disobedience, whenever your obedience is complete (2 Corinthians 10:3-6).

Second, we must effect corporate prayer disciplines. We must infuse Church worship with the unction and gumption that can only come by fervent intercession. We need to pray corporate benediction and blessing for all those who honor God's Word (Psalm 69:13-19). And we need to pray malediction and cursing for all those who impugn God's Word (Psalm 69:20-28). The practice of singing Approbative Psalms—the various hymns of blessing from the Psalter: 5, 7, 9, 20, 23, 25, 65, 75, and 113 — and Imprecatory Psalms—the various hymns of cursing from the Psalter: 2, 10, 35, 55, 69, 79, 83, 94, 109, and 140—has long been the first recourse for the Church in times of distress and dismay.[67] So, why have we failed to instigate seasons of prayer? Why has the Church not gathered its people in mourning and humiliation, in weeping and supplication to pray for the end of the abortion holocaust and the demise of its perpetrators? Why hasn't a profusion of cottage prayer meetings, spontaneous revivals, prayer breakfasts, all night vigils, and fasts flooded the heavenlies with our urgent pleas for relief? And how can we legitimately rail against Planned Parenthood when we have yet to do these things? Really?

Third, we must develop prayer networks and hotlines both on the local and on the national levels. We desperately need to find ways to respond quickly and decisively to the various machinations of Planned Parenthood's medical, legal, educational, and jurisdictional juggernaut. We need to be able to respond to the trumpet call (Joshua 2:15). We need to be able to sound the alarms (Amos 3:6). We need to be able to rush to one another's defense (Galatians 6:2). With phone trees, computer linkups, newsletters, radio broadcasts, electronic bulletin boards, and short wave skip beams, we need to tie all the forces for life together with the strong bonds of prayer.

The bottom line is simply that we can't fight *something* with *nothing*. We can't just say "no" to Planned Parenthood; we must say "yes" to the fullness of the Christian faith and its disciplines. Like Chrysostom, Hus, and Spurgeon, we must say "yes" to fervent intercession. We must say "yes" to prayer.

Fasting

Fasting—or abstinence from food for a time—is not exclusively a Christian practice. It exists in many other religions. It is practiced by some for health reasons. It is even practiced by some for political reasons. So when Jesus commanded His disciples to fast, He was not introducing a novel custom at all (Matthew 6:16, 18). He did however give fasting a distinctive meaning. He connected the practice of fasting with the very mystery of life and death.

According to the Bible, sin is not only the transgression of God's standards leading to judgment and imputed guilt (Romans 3:10-23); it is also the mutilation of life (Romans 5:12). "The wages of sin is *death*" (Romans 6:23). It is for this reason that the Bible's narrative of the original sin is cast against the backdrop of *eating* (Genesis 3:1-7). Food is a means of life. It affords us vitality. It lends us strength. It bolsters our health. But it is *not* the source of life, because life is not merely biological. The fact is, food has no life in and of itself. Only Christ has life and is Life (John 1:4). Calories don't enable food to bestow life. God does. By His direct command. Jesus said, "Man does not live by bread alone" (Matthew 4:4). If he tries, he dies (Proverbs 16:25). To truly live, man must live "by every Word that comes from the mouth of God" (Matthew 4:4).

Adam and Eve rejected the fullness of life preferring "bread alone." They tried to ignore the life-sustaining Word of God (Genesis 3:4-6). As a result, not only were they alienated from God, incurring His wrath, but they died (Genesis 5:5). Though they ate, food could not and would not sustain them. Thus, hunger came to be a reminder to them that they were ultimately dependent on something more than food. They were dependent upon God. Fasting then is an invitation to remember. It is a discipline that enables Believers to reckon their dependency upon God.

Unlike those who fast to secure better health, or to obtain political concessions or even to accrue some ascetic merit, Christians fast in order to renew their fellowship with the Lord God. For us, fasting is not a matter of pragmatism — a ritual or obligation designed to *make something happen*. We don't fast for personal benefit or to make a show of our piety (Isaiah 58:3-5). Rather, we fast "unto the Lord," recognizing our utter and complete reliance on Him (Zechariah 7:5).

Our fasting may be absolute (Ezra 10:6; Deuteronomy 9:9; Exodus 34:28) or partial (Daniel 10:3; 1 Kings 17:1-24). It may be entirely private (Nehemiah 1:1-4, 2:1; Matthew 6:16-18) or demonstrably public (Jeremiah 36:6; Joel 2:15). It may be occasional (Ezra 10:6; Esther 4:16; Acts 13:3) or seasonal (Leviticus 23:27; Psalm 35:13; Zechariah 9:19). But one thing is certain: if we are seriously seeking to do the will of God, obeying His Word and walking in dependence on Him, we *will* fast (Matthew 6:18).

We should fast in times of distress (Esther 4:3, Nehemiah 1:4). We should fast during seasons of repentance (Ezra 10:6; Nehemiah 9:1). We should fast while seeking God's direction (Acts 13:3; Luke 2:37). We should fast while awaiting an outpouring of grace (Psalm 69:10; Joel 2:12), an endowment with power (Judges 20:1-48; Mark 9:29), and a liberation from captivity (Isaiah 58:6; Matthew 17:21). It is only as we humbly fast that we have the spiritual wherewithal to guide and guard the land as prophets and priests (2 Chronicles 7:14).

> Blow a trumpet in Zion, consecrate a fast, proclaim a solemn assembly, gather the people, sanctify the congregation, assemble the elders, gather the children and the nursing infants. Let the bridegroom come out of his room and the bride come out of her bridal chamber (Joel 2:15-16).

We can't fight *something* with *nothing*. We can't simply say "no" to Planned Parenthood; we must say "yes" to the fullness of the Christian faith and disciplines. Like Chrysostom, Hus, and Spurgeon, we must say "yes" to fasting.

It has been so long since the Church has taken seriously its mandate to fast we have all but forgotten *how*! So what can we do to reclaim this lost legacy of obedience, commitment, dependency, and power?

First, we must begin to teach God's people the meaning, the purpose, the importance, and the practice of fasting. Sermons need to be preached. Books need to be distributed.[68] Bible studies need to be taught. Families need to be discipled. And congregations need to be catalyzed. Techniques, health principles, and spiritual exercises need to be communicated to every Believer so that the Church can once again bear its mantle of strength in the world.

Second, we must renew an *individual* commitment to fasting. Like the heroes of faith in bygone days, we each need to fall on our faces before God in distress, humiliation, weeping, and mourning for the awful perversity that is ravaging our land. Planned Parenthood's juggernaut should drive us to sackcloth and ashes. It should stir in us a desperation to seek God with vigor. It should throw us passionately before Him, utterly reliant, completely dependent upon His sustaining grace. It should provoke us to regular fasting, to seasons of fasting, to unremitted fasting.

Third, we must call our Churches to days of public fasting and supplication. We must sanctify our time as congregations. No Christian's time is his own. It is not ours to dispose of as we choose. We have "been bought with a price" (1 Corinthians 6:20), therefore, we are to set our days, weeks, and years apart to the Lord for His glory (Romans 14:6-12). In the Old Testament, the days were divided into eight periods: dawn, morning, midday, dark, evening, and three night watches. These were distinguished by times and seasons of prayer (Psalm 55:17; Daniel 6:10). In the New Testament, the value of this kind of discipline was affirmed by the early Christians who punctuated their urgent task of evangelization with the patient discipleship of regular spiritual refreshment (Acts 3:1). Similarly, the weeks of God's people were ordered with purpose and balance. Centered in the Old Testament around Sabbath sacrifices, and in the New Testament around the Lord's Day sacraments, the weeks established Biblical priorities for the people by giving form to function and function to form (Deuteronomy 5:12; Hebrews 10:24-25). These disciplines enabled them to wait on the Lord and thus to "run and not be weary" and to "walk and not be faint" (Isaiah 40:31). Even the years were given special structure and significance. In ancient Israel, feasts, festivals, and fasts paced the Believers' progression through the months (Exodus 13:6-10; Psalm 31:15). The early Church continued this stewardship of time, punctuating years with the Christian holidays: Advent, Christmas, Epiphany, Lent, Easter, Ascension, and Pentecost — each marked by feasts, festivals, and, of course, fasts. Thus, God's people were enabled and equipped to run the race (Philippians 2:16), to fight the fight (Ephesians 6:10-18), to finish the course (2 Timothy 4:7), and to keep the faith (2 Timothy 3:10). If we are to attain to even just a little of their potency, power, and prowess, it is crucial that we return to these patterns of humility and dependence.

We can't fight *something* with *nothing*. We can't simply say "no" to Planned Parenthood; we must say "yes" to the fullness of the Christian faith and disciplines. Like Chrysostom, Hus, and Spurgeon, we must say "yes" to utter dependence upon God. We must say "yes" to fasting.

Where the Rubber Meets the Road

Mark Lincoln is the pastor of a small Presbyterian Church in central California. Active in the pro-life movement for more than a decade, he recently has gone through a time of tremendous discouragement, frustration, and burnout. "I guess I just got to the point where I had come to the end of myself," he said. "I had worked for years and had very little fruit to show for it. Our Church's crisis pregnancy center was floundering — understaffed, underfinanced, and underexposed. Several of the members of the Church had been arrested and then convicted of trespassing on the property of Planned Parenthood during a prayer protest. Our workers were exhausted and our resources were depleted. And we didn't have a thing to show for any of that. We were all full of heartache and despair."

Mark decided to take off several days to spend some time at a retreat center. "I needed to regain some perspective. I needed a new focus. It seemed like the enemies of God were racking up all the victories while the poor pitiful People of God were being ground into the dust. I wanted to know why."

Taking nothing but the Bible and an anthology of Patristic Epistles, Mark began to read and think and pray. "It didn't take me very long to figure out what had gone wrong with our efforts. It seemed to be written on every page of Scripture. It was illumined in the teachings of the Early Church Fathers at every turn. How I had missed it before, I'll never know. It was as plain as day. *We had left our first love.* It was that simple. We had been trying to fight Planned Parenthood our own way, through our own efforts, with our own resources, through our own energies. The well of our strength is finite, while the well of God's grace is infinite. So as admirable as our struggle had been, it was ultimately self-defeating and foolhardy."

Mark came back from the retreat with a renewed commitment. "I knew that it was time for me to get *serious* about halting the holocaust. I knew it was time for me to get *serious* about exposing Planned Parenthood. But I also knew that the only way that I *could* be serious was to do things God's way. Our Church will still picket. We will still lobby, and testify, and mobilize, and carry out rescues, and mount campaigns and all that. But at the core of all we do, we will walk in the way of the Lord. We will exercise spiritual discipline. We will cling to the fullness of the faith."

"Because we can't fight *something* with *nothing*?" I suggested.

"Yeah, right," he said. "Because we can't fight *something* with *nothing*. Not any more, we can't."

Conclusion

In his famous sermon "The Weight of Glory," C. S. Lewis made a penetrating assessment about Christian virtue. He said that "if you asked twenty good men today what they thought the highest of the virtues, nineteen of them would reply, Unselfishness. But if you asked almost any of the great Christians of old he would have replied, Love. You see what has happened? A negative term has been substituted for a positive, and this is of more than philological importance. The negative ideal of Unselfishness carries with it the suggestion not primarily of securing good things for others, but of going without them ourselves, as if our abstinence and not their happiness was the important point."[69]

Lewis understood that Christian virtue—at least as it was comprehended and practiced by the great Believers of the past—was not a negative thing; it was positive.

It would stand us in good stead to recover that sensibility in our day. The fact is, we can accomplish very little if we are merely *anti-abortion* or *anti-Planned Parenthood*. We must be pro-life—in the sense that we embrace the fullness of love and life and faith.

Anything less is less than sufficient unto this day.

"For our titanic purposes of faith and revolution, what we need is not the old acceptance of the world as a compromise, but some way in which we can heartily hate and heartily love it. We do not want joy and anger to neutralize each other and produce a surly contentment; we want a fiercer delight and fiercer discontent. We have to feel the universe at once as an ogre's castle, to be stormed, and yet as our own cottage, to which we can return at evening."

G. K. Chesterton

THIS TOO SHALL PASS

Dabit Deus His Quoque Finem

I looked up and saw war in the sky. Malevolent light beams bathed the clouds in an eerie sunset of blood red and ash gray. That war should have such a lovely reflection made the prospect of encountering it all the more menacing—or at least it should have. But I was driven by an irresistible compulsion. There was nothing to do except go forward.

I was back in town. I was back where I'd had the frightening chase through the alley, around the corner, and down the freeway with a child cradled in my arms. It was six months later and my throat still knotted and my eyes still clouded whenever I thought of it.

My hotel was just a few blocks from the abortuary. As soon as I was settled in and refreshed from my long trip, I yielded to its magnetism and set out walking.

I trembled with emotion. A flood of images crowded my senses. Apprehension, fear, curiosity, longing, anger, grief, and frustration vied for my emotions. With every step, tension mounted within me.

I took in all the dreary particulars of the cityscape. The final remnants of sunlight glittered ominously through a chainlink fence, still wet from a late afternoon rain. Puddles pocked the asphalt walk, leaden like pools of mercury. I recognized all the elements of the scene. Yet there was a lack of coherence about it. There always is when the dread of war smears its thick urgency upon a land.

As I came upon the final block, I suddenly became dizzy with disorientation.

Is this it?

No, this can't be it. Where is the building?
It's gone. The clinic is gone.
How can that be?
I know this is it.
What's going on here?

I checked the address. I double checked. There was no question about it. This was it. But the clinic was gone. Completely. Leveled. Vanished. No trace in sight.

I walked toward the lot. Down around the corner was the old retainer wall, still scrawled with graffiti. And out back was the alley, now completely visible from the street.

A sign planted in the middle of the property said that the clinic had moved. Except for the naked and now weed-choked foundation and the remembered geography, that was the only hint that anything had *ever* been here.

I walked back to the alley and stood where the old dumpster had been. And I stooped down to pick up a broken piece of rubbish.

At the touch, a shiver went up and down my spine. And then a shudder. This was a place of eternity. Of war.

Like hymning angels chime, I whispered a prayer. Tears fell from my eyes like rain. And then I turned to go.

I realized then, all anew, that in *time* God would make everything right. Like this place.

I looked up at the sky. The colors of war were still there. But somehow they didn't look as foreboding now. Somehow they looked right. Coherent.

As I walked back to my hotel, I sensed a balancing of my equilibrium—both urgency and patience coexisting there.

And I smiled.

APPENDIX A

MAKING A PRESENTATION

With knowledge comes responsibility (Luke 12:42-48). Now that you know what you do about Planned Parenthood, you have a responsibility to *share* that information with others. Not only that, you have a responsibility to *use* that information to effect justice, mercy, and truth in your family, in your community, and in your circle of influence.

If you are ever given the opportunity to speak before a precinct caucus, or a PTA meeting, or a School Board session, or a County Commissioner's hearing, it is important that you have your facts straight, your material organized, and your focus clearly in view.

Making an effective presentation of the facts about Planned Parenthood need not be a daunting experience. Most of the work is already done for you. All you need to do is to pick and choose your quotes, statistics, and anecdotes and, then, boldly go forth (Matthew 28:19-20; Acts 1:8).

Here are a few tips on how to do just that:

First, write your whole presentation out, even if only in outline form. This will keep you on track and accurate. There is nothing worse than obscure generalities or irrelevant rabbit trails. Stick to your prepared comments. You'll be more confident. And you'll be more convincing.

Second, use hard evidence. There aren't more than one hundred footnotes in each chapter of this book for *nothing*! They are there for you to *use*. So use them! Cull out the startling statistics and the incendiary quotations. Prove your point. Drive home your message. Don't leave anything to speculation. Chapter two was especially written so that you could take whole paragraphs and even whole sections word for word, verbatim, and use them as ammunition in your testimony or presentation.

Third, always make sure you use *local* examples, *local* statistics, and *local* quotations in your talk. Don't let the spokesman for Planned Parenthood brush off your arguments as irrelevant simply because you've failed to do your homework. Go to the library. Stop by the schools. Visit the clinics. Check the facts. Leave absolutely nothing to hearsay. Remember, *lives* depend on your getting everything right.

Fourth, do your best to soften your barrage of statistics, studies, and surveys with real life stories. Bring your point all the way home. Make your presentation personal and passionate. Make it human. Make it real. If at all possible, have several women who have been exploited by the local Planned Parenthood abortuary to collaborate your facts with their anecdotes. Don't let your arguments be dismissed and dispatched as mere ephemeral theory.

Fifth, have plenty of supporting pro-life literature, tracts, books, articles, and research papers available for those who may be interested in further investigation. Never show up empty-handed. Back up your claims with real substance. Challenge your adversaries to read through this entire book. Give them a copy. Subscribe to the *LifeNet* or *Christian Action Council* newsletters in their name.[1] And then watch the sparks begin to fly!

Sixth, be prepared to propose real and practical alternatives. If you tell the school board that Planned Parenthood's sex education programs have to go, but then fail to give them some viable alternate courses of action, you might as well save your breath. Find out about the *Sex Respect* curriculum and the *Life Advocates,* or *Why Wait?* programs for public schools and then be prepared to answer questions on them.[2] Learn about the local abortion alternative centers and then be prepared to defend them. Get involved with one of the many excellent Pro-life organizatons in your area (see Appendix B), and know how to counsel, refer, and advise.

Seventh, be sure that you maintain a polite, courteous, and Christian demeanor throughout. You can say the *right* thing, but say it in the *wrong* way, and you'll lose your audience every time. Part of the success of Planned Parenthood has been its ability to choose winsome, articulate, and attractive spokesmen for itself. It is crucial that you counter that advantage with a double dose of Christian charity and longsuffering. Don't lash out. Don't pop off. Don't retaliate. Be tough and unswerving, but always with an eye toward winning the weak, championing the helpless, and wooing the undecided (Jude 22-23).

RESOURCES

There are a large number of excellent pro-life and charitable organizations that you can look to for help in your struggle for life and truth. Each has a unique area of specialty. Each has literature, presentations, services, resources, and opportunities that you can take advantage of, and each is deserving of your prayerful and financial support.

The following list is by no means comprehensive, but it should give you a good start.

Advocates for Life
P.O. Box 13656
Portland, OR 97213

Americans Against Abortion
P.O. Box 40
Lindale, TX 75771

American Life League (ALL)
P.O. Box 490
Stafford, VA 22554

Americans United for Life
343 S. Dearborn, Suite 1804
Chicago, IL 60604

Birthright
11235 S. Western Ave.
Chicago, IL 60643

Black Americans for Life
419 7th St., N.W., Suite 402
Washington, DC 20004

Christian Action Council (CAC)
422 C St., N.E.
Washington, DC 20002

Couple to Couple League
P.O. Box 11084
Cincinnati, OH 45211

Committee to Protect the
Family Foundation
8001 Forbes Place, Suite 102
Springfield, VA 22151

Concerned Women for America
(CWA)
122 C St., N.W., Suite 800
Washington, DC 20001

Eagle Forum
P.O. Box 618
Alton, IL 62002

Family Research Council
515 Second St. N.E.
Washington, DC 20002

Focus on the Family
801 Corporate Center Drive
Pomona, CA 91764

Free Congress Research and
Education Foundation
721 Second St., N.E.
Washington, DC 20002

Heart Light
P.O. Box 8513
Green Bay, WI 54308

HELP Services Women's Center
P.O. Box 1141
Humble, TX 77338

Human Life Foundation
150 East 35th Street
New York, NY 10157

Human Life International
7845-E Airpark Road
Gaithersburg, MD 20879

Liberty Federation
505 Second Street, N.E.
Washington, DC 20002

Liberty Godparent Foundation
P.O. Box 27000
Lynchburg, VA 24506

LifeNet
P.O. Box 185066
Fort Worth, TX 76181-0066

Life Advocates
4848 Guiton, Suite 209
Houston, TX 77027

March for Life Education
and Defense Fund
P.O. Box 90330
Washington, DC 20090

March Houston for Life
P.O. Box 207
Spring, TX 77383

Moral Majority
2020 Tate Springs Road
Lynchburg, VA 24501

National Right to Life Committee
419 7th St., N.W., Suite 402
Washington, DC 20004

Operation Blessing
CBN Center
Virginia Beach, VA 23463

Operation Rescue
P.O. Box 1180
Binghamton, NY 13902

Orthodox Christians for Life
P.O. Box 805
Melville, NY 11747

Pro-Life Action League
6160 N. Cicero Ave.
Chicago, IL 60646

Pro-Life Action Ministries
611 S. Snelling Ave.
St. Paul, MN 55116

Rutherford Institute
P.O. Box 510
Manassas, VA 22110

Sex Respect
P.O. Box 349
Bradley, IL 60915

Why Wait?
P.O. Box 1000
Dallas, TX 75221

Women Exploited (WE)
2100 W. Ainsley
Chicago, IL 60640

Women Exploited By Abortion
(WEBA)
202 S. Andrews
Three Rivers, MI 49093

A number of organizations specialize in distributing pro-life books, tracts, films, and slide presentations. Again, the following list is by no means comprehensive, but it should point you in the right direction.

American Portrait Films
1695 W. Crescent Ave., Suite 500
Anaheim, CA 92801

Catholics United for Life
(CUL)
New Hope, KY 40052

Christian Action Program
P.O. Box 8204
Fort Worth, TX 76124

Christian Worldview (CWV)
P.O. Box 185066
Fort Worth, TX 76181-0066

Couple to Couple League
3621 Clenmore Avenue
Cincinnati, OH 45211

Crossway Books
9825 West Roosevelt Road
Westchester, IL 60153

Dominion Press
P.O. Box 8204
Fort Worth, TX 76124

Hayes Publishing
6304 Hamilton Ave.
Cincinnati, OH 45224

The Human Life Review
150 East 35th Street
New York, NY 10157

Life Cycle Books
2205 Danforth Ave.
Toronto, Ontario M4L1K4

LifeNet
P.O. Box 185066
Fort Worth, TX 76181-0066

Michael Fund
400 Penn Ctr. Blvd., Room 1022
Pittsburgh, PA 15235

New Vision Books
P.O. Box 920970-A16
Houston, TX 77018

Servant Publications
P.O. Box 8617
Ann Arbor, MI 48107

Thoburn Press
P.O. Box 6941
Tyler, TX 75711

Wolgemuth & Hyatt, Publishers
P. O. Box 1941
Brentwood, TN 37027

There is nothing as valuable as primary source documents.
You can write to the various pro-abortion, anti-family organizations below and receive some of the most remarkable literature
you could ever imagine.

Abortion Rights Association
100 E. Ohio
Chicago, IL 60611

Alan Guttmacher Institute
360 Park Ave., South
New York, NY 10010

National Abortion Rights
Action League
825 15th St., NW
Washington, DC 20005

National Organization
for Women
425 13th St., NW
Washington, DC 20004

Planned Parenthood Federation
of America
515 Madison Ave.
New York, NY 10022

Planned Parenthood—
World Population
810 7th Ave.
New York, NY 10019

Religious Coalition for Abortion Rights
100 Maryland Ave., NE
Washington, DC 20002

END NOTES

Introduction — Ad Vitum

1. Although books like David Kennedy's *Birth Control in America: The Career of Margaret Sanger* (New York: Yale University Press, 1970), Linda Gordon's *Woman's Body, Woman's Right: A Social History of Birth Control in America* (New York: Penguin Books, 1974), and Elasah Drogin's *Margaret Sanger: Father of Modern Society* (New Hope, KY: CUL Publications, 1979, 1986) have done a good deal of preliminary or specialized analysis, a *comprehensive* look at Planned Parenthood has always been lacking.
2. See Faye Wattleton, *How to Talk to Your Child About Sexuality* (Garden City, NJ: Doubleday and Company, 1986), p. iv.
3. See Abraham Stone and Norman E. Himes, *Planned Parenthood: A Practical Guide to Birth Control Methods* (New York: Collier Books, 1951, 1965).
4. Throughout this book when I speak of Planned Parenthood, I am speaking in general terms — of the movement — and not of every single individual affiliate, clinic, or chapter. In order to determine which policies, practices, principles, and procedures are normative for the movement, I looked for published information that the national organization had released to all the affiliates, or for trends common to several affiliates.
5. Although there can be no guarantees in this very litigious society, every effort has been made to ensure that no individuals have been isolated, ridiculed, slandered, libeled, or denigrated in any way, shape, or form in this book. Additionally, several researchers and legal counselors have poured over the text and the documentation to ensure both the integrity of the work and the authenticity of its claims. The purpose of *Grand Illusions* is very simply to survey the known data from the Planned Parenthood movement and then to apply Biblical principles to the interpretation of that data. It is not an attempt to influence the flow of interstate commerce or the development of any particular judicial or legislative action.
6. These may be published at a later date as a separate book.
7. Many of the most damning documents we were compelled for legal reasons to eliminate from our study.
8. Several other researchers are currently at work on important manuscripts exposing Planned Parenthood's work including Robert G. Marshall for Crossway and Jacqueline Kasun for Ignatius Press. In addition, Marvin Olasky, Associate Professor of Journalism at the University of Texas, has just released a remarkable study of press coverage of abortion entitled *Dead Beat: The Press and Abortion, 1838-1988* (New York: Lawrence Erlbum Associates, 1988).
9. G. K. Chesterton, *What's Wrong With the World* (New York: Dodd, Mead, and Company, 1910), p. 1.

10. Aleksandr I. Solzhenitsyn, *A World Split Apart* (New York: Harper and Row, 1978), pp. 47-49.
11. Francis A. Schaeffer, *A Christian Manifesto* (Westchester, IL: Crossway Books, 1981), p. 24.
12. See Joseph Fletcher, *Situation Ethics: The New Morality* (Philadelphia: The Westminster Press, 1966).

Chapter 1—In the Heat of the Fight

1. Like all the other stories, illustrations, and vignettes in this book, this one is entirely factual. Certain personal, geographical, and architectural alterations have been symbolically altered in order to protect innocent parties from legal liability and/or harassment. But otherwise, the events and conversations are absolutely accurate.
2. The clinic was not institutionally affiliated with Planned Parenthood—it was not listed in the Planned Parenthood Federation of America directory and it did not use the Planned Parenthood registered service mark. Even so, it was clearly a part of the generic Planned Parenthood movement. Its media center was named for Planned Parenthood's founder, Margaret Sanger, its lobby was stocked with Planned Parenthood literature, and its board participated in a number of legal, professional, and associational Planned Parenthood umbrella groups.
3. Proverbs 8:35-36; Matthew 16:25.
4. David Funderburg, "We Must Cry Out for the Young" (Houston: March Houston for Life, 1986), from the EP *March Houston for Life*, available from MHL, P.O. Box 207, Spring, TX 77383.
5. Psalm 73:1-28.
6. Matt Scudder is a fictional detective in Lawrence Block's series of books published by Arbor House in hardback and by Pocket Books in paperback.
7. Ecclesiastes 11:6.
8. Though it was fairly late, I was able to get at least a cursory understanding of the city's disposal situation by contacting several twenty-four hour operations. It was not a comprehensive survey, but it was quite enlightening.
9. Genesis 3:24; Exodus 14:26-35.
10. Genesis 4:9-16.
11. Hebrews 4:1-11.
12. Psalm 61:1-4.
13. Psalm 11:3.
14. Romans 8:19-22.
15. Romans 3:9-24.
16. 1 Corinthians 12:4-7.
17. Hebrews 10:24-25.
18. John 3:20.
19. Psalm 38:20.
20. Psalm 109:4.
21. Proverbs 24:11-12.
22. Ezekiel 3:17-19.
23. 2 Corinthians 5:20.
24. Daniel 5:25.
25. Isaiah 6:5.
26. Isaiah 6:8.

27. Romans 3:13; Revelation 9:21.
28. Proverbs 8:35-36.
29. Revelation 6:10.
30. Psalm 10:2.
31. Again, the only operations I was able to contact were all-night labs and disposal waste companies, but with the scant information I was able to cull from them, I was able to accurately extrapolate the facts.
32. 2 Chronicles 28:3; Isaiah 30:33; Jeremiah 7:30-33.
33. Mark 5:1-5.
34. Psalm 17:9-12.

Chapter 2 — All That Glitters

1. Curt Young, *The Least of These* (Chicago: Moody Press, 1984), p. 30.
2. LeBeth Myers, *Women Around the Globe: International Status Report* (London: Guyon Social Resource Center, 1986), p. 137.
3. Debbie Taylor et al. *Women: A World Report* (New York: Oxford University Press, 1985), p. 10; and Paul B. Fowler, *Abortion: Toward an Evangelical Consensus* (Portland: Multnomah Press, 1987), p. 11.
4. Frederick S. Jaffe, Barbara L. Lindheim, and Philip R. Lee, *Abortion Politics: Private Morality and Public Policy* (New York: McGraw-Hill, 1981), p. 7.
5. Numbers 13:33.
6. "Celebrating Seventy Years of Service," 1986 Annual Report, Planned Parenthood Federation of America, pp. 23, 32.
7. "Seventy Years of Family Planning in America: A Chronology of Major Events," Planned Parenthood Federation of America, pp. 3, 8.
8. The myth persists that Margaret Sanger, Planned Parenthood's founder, was a trained "public health nurse" (as the 1986 Planned Parenthood Annual Report puts it), but that is patently untrue. See Madeline Gray, *Margaret Sanger: A Biography of the Champion of Birth Control* (New York: Richard Marek Publishers, 1979), p. 326.
9. "Celebrating," p. 14.
10. "Serving Human Needs, Preserving Human Rights," 1983 Annual Report, Planned Parenthood Foundation of America, p. ii.
11. "Celebrating," p. 32.
12. Ibid.
13. Planned Parenthood Affiliates, Chapters, and State Public Affairs Offices Directory, 1984.
14. Ibid.
15. "Celebrating," pp. 22-23.
16. Ibid., pp. 9, 12.
17. Ibid., pp. 9-11.
18. Ibid., pp. 18-19, 25-27.
19. Ibid., pp. 9-10.
20. "Serving," p. 4.
21. "Celebrating," p. 22.
22. Ibid., pp. 10, 21, 27.
23. Ibid., p. 24.
24. "Serving," pp. 14-16.
25. Ibid., pp. 5-6.
26. "Celebrating," pp. 3, 23.

27. Ibid., p. 13.
28. Ibid., pp. 8-9.
29. Ibid., pp. 16, 23.
30. Ibid., p. 9.
31. "Serving," p. 13.
32. A full-page advertisement placed in the *New York Times* and several other news-papers around the country during 1984 by Planned Parenthood Federation of America stated, "We . . . have spent the better part of this century supporting and fighting for everyone's freedom to make their own decisions about having children. Without government interference." See also *Planned Parenthood Review* 2:4 (Winter, 1982).
33. Throughout this chapter and then beyond into the remainder of this book the term *illusion* is used in a theological sense: contrary to the facts of the Bible and to the created order of Almighty God. It is not intended to impugn any one in-dividual's character or integrity.
34. In 1969 Planned Parenthood President Alan Guttmacher asserted that "eventu-ally coercion may become necessary." It was shortly thereafter that his head of research, Frederick Jaffe, issued a now infamous memo entitled, "Examples of Proposed Measures to Reduce U.S. Fertility." See Richard D. Glasow's analy-sis in "Ideology Compels Fervid PPFA Abortion Advocacy," *National Right to Life News* (March 28, 1985), p. 5.
35. Ibid.
36. Ibid.
37. Ibid.
38. See Frederick S. Jaffe, "Activities Relevant to the Study of Population Policy for the U.S.," Memorandum to Bernard Berelson, March 11, 1969, quoted in *Family Planning Perspectives* special supplement no. 1129, 10-70/30, p. ix.
39. See Stephen Jay Gould, *The Mismeasure of Man* (New York: W.W. Norton and Company, 1981), especially pages 335-336; and Charles Valenza, "Was Margaret Sanger a Racist?" *Family Planning Perspectives* 17:1, (January/February 1985) pp. 44-45.
40. In Guttmacher's 1969 remarks, he suggested that coercive measures would likely be necessary first in "India and China." Again, see Glasow's analysis in "Ideology Compels Fervid PPFA Abortion Advocacy." Although direct insti-tutional causality may be difficult to prove, direct generic causality is in-disputable.
41. See Stephen Mosher's important studies on the Chinese birth control atrocities, *Broken Earth* (New York: Free Press, 1983), and *Journey Into the Forbidden China* (New York: Free Press, 1985). Also see Michael Weisskopf's articles that first appeared in the Washington Post and then were widely reprinted: "Abortion Policy Tears at China's Society" (January 7, 1985), and "China's Birth Policy Drives Some to Kill Baby Girls" (January 14, 1985).
42. Remarks made at the Planned Parenthood sponsored "Horizons in Reprod-uctive Health Conference" at the luxurious Hotel del Coronado resort in San Diego in 1985. See Paul L. Bail's analysis in "Planned Parenthood Speakers Support Red Chinese Forced Abortion," American Life Lobby *Issues*, June, 1985.
43. Douglas Johnson, "New Battle Looms Over U.S. Aid for U.N. Agency Sup-porting Coerced Abortion," *National Right to Life News* (May 1, 1986), p. 1; and *Planned Parentwood Review*, 5:1 (Winter 1984/85).
44. Report to donors, International Planned Parenthood Federation, October, 1983.

45. See, for example, *Newsweek Magazine*'s extensive coverage: March 29, 1982; July 12, 1982; April 30, 1984.

46. See William M. O'Reilly, *The Deadly Neo-Colonialism* (Washington, D.C.: Human Life International, 1986); *Planned Parenthood Review* 2:4 (Winter 1982), p. 16; "The Facts About IPPF," (The Human Life Center, University of Steubenville, Steubenville, Ohio); and "Serving: Performance of Projects Funded by Family Planning International Assistance in 1985," Planned Parenthood Federation of America. Again, the issue of direct causality can be resolved only on the generic level.

47. *Report of the Working Group on the Promotion of Family Planning as a Basic Human Right*, International Planned Parenthood Federation, London, 1984, pp. 21-23; and Donald P. Warwick, *Bitter Pills: Population Policies and Their Implementation in Eight Developing Countries* (London: Cambridge University Press, 1982), especially p. 64.

48. In *Planned Parenthood of Central Missouri v. Danforth* (1976), the U.S. Supreme Court ruled that parental consent was unconstitutional.

49. In the same decision, the Supreme Court upheld Planned Parenthood's contention that to require the consent of a husband before his wife could undergo an abortion was a violation of the mythical "right to privacy."

50. In 1986, Planned Parenthood affiliates in several states including Ohio, Washington, and New Jersey won injunctions and restraining orders that "sharply restricted" the activities of pro-life protestors and in several instances barred their dissent altogether. See "Celebrating," pp. 19-21.

51. In *Planned Parenthood v. Kempiners* (1981), a federal district court struck down an Illinois law that provided funds to agencies that offer assistance to pregnant women but that do not refer or counsel for abortion. In other cases across the country, in Fort Worth, San Francisco, Fargo, and Los Angeles, Planned Parenthood has hounded and harassed institutions and services that remain recalcitrant on the dogmas of birth control, abortion, and family limitation. See the articles by Marlene J. Perrin in *USA Today*, July 23, 1986.

52. Bart Ligon, *Legal Restraints: Professional Equity and the Conservative Conscience in the 1980's* (New Orleans: St. Augustine Review Press, 1986), pp. 19-23.

53. In the *City of Akron v. Akron Center for Reproductive Health* (1983), Planned Parenthood filed an amicus brief arguing successfully that city ordinances, state restrictions, and other official regulations of the abortion trade were unconstitutional.

54. When Ronald Reagan finally made good on his campaign promise to limit federal funding to abortion providers seven years into his administration, a massive Planned Parenthood lobbying campaign persuaded the members of the Senate's Appropriations Subcommittee on Labor, Health and Human Services, and Education to veto his plans. See the AP wire story that appeared in newspapers all across the country on September 12, 1987, including *The Tennessean*, *The Houston Chronicle*, and *The Washington Times*.

55. Obviously, Planned Parenthood has one of the most comprehensive legal and judicial programs in the country. See "Celebrating," p. 27, and "Serving," p. 13.

56. David C. Reardon, *Aborted Women: Silent No More* (Westchester, IL: Crossway Books, 1987), p. 28.

57. Ibid., p. 19.

58. Ibid.

59. Ibid.

60. Ibid.

61. Ibid.

62. Ibid.

63. Ibid.
64. "Serving Human Need," *Planned Parenthood Review* 3:4 (Winter 1983/84), pp. 2, 13-14. "It Makes Sense," Planned Parenthood of Houston and Southeast Texas, p. 4.
65. Again, the term *illusion* is used in a theological sense here.
66. See Linda Gordon, *Woman's Body, Woman's Right: A Social History of Birth Control in America* (New York: Penguin Books, 1974); and Elasah Drogin, *Margaret Sanger: Father of Modern Society* (New Hope, KY: CUL Publications, 1986).
67. See, for instance, Margaret Sanger's articles in *The Birth Control Review*, May, 1919; May, 1923; October, 1926; and April, 1932.
68. Margaret Sanger, "Plan for Peace," *Birth Control Review* 16:4 (April, 1932).
69. Margaret Sanger, *The Pivot of Civilization* (New York: Brentano's Inc., 1922), pp. 105-123.
70. Ibid., p. 108.
71. Ibid., p. 114.
72. Ibid., p. 115.
73. Ibid., pp. 116-117.
74. See Gordon, pp. 329-355; Drogin, pp. 17-29; "Ethnic Group and Welfare Statutes of Women Sterilized in Federally Funded Family Planning Programs," *Family Planning Perspectives* 6:4 (Fall, 1974); and *Low Income Task Force Report*, "Planned Parenthood: Objective 2000," Planned Parenthood of Houston and Southeast Texas January 5, 1987.
75. Margaret Sanger, "Birth Control," *The Birth Control Review*, May, 1919.
76. See Erma C. Craven's eye-opening essay, "Abortion, Poverty, and Black Genocide," in Thomas Hilger and Dennis J. Horan *Abortion and Social Justice* (New York: Althea Books, 1981).
77. See Tim Zentler, for Planned Parenthood of Humboldt County, quoted in *The Union*, June 14, 1983; Martha Burt, *Public Costs for Teenage Childbearing*, Center for Population Options, Washington, D.C., 1986; and "Serving Human Need," *Planned Parenthood Review* 3:4 (Winter, 1983).
78. See the letter from Planned Parenthood of Northeastern Indiana board member Len Goldstein to *The Fort Wayne Journal-Gazette*, November 5, 1987.
79. *Pivot of Civilization*, p. 96.
80. Jaffe, p. ix.
81. Ibid.
82. "Planned Parenthood" brochure from Planned Parenthood of Houston and Southeast Texas, 1986, p. 2.
83. Again, the term *illusion* is used in a theological sence here.
84. "Celebrating," p. 32. This is one of the reasons why accumulating accurate data and statistics on Planned Parenthood is so difficult, and why comprehensive information about its activities and funding sources is so easy to conceal.
85. What else can you call the world's number one dispenser of abortion and birth control devices than a "family banning" organization? See Franky Schaeffer, *A Time for Anger: The Myth of Neutrality* (Westchester, IL: Crossway Books, 1982), p. 99.
86. See Chapter 7. Although most of the Planned Parenthood agencies meet the legal IRS standards for non-profit status—putting them on a par with, for instance, a local church—they accrue to themselves vast, vast sums of money. Legal designations aside, by any other standard, Planned Parenthood's abortion and contraceptive industry is phenomenally profitable. "Non-profit" is thus very much in question as well.

87. Robert Ruff, *Aborting Planned Parenthood* (Houston: New Vision Books, 1988). The book is available from Life Advocates, 4848 Guiton, Suite 209, Houston, TX 77027 or from New Vision Books, P.O. Box 920970-A16, Houston, TX 77018.
88. Ibid.
89. Let me note as a matter of clarity that Planned Parenthood is only one of nearly five thousand clinics, hospitals, and other health service providers that receive Title X funding. But as in the Title V, Title XX, Title XIX, and all the other federal appropriations bills mentioned in this chapter, Planned Parenthood *is* the single largest recipient in any and all of its sundry incarnations. Additionally, we should note that in only fourteen states in the United States, and about seventy-six foreign countries, is it actually legal for Planned Parenthood to spend its tax bequest on abortions or abortion-related activities. On this point, Franky Schaeffer's comments from his book *A Time for Anger* are instructive: "Planned Parenthood's most consistent claim is that it does not use federal money to fund abortion. This is probably technically true. But the family planning centers of Planned Parenthood operate in conjunction with medical clinics, *which do* perform abortions. Planned Parenthood's propaganda helps to convince women to have abortions, so their claim is rather like a pimp saying he has nothing to do with prostitution" (p. 99).
90. Robert G. Marshall, *School Birth Control: New Promise or Old Problem* (Stafford, VA: American Life League, 1986), p. 1.
91. Talon Gartrell, *Abortion and the States: A Case Against the Technical Elimination of Federal Jurisdiction and Roe vs. Wade* (Manassas, VA: Life Work Publications, 1987), p. 3.
92. Alan Guttmacher Institute, *Issues in Brief*, 4:1, (March, 1984).
93. Ibid.
94. Ibid.
95. Ibid.
96. Ibid.
97. Ibid.
98. Gartrell, p. 12.
99. Ibid., p. 12.
100. Ibid., p. 2.
101. "Celebrating," pp. 14-16; Gartrell, pp. 2-4; and William M. O'Reilley, *The Deadly Neo-Colonialism* (Washington, D.C.: Human Life International, 1986).
102. "Celebrating," pp. 2-3.
103. Again, the term *illusion* is used in a theological sense here.
104. See Ruff, pp. 9-34; and Stan Weed, "Curbing Births, Not Pregnancies," *Wall Street Journal*, October 14, 1986.
105. J. C. Wilke, *Abortion: Questions and Answers* (Cincinnati: Hayes Publishing Co., 1985), pp. 90-131.
106. Sara E. Rix ed., *The American Woman 1987-88: A Report in Depth* (New York: W. W. Norton and Co., 1987), p. 251.
107. Louis Harris and Associates, *American Teens Speak: Sex, Myths, TV, and Birth Control* (New York: Planned Parenthood Federation of America, 1986), p. 19.
108. Rix, p. 254.
109. David Chilton, *Power in the Blood: A Christian Response to AIDS* (Brentwood, TN: Wolgemuth and Hyatt, Publishers, 1987), p. 50.
110. See Deborah Maine, "Does Abortion Affect Later Pregnancies?" *Family Planning Perspectives*, 11:2, (March/April 1979), pp. 98-101; Kevin Hume, M.D., *Cancer and the Pill: Five Studies and a Review of Literature* (Stafford, VA: Anastasia

Books, 1985); Robert G. Marshall, "A Scandal of Collusion," *A.L.L. About Issues*, April, 1986, pp. 6-7; and Ellen Grant, M.D., *The Bitter Pill: How Safe is the Perfect Contraceptive?* (London: Elm Tree Books, 1985).

111. See Gray, pp. 405, 443; and Gordon, pp. 249-300.

112. Mark D. Hayward and Junichi Yagi, "Contraceptive Failure in the United States: Estimates from the 1982 National Survey of Family Growth," *Family Planning Perspectives* 18:5, (September/October 1986), table 5; and Melvin Zelnik, Michael A. Koenig, and Kim. J. Young, "Sources of Prescription Contraceptives and Subsequent Pregnancy Among Young Women," *Family Planning Perspectives*, 16:1, (January/February 1984), pp. 6-13; and Ruff, pp. 66ff.

113. Ibid.

114. Ibid.

115. Ibid.

116. Ibid.

117. These rates were derived by Robert Ruff using the binomial probability formula to extrapolate Planned Parenthood's published first-year failure rates over extended intervals. See Ruff, pp. 66ff.

118. Ibid.

119. Ibid.

120. Ibid.

121. "Celebrating," pp. 9-10, 22-23, 24-26; and Wattleton, pp. 87-90, 182-87.

122. Again, the term *illusion* is used in a theological sense here.

123. See Planned Parenthood publications for youth such as *The Great Orgasm Robbery* and *Who Changed the Combination?* (Denver: Rocky Mountain Planned Parenthood, 1977, 1979).

124. Ruff, p. 88.

125. Ibid., p. 89.

126. Chilton, p. 51.

127. Hayward and Yagi, table five.

128. Robert A. Hatcher, M.D. ed., *Contraceptive Technology 1986-1987*, 13th Revised Edition, (New York: Irvington Publishers, 1986), pp. 139ff.

129. Ruff, p. 89.

130. "Celebrating," pp. 8-13.

131. Again, the term *illusion* is used in a theological sense here.

132. Only thirty-two percent of teens who have had no sex education are sexually active, compared to forty-six percent of those who have had "comprehensive" sex education courses. See Harris, p. 6; also see Ruff, p. 15.

133. Harris, p. 7; also see William Marsiglio and Frank L. Mott, "The Impact of Sex Education on Sexual Activity, Contraceptive Use and Premarital Pregnancy Among American Teenagers," *Family Planning Perspectives* 18:4, (July/August, 1986); and Ruff, p. 16.

134. "The Effects of Sex Education on Adolescent Behavior," *Family Planning Perspectives*, 18:4, (July/August, 1986), pp. 162-169.

135. See Jacqueline R. Kasun, "Teenage Pregnancy: Media Effects Versus Facts," American Life League, 1986; Fred Glahe and Joseph Peden, *The American Family and the State* (San Francisco: Pacific Institute for Public Policy Research, 1986); "Eleven Million Teenagers: What Can Be Done About the Epidemic of Adolescent Pregnancy in the United States?," Planned Parenthood Federation of America, 1976; and Wattleton, pp. 3-4, 60, 86.

136. See, for example, the tremendous reception that alternative programs for the public schools have received: like *Sex Respect* (Respect, Inc., P.O. Box 349, Bradley, IL 60915) and *Why Wait?* (Josh McDowell Ministry, P.O. Box 1000,

Dallas, TX 75221); also note the success of alternative books like Connie Marshner's *Decent Exposure* (Brentwood, TN: Wolgemuth and Hyatt, Publishers, 1988) and Josh McDowell's *How to Help Your Child Say "No" To Sexual Pressure* (Waco, TX: Word Books, 1986).

137. Roberta Weiner, ed., *Teen Pregnancy: Impact on The Schools* (Alexandria, VA: Capitol Publications, 1987), p. 17.

138. Ibid., pp. 17, 24.

139. Wendy Baldwin, *Adolescent Pregnancy and Childbearing Rates, Trends, and Research Findings from the CPR-NICHD* (Bethesda, MD: Demographic and Behavioral Science Branch, NICHD, 1985), p. 5.

140. Weiner, p. 10.

141. Harris, pp. 8, 18, 60; Ruff, p. 48; and Marsiglio and Mott, p. 141.

142. Marshner, p. 42.

143. "Celebrating," pp. 3, 18-21; also see Alan F. Guttmacher, *Pregnancy, Birth, and Family Planning* (New York: Signet, 1973), pp. 163-75; and Alan F. Guttmacher and Irwin H. Kaiser, *Pregnancy, Birth, and Family Planning* (New York: Signet, 1986, pp. 203-20; 463-64.

144. Again, the term *illusion* is used in a theological sense here.

145. See the testimony of several veterans of both the back alley and Planned Parenthood in John T. Wilson's *Abortion and Repentance* (Los Angeles: Advocates for Life Press, 1979), pp. 19-23, 36-39, 44-46.

146. See Ruff, pp. 36-42.

147. The *VPT Consent Form* for Planned Parenthood of Houston and Southeast Texas speaks of the "inherent risks" in abortion procedures. The *Minor Consent to Abortion Form* informs the applicant that "complications could develop that might require hospitalization" and speaks of "major complications" and "severe consequences" of abortion.

148. Not *all* abortions are legal, of course. In fact, according to a number of studies, criminal and self-inflicted abortions did not decrease following liberalization of abortion statutes. See L. Huldl, "Outcome of Pregnancy When Legal Abortion is Readily Available," *Lancet*, March 2, 1968, pp. 467-468; and Thomas W. Hilgers and Dennis Horan, *Abortion and Social Justice* (New York: Sheed and Ward, 1972).

149. See Thomas W. Hilgers, Dennis Horan, and David Mall ed., *New Perspectives on Human Abortion* (Frederick, MD: Aletheia Books, 1981), pp. 69-150; Jeff Lane Hensley, *The Zero People* (Ann Arbor, MI: Servant Books, 1983), pp. 97-105; and Susan M. Stanford and David Hazard, *Will I Cry Tomorrow?* (Old Tappan, NJ: Fleming H. Revell Co., 1986); also see George Grant, *The Dispossessed: Homelessness in America* (Westchester, IL: Crossway Books, 1986), pp. 74-75; and Wilke, pp. 90-131.

150. *The New American*, January 20, 1986.

151. G. T. Burkman et al., "Culture and Treatment Results in Endometritis Following Elective Abortion," *American Journal of Obstetrics and Gynecology* 128:5 (1977) pp. 556-599.

152. C. Gassner and C. Ballard, "Emergency Medicine After Abortion Abscess," *American Journal of Obstetrics and Gynecology*, 128:4 (1977), p. 716.

153. Ibid., p. 183.

154. Ibid.

155. D. Trichopoulos et al., "Induced Abortion and Secondary Infertility," *British Journal OB/GYN* 83, (August, 1976): 645-650.

156. K. A. Stallworthy et al., "Legal Abortion: A Critical Assessment of its Risks," *The Lancet*, December 4, 1971.

157. American Association of Blood Banks and The American Red Cross, "Circular Information," 1984, p. 6.

158. W. Cates et al., "Thromboembolism and Abortion," *American Journal of Obstetrics and Gynecology* 132:4 p. 169, quoted in R. L. Turner, *Complications and Consequences of Abortion* (Los Angeles: Advocates for Life Press, 1983), p. 4.

159. L. Duenhoelter and B. Grant, "Complications Following Prostaglandin F-2A Induced Midtrimester Abortion," *American Journal of Obstetrics and Gynecology*, vol. 146, quoted in Turner, p. 5.

160. Direct casuality is difficult to prove, but no other single factor has affected the health care world to separate men and women other than abortion. Even the changing shape of the workforce to include more women has been neutralized as a factor in costs by group health insurance stabilization.

161. Julia Wittleson, *The Feminization of Poverty* (Boston: Holy Cross Press, 1983), p. 81.

162. "Factsheet: Planned Parenthood," National Right to Life, 1986; see also Brief for Planned Parenthood Federation of America, "Amicus Curiae," *Thornburgh v. American College of Obstetrics and Gynecologists*, Docket number 84-495, U.S. Supreme Court, August 31, 1985; and "Planned Parenthood Takes a Fighting Stand," *New York Times*, February 3, 1978.

163. One of the five general goals of Planned Parenthood is "to combat the world population crisis by helping to bring about a population of stable size in an optimum environment in the United States," Planned Parenthood Federation of America, *Federation Declaration of Principles*, 1980, p. 12; also see Julian L. Simon, *The Ultimate Resource* (Princeton, NJ: Princeton University Press, 1981), pp. 326-331.

164. Again, illusion is used in a theological sense here.

165. See Julian L. Simon and Herman Kahr ed., *The Resourceful Earth: A Response to Global 2000* (Oxford: Basil Blackwell, 1984); Rousas J. Rushdoony, *The Myth of Over-Population* (Fairfax, VA: Thoburn Press, 1969); Frances Moore Lappe and Joseph Collins, *World Hunger: Twelve Myths* (New York: Grove Press, 1986); William Byron, ed., *The Causes of World Hunger* (New York: Paulist Press, 1982); and Claire Chambers, *The Siecus Circle: A Humanist Revolution* (Boston: Western Islands, 1977); also see Hilgers, Horan, and Mall, pp. 450-465; Hensley, pp. 33-41; and Simon, pp. 159-288.

166. See Guttmacher, pp. 112, 302, 305-6; Guttmacher and Kaiser, pp. 465-66; and Mary S. Calderone and Eric W. Johnson, *The Family Book About Sexuality* (New York: Bantam Books, 1983), pp. 86-7, 114-16, 183.

167. See Ben J. Wattenberg, *The Birth Dearth* (New York: Pharos Books, 1987); and My T. Vu ed., *World Population Projections* (New York: World Bank Policy and Research Division, Population, Health, and Nutrition Department, 1986).

168. Charles Westoff, "Fertility in the United States," *Science Magazine*, October, 1986; also see Rushdoony, p. 39.

169. Wattenberg, p. 172.

170. Ibid., p. 15.

171. Ibid., p. 16.

172. Ibid., p. 16.

173. Ibid., p. 11.

174. Anthony Wolfe, "Population Implosion," *Saturday Review*, June 26, 1976; Donald Bogue and Amy Tsui, "Declining World Fertility: Trends, Causes, and Implications," *Population Bulletin Thirty-Three*, October, 1978; and Donald Bogue and Amy Tsui, "Zero World Population Growth," *The Public Interest*, Spring, 1979.

175. Hilgers, Horan, and Mall, p. 452.
176. Ibid., p. 454.
177. Simon, pp. 309-326.
178. Ibid., pp. 326-331.
179. Simon and Kahn, pp. 7, 12-13, 50-66.
180. As in the case of the word *illusion*, the term *lie* is used in a theological sense here and is not intended to impugn or denigrate any one individual's integrity or character.
181. Planned Parenthood as a generic movement is in theological opposition to Biblical Truth as defined by historical orthodoxy (see Chapter 10). This then, is the root of the conflict. And this is the background for the theological use of the term *lie* in relation to the Planned Parenthood movement.
182. J. I. Packer, "Foreword" in Michael Scott Horton, *Mission Accomplished* (Nashville: Thomas Nelson, 1986), p. 11. Here he uses the term in a popular, not a scholarly sense, where theological truth and error *are* at issue.
183. See Plato, *Great Dialogues of Plato* (New York: Mentor, 1956); and Thucidides, *History of the Pelopenesian War*, W. H. D. Rouse, Trans. (New York: Times Books, 1946).
184. See Plutarch, *Makers of Rome*, trans. Lou Scott-Kilvert (New York: Penguin, 1965); and Augustine, *The City of God*, trans. Robert A. B. Lawton (New York: Epoch Publications, 1957).
185. See Sergios Kasilov, *Icons of History*, trans. Vladimir Lloeslav (Paris: YMCA Press, 1962); and Basil Argyros, *Myth and Man*, trans. Cornelius Dolabella (New York: Caladea Press, 1961).
186. See Niccolo Machiavelli, *The Prince*, trans. Daniel Donno (New York: Bantam Books: 1966); and Thomas More, *Utopia*, trans. Peter K. Marshall (New York: Washington Square Press, 1965).
187. See Aleksandr Solzhenitsyn, *One Day in the Life of Ivan Denisovich*, trans. Max Hayward and Ronald Hingley (New York: Bantam Books, 1963); and Colin Thubron, *Where Nights are Longest* (New York: Random House, 1983).

Chapter 3 — Bad Seed: The Historical Legacy

1. Quoted in Harold Tribble Cole, *The Coming Terror: Life Before the Great War* (New York: Languine Bros., Publishers, 1936), p. 23.
2. Based on figures from Paul B. Fowler, *Abortion: Toward an Evangelical Consensus* (Portland: Multnomah Press, 1987), p. 59; and Debfaie Taylor et al., *Women: A World Report* (London: Oxford University Press, 1985), p. 10.
3. Sobornostic Collectivism was a school of thought developed along Machiavellian lines by Lenin's followers around the world during the first half of the twentieth century.
4. Eugenic Racism was a pseudo-scientific philosophy of genetic manipulation developed in the nineteenth century.
5. Agathistic Distributism was a theory of economic nationalism propounded by facist thinkers in Spain, France, and Italy during the late ninteenth century.
6. Abraham Stone, M.D., *The Margaret Sanger Story and the Fight for Birth Control* (Westport, CN: Greenwood Press Publishers, 1975).
7. Faye Wattleton, president PPFA, speech, February 5, 1979.
8. Diana Shaman, "Margaret Sanger: the Mother of Birth Control," *Coronet Magazine*, March, 1966.
9. Lawrence Lader and Milton Meltzer, *Margaret Sanger: The Mother of Birth Control* (New York: Thomas Crowell Company, 1969), p. 163.

10. Madeline Gray, *Margaret Sanger: A Biography of the Champion of Birth Control* (New York: Richard Marek Publishers, 1979).
11. Funeral eulogy quoted in Elasah Drogin, *Margaret Sanger: The Father of Modern Society* (New Hope, KY: CUL Publications, 1986), p. 95.
12. Ibid.
13. Lader and Meltzer, p. 163.
14. Rev. Martin Luther King, Jr., "Family Planning: A Special and Urgent Concern," Planned Parenthood-World Population (PPFA, 1973).
15. Donald Ben-Feinberg, *Sangerizing the Negroes and Jews* (New York: Shalom Books, 1949), p. 29.
16. Jordan H. Thompson, *The Politics of Birth Control* (New York: Bolastrade Publications Co., 1968), p. 131.
17. Ben-Feinberg, p. 32.
18. Thompson, pp. 63-64.
19. Gray, p. 423.
20. Shannon, p. 7.
21. Gray, pp. 64-81.
22. Sanger was compulsive about concealing her true age. In her autobiographies and on various passports she never gave the same birth date twice. She even altered her record in the Higgins family Bible. The September 14, 1879 date was arrived at by historians only after a careful examination of several palimpsests in her personal documents. See Gray, pp. 9, 13, 37.
23. Exodus 34:6-7.
24. 1 Timothy 5:8.
25. Gray, p. 16.
26. Margaret Sanger, *An Autobiography* (New York: W. W. Norton and Company, 1938), p. 22.
27. It is at least worth noting that each of the other major villains of the twentieth century had similar spiritual experiences. In his youth, Stalin studied for the Orthodox priesthood. Mussolini displayed extreme piety as a youngster. Hitler was obsessed with the study of Lutheran theology. But each of them apostacized, later stoking red hot fires of bitterness and rage against the Church.
28. Gray, p. 23.
29. In her autobiography, Sanger often touted her credentials as a trained nurse. She even inflated her work experience, saying that she had practiced nursing in both White Plains and New York City. The fact is, she never advanced beyond the status of a nurse-probationer—the equivalent of an orderly today. See Sanger, pp. 46-57, 86-92; and Gray, pp. 26-32, 326.
30. See Robert A. Rosenstone, *Romantic Revolutionary: A Biography of John Reed* (New York: Vintage Books, 1975).
31. Arthur S. Link and Richard L. McCormick, *Progressivism* (Arlington Heights, IL: Harlan Davidson, Inc., 1983), pp. 41-42.
32. Linda Gordon, *Woman's Body, Woman's Right: Birth Control in America* (New York: Penguin Books, 1974), p. 208.
33. Link and McCormick, p. 41.
34. Emma Goldman, *Living My Life* (New York: Alfred A. Knopf, 1931).
35. Goldstein, p. 72.
36. Gray, p. 58.
37. Arthur B. Logan and Thomas de Tilati, *Morality and the Village Elite* (New York: St. Regis Press, 1949), pp. 61-72.
38. Ibid., and Joseph Finder, *Red Carpet* (Fort Worth: American Bureau of Economic Research, 1983), pp. 17-19.

39. Gray, pp. 58-59.
40. Gray, p. 59.
41. Albert Gringer, *The Sanger Corpus: A Study In Militancy*, unpublished masters thesis, Lakeland Christian College, 1974, Appendix iv., pp. 473-502.
42. Ibid.
43. Ibid.
44. Ibid.
45. William H. Bradenton, *The Comstock Era: The Reformation of Reform* (New York: Laddel Press, 1958), p. 126.
46. Gray, p. 280.
47. Cited in Allan Chase, *The Legacy of Malthus: The Social Costs of the New Scientific Racism* (New York: Alfred Knopf, 1977), p. 6.
48. Paul Johnson, *A History of the English People* (New York: Harper and Row Publishers, 1985), p. 276.
49. Ibid.
50. Ibid.
51. Ibid., p. 270.
52. For a description and definition of each of these Malthusian off-shoots, see Stephen Jay Gould, *The Mismeasure of Man* (New York: W. W. Norton and Company, 1981).
53. For more on each of these perversions, see Phyllis Grosskurth, *Havelock Ellis: A Biography* (New York: Alfred A. Knopf, 1980).
54. Margaret Sanger, *The Pivot of Civilization* (New York: Brentano's, 1922), p. 264.
55. Gray, pp. 61, 71, 163, 224, 227, 487.
56. Proverbs 7:6-23.
57. Gray, p. 199.
58. Ibid., p. 201.
59. Gordon, pp. 257-272, 341.
60. Gray, pp. 284-288.
61. Gordon, pp. 396-397.
62. Ibid., pp. 264-66, 261, 320-21, 326-29.
63. Ibid., pp. 329-34.
64. Margaret actually resisted changing the name at first. She felt that *birth control* was her own proprietary label. But she soon accepted the fund raising reality that her reputation needed a white washing.
65. Gray, p. 406.
66. Ibid., pp. 306, 389.
67. Ibid., pp. 408, 429-30.
68. Ibid., p. 442.
69. Quoted in Morgan Scott LaTrobe, *The Path of Destruction* (Cleveland: The Ohio Life Alliance Fund, 1974), p. 4.
70. Faye Wattleton, "Humanist of the Year Acceptance Speech," *The Humanist Magazine*, July-August, 1986.
71. Margaret Sanger, *Women and the New Race* (New York: Brentano's, 1920. Reprint. Geo. W. Halter, 1928), p. 67.
72. PPFA service reports 1982-1986. Also see National Right to Life's special tabloid, "Til Victory is Won: Planned Parenthood's Abortion Crusade," 1982.
73. Ibid.
74. Ibid.
75. Gray, pp. 227-8.
76. See such PPFA recommended literature as Wardell B. Pomeroy, *Boys and Sex* (New York: Dell Publishing, 1968, 1981), pp. 43-57.

77. See PPFA's medical director's books re: Mary S. Calderone and Eric W. Johnson, *The Family Book About Sexuality* (New York: Bantam Books, 1983), pp. 120-123.

78. Ibid., pp. 123-130; Pomeroy, pp. 58-79; and Faye Wattleton and the Planned Parenthood Staff, *How to Talk to Your Child About Sexuality* (New York: Doubleday and Co., 1986), pp. 90-93.

79. See Wardell B. Pomeroy, *Girls and Sex* (New York: Dell Publishing Co., 1969, 1981), pp. 44-81.

80. See Wattleton, pp. 74-106; Calderone and Johnson, pp. 11-14, 118-134, 182-186.

81. Claire Chambers, *The SIECUS Circle: A Humanist Revolution* (Boston: Western Islands, 1977), pp. 323-335.

82. *Wall Street Journal*, December 19, 1984.

83. Leon Trotsky, *My Life* (New York: Scribner's, 1931), p. 274.

84. Ibid.; also see Robert Wistrick, *Trotsky: Fate of A Revolutionary* (New York: Stein and Day Publishers, 1979).

85. Ibid.; also see Finder, pp. 13-14, and Robert A. Rosenstone, *Romantic Revolutionary: A Biography of John Reed* (New York: Vintage Books, 1975).

86. Ibid.; also see Theodore Draper, *American Communism and Soviet Russia* (New York: Viking Penguin, 1960).

87. 1 Timothy 3:3; Titus 1:7; 1 Peter 5:2.

88. Robert G. Marshall, "The Real Costs of Federal Birth Control Programs Reauthorizing Title X, US PHSA: Congressional Options," *Family Policy Insights*, 4:6, (September, 1985); see Gordon, p. 320.

89. Quoted in David Goldstein, *Suicide Bent: Sangerizing America* (St. Paul: Radio Replies Press, 1945), p. 103.

90. See Mary Dunn, "Apple Pie and the American Flag," Catholic Twin Circle, November 8, 1981.

91. See Drogin, pp. 54-55.

92. See Sandy McKasson, *The Mysteries of Iniquity: A Critical Look at Modern Sexual Morality* (Dallas: LifePress, 1988).

93. See Robert Ruff, *Aborting Planned Parenthood* (Houston: New Vision Books, 1988).

94. Gray, pp. 37, 44, 76, 80, 325-26.

95. Ibid., pp. 26-31, 48, 326.

96. Ibid., pp. 76, 80.

97. Ibid., pp. 10, 405, 408, 416-18, 427, 434, 436, 439.

98. Ibid., pp. 37, 44, 76, 80, 325-26.

99. Ibid., p. 37.

100. See Ruff, pp. 31-34.

101. Robert G. Marshall, *School Birth Control* (Stafford, VA: American Life League, 1986).

102. J. C. Wilke, *Abortion: Questions and Answers* (Cincinnatti: Hayes Publishing Co., 1985).

103. Planned Parenthood of Houston and Southeast Texas, Annual Report, 1985.

Chapter 4 — Back Alley Butchers: The Medical Legacy

1. "Celebrating Seventy Years of Service," 1986 Annual Report, Planned Parenthood Federation of America, pp. 3, 18, 22-23.

2. Planned Parenthood of Houston and Southeast Texas, *VPT Consent* Liability Release Form.

3. Planned Parenthood of Houston and Southeast Texas *Minor Consent to Abortion* Form.

4. See David C. Reardon, *Aborted Women: Silent No More* (Westchester, IL: Crossway Books, 1988); Deborah Maine, "Does Abortion Affect Later Pregnancies," Family Planning Perspectives, 11:2, (March/April 1979), pp. 98-101; and Thomas Hilgers, Dennis J. Horan, and David Mall, *New Perspectives on Human Abortion* (Frederick, MD: University Publications of America, 1981), pp. 45-181.

5. Author interview conducted in Los Angeles, July, 1987.

6. Based on California Obstetrical/Gynecological tabulated responses to a five-year statistical survey.

7. Leslie Iffy, M.D., "Abortion Statistics in Hungary," *Obstetrics and Gynecology* 45:115, 1975; Alras Klinger, "Demographic Consequences of the Legalization of Induced Abortion in Eastern Europe," *International Journal of Gynecology and Obstetrics*, 8:680, 1970; A. Arvay, M. Gorgey, and L. Kapn, "La Relation Entre Les Avortements et Les Accouchements Prematures," *La Review de La Francais Gynecolog et Obstetricie* 62:81, 1967; and O. Pohonka and I. Torok, "A Gestatios Esemenyekj Alakulasa es a Koraszules-Kerdes Osszefuggese Hazankban 1934 es 1970 Kozott," *Orviatte Hetiliak a Hungary* 117: 965, 1976; all cited in Luc Segond, *La Vie Etait La Lumiere* (Bruxelles: Societe Biblique de Belgique, 1979), pp. 131-132; also see Hilgers, Horan, and Mall, pp. 69-127; as well as Reardon, pp. 103-105.

8. K. G. B. Edstrom, "Early Complications and Late Sequelae of Induced Abortion: A Review of the Literature," *Bulletin of the World Health Organization* 52:3332, 1975; and Y. Moriyama and O. Hirokawa, "The Relationship Between Artificial Termination of Pregnancy and Abortion on Premature Birth," *Harmful Effects of Induced Abortion* (Tokyo: Family Planning Federation of Japan, 1966); all cited in Luc Segond, *La Vie Etait La Lumiere* (Bruxelles: Societe Biblique de Belgique, 1979), pp. 131-132; also see Hilgers, Horan, and Mall, pp. 69-127; as well as Reardon, pp. 103-105.

9. S. N. Pautekakis, G. C. Papadimitriou, and S. A. Dixiadis, "The Influence of Induced and Spontaneous Abortions on the Outcome of Subsequent Pregnancies," *American Journal of Obstetrics and Gynecology*, 116: 799, 1973; and G. Papaevangelou et al, "The Effect of Spontaneous and Induced Abortion on Prematurity and Birthweight," *The Journal of Obstetrics and Gynecology in the British Commonwealth* 80: 418 1973; all cited in Luc Segond, *La View Etait La Lumiere* (Bruxelles: Societe Biblique de Belgique, 1979), pp. 131-132; also see Hilgers, Horan, and Mall, pp. 69-127; as well as Reardon, pp. 103-105.

10. J. A. Richardson and G. Dixon, "The Effects of Legal Termination on Subsequent Pregnancy," *The British Medical Journal* 1:1303, 1976; C. S. W. Wright, S. Campbell, and J. Beazley, "Second Trimester Abortion After Vaginal Termination of Pregnancy," *Lancet* 1:1278, 1972; and Lela Lampe, "Az Elso Terhesseg," *Ovriatte Hetilizak a Hungary* 119: 1331, 1978; all cited in Luc Segond, *La Vie Etait La Lumiere* (Bruxelles: Societe Biblique de Belgique, 1979), pp. 131-132; also see Hilgers, Horan, and Mall, pp. 69-127; as well as Reardon, pp. 103-105.

11. S. Harlap and A. M. Davies, "Late Sequelae of Induced Abortion: Complications and Outcome of Pregnancy and Labor," *American Journal of Epidemiology* 102: 217, 1975; and WHO Task Force on the Sequelae of Abortion, " The Outcome in the Subsequent Pregnancy," *Workshop on Risks, Benefits, and Controversies in Fertility Control* Arlington, VA: Program of Applied Research on Fertility Regulation, 1977); all cited in Luc Segond, *La Vie Etait La Lumiere* (Bruxelles: Societe Biblique de Belgique, 1979), pp. 131-132; also see Hilgers, Horan, and Mall, pp. 69-127; as well as Reardon, pp. 102-105.

12. J. W. Van der Slikke and P. E. Treffers, "The Influence of Induced Abortion on Gestational Duration in Subsequent Pregnancies," *The British Medical Journal* 1:270, 1978; all cited in Luc Segond, *La Vie Etait La Lumiere* (Bruxelles: Societe Biblique de Belgique, 1979), pp. 131-132; also see Hilgers, Horan, and Mall, pp. 69-127; as well as Reardon, pp. 103-105.

13. D. Koller and S. N. Eikhom, "Late Sequelae of Induced Abortion in Primigravidae," *Acta Obstetrics and Gynaecology in Scandinavia* 56: 311, 1977; all cited in Luc Segond, *La Vie Etait La Lumiere* (Bruxelles: Societe Biblique de Belgique, 1979), pp. 131-132; also see Hilgers, Horan, and Mall, pp. 69-127; as well as Reardon, pp. 103-105.

14. Harlap and Davies, p. 217.

15. C. J. Hogue, "Low Birth Weight Subsequent to Induced Abortion: A Historical Prospective Study of 948 Women in Skopje, Yugoslavia," *American Journal of Obstetrics and Gynecology* 123:675, 1975; also see Leslie Iffy, Gary Frisoli, and Antol Jakobovitts, "Perinatal Statistics: The Effect Internationally of Liberalized Abortion," cited in Hilgers, Horan, and Mall, p. 116.

16. J. R. Daling and I. Emanuel, "Induced Abortion and Subsequent Outcome of Pregnancy," *New England Journal of Medicine* 297:1241, 1977; also see Iffy, Frisoli, and Jakobocvitts, p. 116; all cited in Luc Segond, *La Vie Etait La Lumiere* (Bruxelles: Societe Biblique de Belgique, 1979), pp. 131-132; also see Hilgers, Horan, and Mall, pp. 69-127; as well as Reardon, pp. 103-105.

17. G. L. Burkman et. al., "Culture and Treatment Results in Endometritis Following Elective Abortion," *American Journal of Obstetrics and Gynecology*, 128:5, 1977, pp. 556-559.

18. K. L. Barret et al, "Induced Abortion: A Risk Factor for Placenta Previa," *American Journal of Obstetrics and Gynecology*, December, 1981, pp. 769-772.

19. Felix Healt, "Adolescent Pregnancy and Prenatal Care," *Family Practice News*, December 15, 1975.

20. See Hilgers, Miulenburg, and O'Hare in Hilgers, Horan, and Mall, pp. 1-5, 69-91, 164-181, 199-204, and 217-235.

21. J. Queena, "RH Sensitization, Abortion, and Later Pregnancies," *Medical World News*, April 30, 1971, p. 36.

22. S. Funderburk et al., "Suboptimal Pregnancy Outcome with Prior Abortions and Premature Births," *American Journal of Obstetrics and Gynecology*, September 1, 1976, pp. 55-60.

23. L. Talbert, "DIC More Common Threat with Use of Saline Abortion," *Family Practice News*, 5:19, (October, 1975).

24. See WHO Task Force; and Hilgers, Horan, and Mall, pp. 92-163

25. Howard W. Ory, "Mortality Associated with Fertility and Fertility Control," *Family Planning Perspectives*, March/April 1983, p. 60; and Faye Wattleton, *How to Talk With Your Child About Sexuality* (New York: Doubleday and Co., 1986), p. 180.

26. Ibid.

27. Matthew J. H. Bulfin, "Complications of Legal Abortion: A Perspective from Private Practice," in Hilgers, Horan, and Mall, p. 145.

28. Personal interview conducted in Los Angeles, July, 1987.

29. "Celebrating," p. 72; and see "A Risky Business: Reproductive Health Care in Litigation," Planned Parenthood Federation of America brochure.

30. K. Wilson Pike-Lastin, "Planned Parenthood Officials Discuss Risk Prevention," *New Jersey Life News-Forecast, 1987*, New Jersey Citizens for Life, 1987, pp. 4-6.

31. *Roe v. Wade* was simply the first in a long string of legal maneuvers which have served to limit Planned Parenthood's juridical exposure.

32. Exodus 20:13.
33. See "A Risky Business."
34. J. D. Barklay, A. Forsythe, and T. L. Parker, "Abortion Methodologies: Frequency and Risk," *The Medical Life-Line*, March, 1986, pp. 12-19; J. C. Wilke, *Abortion: Questions and Answers* (Cincinnatti: Hayes Publishing Co., 1985), pp. 83-131; The Boston Women's Health Collective, *The New Our Bodies, Ourselves* (New York: Simon and Schuster, 1984), pp. 291-316; "Abortion: Some Medical Facts," National Right to Life Trust Fund 1986; and "Questions and Answers About Abortion," Planned Parenthood League of Massachusetts, 1986.
35. Ibid.
36. Ibid.; and S. K. Henshaw and K. O'Reilly, "Characteristics of Abortion Patients in the U.S.," *Family Planning Perspectives*, 15:1, (January/February 1985), p. 5.
37. Ibid.
38. Ibid.; and U.S. Senate Report of the Committee on the Judiciary, *Human Life Federalism Amendment*, Senate Joint Resolutions, 98th Congress, June 6, 1983, p. 6.
39. Ibid.
40. Ibid.
41. Ibid.
42. Sallie Tisdale, "We Do Abortions Here: A Nurse's Story," *Harper's Magazine*, October, 1987, pp. 66-70.
43. Ibid.
44. B. Duenhoelter and E. Grant, "Complications Following Prostaglandin F-2 A Induced Mid-trimester Abortion," *American Journal of Obstetrics and Gynecology*, 46:3, (September, 1975), pp. 247-250.
45. "Plan Your Children For Health and Happiness," Planned Parenthood Federation of America, 1963.
46. Apparently the Houston affiliate was transferring its records from "hard" copy to either computer or microfiche.
47. The results of this study have been fully documented in Robert Ruff, *Aborting Planned Parenthood* (Houston: New Vision Books, 1988). The book is available from Life Advocates, 4848 Guiton, Suite 209, Houston, TX 77027 or from New Vision Books, P.O. Box 920970-A16, Houston, TX 77018.
48. Ibid., p. 96.
49. Ibid.
50. Ibid.
51. Ibid.
52. Ibid.
53. Ibid., p. 92.
54. Ibid., p. 96.
55. Exodus 20:13.
56. *Our Bodies, Ourselves*, p. 221.
57. Ibid.
58. Ibid., p. 220; and Linda Gordon, *Woman's Body, Woman's Right: A Social History of Birth Control in America* (New York: Penguin Books, 1976), pp. 249-300, 341-390.
59. *Our Bodies, Ourselves*, pp. 220-221.
60. Barbara Seaman, *The Doctor's Case Against the Pill* (New York: Dell Publishing Co., 1979).
61. For an overview of the vast amount of literature, see: Kevin Hume, *Cancer and the Pill: Five Studies and a Review of Literature* (Stafford, VA: Anastasia Books, 1985); Ellen Grant, *The Bitter Pill: How Safe is the Perfect Contraceptive?* (London:

Elm Tree Books, 1985); Becky O'Malley, "Who Says Oral Contraceptives are Safe?", *The Nation*, February 14, 1981; Robert Hatcher et al., *Contraceptive Technology*, 11th rev. ed. (New York: Irvington Publishers, 1982); Kristin Luker, *Taking Chances: Abortion and the Decision Not to Contracept* (Berkeley, CA: University of California Press, 1975); Andrea Borgoff Eagen, "The Contraceptive Sponge: Easy—But is it Safe?" *Ms. Magazine* 12:7, 1984, pp. 94-5; S. Shapiro et. al., "Birth Defects in Relation to Vaginal Spermicides," *Journal of the American Medical Association* 247:17, 1982, pp. 2381-84; Judy Norsigian, "Redirecting Contraceptive Research," *Science for the People*, January/February, 1979, pp. 27-30; and Katherine Roberts, "The Intrauterine Device as a Health Risk," *Women and Health*, pp. 27-30.

62. Seaman, p. 11.
63. Madeline Gray, *Margaret Sanger: A Biography of the Champion of Birth Control* (New York: Richard Marek Publishers, 1979), p. 432.
64. Ibid., p. 318.
65. Ibid., pp. 413-14, 432.
66. *Our Bodies, Ourselves*, p. 237.
67. Ibid., p. 238.
68. Garrison Lawford, *Drugstore Guidebook* (New York: Cherry Ridge Publications, 1986), p. 411.
69. *Our Bodies, Ourselves*, p. 237.
70. Ibid.
71. Ibid., pp. 242-44.
72. For example, see: World Health Organization, *Oral Contraceptives: Technical and Safety Aspects* (New York: United Nations Book Shop), p. 20; Boston Collaborative Drug Surveillance Program, "Oral Contraceptives and Venous Thrombo-Embolic Disease, Surgically Confirmed Gall Bladder Disease, and Breast Tumors," *Lancet*, January, 1973, pp. 1399-1404; O. P. Heinonen et al., "Cardiovascular Birth Defects and Antenatal Exposure to Female Sex Hormones," *New England Journal of Medicine* 296:2 (January, 1977), pp. 67-70.
73. *Our Bodies, Ourselves*, pp. 241-244.
74. That rate applies to teens. Older women tend to have lower in—use failures. See, William R. Grady, Mark Hayward, and Junichi Yagi, "Contraceptive Failure in the United States: Estimates from the 1982 National Survey of Family Growth," *Family Planning Perspectives* 18:5, (November/December, 1986).
75. Ruff, p. 89.
76. *Our Bodies, Ourselves*, p. 249.
77. Ibid.
78. Maria Berta and Gordon Myron, "Common Complications from IUDs," *Resident and Staff Physician*, June, 1976.
79. Mark Dowie and Tracy Johnson, "A Case of Corporate Malpractice," *Seizing Our Bodies: The Politics of Women's Health* (New York: Random House, 1977).
80. W. Cates et al., "The Intrauterine Device and Deaths from Spontaneous Abortion," *New England Journal of Medicine*, 295, 1976, p. 1155.
81. *Our Bodies, Ourselves*, p. 249.
82. Etienne-Emile Boulieu and Sheldon Segal, eds., *The Anti-Progestin Steriod RU-486 and Human Fertility Control* (New York: Plenum Press, 1985); and Judie Brown, "NIH is Paying for Death Pill Development," *A.L.L. About Issues*, March, 1986, pp. 6-8.
83. Ronald C. Kleinman, "The Anti-Progesterone RU-486," *IPPF Medical Bulletin*, 20:5 (October, 1986).
84. In pregnancies more than six weeks, amenorrhoea; see Kleinman, pp. 1-2.
85. Ibid.

86. Ibid.

87. Boulieu and Segal, p. 20.

88. Gray, pp 200-201.

89. Alan Guttmacher Institute, "Crisis in Product Liability Insurance Impacting Current, Future Contraceptive Methods," *Washington Memo*, May 28, 1986, pp. 1-2.

90. See Eagan, pp. 94-95; and Shapiro, pp. 2381-84.

91. Howard J. Tatum and Elizabeth B. Connell-Tatum, "Barrier Contraception: A Comprehensive Review," *Fertility and Sterility* 36:1, (July, 1981), pp. 1-12.

92. Michael Woods, "The National Institutes of Health," *The World and I*, September, 1987, p. 280.

93. Ibid., pp. 280-81.

94. Deuteronomy 28:58-66

95. James C. Morh, *Abortion in America: The Origins and Evolution of National Policy* (New York: Oxford University Press, 1978).

96. Deuteronomy 28:1-14

97. See David Chilton, *Power in the Blood: A Christian Response to AIDS* (Brentwood, TN: Wolgemuth and Hyatt, Publishers, 1987).

98. See Lan Ti Kwo, *The New Frontier: Medicine at the Crossroads* (Boston: Medical Technology Press, 1982).

99. Ibid.

100. Joe Levine, "Help from the Unborn," *Time*, January 12, 1987.

101. Elizabeth Mehren, "Surrogate Mothers: Let's Stop This," *Los Angeles Times*, September 1, 1987.

102. Francis A. Schaeffer and C. Everett Koop, *Whatever Happened to the Human Race* (Old Tappan, NJ: Fleming Revell, 1979), pp. 89-118.

103. William Winslade and Judith Wilson Ross, "High-Tech Babies: A Growth Industry," *Galveston Gazette*, June 17, 1983.

104. Schaeffer and Koop, pp. 55-87.

105. W. H. Hibbard, "The Real Neuromancer," *Late Breaking News*, August 14, 1986.

106. Ted Howard and Jeremy Rifkin, *Who Should Play God?* (New York: Dell Publishing Co., 1977).

107. Golda Lamartia and Thomas Gibson, *Time Enough for Sorrow: The Deinstitutionalization of America's Mentally Ill* (Los Angeles: Kardia Publications, 1984).

108. Jeremy Rifkin, *Algeny* (New York: Viking Press, 1983).

109. Tol Abelard and Rus Contola, *War: The Next Phase, The Next Century* (London: Shambalah Bookworks, 1981).

110. Michael J. Wilson, John F. X. Uhelu, and Robert L. Quay, *Daeliaforcation: Experiments and Procedures* (London: The Research Council of the Institutes of Immunology, 1979).

111. Marvin Morrow, *Big Business: The Corporatization of Health Care* (Dallas: White Paper Reports, 1982).

112. Jim Lester, "Biocleatics: How Safe are the High-Tech Procedures?" *Watchcourt Review of Technical Literature*, 2:4, pp. 16-43.

113. Lucas Berry and Davis Lowery, "Human Experimentation in Berkeley Draws Fire," *Local Times*, February 8, 1978.

114. Roger Howard and Shannon Lee-Bailey, "Neuroclatology: Defining the Parameters," *Pathology Texts*, 16:4, 1984.

115. Daniel J. Kevles, *In the Name of Eugenics* (New York: Penguin Books, 1985).

116. Garson L. B. Trang, "Renatalization of Cell Life and Synthetic Steroids," *Harper Standard*, July, 1977.

117. Stephen J. Gould, *The Mismeasure of Man* (New York: W. W. Norton and Co., 1981).

118. Robert J. Lifton, *The Nazi Doctors* (New York: Basic Books, 1986).
119. Although this genealogy may have a few generational gaps, its veracity is highly likely. See Barbara De Jong, *Tracing the Jewish Diaspora* (Amsterdam: The English Press, 1967); Ronald L. Numbers and Darrell W. Amundsen, ed., *Caring and Curing: Health and Medicine in the Western Religious Traditions* (London: Collier Macmillan Publishers, 1986); F. F. Cartwright, *A Social History of Medicine* (New York: Longman, 1977); and Latimer Wright, *Music in My Ears: Jews and Greeks, Barbarians and Gentiles* (New York: the Albert Kroc House, 1967).
120. See Numbers and Amundsen; and Chilton, pp. 177-182.
121. Demetrios J. Constantelos, *Byzantine Philanthropy and Social Welfare* (Paris: Orthodox Classics, 1968).
122. Timothy S. Miller, *The Birth of the Hospital in the Byzantine Empire* (Paris: Orthodox Classics, 1985).
123. John Scarborrough, ed., *Byzantine Medicine* (Paris: Orthodox Classics, 1984).
124. See Numbers and Amundsen, pp. 65-107.
125. Rupert Masson, "Raison D'Être," *L'Autre*, January, 1962.
126. See Numbers and Amundsen, pp. 47-52.
127. Leo Kuper, *Genocide: Its Political Use in the Twentieth Century* (New Haven, CN: Yale University Press, 1981).
128. The word *absolute* here is of utmost importance.
129. Reardon, p. 232.
130. Ibid., p. 233.
131. Ibid., pp. 233-34.

Chapter 5 — A Race of Thoroughbreds: The Racial Legacy

1. Daniel J. Kevles, *In the Name of Eugenics: Genetics and the Uses of Human Heredity* (New York: Penguin Books, 1985), p. 110.
2. Ibid.
3. Dana Atwell and Irene Paige, *Eugenic Sterilization* (New York: Case Memorial Foundation, 1958), pp. 43-44.
4. *Buck v. Bell*, 274 U.S., 201-3, (1927).
5. Stephen Jay Gould, *The Mismeasure of Man* (New York: W. W. Norton, 1981), p. 336.
6. Atwell and Paige, p. 45.
7. Gould, p. 336.
8. Kevles, p. 111.
9. Madeline Gray, *Margaret Sanger: A Biography of the Champion of Birth Control* (New York: Richard Marek Publishers, 1979), pp. 240-41; Linda Gordon, *Woman's Body, Woman's Right: A Social History of Birth Control in America* (New York: Penguin, 1974), pp. 229-340, 353-359; Elasah Drogin, *Margaret Sanger: Father of Modern Society* (New Hope, KY: CUL Publications, 1986), pp. 11-38; John W. Whitehead, *The End of Man* (Westchester, IL: Crossway Books, 1986), pp. 161-200.
10. See Allan Chase, *The Legacy of Malthus: The Social Costs of the New Scientific Racism* (New York: Alfred A. Knopf, 1977).
11. See Whitehead, pp. 161-165.
12. See Kevles, pp. 57-69.
13. Ibid.
14. Ibid.

15. See Germaine Greer, *Sex and Destiny: The Politics of Human Fertility* (New York: Harper and Row, 1984).
16. See Whitehead, pp. 166-167.
17. Ibid.
18. Ibid.
19. Greer, p. 309.
20. Whitehead, p. 167; and Kevles, p. 111.
21. Ibid., p. 168; Drogin, p. 12; and Kevles, p. 200.
22. Greer, p. 377; Kevles, pp. 56, 199, 200, 210.
23. Kevles, pp. 63-64.
24. G. K. Chesterton, *Eugenics and Other Evils* (London: Cassell, 1922), p. 7.
25. Ibid., p. 54.
26. "C. K. C. Review," *The Speaker*, February 2, 1901, p. 488.
27. Chesterton, p. 151; also see Daniel Grasman, *The Scientific Origins of National Socialism* (London: Macdonald and Co., 1971).
28. Romans 3:10-18.
29. Greer, p. 308.
30. See Kevles, pp. 57, 91-92; Joseph Finder, *Red Carpet* (Fort Worth: American Bureau of Economic Research), pp. 15-39; and Eugene Lyons, *The Red Decade* (New Rochelle, NY: Arlington House, 1941, 1970), pp. 127, 247.
31. See Robert Jay Lifton, *The Nazi Doctors: Medical Killing and the Psychology of Genocide* (New York: Basic Books, 1986), pp. 27-29; and Drogin, pp. 23-26.
32. Margaret Sanger, *The Pivot of Civilization* (New York: Brentano's, 1922).
33. Ibid., pp. 23, 176.
34. Ibid., p. 108.
35. Ibid., pp. 110, 181, 264, 265.
36. *Birth Control Review*, 3:5,(May, 1919), and 5:11, (November, 1921).
37. David Kennedy, *Birth Control in America: The Career of Margaret Sanger* (New Haven, CN: Yale University Press, 1970), pp. 113-117, 118; Drogin, p. 23; and Gordon, pp. 281-288.
38. Ibid.
39. Ibid.
40. See for example Warren Thompson's monthly *BCR* Series: "Race Suicide in the U.S.," extending from August, 1920 to March, 1921.
41. *Birth Control Review*, October, 1920, pp. 14-16.
42. *Birth Control Review*, September, 1923, pp. 219-20.
43. *Birth Control Review*, April, 1932, p. 107; See Drogin,p. 22.
44. *Birth Control Review*, April, 1933, p. 102.
45. *Birth Control Review*, 17:4, 1933, p. 85.
46. Kennedy, p. 118.
47. *Birth Control Review*, April, 1932.
48. Sanger, p. 175.
49. Kennedy, p. 116.
50. Gordon, p. 332.
51. Ibid.
52. Ibid.
53. Ibid.; and Debra Braun, *Exposed: Planned Parenthood* (St. Paul, MN: Peace of Minnesota, 1986), p. 5.
54. Ibid., pp. 332-333.
55. Ibid., p. 333.
56. Ibid., p. 330.
57. Sanger, p. 108.

58. Ibid.; and Kenneth Kammeyer, Norma Yetman, and McKee McClendon, "Family Planning Services and Distribution of Black Americans," *Population Studies: Selected Essays* (Chicago: Rand McNally, 1975).
59. Ibid.
60. Although Planned Parenthood is a primary instigator in the SBC movement, only rarely does an affiliate become institutionally involved in their day to day operation.
61. Carla R. de Vries, Benjamin Goldstein, and Linda Evankirov, *Teen Pregnancy: Crisis, Solution, and Opposition* (Boston: Educational Software Information Group, 1987), p. 14; and Roberta Weiner, *Teen Pregnancy: Impact on the Schools* (Alexandria, VA: Capitol Publications, 1987).
62. Ibid.
63. Note, for example, the organization of Black Americans for Life, 419 7th St. NW, Suite 402, Washington, D.C. 20004, (202) 626-8815.
64. *A.L.L. About Issues*, March/April 1987, pp. 8-9.
65. See, for example, "Celebrating Seventy Years of Service," 1986 Annual Report, Planned Parenthood Federation of America, p. 3.
66. See, for example, Stan E. Weed, "Curbing Births, Not Pregnancies," *Wall Street Journal*, October 14, 1986; Jacqueline Kasun, *Teenage Pregnancy: What Comparisons Among States and Countries Show* (Stafford, VA: American Life League, 1986); Jacqueline Kasun, *Teenage Pregnancy: Media Effects Versus Facts* (Stafford, VA: American Life League, 1984); Charles Murray, *Losing Ground* (New York: Basic Books, 1984); James H. Ford and Michael Schwartz, "Birth Control for Teenagers: Diagram for Disaster," *Linacre Quarterly*, February, 1979; Barrett Mosbacker, *Teen Pregnancy and School-Based Health Clinics* (Washington, D.C.: Family Research Council, 1987).
67. Chase, p. 411.
68. A. L. Thornton, "U.S. Statistical Survey: A Reanalysis of the 1980 Census Figures for Population Distribution and Composition," *Demographics Today*, March, 1983, p. 62.
69. Chase, p. 411.
70. Sanger, pp. 90, 177.
71. Statistical analysis based on U.S. Department of Health and Human Service figures, developed by R. G. Calhoun, University of Houston, 1986.
72. Ibid.
73. Ibid.
74. Ibid.
75. "Celebrating," p. 23.
76. Thornton, p. 101.
77. *Family Planning Perspectives*, 7:3, (May-June 1975); and Drogin, p. 68.
78. Ibid.
79. Gordon, p. 399.
80. Gordon, pp. 399-400.
81. Chase, pp. 17-18.
82. Chase, p. 17.
83. John Rodgers, "Rush to Surgery," *New York Times Magazine*, September 21, 1975, p. 40.
84. Ibid., p. 34.
85. Chase, p. 17.
86. Rodgers, p. 40.
87. "No Se Arriesguen: Visiten Planned Parenthood para el Control de la Natalidad," brochure and coupon from Planned Parenthood of Houston and Southeast Texas, distributed 1986-1987.

88. *Fort Wayne Journal-Gazette*, November 5, 1987.
89. Gordon, p. 399.
90. John L. Keller, *Scientific Racism: Malthusianism, Eugenics, and Recapitulation Beyond Nazi Germany* (New York: Capitol Research Associates, 1967), p. xii.
91. Ibid.
92. Ibid., p. xiii.
93. Drogin, p. 23.
94. Keller, p. xiii.
95. From the United States's *Declaration of Independence*, July 4, 1776.
96. *The Washington Times*, February 3, 1988.
97. *The Tennessean*, February 3, 1988.
98. Ibid.
99. *The Washington Times*, February 3, 1988.
100. Ibid.
101. *USA Today*, February 3, 1988.
102. *The Washington Times*, August 10, 1984.

Chapter 6 — Selling Sex: The Educational Scandal

1. Catherine Toleson's story first came to my attention in Gregg Harris' book, *The Christian Home School* (Brentwood, TN: Wolgemuth & Hyatt, 1988), pp. 37-38. Subsequently, I spoke with her, and her parents, to confirm the details of her remarkable story. Although I have been unable to obtain a copy of the film she saw, Catherine's story is not too terribly different from dozens of others I have heard over the years (though admittedly much more graphic). It appears to be absolutely factual.
2. Note the diatribes against traditional values and morality in the Planned Parenthood-recommended books: Wardell B. Pomeroy, *Girls and Sex* (New York: Dell Publishing, 1981); Mary S. Calderone and Eric W. Johnson, *The Family Book About Sexuality* (New York: Bantam Books, 1981); and Ruth Bell, et. al., *Changing Bodies, Changing Lives* (New York: Random House, 1980). Also note the anti-Christian bias in the literature actually published by various Planned Parenthood agencies: Sheri Tepper, *You've Changed the Combination* (Denver: Rocky Mountain Planned Parenthood, 1974); Sheri Tepper, *The Perils of Puberty* (Denver: Rocky Mountain Planned Parenthood, 1974); Sheri Tepper, *The Problem With Puberty* (Denver: Rocky Mountain Planned Parenthood, 1975); Sheri Tepper, *The Great Orgasm Robbery* (Denver: Rocky Mountain Planned Parenthood, 1977); "Starting Early Xperience: A Parent's Guide to Early Childhood Education," (Denver: RAJ Publications of the Rocky Mountain Planned Parenthood, 1981); and William Bulay and Eileen Garcia, *Sex In Perspective*: Curriculum for Sex Education (Houston: Planned Parenthood of Houston and Southeast Texas, 1982).
3. Ibid.; and "Planned Parenthood Must Be Stopped," American Life Lobby, 1983.
4. Havelock Ellis, *Studies in the Psychology of Sex*, 7 volumes (Philadelphia: F. A. Davis, 1897-1928).
5. Sigmund Freud, *The Future of An Illusion* (Garden City, NY: Anchor Books, 1964).
6. Bertrand Russell, *Marriage and Morals* (New York: Pocket Books, 1959).
7. Alfred Kinsey, *Sexual Behavior of the Human Male* (Philadelphia: Saunders Publishers, 1948).

8. William Masters and Virginia Johnson, *Human Sexual Response* (Boston: Little, Brown, and Co., 1966).
9. William Masters and Virginia Johnson, *Human Sexual Inadequacy* (Boston: Little, Brown, and Co., 1970).
10. Alex Comfort, *The Joy of Sex* (New York: Simon and Schuster, 1974).
11. Alan F. Guttmacher, *Pregnancy, Birth, and Family Planning* (New York: Signet, 1973).
12. Wardell B. Pomeroy, *Boys and Sex* (New York: Dell, 1981).
13. Mary S. Calderone, *Questions and Answers About Love and Sex* (New York: St. Martin's Press, 1979).
14. Shere Hite, *The Hite Report* (New York: Dell, 1976).
15. Ruth Westheimer, *Dr. Ruth's Guide to Good Sex* (New York: Warner Books, 1983).
16. Sol Gordon, *Ten Heavy Facts About Sex* (Syracuse, NY: Ed-U Press, 1975).
17. Sheri Tepper, *After Long Silence* (New York: Bantam Books, 1987).
18. Margaret Sanger, *An Autobiography* (New York: W. W. Norton, 1938).
19. See note number two above; and "Sexuality Alphabet," Planned Parenthood Federation of America, 1982.
20. Ibid.
21. Ibid.
22. Margaret Lundstrom, "Women Exploited by Planned Parenthood: From the Classroom to the Boardroom, The Deception Continues," *Lifeways Newsletter*, April 1982, pp. 6-8.
23. Barrett L. Mosbacker, *School-Based Clinics* (Westchester, IL: Crossway Books, 1987), p. 79.
24. Lena Levine, "Psycho-sexual Development," *Planned Parenthood News*, Summer 1953, p. 10.
25. Tepper, *Perils*.
26. Tepper, *Combination*.
27. Tepper, *Robbery*.
28. Calderone and Johnson, p. 226.
29. Leonard Gross, "Sex Education Comes of Age," *Look Magazine*, March 8, 1966.
30. Judges 21:25.
31. Sandalyn McKasson, "Sex and Seduction in the Classroom," in Richie Martin, ed., *Judgment in the Gate: A Call to Awaken the Church* (Westchester, IL: Crossway Books, 1986), p. 102.
32. Barbara Morris, *Change Agents in the Schools* (Upland, CA: Barbara M. Morris Report, 1979), p. 144.
33. Lleland Hindeman, *Values Clarification: The Children Trap* (Morris, CA: Christian Awareness Publications, 1977), p. 42.
34. McKasson, p. 95.
35. Hindeman, p. 49.
36. *Peer Education in Human Sexuality*, Planned Parenthood of Metropolitan Washington, p. 16.
37. Hindeman, p. 48.
38. Carol Craig, *Decisions About Sex* (White Plains, NY: Planned Parenthood of Westchester, 1975), p. 4.
39. Eleanor S. Morrison and Miln Underhill Price, *Values in Sexuality* (New York: Hart Publishing Company and A & W Publishers, 1974), p. 100.
40. McKasson, p. 97.
41. Ibid., p. 98.
42. Ibid.
43. R. J. Corsini, *Role Playing in Psychotherapy* (Chicago: Aldime Books, 1966).

44. McKasson, p. 100.

45. Ibid., p. 101.

46. Ibid., pp. 97, 99.

47. Morrison and Price, pp. 167-168.

48. Glen E. Richardson, "Educational Imagery: A Missing Link in Decision Making," *The Journal of School Health*, October, 1981, p. 561.

49. "What is Sexual Fantasy?" *What's Happening* (Atlanta: Emory University, Grady Memorial Family Planning Program, 1976), p. 4.

50. Jacqueline Kasun, "Turning Children into Sex Experts," *The Public Interest*, Spring 1979, p. 14.

51. "Control," Planned Parenthood Association of the Chicago Area, April 8, 1978, p. 2.

52. See Carol Cassell, *Three-Year Plan and Long-Range Program Goals* (New York: Planned Parenthood Federation of America, Department of Education, 1979).

53. See Randy C. Alcorn, *Christians in the Wake of the Sexual Revolution* (Portland: Multnomah Press, 1985), pp. 61-77, 108-109; Sandy McKasson, "Sex and Seduction in the Classroom," in Richie Martin, ed., *Judgment in the Gate* (Westchester, IL: Crossway Books, 1986), pp. 90-119; and Tim LaHaye, *The Battle for the Public Schools* (Old Tappan, NJ: Fleming H. Revell Company, 1983), pp. 99-164.

54. Lawrence LaDuc, "Statistical Correlations Between Sexuality Education and Family Planning Services: Deterrent or Feeder System?" *Sexual Ethics in Britain*, 2:3, (Fall 1978), pp. 14-17.

55. "Serving Human Needs, Preserving Human Rights," 1983 Annual Report, Planned Parenthood Federation of America, p. 6; and Cassell, pp. 3-7.

56. Ibid.

57. Ibid.

58. Ibid.; and "Celebrating Seventy Years of Service," 1986 Annual Report, Planned Parenthood Federation of America, pp. 24-25.

59. Ibid.

60. Ibid.

61. Ibid.

62. Ibid.

63. Ibid.

64. Richard Weatherly, et al., "Comprehensive Programs for Pregnant Teenagers and Teenage Parents: How Successful Have They Been?" *Family Planning Perspectives*, 18:2, (March/April 1986), pp. 76-77.

65. Roberta Weiner, *Teen Pregnancy: Impact On the Schools* (Alexandria, VA: Capitol Publications, 1987), p. 17.

66. Mosbacker, p. 74.

67. Jacqueline R. Kasun, "The Truth About Sex Education," in Mosbacker, p. 29.

68. Mosbacker, pp. 75-78.

69. Deborah Dawson, "The Effects of Sex Education on Adolescent Behavior," *Family Planning Perspectives* 18:4, (July/August 1986), p. 169.

70. See Robert Ruff, *Aborting Planned Parenthood* (Houston: New Vision Books, 1988).

71. Mosbacker, p. 75.

72. Josh McDowell and Dick Day, *Why Wait? What You Need to Know About the Teen Sexuality Crisis* (San Bernardino, CA: Here's Life Publishers, 1987), p. 23.

73. Melvin Zelnik and John Kantner, "Sexual Activity, Contraceptive Use, and Pregnancy among Metropolitan Area Teenagers: 1971-1979," *Family Planning Perspectives*, Volume 12, Number 5, September/October 1980, pp. 233-234.

74. McDowell and Day, p. 23.

75. Judie Brown, "Planned Parenthood: The Deception," *A.L.L. About Issues*, February 1985, p. 25.

76. David Chilton, *Power In the Blood: A Christian Response to AIDS* (Brentwood, TN: Wolgemuth & Hyatt Publishers, 1987), p. 50.

77. Zelnik and Kantner, pp. 233-234.

78. See, for instance, William Marsiglio and Frank Mott, "The Impact of Sex Education on Sexual Activity, Contraceptive Use, and Pre-Marital Pregnancy among Teenagers," *Family Planning Perspectives*, Volume 18, Number 4, July/August 1986, p. 151; Zelnik and Kantner, pp. 230-237; Douglas Kirby, "Sexuality Education: A More Realistic View of Its Effects," *Journal of School Health*, Volume 55, Number 10, December 1985; and Scott Thompson, "Sex Education: A Charade," *San Diego Union*, April 27, 1981.

79. Thompson, p. 15.

80. "Planned Parenthood-Style Sex Education," *American Bureau of Educational Research Newsletter*, Fall 1981, p. 2.

81. Weiner, p. 30.

82. Ibid., pp. 19-20.

83. Lana D. Muraskin, "Sex Education Mandates: Are They the Answer?" *Family Planning Perspectives* 18:4, (July/August 1986), p. 173.

84. Mosbacker, p. 77.

85. Quoted in Harold Tribble Cole, *The Coming Terror: Life Before the Great War* (New York: Languine Brothers Publishers, 1936), p. 92.

86. George Orwell, *1984* (New York: Harcourt Brace Jovanovich, 1949).

87. Ibid., p. 251.

88. Ibid., p. 257.

89. Cole, p. 92.

90. Tristram Gylberd, *The Oaken Rithel: An Epic Poem* (New York: Saxony Limbarte, 1972), p. 6.

91. Cole, p. 92.

92. Allan Bloom, *The Closing of the American Mind* (New York: Simon & Schuster, 1987).

93. See Robert G. Marshall, *The Two Faces of Planned Parenthood* (Stafford, VA: American Life Education and Research Trust, 1984); and "Sexuality Alphabet," pp. 3-4.

94. Luke 19:12-27.

95. "Would You—Could You—Can You?" Discussion Group Guide, Planned Parenthood of West Central Ohio, 1986, p. 2; "Sexuality Alphabet," pp. 4-7; and Alcorn, p. 73.

96. Colossians 3:5-10.

97. "Guidelines for Discussion-Based Sexuality Education," Memorandum 2/6/84, Planned Parenthood-Essex County, p. 1; and "Sexuality Alphabet," p. 7.

98. Acts 17:10-12.

99. Bulay and Garcia, Session V, "Values"; and "Sexuality Alphabet," pp. 5-7.

100. Deuteronomy 30:15-20.

101. "Celebrating," pp. 3, 18-19.

102. Psalm 127:3-5.

103. Warren Hearn, "Is Pregnancy Really Normal?" *Family Planning Perspectives*, 3:1, (January 1971), p. 9; and Willard Cates, "Abortion As A Treatment for Unwanted Pregnancy: The Number Two Sexually-Transmitted Condition," an address presented to the Association of Planned Parenthood Physicians, Miami, Florida, November 11-12, 1976.

104. Proverbs 15:13.
105. "Sexuality Alphabet," p. 14; and LaHaye, p. 107.
106. Psalm 11:7.
107. "Control," p. 2; and LaHaye, p. 119.
108. Proverbs 17:17.
109. Peter J. Leithart, "Modern Sex-Speak," *Chalcedon Report*, Number 270, January 1988, p. 3.
110. Alcorn, pp. 68-73; and LaHaye, pp. 133-136.
111. Orwell, p. 246.
112. Alcorn, pp. 68-73.
113. Leithart, p. 3.
114. Cole, p. 92.
115. See Chapter 4 for a detailed discussion of the medical risks of abortion and birth control.
116. See Phyllis Schlafly, ed., *Child Abuse in the Classroom* (Westchester, IL: Crossway Books, 1984).
117. "What is Peer Education in Human Sexuality" brochure, Planned Parenthood of Greater Metropolitan Washington, p. 1.
118. Louis Harris and Associates, *American Teens Speak: Sex, Myths, TV, and Birth Control*, "The Planned Parenthood Poll" (New York: Louis Harris and Associates, 1986).
119. Ibid., p. 71.
120. Ibid., pp. 71-72.
121. Ibid., p. 15.
122. Ibid., p. 24; and see Robert Ruff's analysis in *Aborting Planned Parenthood* (Houston: New Vision Books, 1988), p. 19.
123. Ibid., p. 18.
124. Ibid., p. 53.
125. David C. Reardon, *Aborted Women: Silent No More* (Westchester, IL: Crossway Books, 1987), p. xxiv.
126. Ibid., p. xxv.
127. Ibid., p. 17.
128. Ibid., p. 19.
129. Note; Planned Parenthood Association of Nashville, Board President, Nancy A. Ransom's "Planned Parenthood, An Excellent Resource," a letter to the Editor, *The Tennessean*, January 22, 1988.
130. Reardon, p. 19.
131. Ibid.
132. Ibid.
133. Sam Gitchel and Lorri Foster, *Let's Talk About Sex: A Read-and-Discuss Guide for People Nine to Twelve and Their Parents* (Fresno, CA: Planned Parenthood of Central California, 1986), pp. 17-18.
134. Dan Smoot, "Contributing to the Delinquency of Minors," *Dan Smoot Report*, March 31, 1969, p. 51.
135. Samuel L. Blumenfeld, "The Fraud of Educational Reform," *The Journal of Christian Reconstruction*, 11:2, 1987, p. 22.
136. Ibid., p. 26.
137. R. J. Rushdoony, "Education: Today's Crisis and Dilemma," *The Journal of Christian Reconstruction*, 11:2, 1987, p. 68.
138. Robert L. Dabney, *Discussions* (Harrisonburg, VA: Sprinkle Publications, 1879), p. 195.

139. See Robert Thoburn, *The Children Trap, Biblical Principles of Education* (Fort Worth: Dominion Press, 1986); and Gregg Harris, *The Christian Home School* (Brentwood, TN: Wolgemuth and Hyatt, Publishers, 1988).
140. Thoburn, p. 79.
141. Ibid., p. 123.
142. Ibid., p. 23.
143. Ibid., pp. 86-89.

Chapter 7 — Robber Barons: The Financial Scandal

1. See Robert Ruff *Aborting Planned Parenthood* (Houston: New Vision Books, 1988) pp. 9-34. This important book is available from Life Advocates, 4848 Guiton, Suite 204, Houston, TX 77027 or New Vision Books, P.O. Box 920970-A16, Houston, TX 77018.
2. See Erma C. Craven "Abortion, Poverty, and Black Genocide," in Thomas Hilger and Dennis J. Horan *Abortion and Social Justice* (New York: Althea Books, 1981); Tim Zentler, for Planned Parenthood of Humboldt County, quoted in *The Union*, 14 June 1983; Martha Burt, *Public Costs for Teenage Childbearing* (Washington, D.C.: Center for Population Options, 1986); Charles Murray, *Losing Ground: American Social Policy 1950-1980* (New York: Basic Books, 1984); George Gilder, *Men and Marriage* (Gretna, LA: Pelican Publishing Company, 1986); George Grant, *The Dispossessed: Homelessness in America* (Westchester, IL: Crossway Books, 1986); and George Grant, *In the Shadow of Plenty* (Nashville: Thomas Nelson, 1986).
3. *USA Today* February 3, 1988.
4. *USA Today* August 10, 1987.
5. Ken McKee, "Planned Parenthood and Title X," *All About Issues*, March 1984, pp. 8-9.
6. W. Douglas Badger, "Legislative History of Section 1008 of the Public Health Service Act," *Action Line*, February 1985.
7. Ibid.
8. See Frederick S. Jaffe, Barbara L. Lindheim, and Philip R. Lee, *Abortion Politics: Private Morality and Public Policy* (New York: McGraw-Hill Book Company, 1981); Kristin Luker, *Abortion and the Politics of Motherhood* (Los Angeles: University of California Press, 1984); and Linda Gordon, *Woman's Body, Woman's Right: A Social History of Birth Control in America* (New York: Penguin Books, 1977).
9. Ibid.
10. McKee, p. 8.
11. Ibid.
12. Gordon Lammers, "Title X and the Radical Eugenic Programs of Planned Parenthood," *The Life Advocate*, March 1986, pp. 4-11; and Jaffe, Lindheim, and Lee, p. 120.
13. McKee, pp. 8-9.
14. 1 Timothy 3:3; 3:8; Titus 1:7; 1 Peter 5:2.
15. Ruff, pp. 9-34.
16. Each Planned Parenthood affiliate sets its own billing procedure. Thus, each affiliate's financial profile is slightly different. Some receive Title XX dollars only (as in the Houston affiliate). Some receive Title X dollars only (as in the New York affiliate). And some receive no *direct* federal subsidies at all (as in the New Orleans affiliate). But each organization in the Planned Parenthood net-

work shares a basic financial philosophy and each benefits from subsidies delivered at the national level.

17. Ibid.
18. Ibid., p. 24.
19. Ibid. The subsidized service visit may include additional procedures.
20. Ibid., p. 25.
21. Ibid.
22. Ibid., p. 25. The subsidized service visit may include additional procedures.
23. Ibid.
24. Ibid. The subsidized service visit may include additional procedures.
25. Ibid.
26. Ibid., p. 26.
27. Ibid. The subsidized service visit may include additional procedures.
28. Lammers, pp. 10-11.
29. Again, this varies from affiliate to affiliate around the country and is dependent upon the level and the extent of the tax subsidies available: see Ruff, pp. 20, 25.
30. See Ley W. Sommerton, *Highway Robbery at the Pentagon* (Chicago: Bailerton Peace Fund Press, 1985).
31. See Judie Brown, *Planned Parenthood Must Be Stopped* (Stafford, VA: American Life Lobby, 1980).
32. Ruff, p. 11.
33. Ibid.
34. Jaffe, Lindheim, and Lee, pp. 165-66: and Ruff, p. 4.
35. Ruff, p. 11.
36. Mary A. Black, "Assessing Title XX Eligibility"; and Planned Parenthood of Houston and Southeast Texas "Title XX," *Planned Parenthood Memorandum*, December 11, 1985.
37. See Black, p. 2.
38. J. Robert Dumouchel, *Government Assistance Almanac 1988* (Washington, D.C.: Regnery Gateway, 1988), p. 443.
39. Ibid., p. 442.
40. Ibid., p. 444.
41. Ibid., p. 445.
42. Ibid.
43. Lammers, pp. 9-10.
44. The term *looting* here is a derivation from the Biblical meaning of *filthy lucre*.
45. Ibid.
46. See Black, pp. 1-3.
47. Ruff, p. 11.
48. Jaffe, Lindheim, and Lee, pp. 129-131, 141-145, 186-197.
49. Richard D. Glasow, "A Look at PPFA Finances," *Til Victory is Won: Planned Parenthood's Abortion Crusade* (Washington, D.C.: National Right to Life Educational Trust Fund, 1981), p. 5.
50. "Seventy Years of Family Planning in America: A Chronology of Major Events," Planned Parenthood Federation of America, p. 22.
51. Ibid., p. 23.
52. Ibid.
53. *The New American*, April 21, 1986.
54. *USA Today*, August 10, 1987; February 3, 1988.
55. See Planned Parenthood's aggressive litigal programs as outlined in Jaffe, Lindheim, and Lee, pp. 185-208; "Serving Human Needs, Preserving Human Rights," 1983 Annual Report, Planned Parenthood Federation of America, pp.

11-13; and "Celebrating Seventy Years of Service," 1986 Annual Report, Planned Parenthood Federation of America, pp. 25-27.

56. George F. Will, *The New Season* (New York: Simon and Schuster, 1987) p. 156.

57. Irwin Schiff, *The Social Security Swindle* (Hamden, CT: Freedom Books, 1984) pp. 11-13.

58. Madeline Gray, *Margaret Sanger: A Biography of the Champion of Birth Control* (New York: Richard Marek Publications, 1979) pp. 197-199.

59. This was in the early days when Planned Parenthood was still operating under the name The American Birth Control League; see Gray pp. 238, 244-246; pp. 276; 434.

60. Ibid., pp. 200-201.

61. Ibid., p. 398, 429-432, 266.

62. Ibid., p. 337.

63. Ibid., pp. 344, 347, 413-415.

64. Ibid., pp. 276-277, 368.

65. Ibid., pp. 277, 368.

66. "Seventy Years," pp. 2-5.

67. Gray, pp. 277-278, 298-299, 303, 365, 368, 405, 445.

68. Diana Shannan, "Margaret Sanger: The Mother of Birth Control," *Coronet*, March, 1966.

69. Glasow, p. 5.

70. Ibid.

71. Ibid.

72. Ibid.

73. Ruff, p. 12.

74. Robert G. Marshall, *School Birth Control: New Promise or Old Problem* (Stafford, VA: American Life League, 1986), p. 1.

75. Talon Gartrell, *Abortion and the States: A Case Against the Technical Elimination of Federal Jurisdiction and Roe v. Wade* (Manassas, VA: Life Work Publications, 1987), pp. 3-4.

76. "Planned Parenthood," brochure from Planned Parenthood of Houston and Southeast Texas, 1986, p. 2.

77. Jaffe, Lindheim, and Lee, pp. 200-208.

78. William Puckett, *What the Limits Are: Abortions and Tax Dollars* (Denver: Life Advocates Booklets, 1984), p. 2.

79. Ibid., pp. 2-3.

80. Ibid., p. 3.

81. Ibid., pp. 4-5.

82. Gartrell, pp. 7-8.

83. Ibid., p. 9.

84. Ibid.

85. Ibid., p. 11.

86. Ibid.

87. "Questions and Answers about Title X and Family Planning," *Issues in Brief,* 4:1 (March, 1984), p. 2.

88. Black, pp. 1-3.

89. Ibid.

90. Ruff, p. 13.

91. See, for example, *PPFA vs. Heckler*, United States District Court of Appeals, Washington D.C., 1983; and Dennis H. Horan, Edward R. Grant, and Paige C. Cunningham, *Abortion and the Constitution* (Washington, D.C.: Georgetown University Press, 1987).

92. See Bernard N. Nathanson, *The Abortion Papers: Inside the Abortion Mentality* (New York: Frederick Fell Publishers, 1983); and Colonel V. Doner, *A Christian Parent's Guide to TV* (Shreveport: Huntington House, 1988).

93. See Barrett Mosbacker ed. *School Based Clinics* (Westchester, IL: Crossway Books, 1987) pp. 208-209.

94. "Parental Notification Statutes," *Planned Parenthood Public Affairs Newsletter*, September 16 1983, pp. 2-3.

95. Mosbacker, p. 70.

96. Ibid., pp. 33, 71-72.

97. *USA Today* August 10 1987, February 3 1988.

98. "Teen Pregnancy and Parental Consent Laws" Tennessee Volunteers For Life, 1988, p. 2.

99. Ibid.

100. Ibid.

101. Ibid.

102. Ruff, p. 22.

103. Angela Bonavoglia, "Kathy's Day in Court," *Ms. Magazine*, April 1988, pp. 46-52. These seven states are Alabama, Indiana, Louisiana, Massachusetts, Missouri, North Dakota, and Rhode Island. Three other states have enforceable parental notification laws: Maryland, Utah, and West Virginia.

104. Planned Parenthood Affiliates, Chapters, and State Public Affairs Offices Directory, 1984.

105. See "Celebrating," pp. 22-23; and "Serving," pp. 4-5.

106. Marshall, p. 5. It must be noted that while Planned Parenthood affiliates for the most part actively support SBCs and often even supply SBCs, they usually do not operate them. SBC operations are generally independent. Thus, while they are generically dependent on Planned Parenthood, they are very often institutionally independent.

107. Judie Brown, Robert G. Marshall, and Herbert Ratner, *Stop School Based Sex Clinics* (Stafford, VA: American Life League, 1987), pp. 3-5.

108. Sodja Goldsmith, "Medicalized Sex," *The New England Journal of Medicine*, 24 September, 1970.

109. Susan Proctor, "A Developmental Approach to Pregnancy Prevention with Early Adolescent Females" *Journal of School Health* 56:8, (October, 1986.)

110. Joy Dryfoos "School-Based Health Clinics: A New Approach to Preventing Adolescent Pregnancy" *Family Planning Perspectives* 17:2, (March/April, 1985), p. 71.

111. Richard Weatherby, "Comprehensive Programs for Pregnant Teenagers and Teenage Parents: How Successful Have They Been?" *Family Planning Perspectives* 18:2, (March/April, 1986), p. 76.

112. Dryfoos, pp. 72-73.

113. Douglas Kirby, "School-Based Health Clinics: An Emerging Approach to Improving Adolescent Health and Addressing Teenage Pregnancy," *Center for Population Options Report*, April 1985, pp. 18-21.

114. *Planned Parenthood Review*, Winter, 1986.

115. Paul Ramsey, quoting Michael Bracken of Yale School of Medicine in "Adolescent Morality: A Theologian's Viewpoint," *Postgraduate Medicine*, July 1982.

116. Alan F. Guttmacher, "Planned Parenthood: Profile and Prospectus," *Family Planning Perspectives* 3:1 (January 197.)

117. Cited in Robert Byrne, *The Other 637 Best Things Anybody Ever Said* (New York: Fawcett Crest, 1984).

118. As with the use of the word *lie*, the word *crime* is intended here in its theological sense.

Chapter 8 — Strange Bedfellows: The Institutional Scandal

1. *Wall Street Journal*, November 13, 1987.
2. Ibid.
3. Ibid.
4. See: Robert Axelrod, *The Evolution of Cooperation* (New York: Basic Books, 1984); Michael B. Katz, *In the Shadow of the Poorhouse* (New York: Basic Books, 1986); Frank R. Breul and Steven J. Diner, *Compassion and Responsibility* (Chicago: University of Chicago Press, 1980); Larry Jones, *Feed the Children* (Oklahoma City: Feed the Children, 1986); and George Grant, *The Dispossessed: Homelessness in America* (Westchester, IL: Crossway Books, 1986).
5. See: John White, *The Golden Cow* (Downer's Grove, IL: Inter-Varsity Press, 1979); John Perkins, *A Quiet Revolution* (Waco, TX: Word Books, 1976); Leonard M. Greene, *Free Enterprise Without Poverty* (New York: W. W. Norton, 1981); Frank Tillapaugh, *Unleashing the Church* (Ventura, CA: Regal Books, 1982); Ronald H. Nash, *Poverty and Wealth* (Westchester, IL: Crossway Books, 1986); and George Grant, *In the Shadow of Plenty: Biblical Principles of Welfare and Poverty* (Nashville: Thomas Nelson, 1986).
6. See: Henry Hazlitt, *The Conquest of Poverty* (New Rochelle, NY: Arlington House, 1973); David Chilton, *Productive Christians In an Age of Guilt-Manipulators* (Tyler, TX: Institute for Christian Economics, 1981, 1985); Walter E. Williams, *The State Against Blacks* (New York: McGraw-Hill Book Company, 1982); Lawrence Mead, *Beyond Entitlement* (New York: Free Press, 1986); and George Grant, *Bringing In the Sheaves: Transforming Poverty Into Productivity* (Atlanta: American Vision Press, 1985).
7. See: William Showcross, *The Quality of Mercy* (New York: Touchstone Books, 1984); Richard D. Lamm and Gary Imhoff, *The Immigration Time Bomb* (New York: Truman Talley-E. P. Dutton, 1985); and Grant, *The Dispossessed*.
8. *Relief: International Report*, August 1987.
9. See: Sven Rydenfelt, *A Pattern for Failure: Socialist Economies in Crisis* (New York: Harcourt Brace Jovanovich, 1984); Lloyd Billingsley, *The Generation That Knew Not Josef* (Portland: Multnomah Press, 1985); Otto Scott, *The Other End of the Lifeboat* (Chicago: Regnery Books, 1985); Leo Kuper, *Genocide: Its Political Use in the Twentieth-Century* (New Haven, CT: Yale University Press, 1982); Richard L. Rubenstein, *The Age of Triage* (Boston: Beacon Press, 1983); and Thomas Sowell, *Marxism* (New York: William Morrow, 1985).
10. See Grant, *In the Shadow of Plenty*, pp. 52-53.
11. Ibid., pp. 54-55.
12. Cathy Fonseca Marshall, "A Few Rotten Recipients Spoil the Whole Fund," *A.L.L. About Issues*, September 1983, pp. 20-21.
13. "Celebrating Seventy Years of Service," 1986 Annual Report, Planned Parenthood Federation of America, p. 29 (computed by adding Federation and Affiliate private contributions, bequests, endowments, and Institute funding).
14. Michael Patrick Dugan, "United Way Funding of Abortion," *Texas Nurses for Life News*, Spring 1987, p. 1.
15. Ibid.
16. Ibid.; also see Richard D. Glasow, "A Look at PPFA Finances," *Til Victory is Won: Planned Parenthood's Abortion Crusade* (Washington, D.C.: National Right to Life Educational Trust Fund, 1981), p. 5.
17. See "Stop United Way Support of Anti-Life Agencies," information packet, American Life League, 1986; and "March of Dimes" information packet, American Life Lobby, 1985.

18. See Madeline Gray, *Margaret Sanger: A Biography of the Champion of Birth Control* (New York: Richard Marek, 1979), pp. 37-113.
19. See David Kennedy, *Birth Control in America: The Career of Margaret Sanger* (New Haven, CT: Yale University Press, 1970), pp. 112-170.
20. Linda Gordon, *Woman's Body, Woman's Right: A Social History of Birth Control in America* (New York: Penguin Books, 1976), pp. 249-390.
21. Donald Ben-Feinberg, *Sangerizing the Negroes and Jews* (New York: Shalom Books, 1949), p. 38.
22. Galatians 5:19-21; Jude 4; Romans 8:5-17.
23. Gordon, pp. 301-340.
24. Gray, pp. 373, 386.
25. Ibid., pp. 303-304.
26. Ibid., p. 427.
27. Ibid., p. 423.
28. Ibid, pp. 426-427.
29. Ibid., p. 430.
30. Ibid., p. 441.
31. Ibid., pp. 430, 438.
32. Diana Shaman, "Margaret Sanger: The Mother of Birth Control," *Coronet*, March 1966.
33. Gray, p. 441.
34. Julian L. Simon, *The Ultimate Resource* (Princeton, NJ: Princeton University Press, 1981), p. 328.
35. Gray, pp. 29, 37-39, 40-41, 52.
36. Ibid., pp. 45, 47-52, 56, 78, 101.
37. Ibid., pp. 37-39, 40-41, 47-52.
38. Ibid., p. 438.
39. Ben-Feinberg, p. 69.
40. Gordon, pp. 341-390.
41. *The New American*, April 21, 1986.
42. Ibid.
43. Ironically, Planned Parenthood has not restrained itself to abide by the IRS Code's 501(c)3 conditions. It continues to improperly pursue an aggressive program of political lobbying. At the same time, it has attempted to deny Churches and pro-life groups the same privilege. It reaps the benefits of tax exemption without upholding its responsibilities. See "Church Battles Challenges," *Rutherford Institute News Release*, January 21, 1988.
44. *Planned Parenthood Review*, 3:3, (Fall 1983), p. 8.
45. "Planned Parenthood of Houston and Southeast Texas Professional Affiliations," *Memorandum*, May 2, 1986.
46. Ibid.
47. Karen E. Koek and Susan Boyles Martin, ed., *Encyclopedia of Associations*, 22nd ed. (New York: Gale Publishers, 1988), p. 1015.
48. Ibid.
49. Ibid.
50. Ibid.
51. "Help for Hard Times: United Way Services" brochure (Houston: United Way of the Texas Gulf Coast, 1982).
52. Ibid.
53. Dugan, p. 2. This figure is an estimated total of both national and local giving patterns.
54. "Effectively Fighting United Way," *A.L.L. About Issues*, December 1981, pp. 24-25; and see Marshall, pp. 20-21.

55. Dugan, p. 2.
56. "United Way and PP: Bedfellows of Destruction," *A.L.L. About Issues*, July 1982, pp. 44-45.
57. Ibid., p. 44.
58. Koek and Martin, p. 1117.
59. Ibid.
60. Ibid.
61. Ibid.
62. "March of Dimes" information packet, American Life Lobby, 1985, pp. 10-14.
63. Ibid., p. 11.
64. Robert Peters, "March of Dimes: No Excuses," *A.L.L. About Issues*, July 1985, pp. 32-33.
65. Ibid., p. 63.
66. "March of Dimes and the Unborn: What You Need to Know Before You Give" brochure, Minneapolis Human Life Alliance, 1977, p. 1.
67. Ibid., p. 2.
68. "The March of Dimes and Abortion," *A.L.L. About Issues*, October 1982, pp. 3-4.
69. "March of Dimes" information packet, American Life Lobby, 1985, p. 10.
70. *MOD News*, June 23, 1980.
71. P. G. Stubblefield, et al., "Fertility After Induced Abortion: A Prospective Follow-Up Study," *Obstetrics and Gynecology* 62:2, (February 1984), pp. 186-193.
72. "March of Dimes" information packet, American Life Lobby, 1985, p. 12.
73. Linda Wallace, "The March of Dimes-Planned Parenthood Connection," *Texas Nurses for Life News*, Fall 1983, p. 3.
74. Ibid., p. 4.
75. Ibid,. p. 3.
76. Ibid., p. 4.
77. For more information about The Michael Fund, write to International Foundation for Genetic Research, 400 Penn Center Boulevard, Room 1022, Pittsburgh, PA 15235.
78. See Marvin Olasky, *Patterns of Corporate Philanthropy: Public Affairs Giving and the Forbes 100* (Washington, D.C.: Capitol Research Center, 1987).
79. Anthony Sutton, *The Best Enemy Money Can Buy* (Billings, MT: Liberty House Press, 1986).
80. Igor Shafarevich, *The Socialist Phenomenon* (New York: Harper & Row, 1980); A. J..A. Peck, *Rhodesia Accuses* (Boston: Western Islands, 1966); Joseph Finder, *Red Carpet* (Ft. Worth: American Bureau of Economic Research, 1983); Barry Rubin, *Paved With Good Intentions* (New York: Oxford University Press, 1980).
81. Marvin Olasky, "Big Corporations Finance the Left," *Conservative Digest*, January 1988, pp. 57-62.
82. Ibid., p. 57.
83. Ibid., pp. 57-58.
84. Ibid., p. 59.
85. Ibid., p. 61.
86. Ibid., p. 57.
87. Ibid., p. 58.
88. Ibid., pp. 57-58.
89. Cindy Gorman, "Corporate Development and the Planned Parenthood Affiliate," *Texas Nurses for Life News*, Winter 1986, p. 2.
90. See: Harold L. Sheppard, ed., *Poverty and Wealth in America* (Chicago: Quadrangle Books, 1970); Carroll Quigley, *Tragedy and Hope: A History of the World in*

Our Time (New York: The Macmillan Co., 1966); Anthony C. Sutton, *America's Secret Establishment* (Billings, MT: Liberty House Press, 1986); Richard Kelly Hoskins, *War Cycles, Peace Cycles* (Lynchburg, VA: The Virginia Publishing Co., 1985); and Arthur S. Link and Richard L. McCormick, *Progressivism* (Arlington Heights, IL: Harlan Davidson, 1983).

91. See Larry Abraham, *Call It Conspiracy* (Seattle: Double A Publications, 1985).

92. See Gary North, *Conspiracy: A Biblical View* (Westchester, IL: Crossway Books, 1986).

93. See William McIlhany, *The Tax-Exempt Foundations* (Westport, CT: Arlington House, 1980).

94. Walter Adams-Lowe, *The Foundation Directory* (Indianapolis: Foundation Library Press, 1987), p. 1151.

95. Ibid.

96. Ibid, pp. 2164-2166.

97. Ibid., p. 2166.

98. Ibid., p. 2165.

99. Ibid.

100. Ibid., p. 1841.

101. Ibid.

102. Ibid.

103. See McIlhany, pp. 14-26.

104. Gray, p. 430.

105. Ibid., p. 438.

106. Ibid., p. 429.

107. *The Tennessean*, March 15, 1988.

Chapter 9 — The Camera Blinked: The Media Legacy

1. Peter Prichard, *The Making of McPaper: The Inside Story of USA Today* (Kansas City: Andrews, McMeel, and Parker, 1987), p. xiii.

2. See George Grant, *The Changing of the Guard: Biblical Principles of Political Action* (Ft. Worth: Dominion Press, 1987).

3. Rael Jean Isaac and Erich Isaac, *The Coercive Utopians: Social Deception by America's Power Players* (Chicago: Regnery Gateway, 1983), p. 251.

4. Alvin Toffler, *Future Shock* (New York: Bantam Books, 1971), p. 155.

5. Ibid.

6. E. F. Schumacher, *Small is Beautiful: Economics As If People Mattered* (New York: Harper and Row, 1975), p. 82.

7. James W. Sire, *How To Read Slowly: A Christian Guide to Reading With the Mind* (Downers Grove, IL: Inter-Varsity Press, 1978), pp. 14-15.

8. Allan Brownfield, "Journalists: How Much Can We Trust Them?" *Human Events*, May, 1987.

9. Ibid.

10. Ibid.

11. Ibid.

12. See Marvin Olasky, *Prodigal Press: The Anti-Christian Bias of The American News Media* (Westchester, IL: Crossway Books, 1988); and Marvin Olasky, *Dead Beat: The Press and Abortion, 1838-1988* (New York: Lawrence Erblum Associates, 1988); also see Colonel V. Doner, *A Christian Parent's Guide to TV* (Shreveport: Huntington House, 1988).

13. S. Robert Lichter and Stanley Rothman, "Media and Business Elites," *Public Opinion*, October/November 1981, pp. 42-44.
14. Ibid.; also see Olasky, *Prodigal Press* and *Dead Beat*.
15. Ibid.
16. Ibid.
17. Ibid.
18. Ibid.
19. Ibid.
20. Franky Schaeffer, *A Time For Anger: The Myth of Neutrality* (Westchester, IL: Crossway Books, 1982), p. 27.
21. See John Naisbitt and Patricia Aburdene, *Re-Inventing the Corporation* (New York: Warner Books, 1985).
22. *Values in Media Alert*, Spring 1986, p. 2.
23. See John Naisbitt, *Megatrends* (New York: Warner Books, 1982); Marvin Olasky argues in *Prodigal Press* that this decentralization trend will in the end mean a reshaping of the national news centers in New York, but not their elimination.
24. See Bernard N. Nathanson, *The Abortion Papers: Inside the Abortion Mentality* (New York: Frederick Fell Publishers, 1983), pp. 7-109.
25. *The Tennessean*, February 20, 1988.
26. Standard and Poor's, *Standard Corporation Descriptions*, 48:2 (New York: McGraw-Hill Company, 1987), p. 2565.
27. Ibid.
28. Ibid.
29. Ibid., p. 2566.
30. Ibid.
31. See Franky Schaeffer, *Bad News for Modern Man* (Westchester, IL: Crossway Books, 1984), pp. 32-42, 158-164.
32. Nathanson, pp. 87-90.
33. Standard and Poor's, p. 1490.
34. Ibid.
35. Ibid.
36. David Halberstam, *The Powers That Be* (New York: Dell Publishing, 1979), pp. 30, 182-183.
37. Ibid., pp. 38, 43, 52-53.
38. See James Hitchcock, "The Mass Media," *The Human Life Review* 9:2, (Spring 1983), pp. 39-52.
39. Marla Deane, "Planned Parenthood's Romance With the Networks," *Texas Nurses for Life News*, Winter 1984, p. 3.
40. Ibid., p. 2; and Schaeffer, *Bad News*, pp. 158-164.
41. Halberstam, p. 1025.
42. Ibid., p. 1026.
43. Standard and Poor's, p. 2289.
44. Ibid.
45. Ibid.
46. Ibid.
47. Ibid.
48. Deane, p. 3.
49. Ibid., p. 2.
50. Halberstam, p. 1025; and Deane, p. 2.
51. Halberstam, pp. 291, 298, 307-309.
52. Standard and Poor's, p. 2301.
53. Ibid.

54. Ibid.
55. Ibid.
56. Ibid.
57. Ibid.
58. Nathanson, p. 47.
59. Ibid., pp. 46-67; and Bernard Nathanson, *Aborting America* (New York: Double-day and Company, 1979), pp. 61, 146-151.
60. Ibid.
61. Ibid.
62. Gans, p. 216.
63. Nathanson, *Papers*, p. 80.
64. Ibid.
65. Ibid.
66. Gans, pp. 193-195; and Nathanson, *Papers*, p. 80.
67. Deane, p. 3.
68. Ibid., p. 2.
69. Nathanson, *Papers*, p. 80.
70. Prichard, pp. 51-52.
71. Ibid., pp. 52-53.
72. Ibid., p. 349.
73. Ibid., p. 348.
74. Ibid., p. 346.
75. Ibid., p. 77.
76. Ibid.
77. Ibid., p. 340.
78. *Wall Street Journal*, February 4, 1988; and Deane, p. 3.
79. See Marvin Olasky, "Abortion Rights: Anatomy of A Negative Public Relations Campaign," *Public Relations Review*, Fall, 1987, pp. 12-23.
80. Standard and Poor's, p. 3706.
81. Ibid.
82. Ibid.
83. Ibid., p. 3707.
84. Ibid., p. 3706.
85. Ibid.
86. Nathanson, p. 69.
87. Ibid., p. 70.
88. Ibid.
89. Schaeffer, *Anger*, p. 27; also see Marvin Olasky's marvelously balanced and historically grounded treatment of this subject in *Prodigal Press*.
90. Olasky, "Abortion Rights," p. 12.
91. Ibid., pp. 14-18.
92. *USA Today*, July 23, 1986; and Olasky, "Abortion Rights," p. 4.
93. Olasky, "Abortion Rights," p. 14.
94. Ibid.
95. Ibid., pp. 14-15.
96. Ibid; and Faye Wattleton, Planned Parenthood Federation of America Press Release, January 22, 1987.
97. Olasky, "Abortion Rights," pp. 15-16.
98. Ibid., p. 14.
99. "CPCs Under Fire," *Action Line Special Report*, 9:10, 27 December 1986; and Olasky, "Abortion Rights," pp. 12, 15-16.
100. Ibid.

101. *USA Today,* July 23, 1986; *Newsweek,* September 1, 1986.
102. Olasky, "Abortion Rights," pp. 16-17.
103. Ibid., p. 17.
104. Ibid.
105. Ibid, pp. 14, 20.
106. *Newsweek,* September 1, 1986.
107. *Action Line,* pp. 3-4.
108. Charlotte Low, "The Pro-Life Movement in Disarray: Lessons in Political Ineptitude," *The American Spectator,* October 1987, pp. 23-26.
109. Edward Jay Epstein, *Between Fact and Fiction: The Problem of Journalism* (New York: Vintage Books, 1975), p. 3.
110. Ibid., p. 4.
111. James Hitchcock, "The Mass Media," *The Human Life Review* 9:2, (Spring 1983), p. 42.
112. Lauren Filmer, *The Hidden Powers and Principalities: The Influence of Media Today* (New York: Modern Press, 1981).
113. Hitchcock, p. 42.
114. Tom Goldstein, *The News At Any Cost: How Journalists Compromise Their Ethics to Shape the News* (New York: Touchstone Books, 1985), pp. 59-83.
115. Ibid.
116. See Paul R. Ehrlich, *The Population Bomb* (New York: Ballantine Books, 1968).
117. See Julian L. Simon, *The Ultimate Resource* (Princeton, NJ: Princeton University Press, 1981).
118. See Ben J. Wattenberg, *The Birth Dearth* (New York: Pharas Books, 1987).
119. See Julian L. Simon and Herman Kahn, eds., *The Resourceful Earth* (New York: Basil Blackwell, 1984).
120. See Steven W. Mosher, *Broken Earth* (New York: The Free Press, 1983).
121. See *Newsweek,* March 29, 1982; July 12, 1982; and April 30, 1984.
122. See Han Woelmier, *Lex Draconia* (Berlin: Schmidt and Hoche, 1984).
123. See Sylvia Ann Hewlett, *A Lesser Life: The Myth of Women's Liberation in America* (New York: William Morrow and Company, 1986).
124. See Anne Speckhard, *Post Abortion Counseling: A Manual for Christian Counselors* (Falls Church, VA: Christian Action Council, 1987).
125. David C. Reardon, *Aborted Women: Silent No More* (Westchester, IL: Crossway Books, 1987), pp. 23-24.
126. See Linda Bird Franke, *The Ambivalence of Abortion* (New York: Laurel Books, 1978).
127. See Robert Jay Lifton, *The Nazi Doctors: Medical Killing and the Psychology of Genocide* (New York: Basic Books, 1986).
128. See Francis A. Schaeffer and C. Everett Koop, *Whatever Happened to the Human Race?* (Old Tappan, NJ: Fleming H. Revell, 1979).
129. Hans Berukel, "U.S. Government Funded Experiments on Live Aborted Babies," *International Life Times,* November 7, 1980, p. 9.
130. Olga Fairfax, "101 Uses For A Dead (or Alive) Baby," *The Forum,* January, 1984, p. 6.
131. *The Washington Post,* September 1, 1987.
132. See Barbara Katz Rothman, *The Tentative Pregnancy: Prenatal Diagnosis and the Future of Motherhood* (New York: Viking, 1986); and Germaine Greer, *Sex and Destiny: The Politics of Human Fertility* (New York: Harper Colophon Books, 1984).
133. See Marvin Olasky, "When the *Times* Damned Abortion," *The Human Life Review* 12:3, (Fall 1986); Marvin and Susan Olasky, "From Crime to Compas-

sion," *The Human Life Review* 12:2, (Summer 1986); and Olasky's remarkable books *Prodigal Press* and *Dead Beat*.

134. Madeline Gray, *Margaret Sanger: A Biography of the Champion of Birth Control* (New York: Richard Marek, 1979), pp. 71-72, 77.
135. See James C. Mohr, *Abortion in America: The Origins and Evolution of National Policy, 1800-1900* (New York: Oxford University Press, 1978).
136. Ibid., pp. 47-57.
137. Ibid., pp. 77-85.
138. Olasky, *Times*, p. 74.
139. Ibid.
140. Mohr, p. 52.
141. Olasky, *Times*, p. 81.
142. Mohr, p. 55.
143. Matthew 6:24.
144. Linda Gordon, *Woman's Body, Woman's Right: A Social History of Birth Control in America* (New York: Penguin Books, 1974), p. 53.
145. Olasky, *Times*, p. 76.
146. Ibid.
147. Ibid.
148. Ibid.
149. Ibid.
150. Gordon, pp. 51-60; and Mohr, pp. 200-225.
151. Olasky, *Times*, pp. 79-83.
152. *The Liberty Report*, February, 1988.
153. *Insight*, March 21, 1988.
154. Ibid.

Chapter 10 — A Divine Tragedy: The Religious Legacy

1. Steven Runciman, *The Fall of Constantinople 1453* (New York: Cambridge University Press, 1965), p. xi.
2. Talon Gartrell, *Abortion and the States: A Case Against the Technical Elimination of Federal Jurisdiction and Roe v. Wade* (Manassas, VA: Life Work Publications, 1987), p. 5.
3. Ibid., p. 7.
4. See Randy C. Alcorn, *Christians in the Wake of the Sexual Revolution: Recovering Our Sexual Security* (Portland: Multnomah Press, 1985).
5. See Joseph M. Scheidler, *Closed: Ninety-Nine Ways to Stop Abortion* (Westchester, IL: Crossway Books, 1985).
6. See George Grant, *The Changing of the Guard: Biblical Principles of Political Action* (Fort Worth, TX: Dominion Press, 1987).
7. See Curt Young, *The Least of These: What Everyone Should Know About Abortion* (Chicago, IL: Moody Press, 1983).
8. See Dennis J. Horan, Edward R. Grant, and Paige G. Cunningham, eds., *Abortion and the Constitution: Reversing Roe v. Wade Through the Courts* (Washington, D.C.: Georgetown University Press, 1987).
9. See Robin Lane Fox, *Pagans and Christians* (New York: Alfred A. Knopf, 1987).
10. See Linda Gordon, *Woman's Body, Woman's Right: A Social History of Birth Control in America* (New York: Penguin Books, 1974).
11. See Thomas A. Shannon and Jo Ann Manfra, eds., *Law and Bioethics: Texts with Commentary on Major U.S. Court Decisions* (New York: Danlist Press, 1982).

12. See Herbert Aptekar, *Infanticide, Abortion, and Contraception in Savage Society* (New York: William Godwin, Publisher, 1931).
13. See Will Durant, *Caesar and Christ* (New York: Simon and Schuster, 1944).
14. See Michael J. Gorman, *Abortion and the Early Church: Christian, Jewish, and Pagan Attitudes in the Greco-Roman World* (Downers Grove, IL: InterVarsity Press, 1982).
15. See Norman E. Himes, *Medical History of Contraception* (New York: Gamut Press, 1963).
16. See George Devereux, "A Typological Study of Abortion in 350 Primitive, Ancient, and PreIndustrial Societies," in Harold Rosen ed., *Abortion in America* (Boston: Beacon Press, 1967).
17. See David Bakan, *The Slaughter of the Innocents* (Boston: Beacon Press, 1972).
18. See Paul H. Gebhard, Wardell B. Pomeroy, Clyde E. Martin, and Cornelia V. Christenson, *Pregnancy, Birth, and Abortion* (New York: Harper Brothers, 1958).
19. See Augustus Ambrose, *The Women of Gilead: The Abuse of Women and Children in History* (New York: Uptown Bookseller, 1957).
20. Plato, *The Republic,* 5.9; Aristotle, *Politics,* 7.1.1.; and Aristotle, *Historia Animalium,* 7.3.
21. Juvenal, *Satire,* 6.592-601; and Chrysostom, *Homily Twenty-Four on Romans,* 3.4.1.
22. Soranos, *Gynecology,* 1.19.
23. Ambrose, *Hexameron,* 5.18.58; and Hippolytus, *Refutation of All Heresies,* 9.7.
24. Justinian, *Digest,* 48.19.39.
25. Calaetus, *Dogmas,* 14.9.2.
26. A. L. Cameron, "The Exposure of Children and Greed Ethics," *The Classical Review* 46:3 (July 1932), pp. 105-114.
27. Robert M. Grant, *Augustus to Constantine* (New York: Harper and Row, 1970), pp. 97-99, 272.
28. Justinian, *Digest,* 47.11.4; 48.8; 48.19.38-39.
29. Albert Karmer, *Witness to Truth: The Early Church and Social Reform in the Empire* (New York: Ballister Historical Review, 1951), pp. 92-111.
30. See Gorman, pp. 47-90.
31. *Didache,* 2.2.
32. *Epistle of Barnabas,* 19.5.
33. Athenagoras, *A Plea for the Christians,* 35.6.
34. Clement, *Paedagogus,* 2:10.96.1.
35. Tertullian, *Apology* 9.4.
36. Basil, *Canons,* 188.2.
37. Ambrose, *Hexameron* 5.18.58.
38. Jerome, *Letter to Eustochium* 22.13.
39. Augustine, *On Marriage,* 1.17.15.
40. Origen, *Against Heresies,* 9.2.; and *Homily Ten,* 21.22.
41. Hippolytus, *Refutation of All Heresies,* 9.7.
42. Cyprian, *Letters,* 48.3.
43. Methodius, *Fragments,* 6.1.3.
44. Chrysostom, *Homily Twenty-Four on Romans,* 3.4.1.
45. Minucius Felix, *Octavius,* 30.16.
46. Gregory Nazianzus, *Oratory,* 43.66.
47. See Karmer, p. 109.
48. See Fox, pp. 343, 351, 382.
49. See Karmer, p. 142.
50. Psalm 68:6.

51. Ronald L.Numbers and Darrel W. Amundsen, eds., *Caring and Curing: Health and Medicine in the Western Religious Traditions* (MacMillan Publishing Company, 1986), pp. 40-64.
52. Ibid., pp. 146-172.
53. See George Grant, *The Dispossessed: Homelessness in America* (Westchester, IL: Crossway Books, 1986).
54. See George Grant, *Bringing in the Sheaves: Transforming Poverty Into Productivity* (Atlanta: American Vision Press, 1985).
55. See David Chilton, *Power in the Blood: A Christian Response to AIDS* (Brentwood, TN: Wolgemuth & Hyatt, Publishers, 1987).
56. See George Grant, *In the Shadow of Plenty: Biblical Principles of Welfare and Poverty* (Nashville, TN: Thomas Nelson, 1986).
57. See Sidney Lens, *Poverty: Yesterday and Today* (New York: Thomas Crowell, Co., 1973).
58. See Robert Hunter, *Poverty* (New York: The MacMillan Company, 1907).
59. See Cecil Woodham Smith, *The Great Hunger* (London: Hamish Hamilton, Ltd., 1962).
60. See Karl de Schweinitz, *England's Road to Social Security* (New York: A. S. Barnes and Company, 1943).
61. See Clarence B. Carson, *The War on the Poor* (New Rochelle, NY: Arlington House, 1969).
62. See Stanley S. Harakas, *Moral Issues Facing the Orthodox Christian* (Minneapolis: Light and Life Publishing Company, 1982).
63. See Alexander Schmemann, *The Historical Road of Eastern Orthodoxy* (New York: St. Vladimir Seminary Press, 1963).
64. See Francis A. Schaeffer and C. Everett Koop, *Whatever Happened to the Human Race?* (Old Tappan, NJ: Fleming Revell, 1979).
65. See Francis A. Schaeffer, *How Should We Then Live?* (Old Tappan, NJ: Fleming Revell, 1976).
66. See John Kowalczyk, *An Orthodox View of Abortion* (Minneapolis: Light and Life Publishing Company, 1979).
67. Re: "right belief."
68. Re: "right living."
69. Re: "right heritage."
70. "We Affirm" brochure, Religious Coalition for Abortion Rights Educational Fund, 1986.
71. See T. J. Bosgra, *Abortion, the Bible, and the Church: A Survey of One Hundred Fifty Denominational Views* (Honolulu: Hawaii Right to Life Educational Foundation, 1980).
72. See Edmund W. Robb and Julia Robb, *The Betrayal of the Church* (Westchester, IL: Crossway Books, 1986).
73. David M. Rogge, "The Loving Solution," *Emphasis*, Summer 1983, p. 45.
74. Phyllis Cooksey, "Motivation Moves Minnesota," *Emphasis*, Summer 1983, pp. 11-12.
75. Thomas McCloskey, "A Methodist Model," *Emphasis*, Summer 1983, pp. 21-22.
76. Richard N. Chrisman, "Clergy Involvement Sought," *Planned Parenthood Review*, 5.1, (Winter 1984), pp. 46-47.
77. Eugene Navias, "Universal Appeal," *Emphasis*, Summer 1983, pp. 27-28.
78. "We Affirm," p. 6; and *New York Times*, August 3, 1986.
79. "Planned Parenthood Education Branch" brochure, Cypress Creek Christian Community Center, 1982.
80. Martha Ehrlich, *Carrying the Torch: Religion and the Left* (Atlanta: St. George's Press, 1981), p. 121.

81. Madeline Gray, *Margaret Sanger: A Biography of the Champion of Birth Control* (New York: Richard Movek, Publishers, 1979), p. 330.
82. Ibid.
83. Donald Ben-Feinberg, *Sangerizing the Negroes and Jews* (New York: Shalom Books, 1949), p. 37.
84. Ibid., p. 38.
85. Ibid., p. 37.
86. Ibid., p. 38.
87. Ibid., p. 40.
88. Ibid., p. 41.
89. David Goldstein, *Suicide Bent: Sangerizing America* (St. Paul: Radio Replies Press, 1945), pp. 39-42.
90. Ben-Feinberg, p. 40.
91. Gordon, pp. 301-340.
92. Ben-Feinberg, p. 41.
93. See Francis A. Schaeffer, *The Great Evangelical Disaster* (Westchester, IL: Crossway Books, 1984).
94. See Timothy Ware, *The Orthodox Church* (New York: Penguin Books, 1963).
95. See Philip Schaff, *The Principle of Protestantism* (New York: Hartford Theological Reprints, 1962).
96. See Francis A. Schaeffer, *Reclaiming the World* (Grand Rapids, MI: Gospel Films, 1982).
97. See Franky Schaeffer, *Addicted to Mediocrity* (Westchester, IL: Crossway Books, 1980).
98. See Franky Schaeffer, *Bad News for Modern Man* (Westchester, IL: Crossway Books, 1984).
99. See Os Guiness, *The Gravedigger Files* (Downers Grove, IL: InterVarsity Press, 1982).
100. Ben-Feinberg, p. 38.
101. Ibid., p. 39.
102. See John White, *Flirting With the World* (Wheaton, Illinois: Harold Shaw Publishers, 1982).
103. See Leonard J. Nelson, ed., *The Death Decision* (Ann Arbor, MI: Servant Books, 1984).
104. See, for example, the devastating infiltration of Planned Parenthood rhetoric in these Evangelical publications: Peter DeJong and William Smit, *Planning Your Family: How to Decide What's Best For You* (Grand Rapids, MI: Zondervan Publishing House, 1987); D. Gareth Jones, *Brave New People: Ethical Issues at the Commencement of Life* (Downers Grove, IL: InterVarsity Press, 1984), later republished by William B. Eerdmans when a pro-life outrage and outcry began to threaten InterVarsity's campus ministries; and Caroline Berry, *The Rites of Life: Christians and Bio-Medical Decision Making* (London: Hodder and Stoughton, 1987).
105. *World*, February 15, 1988, p. 5.
106. Ibid.
107. Ibid.
108. These records were obtained when several affiliates apparently began to "clean house," transferring their records from "hard" copy to disk and microfiche. Over 55,000 full medical charts and 110,000 clinic visit records were gathered from fourteen different locations. Analysis was complete on only 35,000 at the time of this writing.
109. Ibid.

110. Ibid.
111. Ibid.
112. Cited in Rus Walton, *Biblical Solutions to Contemporary Problems: A Handbook* (Brentwood, TN: Wolgemuth and Hyatt, Publishers, 1988).
113. Revelation 22:12.

Chapter 11—Slaying Dragons: The Character to Confront

1. Allan Gould-Trevorsen, *The Cathari: Medieval Manichees and the Church's Response* (London: Sts. Peter and Paul's Book Shoppe, 1937), p. 62.
2. Walter Gannick, *Bernard of Clairveaux: A Biography* (Suffolk: Wilson, James, and Thompson, Ltd., 1951), p. 219.
3. Gould-Trevorsen, p. 113.
4. Ibid., p. 114.
5. Ibid., pp. 201-227.
6. See Trevor Ravenscroft, *The Spear of Destiny* (London: Neville Spearman, Ltd., 1973).
7. See Walter Johannes Stein, *Occultism and the Anglo-American Establishment* (Boston: Grail Chapel Press, 1927).
8. See Elasah Drogin, *Planned Parenthood: An Anti-Christian Witchcraft Cult?* (Coarsegold, CA: CUL Dominican Community, 1981).
9. Madeline Gray, *Margaret Sanger: A Biography of the Champion of Birth Control* (New York: Richard Marek Publishers, 1979), pp. 108, 112-113, 249-250, 266, 290, 306, 389.
10. The Greek word for *sorcery* or *witchcraft* throughout the Bible is *pharmakea*. That is also the word that is consistently used in ancient literature for *abortifacient*. There is a Scriptural connection, then, between occultic sorcery and abortion. Considering the backdrop of Baal and Molech worship and their occultic and child sacrifice elements, this connection should not be too terribly surprising.
11. See George Grant, *The Dispossessed: Homelessness in America* (Westchester, IL: Crossway Books, 1986).
12. Gannick, p. 191.
13. Gould-Trevorsen, p. 119.
14. Ibid., p. 118.
15. Ibid., p. 114.
16. Gannick, p. 191; and Gould-Trevorsen, p. 122.
17. See Joe Scheidler's very helpful and intensely practical book *Closed: 99 Ways to Stop Abortion* (Westchester, IL: Crossway Books, 1985). p. 150, or call his hotline (312) 777-2525.
18. Call *American Press International*, 1-800-356-7111, and ask for information about *Right/Net, Family/Net*, and the full wire service network.
19. For a comprehensive bibliography and resources list of Christian pro-life and charitable relief organizations conact LifeNet, P.O. Box 185066, Fort Worth, TX 76181-0066.
20. See Connie Marshner, *Decent Exposure: How to Teach Your Children About Sex* (Brentwood, TN: Wolgemuth & Hyatt, Publishers, 1988).
21. See James B. Jordan, ed., *The Reconstruction of the Church* (Tyler, TX: Geneva Ministries, 1985) pp. 19-21.
22. See Peter C. Phan, *The Message of the Fathers of the Church: Social Thought* (Wilmington: Michael Glazier, 1984).

Chapter 12 — Idols for Destruction: A Strategy for Prophets and Priests

1. *The Lakeland Post-Dispatch*, October 14, 1986.
2. Ibid.
3. See Gary DeMar, *Ruler of the Nations: Biblical Principles for Government* (Ft. Worth: Dominion Press, 1987).
4. See John W. Whitehead, *The Separation Illusion: A Lawyer Examines the First Amendment* (Milford, MI: Mott Media, 1977).
5. See Tim LaHaye, *Faith of Our Founding Fathers* (Brentwood, TN: Wolgemuth and Hyatt Publishers, 1987).
6. See Rus Walton, *One Nation Under God* (Nashville, TN: Thomas Nelson Publishers, 1987).
7. Joseph Story, *Commentaries on the Constitution* (Philadelphia: Patriot Publications, 1833, 1967).
8. See John W. Whitehead, *The Second American Revolution* (Elgin, IL: David C. Cook, 1982).
9. See Henry Van Til, *The Calvinistic Concept of Culture* (Philadelphia: Presbyterian and Reformed, 1959).
10. See George Grant, *In the Shadow of Plenty: Biblical Principles of Welfare and Poverty* (Nashville: Thomas Nelson, 1986).
11. See Dennis Peacock, *Winning the Battle for the Minds of Men* (Santa Rosa, CA: Alive and Free, 1987).
12. See John Chrysostom, *On Wealth and Poverty* (New York: St. Vladimir's Seminary Press, 1984).
13. See David Chilton, *Paradise Restored: An Eschatology of Dominion* (Ft. Worth: Dominion Press, 1985).
14. See R. J. Rushdoony, *The Nature of the American System* (Tyler, TX: Thoburn Press, 1978).
15. See R. J. Rushdoony, *This Independent Republic* (Tyler, TX: Thoburn Press, 1978).
16. See John W. Whitehead, *The Stealing of America* (Westchester, IL: Crossway Books, 1983).
17. See Gary North, *Unconditional Surrender* (Tyler: Institute for Christian Economics, 1981, 1988).
18. See Francis A. Schaeffer, *A Christian Manifesto* (Westchester, IL: Crossway Books, 1981).
19. See Gary DeMar, *God and Government: A Biblical and Historical Study* (Atlanta: American Vision Press, 1982).
20. See Otto Scott, *The Secret Six: John Brown and the Abolitionist Movement* (New York: Times Books, 1979).
21. See Clarence B. Carson, *The Sections and the Civil War* (Greenville, AL: American Textbook Committee, 1985).
22. See Robert B. Webster, *The Rise and Fall of the American Republic* (Los Angeles: Freedom Bookhouse, 1979).
23. See James Hitchcock, *What Is Secular Humanism?* (Ann Arbor, MI: Servant Books, 1982).
24. See John W. Whitehead, *The End of Man* (Westchester, IL: Crossway Books, 1986).
25. See James T. Draper and Forrest E. Watson, *If the Foundations Be Destroyed* (Nashville: Oliver-Nelson Books, 1984).

26. See C. Gregg Singer, *A Theological Interpretation of American History* (Philadelphia: Presbyterian and Reformed, 1964).
27. See Erwin W. Lutzer, *Exploding the Myths That Could Destroy America* (Chicago: Moody Press, 1986).
28. See Lynn Buzzard and Paula Campbell, *Holy Disobedience: When Christians Must Resist the State* (Ann Arbor, MI: Servant Books, 1984).
29. Cyril Kadrey, *The Second Millennium: The Kievan Christian Republic* (Paris: YMCA Press, 1961), p. 431.
30. Alexis de Tocqueville, *Democracy In America* 2:141.2.
31. See Francis A. Schaeffer, *How Should We Then Live?* (Old Tappan, NJ: Fleming H. Revell, 1976).
32. Cornelius Van Til, *Defense of the Faith* (Philadelphia: Presbyterian and Reformed, 1967), p. 8.
33. Ibid.
34. *The Shorter Catechism*, Westminster Confession of Faith, 1:1.
35. See James B. Jordan, *The Sociology of the Church* (Tyler, TX: Geneva Ministries, 1986).
36. See Alexander Schmemann, *For the Life of the World* (New York: St. Vladimir's Seminary Press, 1973).
37. Chilton, p. 215.
38. Ibid.
39. See G. K. Chesterton, *What's Wrong With the World* (New York: Dodd, Mead, and Company, 1910).
40. See Gregg Harris, *The Christian Home School* (Brentwood, TN: Wolgemuth & Hyatt, 1988); and Ray Ballman, *The How and Why of Home Schooling* (Westchester, IL: Crossway Books, 1987).
41. Blair Adams, Joel Stein, and Howard Wheeler, *Who Owns the Children? Compulsory Education and the Dilemma of Ultimate Authority* (Austin: Truth Forum, 1986).
42. Jonathan Kozol, *Illiterate America* (Garden City, NY: Anchor Press, 1985), pp. 8-9.
43. Ibid.
44. Robert T. Langle, *Educational Chaos* (Seattle: Child Light Press, 1983), p. 16.
45. Ibid., p. 17.
46. Ibid., p. 2.
47. Harris, pp. 29-30.
48. See Samuel Blumenfeld, *NEA: Trojan Horse in American Education* (Boise: Paradigm, 1984).
49. Kozol, p. 18.
50. Harris, pp. 24-26.
51. For a comprehensive bibliographic guide to the best pro-life literature write to LifeNet, P.O. Box 185066, Fort Worth, TX 76181-0066.
52. See Marvin Olasky, "Abortion Rights: Anatomy of a Negative Campaign," *Public Relations Review* (Fall, 1987).
53. Ibid., pp. 8-10.
54. Once again, Joe Scheidler's book is helpful here: *Closed: 99 Ways to Stop Abortion* (Westchester, IL: Crossway Books, 1985) pp. 100-103.
55. See John Eidsmoe, *God and Caesar: Christian Faith and Political Action* (Westchester, IL: Crossway Books, 1984).
56. See Vern McLellan, *Christians in the Political Arena* (Charlotte, NC: Associates Press, 1986), pp. 142-143.
57. Martin Talbot Graves, *Data on File: The American Political Scene* (Dallas: Christ Over All, 1985), p. 28.

58. Ibid.
59. Ibid., p. 29.
60. Ibid.
61. Ibid.
62. See R. E. McMaster, Jr., *No Time for Slaves* (Phoenix: Reaper Publishing, 1986).
63. Graves, p. 32.
64. Ibid.
65. Ibid.
66. See Stephen R. Hightower, *Committees of Correspondence* (Memphis: The Sound of Liberty, 1967).
67. See Dennis J. Horan, Edward R. Grant, and Paige C. Cunningham, *Abortion and the Constitution* (Washington, D.C.: Georgetown University Press, 1987).
68. Ibid., pp. 265-268.
69. See John C. Calhoun, *A Disquisition on Government* (Indianapolis: Bobbs-Merrill Educational Publishing, 1953).
70. The Rutherford Institute, P.O. Box 510, Manassas, Virginia, 22110.
71. Christian Legal Society, P.O. Box 1492, Springfield, Virginia, 22151.
72. Women who have been exploited by abortion may call the Committee to Protect the Family Foundation, (203) 321-8833, for free legal help.
73. McLellan, pp. 127-128.
74. See Robin Love Fox, *Pagans and Christians* (New York: Alfred A. Knopf, 1986).
75. Schaeffer, *Manifesto*, p. 92.
76. Michael Pesce, *Legal Documents of the Roman Empire* (New York: Black, Albertson, and Bloesch, 1959), pp. 46-47.
77. Ibid., p. 47.
78. Ibid.
79. Ibid., p. 48.
80. Whitehead, *Revolution*, p. 161.
81. See Randall A. Terry *Operation Rescue* (Springdale, PA: Whitaker House, 1988); and Gary North *When Justice Is Aborted* (Tyler, TX: Institute for Christian Economics, 1988).
82. Herbert Schlossberg, *Idols for Destruction: Christian Faith and Its Confrontation With American Society* (Nashville: Thomas Nelson Publishers, 1983), p. 295.
83. Ibid.
84. See "1988—Pro-Life Momentum Builds," *Action Line* 12:1, February 15, 1988.
85. See *Business Week*, February 29, 1988.

Chapter 13—Altars for Construction: An Agenda for the Future

1. The phrase and the concept, though ancient, was first introduced to me by Christian economist Dr. Gary North. See, for example, his *Unconditional Surrender* (Tyler, TX: Institute for Christian Economics, 1981, 1988).
2. Claude L. Fevre, *L'Ecriture de Thyrasymachos* (Paris: Parbleu Libraire-Editeur, 1963), p. 61.
3. Ibid., p. 62.
4. Ibid., p. 61.
5. Ibid.
6. Ibid., p. 74.
7. Quoted in Hardin Blanchard, *The Forerunner of the Reformation: An Analysis of the Hussite Movement* (London: Lollard Publication Board, 1927), p. 137.
8. Ibid., p. 138.
9. Ibid.
10. Ibid.

11. Ibid., p. 139.
12. Ibid.
13. Ibid., p. 172.
14. Quoted in G. Holden Pike, *Charles Haddon Spurgeon: Preacher, Author, and Philanthropist* (New York: Funk and Wagnalls Company, 1892), p. 10.
15. Ibid., p. 11.
16. Ibid., p. 9.
17. Ibid., p. 11.
18. Ibid., p. 9.
19. Ibid., pp. 8-9.
20. Ibid., p. 11.
21. Ibid., p. 12.
22. Anatol Kabosili, *Faith at Work* (Boston: K. L. A. Monastic Orders Publication Review, 1927), p. 63.
23. Ibid., p. 92.
24. Maria L. H. Blumhardt, *Pioneer to Africa: The Life of Otto Blumhardt* (St. Louis: Wittenburg Missionary Press, 1949), p. 6.
25. See George Grant, *Bringing in the Sheaves: Transforming Poverty into Productivity* (Atlanta: American Vision Press, 1985).
26. George Grant, *In the Shadow of Plenty: Biblical Principles of Welfare and Poverty* (Nashville: Thomas Nelson, Publishers, 1986), p. 4.
27. Ibid.
28. Ibid.
29. Ibid.
30. Ibid.
31. Ibid.
32. Ibid.
33. See George Grant, *The Dispossessed: Homelessness in America* (Westchester, IL: Crossway Books, 1986).
34. Grant, *In the Shadow of Plenty*, p. 5.
35. Ibid.
36. Ibid.
37. See Frances Moore Lappe and Joseph Colline, *World Hunger: Twelve Myths* (New York: Grove Press, 1986).
38. See George Grant, "The Reclamation of Biblical Charity," *In Christianity and Civilization: The Reconstruction of the Church*, ed. James B. Jordan, 1985, pp. 299-325.
39. See Ruth Sidel, *Women and Children Last: The Plight of Poor Women in Affluent America* (New York: Penguin, 1986), p. 3.
40. Ibid.
41. Ibid.
42. Ibid., p. 4.
43. Ibid.
44. Ibid.
45. Ibid., p. 11.
46. See Grant, *Shadow*, pp. 123-128.
47. Ibid., p. 136-158.
48. Lenore J. Weitzman, *The Divorce Revolution: The Unexpected Social and Economic Consequences for Women and Children in America* (New York: Free Press, 1985), p. xii.
49. Ibid.
50. Ibid.

51. Sylvia Ann Hewlett, *A Lesser Life: The Myth of Women's Liberation in America* (New York: William Morrow, 1986), p. 14.
52. Ibid.
53. See Grant, *The Dispossessed*, pp. 712-83.
54. See Joni Eareckson Tada, *Friendship Unlimited: How You Can Help a Disabled Friend* (Wheaton, IL: Harold Shaw Publishers, 1987).
55. Joni Eareckson and Gene Newman, *All God's Children* (Grand Rapids, MI: Zondervan, 1987), p. 22.
56. Ibid., p. 32.
57. Ibid., p. 43.
58. See the Christian Action Council. 701 W. Broad Street, Suite 405, Falls Church, VA 22046.
59. See local Adoption Agencies listed in the telephone directory, or write to the Pro-Life Action League, 6160 N. Cicero Ave., Chicago, IL 60646.
60. See Liberty Godparent Home, Box 27000, Lynchburg, VA 24506.
61. See local LifeLine Maternal Clinics or Crisis Pregnancy Centers, or write to the Christian Action Council 422 C. St., N.E., Washington, D.C. 20002.
62. See local chapters of Natural Family Planning Leagues or write to either the Couple to Couple League, P.O. Box 11084, Cincinnati, OH 45211 or American Life League, P.O. Box 490, Stafford, VA 22554.
63. See *Sex Respect* and *Why Wait?*, The Julian Center, P.O. Box 1000, Dallas, TX 75221.
64. See LifeNet, P.O. Box 185066, Fort Worth, TX 76181-0066.
65. See Help Services, P.O. Box 1141, Humble, TX 77347.
66. It is actually *God* who changes things as we humble ourselves before Him. But prayer is the method He has chosen to effect that humbling process.
67. See James B. Jordan, *The Sociology of the Church* (Tyler, TX: Genera Ministries, 1986) pp. 279-282.
68. One of the best books on fasting, although it tends at times to lean toward platonic pietism, is Arthur Wallis's classic *God's Chosen Fast* (Fort Washington, PA: Christian Literature Crusade, 1968). Other books with excellent insights into fasting include Connie Marshner, *Decent Exposure* (Brentwood, TN: Wolgemuth & Hyatt, Publishers, 1988); and Alexander Schmemann, *Great Lent* (Crestwood, NY: St. Vladimir's Seminary Press, 1969).
69. C. S. Lewis, *The Weight of Glory and Other Addresses* (Grand Rapids: Wm. B. Eerdmans, 1965), p. 1.

Appendix A — Making a Presentation

1. LifeNet, P.O. Box 185066, Ft. Worth, TX 76181-0066; CAC, 422 C St., NE, Washington, DC 20002
2. Christian homes and Christian schools will want to approach the whole question of sex education, chastity, and abstinence differently than the public schools would.

INDEX

ABOUT THE AUTHOR

A leader in the pro-life movement for more than a decade, George Grant is the author of five books, including *THE DIS-POSSESSED: Homelessness in America*, *IN THE SHADOW OF PLENTY: Biblical Principles of Welfare and Poverty*, *THE CHANG-ING OF THE GUARD: Biblical Principles for Political Action*, and *BRINGING IN THE SHEAVES: Transforming Poverty into Produc-tivity*.

He lives with his family in the piney woods of east Texas.

For information regarding booking George Grant for speak-ing engagements, please contact:

LifeNet
P.O. Box 185066
Fort Worth, TX 76181-0066

COLOPHON

The typeface for the text of this book is *Baskerville*. Its creator, John Baskerville (1706-1775), broke with tradition to reflect in his type the rounder, yet more sharply cut lettering of eighteenth-century stone inscriptions and copy books. The type foreshadows modern design in such novel characteristics as the increase in contrast between thick and thin strokes and the shifting of stress from the diagonal to the vertical strokes. Realizing that this new style of letter would be most effective if cleanly printed on smooth paper with genuinely black ink, he built his own presses, developed a method of hot-pressing the printed sheet to a smooth, glossy finish, and experimented with special inks. However, Baskerville did not enter into general commercial use in England until 1923.

Copy editing by Lynn Hawley
Cover design by Kent Puckett Associates, Atlanta, Georgia
Typography by Thoburn Press, Tyler, Texas
Printed and bound by Maple-Vail Book Manufacturing Group
Manchester, Pennsylvania
Cover Printing by Weber Graphics, Chicago, Illinois